Books by Maida Heatter

Maida Heatter's New Book of Great Desserts

Maida Heatter's
NEW BOOK
OF GREAT
DESSERTS

Drawings by Toni Evins

 ALFRED A. KNOPF   NEW YORK   1982

THIS IS A BORZOI BOOK
PUBLISHED BY ALFRED A. KNOPF, INC.

The recipe for Apricot Tart has been published in
Food & Wine Magazine. And the recipe for Corn Melba,
in *House & Garden*.

Library of Congress Cataloging in Publication Data

Heatter, Maida.
Maida Heatter's New book of great desserts.

Includes index.
1. Desserts. I. Title. II. Title: New book of
great desserts.
TX773.H353   641.8′6   81–48136
ISBN 0–394–51960–4   AACR2

Manufactured in the United States of America

FIRST EDITION

To Ralph, always

I want to thank Nancy Nicholas;
I am lucky indeed to have such a wonderful
editor. This is our fourth book together.

Contents

Introduction

For almost 40 years I tried (I often gave up and quit, but mostly I kept trying) to duplicate a certain chocolate cake from a bakery in New York City. I finally worked it out just shortly after my chocolate book went to the printer. I knew then that I wanted to write another book which would start with that recipe. That is how this book began.

Then I received a gift of a new Brownie recipe, called Christmas Brownies. Everyone who has eaten them says it is their favorite Brownie. That became the second recipe for this new book.

At about the same time my husband and I were visiting in California, and I thought I was hearing things when my sister-in-law, Helen Sparks, casually asked if I would like a recipe for a drink that tasted like Baileys Original Irish Cream. I love the drink, and I was sure there was a misunderstanding—I could not believe there was a recipe for it. But Helen gave it to me. She had gotten it at a meeting of a wine-tasting group that she and her husband belong to in San Diego; it came from a lady who had brought it from Ireland.

When I read it, I raised an eyebrow—I was very sceptical and not in much of a hurry to try it. But I did.

Then we had a blind taste-testing party with this and Baileys Original Irish Cream for eight people and everyone liked this one better (not to mention the price, which is a fraction of the other).

I knew that I had to make room for the recipe in this book. But since a liqueur is not officially a dessert (although it is a delicious way to end a meal) and since I do not have a section of liqueurs, here's the recipe now.

Homemade Irish Cream Liqueur

1½ PINTS

1 cup Irish whiskey (I use John Jameson)
1 14-ounce can sweetened condensed milk
4 eggs
2 tablespoons vanilla extract
2 tablespoons chocolate extract
1 tablespoon coconut extract
1 tablespoon powdered instant espresso or other powdered (not granular) instant coffee

In a blender, blend all the ingredients at low speed until thoroughly mixed. Transfer to a bottle with a tight cover (I save small bottles to fill with this) and refrigerate overnight or longer. The original recipe said to refrigerate overnight before serving. Serve very cold. Shake well before serving.

I don't know how long this will last (I have kept it for a month), but on the bottle of Baileys they say that the alcohol content acts as a preservative. And they hint that once you have tasted it, you might be surprised at how quickly it is consumed. Yes, it is.

One of the questions people often ask me is "Do you have a good recipe for a fruit tart?" Frankly, I did not want to write recipes for fruit tarts and fruit pies. I love them, but I thought that writing those recipes would be an impossibly big job. To me, making fruit tarts and pies, or writing the recipes for them, calls for a little magic. But when I knew there was going to be another book, I decided to try. And I did. And here they are with all the magic I know included.

Then ice creams and ices took over. What fun! Removing the cover from my churn and seeing that what went in as liquids is now a frozen dessert—that is happiness!

This book does not fit any category, such as "cookies," "chocolate," etc. It is a very personal collection of recipes that intrigue me now. At the beginning of the book you will see that there are many rich, dense, dark chocolate and some nonchocolate desserts, many possibly even richer than in my other books. But then, as this book progressed, I became more and more interested in light desserts (light, lighter, lightest!), quick desserts, fruit desserts, nouvelle cuisine desserts, ice creams, yeast cakes, sweet breads, et cetera, et cetera, et cetera. Many of these desserts tend to be quicker to make, lighter to eat, and slightly more streamlined than in my other books. Flip through. You'll see what I mean.

And although most of these recipes are very easy, a few are more involved and more professional than those in my other books. But I feel that both my readers and I have been promoted to the next grade; I am sure you can make them all and am also sure that you will have fun with them.

Enjoy!

Maida Heatter

Miami Beach, Florida

Maida Heatter's New Book of Great Desserts

Much of the following material entitled Ingredients, Equipment, and Techniques is repeated here from my other books, because it still holds true.

Ingredients

FLOUR

Many of these recipes call for sifted flour. That means that even if the package is labeled "presifted," you should sift it before measuring. If not, since flour packs down while standing, 1 cup unsifted flour is liable to be a few spoonfuls more than 1 cup of just-sifted flour.

The new battery-powered sifter is great. I use mine almost every day, and can use it for six months before having to change the battery. (I keep extra batteries in the refrigerator.)

Sift the flour onto a large piece of wax paper. Make sure that there is no flour left in the sifter. Then transfer the sifter to another piece of wax paper. Use a metal measuring cup and lightly spoon the sifted flour into the cup or lift it on a dough scraper and transfer it to the cup—do not pack or press the flour down—and scrape the excess off the top with a dough scraper or any flat-sided implement. Place the flour in the sifter, add any ingredients to be sifted with it, and sift onto the second piece of wax paper. Again, make sure there is nothing left in the sifter.

It is not necessary ever to wash a flour sifter; just shake it out firmly and store it in a plastic bag.

SUGARS

All sugars should be measured in the graded measuring cups that are made for measuring dry ingredients.

Brown Sugars

Most brown sugars are made of white granulated sugar to which a dark syrup has been added. Dark brown sugar has a mild molasses, and light brown sugar has a milder, lighter syrup (which may also be molasses). Dark brown has a slightly stronger flavor, but they may be used interchangeably. The label on Grandma's Molasses says, "You can easily make your own brown sugar as you need it by blending together ½ cup of granulated sugar with 2 tablespoons of unsulphured molasses. The yield is equivalent to ½ cup of brown sugar."

Brown sugar is moist; if it dries out it will harden. It should be stored airtight at room temperature. If it has small lumps in it they should be strained out. With your fingertips press the sugar through a large strainer set over a large bowl. The Savannah Sugar Refinery is now printing the following directions on their boxes of brown sugar: "If your brown sugar has been left open and becomes hard, place a dampened (not wet) paper towel inside the resealable poly bag and close the package tightly for 12 hours or more. A slice of apple can be used in place of the dampened towel."

Confectioners Sugar

Confectioners sugar and powdered sugar are exactly the same. They are both granulated sugar that has been pulverized very fine and has had about 3% cornstarch added to keep it in a powdery condition. Of these, 4-x is the least fine and 10-x is the finest. They may be used interchangeably. Confectioners sugar should be strained; you can do several pounds at a time if you wish. (It does not have to be done immediately before using as flour does.) Store it airtight.

If directions say to sprinkle with confectioners sugar, place the sugar in a strainer or a shaker and shake over the top of the cake or cookies.

Vanilla Confectioners Sugar

This is a flavored confectioners sugar that is used to sprinkle over cakes and cookies. It adds a nice mild flavor and delicious aroma. To make it, fill a jar that has a tight cover with confectioners sugar. Split one or two vanilla beans the long way and bury them in the sugar. Cover tightly and let stand for at least a few days before using. As the sugar is used it may be replaced; the vanilla beans will continue to flavor the sugar for a month or two.

When you make vanilla confectioners sugar, don't bother to strain the sugar beforehand. The vanilla beans give off a certain amount of moisture which the sugar absorbs, causing the sugar to become lumpy and making it necessary to strain it just before using.

Crystal Sugar

Crystal sugar, also called pearl sugar, or hagelzucker in German, is generally used to sprinkle over certain European cookies and pastries before baking. It is coarser than granulated sugar. It is available at Paprikas Weiss, 1546 Second Avenue, New York, New York 10028. And at H. Roth & Son, 1577 First Avenue, New York, New York 10028. Paprikas Weiss and H. Roth both have catalogs.

WHIPPING CREAM

Plain old-fashioned whipping cream is almost impossible to find nowadays unless you have your own cow. Too bad, because the new super- or ultra-pasteurized (known as UHT—ultra-high-temperature pasteurized) is not as good, at least I don't think so. The reason dairies make it is that it has a 6- to 8-week shelf life. (They call it a "pull date"; the store has to pull it off their shelves if it is not sold by the date stamped on the container.) This product is called either Heavy Whipping Cream or Heavy Cream, depending on the manufacturer. Either type can be used in recipes calling for Heavy Cream.

The process of making ultra-pasteurized cream involves heating the cream to 250 degrees for 1 second. It gives the cream a slight caramel flavor (so mild you might not notice it), and makes it more difficult to whip (it will take longer). It is advisable to chill the bowl and the beaters in the freezer for about half an hour before using. And keep the cream in the refrigerator until you are ready to whip; do not let it stand around in the kitchen—it should be as cold as possible.

It seems to me that baked custards take longer to set if they are made with ultra-pasteurized cream, and ice cream takes longer to churn.

How to Whip Cream

The best way to whip either plain old-fashioned or UHT cream is to place it in a large bowl, set the bowl in a larger bowl of ice and water, and whip with a large, thin-wired, balloon-type whisk. You get more volume that way, and it tastes better.

If that seems like more than you want to fuss with, use an electric mixer or an egg beater, and chill the bowl and beaters before using them. If the bowl does not revolve, then move the beaters around the bowl to whip all the cream evenly at the same time.

When I whip cream with an electric mixer, I always (and I recommend this to everyone) finish the whipping by hand with a wire whisk; there is less chance of overwhipping. At this stage you can use a smaller whisk than if you do it all by hand.

Whipped cream, which can be heavenly, is not quite so delicious if it is whipped until it is really stiff—softer is better.

EGGS

Size

The size of eggs can be very important in certain recipes. In cakes without flour, or with very little, if the egg whites are too large there might be more air beaten in than the other ingredients can support and the cake might fall. On the other hand, in certain gelatin desserts, or in some mousses or soufflés, if the whites are too small there might not be enough air for the dessert to be as light as it should.

In each recipe where it matters, I have indicated the size or choice of sizes that should be used.

To Open Eggs

If directions call for adding whole eggs one at a time, they may all be opened ahead of time into one container and then poured into the other ingredients, approximately one at a time. Do not open eggs directly into the other ingredients—you would not know if a piece of shell had been included.

To Separate Eggs

Eggs separate more safely—there is less chance of the yolk breaking—when they are cold. Therefore, if a recipe calls for separated eggs, it is usually the first thing I do when organizing the ingredients so that they are cold from the refrigerator.

The safest way to separate eggs is as follows: Place three small cups or bowls in front of you (or use shallow drinking glasses; glasses generally have a sharper edge and therefore crack the shell more cleanly). One container is for the whites and one for the yolks. The third might not be needed, but if you should break the yolk when opening an egg, just drop the whole thing in the third bowl and save it for some other use.

Tap the side of the egg firmly (but not too hard or you might break the yolk) on the edge of the bowl or glass to crack the shell, with luck, in a rather straight, even line. Then, holding the egg in both hands (so that the halves each make a cup), separate the halves of the shell, letting some of the white run out into the bowl or glass. Pour the yolk back and forth from one half of the shell to the other, letting all of the white run out. Drop the yolk into the second bowl or glass.

Many professional cooks simply open the egg into the palm of one hand, then hold their fingers, slightly separated, over a bowl. They let the white run through their open fingers and then slide the left-behind yolk into the second bowl.

As each egg is separated the white should be transferred to another container (that is, in addition to the three—it could be another bowl or glass or it might be the mixing bowl you will beat them in), because if you place all of the whites in one container there is a chance that the last egg white might have some yolk in it, which could spoil all of the whites. Generally, a tiny bit of yolk or shell can be removed from the whites with an empty half shell. Or try a piece of paper towel dipped in cold water.

To Beat Egg Whites

The success of many recipes depends on properly beaten whites. After you have learned how, it becomes second nature.

First, the bowl and beaters must be absolutely clean. A little bit of fat (egg yolks are fat) will prevent the whites from incorporating air as they should and from rising properly.

Second, do not overbeat or the whites will become dry and you will not be able to fold them into other ingredients without losing the air you have beaten in.

Third, do not beat them ahead of time. They must be folded in immediately after they are beaten; if they have to wait they separate. (Incidentally, if the whites are being folded into a cake batter, the cake must then be placed in the oven right away.)

You can use an electric mixer, a rotary beater, or a wire whisk. (Although a wire whisk and a copper bowl are said to give the most volume and therefore the best results.)

If you use an electric mixer or a rotary beater, be careful not to use a bowl that is too large or the whites will be too shallow to get the full benefit of the beater's action. If the bowl or beaters do not revolve by themselves (as they do in electric mixers on a stand), move the mixer or beater around the bowl to beat all the whites evenly. If you use a mixer on a stand, use a rubber spatula frequently to push the whites from the side of the bowl into the center.

If you use a wire whisk, it should be a large, thin-wired, balloon-type, at least 4 inches wide at the top. The bowl should be very large, the larger the better, to give you plenty of room for making large circular motions with the whisk. An unlined copper bowl is the best, or you may use glass, china, or stainless steel—but do not beat egg whites in aluminum, which might discolor the whites, or plastic, which is frequently porous and might be greasy from some other use.

A copper bowl should be treated each time before using as follows: Put 1 or 2 teaspoons of salt in the bowl and rub thoroughly with half a lemon, squeezing a bit of the juice and mixing it with the salt. Then rinse with hot water (no soap) and dry. After using a copper bowl, wash it as you would any other, but be sure to treat it before beating egg whites again.

When I beat whites with an electric mixer, if they do not have sugar added (sugar makes them more creamy and slightly lessens the chance of overbeating), I always—and I recommend this to everyone—finish the beating with a wire whisk. There is less chance of overbeating, and the whisk seems to give the whites a slightly creamy consistency. At this stage you can use a smaller whisk than the one mentioned above—use any one that seems to fit the bowl the whites are in.

People always ask me if I bring whites to room temperature before beating them. If I do, it is a rare occasion and was not planned. They are usually cold when I beat them (because I do not plan ahead and do not have the patience to wait, and because I have had equally good results whether cold or at room temperature).

To Freeze Egg Whites or Yolks

Some of these recipes call for yolks and no whites, and some call for only whites. If you have just a few extra of either left over and do not want to save them for something else, add them to scrambled eggs.

Leftover egg whites may be kept covered in the refrigerator for a few days or they may be frozen. I freeze them individually (or occasionally 2 or 4 together) in ovenproof glass custard cups. When they are frozen, hold one cup upside down under running hot water until the frozen egg white can be removed (but not until it melts). Quickly wrap each frozen egg white individually in plastic wrap and return to the freezer. To use, remove the number you want, unwrap, place them in a cup or bowl, and let stand at room temperature to thaw. Or place them, in a cup or bowl, in a slightly warm oven, or in a larger bowl of warm water.

To freeze egg yolks, stir them lightly just to mix, and for every yolk stir in ⅓ teaspoon of granulated sugar or ½ teaspoon of honey. Freeze them in a covered jar, labeling so you will know how many yolks and how much sugar or honey. When thawed, stir to mix well—they will not look exactly the same as before they were frozen (not as smooth) but they will work in recipes.

NUTS

Nuts can turn rancid rather quickly—walnuts and pecans more so than almonds. Always store all nuts airtight in the freezer or refrigerator. In the refrigerator nuts last well for 9 months; in the freezer at zero degrees they will last for 2 years. Bring them to room temperature before using; smell and taste them before you use them (preferably as soon as you buy them)— you will know quickly if they are rancid. If you even suspect that they might be, do not use them; they would ruin a recipe.

If pecans are stored in the freezer they might become limp when they are thawed. If so, do not use them that way; crisp them before using. To crisp, bake the nuts in a shallow pan in a 350-degree oven for 10 to 15 minutes until very hot and crisp but not until darker in color.

To Blanch Almonds
(Blanched almonds are skinned almonds.)

Cover the almonds with boiling water—the skin will loosen almost immediately. Spoon out a few nuts at a time and one by one, hold them under cold running water, squeezing the nuts between your thumb and forefinger. The nuts will pop out and the skin will remain between your fingers. Place the peeled almonds on a towel to dry, then spread them in a single layer in a shallow baking pan and bake in a 200-degree oven for half an hour or so until they are completely dry. Do not let them brown.

If the almonds are to be split, sliced, or slivered, they should remain in the hot water longer to soften; let them stand in the water until the water cools enough for you to touch it. Then, one at a time, remove the skin from each nut and immediately, while the nut is still soft, place it on a cutting board and cut with a small, sharp paring knife. Bake to dry as above. Sliced almonds are those that have been cut into very thin slices; slivered almonds are the fatter, oblong, "julienne"-shaped pieces. Don't expect sliced or slivered almonds that you have cut yourself to be as even as the bought ones.

To Blanch Hazelnuts

Spread the hazelnuts on a baking sheet and bake at 350 degrees for about 15 minutes or until the skins parch and begin to flake off. Then, working with a few at a time, place them on a large, coarse towel (I use a large terry-cloth bath towel). Fold part of the towel over to enclose the nuts. Rub firmly against the towel, or hold that part of the towel between both hands and rub back and forth. The rubbing and the texture of the towel will cause most of the skins to flake off. Pick out the nuts and discard the skins. Don't worry about the few little pieces of skin that may remain.

This is not as quick and easy as it sounds.

Pistachio Nuts

A light sprinkling of chopped green pistachio nuts is an elegant and classy touch. But don't overdo it; less is better than more. Fine pastries in swanky patisseries might have only about a teaspoonful of them in the center of a

9-inch cake, sprinkled on the center of chocolate icing or whipped-cream topping.

Buy shelled, unsalted green pistachios. They are hard to find, but they keep for a long, long time in the freezer. Try wholesale nut dealers or specialty nut shops. In New York they are available (by mail, too) from Paprikas Weiss, 1546 Second Avenue, New York, New York 10028; or H. Roth & Son, 1577 First Avenue, New York, New York 10028.

Chop them coarse or fine on a board using a long, heavy knife. Don't worry about the little pieces of skin that flake off; you can use them with the nuts (or pick out the large pieces of skin if you wish).

DRIED AND/OR CANDIED FRUIT

In most recipes that call for candied fruit of one kind or another, or several kinds, it is perfectly all right to substitute a different kind. For instance, if you wish, dates, raisins, figs, prunes, or apricots may be substituted for candied pineapple or citron, etc.

COFFEE AS A FLAVORING

Often people ask about the instruction "use powdered, not granular, coffee." If a recipe specifies powdered, it is because the granular would stay in granules and would not dissolve. Spice Islands brand, generally available in specialty food stores, makes powdered instant espresso and also a powdered instant coffee. And Medaglia D'Oro instant espresso, which is powdered, is generally available in large cities all around the country.

When a recipe calls for dissolving instant coffee in water, if you leave out the coffee, do not leave out the water.

Equipment

ELECTRIC MIXERS

I use an electric mixer on a stand that comes with two different-size bowls and a pair of beaters (rather than one). Mine is a Sunbeam, and I am so dependent on it that when I do cooking demonstrations, I bring my own with me.

I think it is important, or at least extremely helpful, for many dessert recipes to use a mixer that:

    a. is on a stand;

    b. comes with both a small and a large bowl; and

    c. has space to scrape around the bowl with a rubber spatula while the mixer is going.

I especially recommend that you buy an extra set of bowls and beaters—they are generally available wherever mixers are sold.

Incidentally, although I have a hand-held mixer, I could live without it. (But if I did not have any other I am sure I would learn to love it.) If you are using a hand-held mixer (or an egg beater), when I say "small bowl of electric mixer" that means one with a 7-cup capacity, and "large bowl of electric mixer" means a 16-cup capacity.

THERMOMETERS

Oven Temperature

One of the most important and often most overlooked requirements for good results in baking is correct oven temperature. The wrong temperature can cause a cake to fall, to burn, to be underdone, to refuse to rise; it can ruin a soufflé; it can turn cookies that should be wonderfully crisp into pale, limp, soggy messes; and it could be the cause of almost any other baking disaster that you might have experienced or heard about.

No matter how new or how good your oven is, *please* double-check the temperature every time you bake. Use a small, portable oven thermometer from the hardware store or kitchen shop. Buy the mercury kind—it is best. Light your oven at least 20 minutes ahead of time and place the thermometer in the middle of the oven. Give the oven plenty of time to heat and cycle and reheat before you read the thermometer; read it (and all thermometers) at eye level. If it does not register the heat you want, adjust the thermostat up or down until the mercury thermometer registers the correct heat—no matter what the oven setting says.

When you put unbaked cakes or cookies in the oven they reduce the oven temperature more than you would expect. If you check the temperature on a portable oven thermometer during about the first 10 minutes of baking don't think that your oven suddenly got sick; give it time to reheat.

Other Thermometers

A friend told me she did not know that her refrigerator was too warm until she served a large chocolate icebox cake at a dinner party and found that the middle was thin and runny instead of firm as it should have been. And once I didn't know that my freezer was misbehaving until the very last minute, when a photographer was here to take pictures of a chocolate dessert; I had waited until he was ready to shoot before I took the big, gorgeous chocolate curls that I had made so carefully out of the freezer and found they had flattened and were no longer curls.

Keep a freezer thermometer in your freezer and a refrigerator thermometer in your refrigerator—and look at them often.

And for many of these recipes you will need a candy thermometer (called a candy-jelly-frosting thermometer). This thermometer clips on to the side of a saucepan; bend down and read it at eye level in order to get a correct reading. And make sure the stem is deep enough in the liquid being cooked to give an accurate reading.

CAKE PANS

Bright, shiny surfaces reflect the heat away from the item being baked, preventing the item from browning. Dark, dull metal (black iron, black steel, blue steel, and nonstick finishes) absorb and hold the heat, encouraging a dark crust on the item being baked. This is especially noticeable when baking yeast doughs, or tart pastries in quiche pans. These dark pans are becoming more available lately than they used to be. Marique pans from Belgium and Matfer pans from France—each brand in a variety of sizes and shapes, all dark steel—are generally available in good kitchen shops.

The most popular 8-cup loaf pan measures 9 × 5 × 3 inches. But my favorite, which makes a longer, narrower loaf, measures 10¼ × 3¾ (width at top) × 3⅜ (depth) inches. (It is made of heavy aluminum.) It is generally available at many specialty kitchen shops; it can be bought at, or ordered by mail from, Bobbi & Carole's Cookshop, 7251 S.W. 57th Court, Miami, Florida 33143.

DOUBLE BOILERS

Many of these recipes call for a double boiler. You can buy them in hardware stores or kitchen shops. The thing to look for is one in which the upper section is not too deep (shallow is better) and is smooth (no ridges). I like Revere Ware; it comes in two sizes, and I use both.

If necessary, you can create your own by placing a heatproof bowl over a saucepan of shallow hot water. The bowl should be wide enough at the top so its rim rests on the rim of the saucepan, keeping the bowl suspended over (not touching) the water.

ROLLING PINS

If you have many occasions to use a rolling pin (and I hope that you will—with the pies and tarts, yeast cakes, and many of the cookies in this book), you really should have different sizes and different shapes. Sometimes a very long, thick, and heavy one will be best; for other doughs you will want a smaller, lighter one. The French style, which is extra long, narrow, and tapered at both ends, is especially good for rolling dough into a round shape, as for a pie crust, while the straight-sided pin is better for an oblong shape.

However, in the absence of any rolling pin at all, other things will do a fair job. Try a straight-sided bottle, tall jar, or a drinking glass.

CAKE-DECORATING TURNTABLE

If you ice many cakes, this is a most important piece of equipment. Not that you can't ice a cake without it, but it will not look the same. You will love the smooth, professional-looking results, and the ease of using a turntable. It works on the same principle as a lazy Susan and although a lazy Susan can be used in place of a turntable, it usually does not turn quite so easily.

I put the cake on a cake plate and then put the plate on the turntable.

First put the icing on freely just to cover the cake. Then hold a long, narrow metal spatula in your right hand, with the blade at about a 30-degree angle against the side or the top of the cake. With your left hand slowly rotate the turntable. Hold your right hand still as the cake turns and in a few seconds you will have a smooth, sleek, neat-looking cake. It is fun. And exciting.

I also use the turntable when trimming and then fluting the edge of pie crust (you will love using it for this).

Turntables are available at specialty kitchen equipment shops and at wholesale restaurant and bakery suppliers. They do not have to be expensive. The thing to look for is one that turns very easily. There is no reason why a turntable, if it is not abused, should not last a lifetime or two.

PASTRY BAGS

The best pastry bags for many years have been those that are made of canvas and are coated on one side only with plastic. Use them with the plastic coating inside. The small opening generally has to be cut a bit larger to allow the metal tubes to fit.

And now there are new, thinner, lightweight nylon bags from France named IMPER that are a joy to use.

Either kind should be washed in hot soapy water, then just hung up to dry.

When filling a pastry bag, unless there is someone else to hold it for you, it is generally easiest if you support the bag by placing it in a tall and wide glass or jar.

SMALL, NARROW METAL SPATULA

Many of my recipes call for this tool for smoothing icing around the sides of a cake. Mine is 8 inches long; it has a 4-inch blade and a 4-inch wooden handle. The blade is ⅝ inch wide and has a rounded tip. Although it can bend, it is more firm than flexible. Metal spatulas are generally available in a variety of sizes and shapes in specialty kitchen supply stores. A table knife can be used in place of this small spatula.

Techniques

ABOUT MEASURING

Meticulously precise measurements are essential for good results in baking.

Glass or plastic measuring cups with the measurements marked on the side and the 1-cup line below the top are only for measuring liquids. Do not use them for flour or sugar. With the cup at eye level, fill carefully to exactly the line indicated.

Measuring cups that come in graded sets of four (¼ cup, ⅓ cup, ½ cup, and 1 cup) are for measuring flour, sugar, and other dry ingredients—and for thick sour cream. Fill the cup to overflowing and then scrape off the excess with a dough scraper, a metal spatula, or the flat side of a knife.

Standard measuring spoons must be used for correct measurements. They come in sets of four: ¼ teaspoon, ½ teaspoon, 1 teaspoon, and 1 tablespoon. For dry ingredients, fill the spoon to overflowing and then scrape off the excess with a small metal spatula or the flat side of a knife.

TO ADD DRY INGREDIENTS ALTERNATELY WITH LIQUID

Begin and end with dry. The procedure is generally to add about one-third of the dry, then half of the liquid, a second third of the dry, the rest of the liquid, and then the rest of the dry.

Use the lowest speed on an electric mixer for this (or it may be done by hand using a rubber or wooden spatula—some few people do it with a bare hand). After each addition mix only until smooth. If your mixer is the type that allows you to use a rubber spatula while it is in motion, help the mixing along by scraping the sides of the bowl with the spatula. If the mixer does not allow room, or if it is a hand-held mixer, stop it frequently and scrape the bowl with the spatula; do not beat any more than necessary.

ABOUT FOLDING INGREDIENTS TOGETHER

Many of these recipes call for folding beaten egg whites and/or whipped cream into another mixture. The whites and/or cream have air beaten into them, and folding rather than mixing is done in order to retain the air.

This is an important step and should be done with care. The knack of doing it well comes with practice and concentration. Remember that you want to incorporate the mixtures without losing any air. That means handle as little as possible.

It is important not to beat the whites or whip the cream until they are actually stiff; if you do you will have to stir and mix rather than fold, thereby losing the air.

Do not let beaten egg whites stand around or they will become dry and separate. Do not fold whipped cream into a warm mixture or the heat will deflate the cream. Generally it is best to fold the lighter mixture into the heavier one, and to actually stir a bit of the lighter mixture into the heavier (to lighten it a bit) before you start to fold. Then, as a rule, it is best not to add all of the remaining light mixture at once; do the folding in a few additions. The first additions should not be folded thoroughly.

Although many professional chefs use their bare hands for folding, most home cooks are more comfortable using a rubber spatula. Rubber is better than plastic because it is more flexible. Spatulas come in three sizes. The smallest is called a bottle scraper. For most folding, the medium size is the one to use. But for folding large amounts in a large bowl, the largest rubber spatula can be very helpful. The one I mean might measure about 13 to 16 inches from the end of the blade to the end of the handle; the blade will be about 2¾ inches wide and about 4½ inches long. This large size is difficult to locate; try specialty kitchen equipment shops or wholesale restaurant suppliers.

To fold ingredients together it is best to use a bowl with a rounded bottom, and it is better if the bowl is too large rather than too small. Following the recipe, place part (occasionally all, depending on the recipe) of the light mixture on top of the heavier mixture. Hold the rubber spatula, rounded side toward the bottom and over the middle of the bowl, and cut through to the bottom of the bowl. Bring the spatula toward you against the bottom, then up the side and out, over the top, turning your wrist and the blade as you do this so the blade is upside down when it comes out over the top. Return the spatula to its original position, then cut through the middle of the mixture again. After each fold, rotate the bowl slightly in order to incorporate the ingredients as much as possible. Continue only until both mixtures are combined.

Occasionally a bit of beaten egg white will rise to the top. If it is just one or two small pieces, instead of folding more, simply smooth over the top gently with the spatula.

If the base mixture has gelatin in it, it should be chilled until it starts to thicken.

When folding, it is ideal to have the gelatin mixture, the whipped cream, and/or the egg whites all the same consistency (although in some cases that is not possible).

TO MEASURE THE CAPACITY
OF A CAKE PAN

Fill a large measuring cup with water and pour it into the pan to over-flowing. If it is a two-piece pan, and the water would run out, fill it with sugar or rice or beans instead of water.

ABOUT PREPARING CAKE PANS

In many recipes, after buttering the pan, I dust it with bread crumbs, because in many recipes, but not all, there is less chance of sticking if you use crumbs rather than flour. The crumbs should be fine and dry. They may be homemade (see below) but I always have purchased ones on hand. If you use purchased ones, be sure to buy the ones marked "plain" or "unseasoned," *not* "seasoned." Some brands are O.K. just as they are, some are a bit coarse; they may be ground a little finer in a food processor or blender—but don't overdo it, they should be crumbs, not powder. You can grind a whole boxful in two or three batches and store them ready to use.

To prepare a tube pan: When directions call for buttering the pan and then coating it with flour or crumbs, the only way to get the flour or crumbs on the tube itself is by lifting them with your fingers and sprinkling them around the tube with your fingers.

In all of these recipes, the butter and flour or bread crumbs used to prepare the pans are in addition to those called for in the ingredients.

HOMEMADE DRY BREAD CRUMBS

Remove and discard the crusts from sliced white bread. Place the slices in a single layer on cookie sheets in a 225-degree oven and bake until the bread is completely dry and crisp. Although if it is so stale that it is completely dry, it is not necessary to bake it. Break up the slices coarsely and grind them in a processor or a blender until the crumbs are rather fine, but not as fine as powder.

TO BUTTER A FANCY-SHAPED
TUBE PAN

If you spread the butter with a piece of wax paper it feels clumsy and seems inefficient. If you melt the butter and brush it on, it seems as though most of the butter runs down to the bottom of the pan. It is best to let some butter stand at room temperature to soften. Then use a pastry brush to brush it carefully all over the pan.

COOKIE SHEETS

I use Wear-Ever cookie sheets that measure 15½ × 12 inches and have only one raised rim, and I line them with aluminum foil (instead of buttering the sheets—the foil keeps the cookies from sticking). The usual extra-large roll of 12-inch foil has 200 feet. If you would like a box of Reynolds foil that has 1,000 feet, in a strong box with a wonderful cutting edge, you can buy it (and the above cookie sheets) from Bobbi & Carole's Cookshop, 7251 S.W. 57th Court, Miami, Florida 33143.

HOW TO PREPARE ORANGES, GRAPEFRUITS, AND LEMONS

I use the juice of fresh lemons or oranges in all recipes calling for their juice. If possible, I recommend that you do the same for the best flavor.

In recipes that call for the grated rind of lemons or oranges, the grated rind of fresh fruit has a better flavor than bought dried grated rind.

To Grate the Rind

It is best to use firm, deep-colored, thick-skinned fruit. And it is best if the fruit is cold; the rind is firmer and grates better. Use a standing metal grater—usually they have four sides, or some are round. Hold the grater up to the light and look at the shapes of the holes from the inside. You should use the small holes that are round, not diamond-shaped. Place the grater on a piece of wax paper on the work surface. Wash and dry the fruit. Hold the grater firmly in place with your left hand. With your right hand hold the fruit cupped in your palm at the top of the grater. Now, press the fruit firmly against the grater as you push the fruit down toward the bottom of the grater. Press firmly, but do not overdo it—all you want is the zest (the thin, colored outside part), so do not work over the same spot on the fruit or you will be grating the white underneath; rotate the fruit in your hand as you press it against the grater. Remove the gratings from the inside of the grater with a rubber spatula.

To Pare the Rind

Use a vegetable peeler with a swivel blade to remove the thin, colored outer rind.

To Peel an Orange, Grapefruit, or Lemon

Place the fruit on a board on its side. With a sharp, thin knife, cut off the top and the bottom. Turn the fruit upright, resting on a flat end. Hold the fruit with your left hand as you cut down toward the board with your right hand, curving the knife around the fruit and cutting away a strip of peel—cut right to the fruit itself in order not to leave any of the white underskin. Rotate the fruit a bit and cut away the next strip of peel. Continue all the way around. Then hold the fruit in the palm of your left hand and carefully trim away any remaining white parts.

To Section an Orange, Grapefruit, or Lemon

Work over a bowl to catch the juice. With a small, thin, sharp knife, cut down against the inside of the membrane of one section on both sides, releasing the section and leaving the membrane. After removing one or two sections, continue as follows: Cut against the membrane on the left side of a section and then, without removing the knife, turn the blade up against the membrane on the right side of the section. The section will fall out clean. After removing all the sections, squeeze the leftover membrane in your hand to extract any juice. Carefully remove any seeds.

ABOUT DECORATING CAKES

Cake decorating can be just as much a creative art as painting or sculpting. But to me, the pure untouched simplicity of a smooth, shiny chocolate glaze, or a topping of barely firm whipped cream, is perfection and adding anything to it would detract from an already perfect work of art. The same goes for an un-iced pound cake or loaf cake. Of course there are times when I like to wield a pastry bag and don't ever want to quit. But please don't feel that every cake needs decoration; simplicity is often decoration enough. Anything else might be gilding the lily.

Very often, a few small, fresh, beautiful flowers are a wonderful decoration. Either place them on the plate alongside the cake, or cut the stems short and place a few (or sometimes only one) directly on top of the cake, either resting on the cake, or inserted into it.

HOW TO PREPARE THE SERVING PLATE BEFORE YOU ICE THE CAKE

This is done to keep any icing off the plate. It will result in a clean, neat, professional-looking finished product.

Begin by tearing off a 10-inch piece of wax paper. Fold it crossways into four equal strips (fold it in half and then in half again), then cut through the folds with a sharp knife, making four 10 × 3-inch strips.

Lay the strips in a square pattern around the rim of the plate, put the cake on the plate over the paper, and check to be sure that the papers touch the cake all around.

After the cake is iced (before the icing hardens) remove the papers by pulling each one out toward a narrow end.

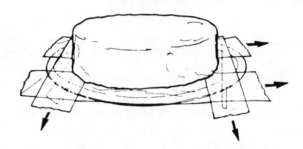

IF YOU PLAN TO TRANSPORT A CAKE

If you plan to transport a cake that is iced, here's a trick I learned during the years when I baked desserts at home and my husband carried them in a station wagon to his restaurant.

Melt about half an ounce of semisweet chocolate and place it in the center of the cake plate. Place the cake directly on the chocolate, which will act as a paste to keep the cake from sliding.

ABOUT WRAPPING COOKIES

Unless I am baking cookies to serve right away, I wrap them in clear cellophane. It gives them an attractive and professional look, keeps them fresh, easy to handle, easy to pack for the freezer, lunch box, or picnic, and makes it handy if you want to slip a few into a little bag, basket, or box as a gift.

Clear cellophane is hard to find. Try wholesale paper companies, the kind that sell paper napkins, etc., to restaurants. Or buy or order it by mail from Bobbi & Carole's Cookshop, 7251 S.W. 57th Court, Miami, Florida 33143. (When you buy it, if you have a choice of widths, it is easier to handle if it is no more than 20 inches wide.)

If you cannot get cellophane, wax paper is better than plastic wrap (which is too hard to handle, takes too long, and will drive you crazy).

It is easier to cut cellophane with a knife than with scissors. Cut off a long piece, fold it in half crossways, cut through the fold with a long, sharp knife, fold again and cut again, and continue to fold and cut until you have the right width pieces. Then cut the other way. (The size depends on the size of the cookies.) If the size is close but a bit too large, do not cut the papers individually (it takes too long). Instead, place the whole pile in front of you and fold one side of the entire pile to the size you want. Place your left hand firmly on the pile, holding the folded side down and at the same time holding the pile so that the papers do not slip out of place. With your right hand cut through the pile with a knife. (If the pile is very large, cut through about a dozen or two at a time.)

Bar cookies should be wrapped individually. Small drop cookies or thin rolled cookies, and some refrigerator cookies, may be wrapped two to a package, placed with their bottoms together.

Wrap one cookie as a sample to be sure that the papers are the right size.

Spread out as many pieces of cellophane as you have room for (or as many as you have cookies for).

1. Place a cookie in the center of each paper.

2. Bring the two long sides together up over the top.

3, 4. Fold over twice so that the second fold brings the cellophane tight against the cookie.

5. Now, instead of just tucking the ends underneath, fold in the corners of each end, making a triangular point.

6. Then fold the triangles down under the cookie.

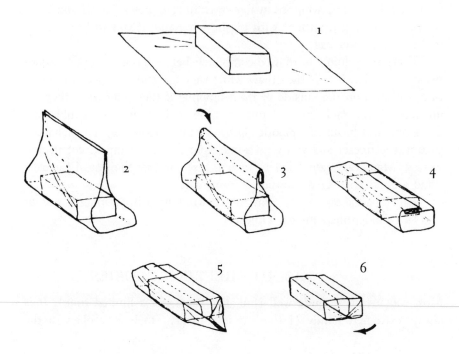

HOW TO WASH A PASTRY BRUSH

If you have used the brush for a sugar glaze, just rinse it under warm running water, separating the bristles a bit with your fingers so the water reaches all of them. If you have used it to butter a pan, it is important to remove every bit of butter or it will become rancid on the brush and I don't know any way to ever get rid of that. First rinse the brush briefly under running hot water. Then rub it well on a cake of soap, first rubbing one side of the bristles and then the other. Rinse well under hot running water, then repeat the soaping and rinsing one or two more times to be sure. Just let it stand bristle side up in a dish drainer or in a glass to dry.

ABOUT FREEZING CAKES

I don't think that any baked dessert tastes as good after freezing as when it is fresh. However, if it is frozen for only a short time (a few days or weeks) the difference might be infinitesimal. I have indicated in many of these recipes that the dessert can be frozen. If it is a big help to you to prepare it ahead, do it. But if you have your choice, fresh is best.

If you want to ice a cake first and then freeze it, it may be frozen directly on the cake plate and left on the plate, or, to keep the cake from sticking to the plate, it may be placed on wax paper or baking-pan liner paper (cut to fit the bottom of the cake) on the plate, and then removed from the plate and wrapped when it is frozen. Freeze until the icing is firm, then wrap it airtight with plastic wrap and, if you wish, rewrap it in foil or a freezer bag.

Everything should be thawed completely before it is unwrapped. (Foods sweat while thawing. If they thaw while they are still wrapped, the moisture will form on the outside of the wrapping; if they thaw after they are unwrapped, the moisture will form on the food itself—that could spoil the looks of a beautiful smooth glaze or icing.) However, if you have a cake in the freezer and you want some right away, unwrap it, cut it, and serve it. Many cakes are delicious frozen. Just don't let the rest of the cake stand around uncovered—rewrap it immediately.

Label packages—if not, you might wind up with a freezer full of UFO's (Unidentified Frozen Objects).

ABOUT FREEZING COOKIES

Most cookies freeze quite well (but, like cakes, for a limited time). It is always extremely handy (I think it is a luxury) to have cookies in the freezer for unexpected company; they usually thaw quickly, and many can be served frozen directly from the freezer.

(Almost always, when I need a quick, or not so quick, gift for someone, my first thought is cookies. And if they are in the freezer, individually wrapped in cellophane, all I have to do is plan some attractive packaging for them.)

The same rule about thawing cakes applies to cookies—thaw before unwrapping.

Any cake or cookie that may be frozen, may be thawed and refrozen—even several times. I do it often. I would rather refreeze it immediately than let it stand around and get stale.

ABOUT CUTTING CAKES, PIES, AND BAR COOKIES

I can do a better job if I stand rather than sit.

Cakes and pies should be cut carefully and neatly with a very sharp knife that is long enough. You may not use the whole blade, but it gives leverage. Some cakes cut best with a sawing motion—try it. Some cut best with a serrated knife—try that, also.

If it is a round cake or a pie, always start cutting each pie-shaped wedge from the exact center. Mark the center with the tip of the knife. Or, to find the center, lightly score the cake or pie in half first in one direction and then in the opposite direction. Then, if you don't trust yourself to cut freehand, mark each quarter lightly with the tip of the knife, marking the outside edge into 2 to 6 portions, depending on the size of the cake or pie and the size of the portions. But always keep your eye on the center so that the slices all radiate out from there.

Talking about size of portions, unless it is for a restaurant—and sometimes even if it is—small portions are better than large.

If it is a loaf cake or a square cake, it may be a big help to use a ruler and toothpick to mark the portions.

Fruitcakes cut best when they are very cold.

So do pound cakes.

Sponge cakes, angel-food cakes, chiffon cakes—all light and airy cakes—should be cut with a serrated French bread knife. Use a sawing motion and do not press down on the cake or you will squash it.

Brownies and many other bar cookies cut best if they are very cold or almost frozen. Work on a cutting surface that is too large rather than one that is too small. Use a very long and very sharp knife. Or try a serrated one. (I once watched a cook cutting—or trying to cut—Brownies that were at room temperature, on a small cutting board, with a small and dull knife, and he was sitting down. It was a mess.)

Occasionally, for certain cakes (for many cheesecakes, for some layer cakes with sticky icing, and for some others) it is best if the knife blade is hot and wet. In the kitchen, work next to the sink. Or, in the dining room, have a tall jar or pitcher of hot water handy. And have a towel to wipe the blade after cutting each slice.

Then there are times when you do not need to wet the blade, but you do need to wipe it before cutting each slice.

Mainly, take your time. And if it isn't going too well, remember all the options—try a different knife, or a wet blade, or simply wipe the blade.

A FINAL WORD

I once put a cake in the oven and then realized that I had forgotten to use the baking powder that the recipe called for. (The cake had beaten egg whites in it and there was no way I could still add the baking powder.) I learned the hard way that it is necessary to organize all the ingredients listed in a recipe—line them up in the order they are called for—before you actually start mixing. As you use an ingredient, set it aside. That way, nothing should be left on the work surface when you are through. A quick look during and after mixing will let you know if something was left out.

Cakes

Plain Cakes

Chocolate Cakes and Cheesecakes

French Chocolate Loaf Cake

10 PORTIONS

In my chocolate book I told the story of my life-long search for the recipe for a particular chocolate cake sold at a French pastry shop in New York City. I confessed that I still could not make it but would keep on trying. And I did.

Eureka!

These ingredients and these directions might not be the same as those in the elusive "Le Trianon"—I probably will never know—but the result is mighty close to, if not the same as, the cake I fell in love with almost forty years ago.

The cake as it is sold today does not taste the same to me as it did years ago. I can still remember the sensation, and my descriptive adjectives: moist, smooth, rich, dense/dark/delicious, a cross between fudge candy, chocolate pudding, and chocolate cheesecake.

That is what this recipe will make.

For the first dozen or so years that I tried to make this, I concentrated on recipes with only 1 or 2 spoonfuls of flour and only about 15 minutes of baking. The results were too much like an icing. Years later, when I used cornstarch instead of flour, more of it, and a longer baking time, I felt that I was getting close, but the cakes always cracked badly and were unattractive, and they had a too-dry outside and a too-wet inside.

One day, out of the blue, my husband suggested baking it in a pan of water. I did not think that would make a bit of difference but I had run out of other things to try. I could not believe my eyes! Without the water the recipe rose in a high mound with a deep crack down the middle and hollows on the sides. With the water it rose only slightly—very flat, very beautiful, no cracks and no hollows.

This cake may be made ahead of time and may be frozen for a month or so. It is possible to serve it directly from the freezer—it will not be too hard to slice—but it is more tender and more delicate at room temperature.

It is a very plain-looking loaf, which may be covered with optional chocolate curls (easily made with milk chocolate), and may be served alone or with whipped cream and berries.

> ¾ cup sifted cornstarch (sift before measuring
>   and do not pack down when measuring)
> 8 ounces semisweet chocolate (see Notes)
> 1 tablespoon instant coffee
> ¼ cup boiling water
> 3 ounces (¾ stick) unsalted butter
> ½ cup granulated sugar
> 4 eggs (graded large), separated
> ⅛ teaspoon salt

Adjust a rack one-third up from the bottom of the oven and preheat oven to 350 degrees. You will need a loaf pan with a 6-cup capacity; mine measures 8½ × 4½ × 2¾ inches.

To line the pan with foil: Place the pan upside down on the work surface. Measure the bottom of the pan—the bottom of my pan measures 7⅝ × 3⅝ inches (yours may vary). Cut two strips of foil; one to fit the length (bottom and sides) and one to fit the width (bottom and sides) of the pan. For the measurements of my pan, one piece is cut a scant 7⅝ × about 10 inches, and one piece is cut a scant 3⅝ × about 14½ inches (both measurements allow a little excess to extend over the rim of the pan when the foil is in place). If the foil is not measured carefully and if it is too wide, it will wrinkle when it is placed in the pan. (I mark the foil with a pencil and tear it against a straight-edge table or counter top.) Now, to shape the foil to fit the pan without wrinkling the foil, carefully place one piece over the upside-down pan, center it, and fold it down on the sides of the pan. Remove the foil and set it aside. Repeat the procedure with the second piece of foil, folding it down on the remaining two sides of the pan. Remove the second piece of foil. Turn the pan upright. Carefully place one piece of the foil in the pan, press it into place, and then place the other piece in the pan and press it into place. There will be two thicknesses on the bottom. The sides of the foil may extend about half an inch or so above the pan, and may be folded down over the rim. (Since the pan flares at the top, the upper corners of the pan will remain unlined—it is O.K.)

During the preparation of the pan, handle the foil carefully and do not wrinkle it—the wrinkles would show up in the finished cake. (Incidentally, I could line several pans in less time than it took me to describe it.)

Now, there are two ways of treating the foil. One is to brush it carefully with melted butter. The other is to set the pan aside until you are ready to pour the batter in, and then spray it generously with Pam or any other vegetable cooking spray. The Pam does a slightly better job than butter; with butter the cake might stick, but it will only be a very little bit.

After sifting and measuring the cornstarch, resift it three more times and set it aside.

Break up or coarsely chop the chocolate and place it in a heavy saucepan with about a 4-cup capacity. Dissolve the coffee in the water and pour it over the chocolate. Cover, place over low heat, and let stand for a few minutes until the chocolate starts to melt. Do not overcook. Stir (preferably with a small wire whisk) until smooth, and then transfer to a small bowl to stop the cooking and set aside to cool slightly.

Meanwhile, in the large bowl of an electric mixer, beat the butter until soft. Gradually add the sugar and beat for 2 or 3 minutes, scraping the bowl occasionally with a rubber spatula. Add the yolks one at a time, scraping the bowl and beating after each addition until incorporated. Then continue to beat for a few minutes until the mixture is pale and creamy.

On low speed add the chocolate, which may still be slightly warm or may be at room temperature. Scrape the bowl and beat only until smooth. Then add the cornstarch, scrape the bowl, and beat only until smooth. Remove from the mixer and set aside.

In the small bowl of the electric mixer, with clean beaters (or if you prefer, in any small bowl with an egg beater), beat the whites and the salt *only* until the whites just stand up straight when the beaters are raised— do not overbeat.

Add 1 rounded tablespoonful of the whites (just guess the amount— don't measure) to the chocolate mixture and stir to mix. Repeat with a second spoonful, and then with a third. Fold in about half of the remaining whites without being too thorough, and then fold in the balance of the whites, folding gently but completely.

If you are using Pam, spray the pan now, rather generously. Pour the batter into the pan.

Lift the pan in both hands and move it gently from left to right and front to back in order to smooth the top of the batter.

Place the cake pan in a larger pan (which must not be deeper than the cake pan; incidentally, if the larger pan is made of aluminum, sprinkle about ½ teaspoon of cream of tartar in the pan to keep it from discoloring). Pour boiling water into the large pan until it is about an inch deep.

Bake for 50 to 55 minutes until a cake tester gently inserted into the middle, all the way to the bottom, comes out just barely clean and dry. Test very carefully several times to be sure. There will be a thin crust on top; the middle of the cake will be soft. *Do not overbake.*

Turn off the heat and open the oven door a few inches; let cool that way for 20 minutes. Then open the oven door all the way and let the cake stand for about an hour until cooled to room temperature. (If you need the oven, let the cake cool in the oven for only half the time, and then let it finish cooling in the kitchen.)

Remove the cake pan from the water and dry the pan. Cover the cake with a flat serving plate or a board. Turn over the plate or board and the cake pan, remove the pan and the foil. Serve the cake upside down. (The cake may now be frozen.)

Before serving, the cake may be covered with chocolate curls (see below), and then sprinkled generously with confectioners sugar sifted through a strainer held over the top.

This may be served as it is, but it is better with a spoonful of softly whipped cream (sweetened only slightly with confectioners or granulated sugar, and flavored slightly with vanilla extract). And with a spoonful of fresh raspberries or strawberries, or with just barely thawed and partially drained frozen raspberries.

Make the portions small.

NOTES: 1. *I especially like Lindt Surfin, Lindt Excellence, and Tobler Tradition, all of which are labeled "bittersweet," which is the same as semisweet; just use the best semisweet you can get.*

The Tobler chocolates are available at Paprikas Weiss, 1546 Second Avenue, New York, New York 10028. Both Tobler and Lindt chocolates are available at Bobbi & Carole's Cookshop, 7251 S.W. 57th Court, Miami, Florida 33143.

I have been told that the original cake—the one I tried to duplicate—is made with Van Leer chocolate. Mr. Malcolm Campbell, of the Van Leer Chocolate Corporation, verified that they do indeed sell a semisweet chocolate to Colette, but he thinks that the cake is made with a combination of chocolates, possibly both semisweet and unsweetened.

2. Correct oven temperature is critical for this cake; if the oven is too warm and the cake overbakes even slightly it loses its wondrous texture and quality. If you do not have a portable oven thermometer to check your oven temperature, please get one.

MILK CHOCOLATE CURLS

These are the easiest chocolate curls, and they're adorable. They are made with a swivel-bladed vegetable peeler and with milk chocolate, which will give the results you want with the least amount of trouble. The ½-pound bar is thicker than most smaller bars; you will use only about an ounce or so, but you will have better results with a thick piece of chocolate.

Work over wax paper. Hold a piece of the chocolate in your left hand, making the curls either from the side of the piece of chocolate or from the bottom; try both. Move the vegetable peeler along the chocolate, moving it toward yourself, pressing it very firmly against the chocolate.

Spoon the curls on the cake, piling on as many as will stay.

The Robert Redford Cake

16 PORTIONS

Chocolate News, *a food publication, recently printed a photo of Robert Redford along with a recipe for a chocolate honey cake which, they said, he had enjoyed at the Hisae restaurant in New York City.*

I broke the 4-minute mile getting to the kitchen to try the recipe, and it was a delicious cake.

Soon after that my husband and I were in New York and went to Hisae. With the first bite I knew the cake was different from the one I had made. This one had less of a honey taste, but it was a sweeter cake. The management was extremely generous about sharing the recipe. (The fact that it is very different from the one in Chocolate News *is a mystery I am not trying to solve.)*

This is the recipe from the restaurant. It is closely related—about like a big sister—to Queen Mother's Cake (see Note), which is in both my first dessert book and my chocolate book. This has honey instead of sugar, it has fewer nuts, and it is a larger cake and makes more portions. It is super dense-compact, moist and rich, not too sweet, and it really should be served with whipped cream and, if possible, berries.

If it weren't for Redford's picture I probably would not have noticed the recipe to begin with. So thank you, Robert Redford; you are a gentleman and a scholar and a man of good taste indeed.

6½ ounces (1¼ cups) blanched hazelnuts or
blanched almonds (see page 9 for
blanching directions)
12 ounces semisweet chocolate (I have made
this with both Tobler Tradition and with
Tobler Mi-Amer, both labeled bittersweet
which means the same as semisweet)
6 ounces (1½ sticks) unsalted butter
½ cup honey
10 eggs (graded large), separated
¼ teaspoon salt

Adjust a rack one-third up in the oven and preheat the oven to 375 degrees. Butter a 10 × 3-inch round cake pan or spring form. Line the bottom with a round of wax paper or baking-pan liner paper cut to fit, butter the paper, and dust all over with fine, dry bread crumbs. Tap to shake out excess crumbs over a piece of paper; set the pan aside.

The blanched hazelnuts or almonds must be ground to a fine powder; it can be done in a food processor, a blender, or a nut grinder. Set the ground nuts aside. Break up or coarsely chop the chocolate and place it in the top of a large double boiler over shallow, warm water on moderate heat. Cover with a folded paper napkin or paper towel (to absorb condensation) and with the pot cover. Let stand until partly melted, then uncover and stir until completely melted. Remove the top of the double boiler, carefully dry the bottom (a drop of moisture in the chocolate would make it "tighten"), and transfer the chocolate to a bowl (to stop the cooking). Stir occasionally until tepid or cooled to room temperature.

Meanwhile, in the large bowl of an electric mixer, beat the butter until it is soft. Gradually add the honey and beat until smooth. Then add the egg yolks, two or three at a time, beating until smooth after each addition. (The mixture will look curdled now, it is O.K.) Beat only until mixed.

Add the chocolate and beat, scraping the bowl with a rubber spatula, and beating only until mixed. (The curdled look will go away now.)

Add the ground nuts and beat only to mix.

Now, to beat the egg whites, you will either need the same bowl and beaters you used for the chocolate mixture (in which case, transfer the chocolate mixture to another large bowl, and thoroughly wash the bowl and beaters), or if you have an additional large bowl for your mixer and an extra set of beaters, use those, or beat the eggs in a large copper bowl with a large, balloon-shaped wire whisk. Either way, add the salt to the whites and beat only until the whites just barely stand up straight when the beater or whisk is raised, or when some of the whites are lifted on a rubber spatula.

With a large rubber spatula, fold about one-quarter of the whites into the chocolate mixture. Then fold in another quarter.

Now, if you have a larger mixing bowl (I use an 8-quart one), transfer the folded mixture to the larger bowl, add the remaining whites, and fold together gently only until the mixtures are blended. If you do not have a larger bowl to finish the folding, it can be done in the large mixer bowl, but not quite as easily—it is a large amount of batter.

Turn the mixture into the prepared pan. Bake at 375 degrees for 20 minutes, then reduce the temperature to 350 degrees and bake for 50 minutes more (total baking time is 70 minutes), until a cake tester comes out clean. Turn the oven off, open the oven door, and let the cake cool in the oven for about 15 minutes. Then remove it from the oven and let it stand at room temperature until completely cool. During the cooling, the cake will sink more in the center than along the rim; that is what it should do.

When the cake is completely cool, cover it with a rack and turn over the pan and rack. Remove the pan and the paper lining. Cover the cake with another rack and invert again, leaving the cake right side up.

Now the top of the cake must be cut with a long, thin, sharp knife to make it level. (It is easiest to do this if you place the cake on a cake-decorating turntable.)

The cake may be iced either side up; if the sides taper in toward the top (which happens sometimes), it is best to ice it right side up, but if the sides are straight it is best to ice it upside down. Place the cake carefully on a large cake platter or a serving board.

To protect the plate while you ice the cake, you will need four 10 × 3-inch strips of wax paper. Use a wide metal spatula to gently raise one side of the cake and slide a strip of the paper partly under the cake. Repeat with the remaining papers, and check to be sure that the papers touch the cake all around.

If you have a cake-decorating turntable, place the cake platter or serving board on it.

Prepare the icing.

ICING

¾ cup heavy cream
12 ounces semisweet chocolate (it may be the
      same as the chocolate in the cake, or it may
      be a different one)

In a heavy saucepan over moderate heat cook the cream until it forms a wrinkled skin on the top. Meanwhile, break up or coarsely chop the chocolate. When the cream is ready, add the chocolate, reduce the heat to low, and stir with a small wire whisk until the mixture is perfectly smooth. Transfer it to a bowl to stop the cooking. Stir occasionally until cool and very slightly thickened.

Pour the cooled icing over the top of the cake. Carefully spread it to allow only a small amount of it to run down the sides of the cake. With a long, narrow metal spatula, spread the top very smoothly (easy if you are working on a cake-decorating turntable) and then with a small, narrow metal spatula, smooth the sides. (The icing on the sides might run down a bit onto the wax papers on the plate; if so, it might be necessary to use a rubber spatula to scoop it up and replace it on the sides, and then to smooth it again.)

Remove the wax-paper strips by pulling each one out toward a narrow end, pulling them slowly and gently.

This may be served soon while the icing is soft, or it may wait overnight at room temperature. (If you make the cake ahead of time it may be frozen. Thaw and ice it the day it is to be served, or a day ahead.)

This cake really is just not complete without whipped cream. Fresh raspberries or strawberries are also a part of the recipe. (If you do not have fresh berries, do not serve any.)

WHIPPED CREAM

The amount of whipped cream to prepare depends on the number of portions you will serve. Plan on 1 cup of heavy cream for each 4 or 5 portions. For each cup of cream, add 2 tablespoons of confectioners or granulated sugar, or 1 tablespoon of honey, and ½ teaspoon of vanilla extract. In a chilled bowl with chilled beaters whip all the ingredients only until the cream holds a soft shape; it should not be stiff. If you whip the cream early in the day for that evening, refrigerate it; it will separate a bit— just whip it a bit with a small wire whisk before serving.

Serve the cream and the berries separately; spoon a generous amount of each alongside each portion, cream on one side of the cake and berries on the other side.

NOTE: *Many people have written to thank me for Queen Mother's Cake, Hungarian Rhapsody, The Orient Express Chocolate Torte (all three are in my chocolate book), and other flourless chocolate cakes—especially be-*

cause they are so good for Passover. They tell me that they make them with kosher chocolate, matzo meal instead of bread crumbs, and pareve margarine. And they say, "It was the hit of the Seder."

Penni's Mocha Nut Loaf

1 9½-INCH LOAF

This is the cake that my friend Penni Linck made for Christmas gifts when she was the wine and food editor of House & Garden. *It is one of the darkest of all chocolate cakes, and is a terrifically good, not too sweet, coffee-flavored, sour-cream loaf that you will love to give away or keep for yourself any time of the year.*

1½ cups sifted all-purpose flour
1 teaspoon salt
1½ teaspoons baking soda
½ cup unsweetened cocoa powder (preferably Dutch process)
¼ cup powdered instant espresso or other powdered (not granular) instant coffee
1 egg (graded large or extra-large)
1¼ cups sour cream
1 cup granulated sugar
2⅔ ounces (5⅓ tablespoons) unsalted butter, melted
5 ounces (1¼ cups) pecans, cut or broken into medium-size pieces

Adjust an oven rack one-third up from the bottom of the oven and preheat oven to 350 degrees. You will need a loaf pan with a 7-cup capacity; mine measures 9½ × 4½ × 3 inches. If necessary, use a larger pan, but not smaller. (It is best to check by capacity, rather than dimensions.) Butter the pan and dust well with fine, dry bread crumbs, then, over a piece of paper, tap firmly to shake out excess crumbs. Set the pan aside.

Sift together the flour, salt, baking soda, cocoa, and powdered instant espresso. Set aside.

In the large bowl of an electric mixer, on low speed, beat the egg, sour cream, and sugar, just to mix. Beat in the melted butter.

On low speed add the sifted dry ingredients—they may be added all at once—scraping the bowl with a rubber spatula and beating only until the mixture is smooth. Remove from the mixer and stir in the nuts.

Turn the mixture into the prepared pan and smooth the top.

Bake for 1 hour until a cake tester gently inserted into the middle comes out clean and dry.

Cool the cake in the pan for 10 or 15 minutes. Then cover it with a rack, turn over the pan and the rack, remove the pan, cover with another rack and turn over again, leaving the cake right side up. Let stand until completely cool.

When the cake is cool, wrap it in plastic wrap and refrigerate or freeze it until it is thoroughly chilled, or refrigerate it for a day or two. It is best to slice the cake when it is cold. Cut it into about 18 to 20 ½-inch slices. The cake may be served cold or at room temperature.

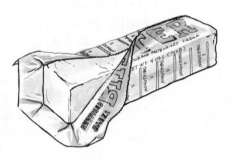

Chocolate Soufflé Cake

10 PORTIONS

One of the most talked-about chocolate cakes in New York City is the Chocolate Soufflé Cake from Fay and Allen's Foodworks (a restaurant and fancy food store). I had heard raves about it. It was described as a soft, moist, rich, dark chocolate mixture with a crisp, brownie-like crust!

In September 1980, my husband and I were on a tour to promote my chocolate book, and were in New York for only a few hectic days. As we were checking out of our hotel I suddenly remembered the Chocolate Soufflé Cake. With the taxi waiting, I rushed to the phone to call Fay and Allen's, and to my surprise and joy, within a few minutes I had the recipe. I spoke to Mr. Mark Allen, the man who bakes the cakes, and the son of the owner. He could not have been nicer or more agreeable. He told me that he got the recipe when he attended the Culinary Institute of America.

It is a flourless mixture similar to a rich chocolate mousse, baked in a large Bundt pan. During baking, a crisp crust forms on the outside; the inside stays moist.

The recipe calls for long, slow baking. You can make this a day ahead or you can freeze it or you can serve it hot, right out of the oven.

> 8 ounces semisweet chocolate (I have made this several times with Maillard's Eagle Sweet, which is semisweet; it is delicious—but you can use any chocolate labeled semisweet, bittersweet, or extra-bittersweet—the less sweet the better)
> 8 ounces (2 sticks) unsalted butter
> 2 tablespoons salad oil
> 8 eggs (graded large), separated
> 1 cup granulated sugar
> 1 teaspoon vanilla extract
> ¼ teaspoon salt
> Optional: confectioners sugar

Adjust a rack one-third up from the bottom of the oven and preheat the oven to 300 degrees. You will need a 10-inch Bundt pan or any other fancy-shaped tube pan with a 12-cup capacity. (Mine is labeled Bundt; it is made by Northland Aluminum Products; it has a nonstick lining.) Butter the pan (even if it has a nonstick lining); the best way is to use room-temperature butter, and brush it on with a pastry brush. Then sprinkle granulated sugar all over the pan; in order to get the sugar on the tube, sprinkle it on with your fingertips. Shake the pan to coat it all with sugar, and then invert it over a piece of paper and tap to shake out excess. Set the pan aside.

Break up or coarsely chop the chocolate and place it in the top of a large double boiler over hot water on moderate heat. Cut up the butter and add it, and the oil, to the chocolate. Cover and let cook until almost completely melted. Then stir, or whisk with a wire whisk, until completely melted and smooth. Remove from the hot water.

In a mixing bowl, stir the yolks a bit with a wire whisk just to mix. Then, gradually, in a few additions, whisk about half of the hot chocolate mixture into the yolks, and then, off the heat, add the yolks to the remaining hot chocolate mixture and mix together (the mixture will thicken a bit as the heat of the chocolate cooks the eggs). Add the sugar and vanilla and stir to mix. Set aside.

In the large bowl of an electric mixer add the salt to the egg whites and beat until the whites hold a point when the beaters are raised but not until they are stiff or dry.

Fold a few large spoonfuls of the whites into the chocolate mixture. Then add the remaining whites and fold together gently only until incorporated.

Gently turn the mixture into the prepared pan.

Bake for 2¼ hours. During baking the cake will rise and then sink; it will sink more in the middle than on the edges. That is as it should be. It is O.K.

Remove from the oven and let stand in the pan for about 5 minutes.

Then cover the cake with an inverted serving plate. Hold the pan and the plate firmly together, and turn them over. The sugar coating in the pan forms a crust and the cake will slide out of the pan easily.

Let stand until cool or serve while still warm. If you wish, cover the top of the cake generously with confectioners sugar, sprinkling it on through a fine strainer held over the cake. Brush excess sugar off the plate.

(On a recent trip to New York I went to Fay and Allen's to eat this cake there. I was thrilled to see that it was precisely the same as the ones I had made. They served it quite warm, just out of the oven, with a generous topping of icy cold whipped cream.)

WHIPPED CREAM

2 cups heavy cream
¼ cup confectioners sugar
1½ teaspoons vanilla extract

In a chilled bowl with chilled beaters whip the ingredients only until the cream holds a shape; it is more delicious if it is not really stiff. (If you whip the cream ahead of time and refrigerate it, it will separate slightly as it stands; just whisk it a bit with a wire whisk before serving.) Serve the cream separately, spooning a generous amount over and alongside each portion.

This is even better if you serve a few fresh raspberries and/or strawberries with each portion.

NOTE: When cutting this cake it will crumble a bit as you cut through the bottom (previously the top) crisp crust. (It did at Fay and Allen's, too.) Don't try to cut thin slices.

Currant Cheesecake

10 TO 12 PORTIONS

This is a large and impressive cream-cheese pie in a graham-cracker crumb crust made in a 10-inch glass pie plate. The cheese filling, which is studded with currants, is unbelievably smooth and mellow. The currants are unusual in a cheesecake, but so is the mixture of cream cheese and butter.
Too good!

It can be made a day or two before serving or just a few hours before. Or, like most cheesecakes, this freezes well.

CRUMB CRUST

2 cups graham-cracker crumbs
3 tablespoons granulated sugar
2 teaspoons cinnamon
4 ounces (1 stick) unsalted butter, melted

Mix the crumbs, sugar, and cinnamon in a mixing bowl. Add the butter and stir/mix with a rubber spatula until the crumbs are evenly moistened. (The mixture will not hold together in the bowl.)

Turn the mixture into a 10-inch ovenproof glass pie plate. With your fingertips distribute the mixture evenly and loosely all over the plate. Then raise the mixture around the sides of the plate; it should still be loose—do not press firmly until the mixture is evenly distributed over the bottom and the sides. Before you start to press it firmly, try to have enough of the crumb mixture on the sides to form a slightly raised rim; there will be a generous amount of filling and the sides must be high enough to hold it all.

Press firmly on the sides first and then on the bottom. Refrigerate briefly.

FILLING

Boiling water
⅔ cup dried currants
24 ounces cream cheese, at room temperature
4 ounces (1 stick) unsalted butter, at
    room temperature
⅛ teaspoon salt
¾ cup granulated sugar
1½ teaspoons vanilla extract
3 eggs (graded large or extra-large)

Adjust a rack to the center of the oven and preheat the oven to 350 degrees.

Pour boiling water over the currants to cover them, let them stand for a minute, drain in a strainer, and then turn out onto a double thickness of paper towels. Fold the towels over the top and press lightly to absorb any remaining water. Set aside.

In the large bowl of an electric mixer beat the cream cheese and butter until they are soft and perfectly smooth. Add the salt, sugar, and vanilla and beat well, scraping the bowl with a rubber spatula, until the mixture is as smooth as honey. Add the eggs one at a time, continuing to scrape the bowl as necessary and beating well after each addition. Remove from the mixer and stir in the currants.

Pour the filling into the crumb crust, watching the edges carefully— if there are any low spots in the crust do not use all of the filling. Smooth the top. Then rotate the pan briskly first in one direction, then the other, to level and smooth the top even more.

Bake for 35 minutes.

Now, to brown the top, turn the broiler on and place the cake 12 inches below the broiler—no closer. Broil, watching carefully, until the top turns a beautiful, rich golden brown. It will take only a minute—watch it every second.

Let the cake cool to room temperature.

It may be served at room temperature or refrigerated for a day or two. Or it may be frozen. However, wonderful as it is any way, it is most tender, delicate, creamy, and delicious at room temperature—the day it is baked.

Long-champs' Cheesecake

10 TO 12 PORTIONS

When the Longchamps' chain of restaurants opened in New York City about 45 years ago, their two most popular desserts were baked apples the size of grapefruits and wonderful cheesecake; they usually sold out of both before the day was over. We lived near the branch on Fifth Avenue and 34th Street and ate there quite often. The manager gave my mother this recipe. Originally, it was prepared in a pastry crust, but I do not have that recipe and I have put it in a crumb crust. It is lighter and less dense than many other cheesecakes and has a fresh-fruit topping. It can be baked a day or two before serving and is absolutely and perfectly marvelous.

CRUMB CRUST

1¾ cups graham-cracker crumbs
⅓ cup granulated sugar
2 teaspoons cinnamon
7 tablespoons plus 1 teaspoon (1 stick minus 2 teaspoons) unsalted butter

Generously butter the sides *only* of a 9 × 2½ or 3-inch spring-form pan. (Leaving the bottom unbuttered makes it easier to transfer the baked cake to a serving plate.)

Stir the crumbs, sugar, and cinnamon in a mixing bowl. Melt the butter, add it, and stir until evenly distributed.

Remove and reserve 1½ cups of the mixture. Press the remainder onto the sides of the pan, but the crust should not be as deep as the pan—it should be 2 inches deep. (If the pan is 2½ inches deep, leave ½ inch uncovered at the top. If the pan is 3 inches deep, leave 1 inch uncovered.) Use your thumbnail to cut around the upper edge of the crust to make it straight. Then press the reserved mixture evenly onto the bottom. Press firmly all over. Place in the refrigerator or freezer until you are ready to use it.

FILLING

> 16 ounces cream cheese, at room temperature
> 1 cup granulated sugar
> ¼ teaspoon salt
> 6 eggs (graded large)
> 1 cup heavy cream
> 1 teaspoon vanilla extract
> Finely grated rind of 2 large lemons

Adjust a rack one-third up from the bottom of the oven and preheat oven to 350 degrees.

In the large bowl of an electric mixer, beat the cheese until it is soft and very smooth. Add the sugar and beat very well, scraping the bowl as necessary with a rubber spatula—the mixture must be smooth. Add the salt and then the eggs, one or two at a time, beating well after each addition. Then beat in the cream and the vanilla. Remove from the mixer and stir in the rind.

Pour the mixture into the prepared crust.

Bake for 1 hour and 20 minutes.

Then, do not remove the cake from the oven, but turn the heat off, open the oven door about 6 or 8 inches, and let the cake stand until cool.

With a small, narrow metal spatula or with a table knife, cut around the cake between the crust and the pan, pressing the blade against the pan. Carefully remove the sides of the pan.

Refrigerate for several hours or for a day or two.

The cake may be served on the bottom of the pan or it may easily be transferred to a flat cake plate. To transfer, use a strong and firm (not flexible), long, narrow metal spatula, or a strong knife with about a 6-inch blade. Insert the spatula or knife between the crust and the pan and gently ease it around to release the cake. It will be easy if the bottom of the pan has not been buttered and if the cake has been chilled enough. Then use either a flat-sided cookie sheet, or the bottom of a loose-bottomed quiche pan, or two wide metal spatulas, and transfer the cake.

TOPPING

This should be done a few hours before serving, at most early in the day for that evening—the less time it stands, the better.

Use either about 2 cups of fresh blueberries or about 3 cups of fresh strawberries.

If you use the blueberries, wash and drain them, then dry them thoroughly—they must be completely dry. Melt about ½ cup of seedless red currant preserves in a small saucepan, stirring over low heat. Let it just come to a boil. Mix it with the berries and spread the mixture over the top of the cake, leaving a 1-inch rim around the outside.

If you use strawberries, wash, hull, and drain them, then dry thoroughly—they must be completely dry. If the berries are small, place them point up all over the cake, leaving a 1-inch rim around the outside. If the berries are large, slice them in half and lay the halves, cut side down, overlapping one another in a ring pattern all over the top (again leaving a 1-inch rim). Large berries or small, it is easiest if you start placing them from the outside rather than from the center. When the fruit is in place, put about ¾ cup of seedless red currant preserves in a small saucepan and stir over low heat until it is melted and comes to a boil. Spoon the preserves slowly and carefully over the berries to coat them completely.

WHIPPED CREAM

¾ cup heavy cream
2 tablespoons confectioners sugar
½ teaspoon vanilla extract
Optional: additional confectioners sugar

In a chilled bowl with chilled beaters, whip the cream with the sugar and vanilla until the cream holds a definite shape, but don't let it get very stiff. Fit a pastry bag with a large star-shaped tube, place the whipped cream in the bag, and form a border around the fruit on the uncovered 1-inch rim by pressing out rosettes of cream, touching one another. Refrigerate.

Just before serving, a tiny bit of confectioners sugar may be sprinkled through a fine strainer over the center only of the fruit.

This is a pleasure to serve, it looks gorgeous, it cuts beautifully and does not stick to the knife.

NOTE: *I believe that the Longchamps' chain has been sold many times and I don't suppose they still serve this cheesecake.*

Fancy Cakes

Walnut Tart from Saint-Paul-de-Vence

16 PORTIONS

This is called a tart and is made with pastry, but it is really a very fancy cake.

A few years ago I taught cooking classes at Ma Cuisine, a cooking school connected to Ma Maison, a wonderful restaurant in Los Angeles. One day we wound up a beautiful lunch in the restaurant with a divine chocolate-walnut-honey pastry that was brand new to me and so good I couldn't stand it. A gentleman who was one of the students in my classes there heard me rave about it and gave me what he said was the recipe. And then one of the food magazines printed the recipe. Then a big new French cookbook printed it. All three recipes were the same, and none of the three worked for me.

I recently came across a four-year-old pamphlet published by the Cuisinart people. And there was the recipe again. This time from Gino Cofacci, one of the best pastry chefs in New York. Gino got it from Le Mas des Serres, a restaurant in a picturesque little medieval walled village on the French Riviera. Gino's recipe was different from the other three (see Notes) and hallelujah—it worked!

It is a French pastry dough formed in a quiche pan, surrounding a rich walnut and honey mixture. After it is baked and cooled it is inverted, iced with chocolate, and decorated with walnuts. It is a large dessert that makes 16 portions, and Mr. Cofacci says that it will keep in the refrigerator for a week or two. Or you can freeze it, even with the icing. And I have kept it at room temperature for a few days. Heaven!

This is not quick and easy, and is not a recipe for a beginning baker. When you make this, you will be so pleased that my congratulations will be lost in the excitement; however, I do congratulate you.

Just a note to give an idea of how special I consider this dessert: When I was invited to dinner at Julia and Paul Child's, this is the dessert I brought.

The following is my own adaptation of the recipe.

You will need an 11 × 1-inch loose-bottomed quiche pan. The pan must be made of blue or black steel (in a shiny pan the bottom will not brown). Mine is made in France by Matfer, and is available in many kitchen shops. It may be bought at, or ordered by mail from, Bridge Kitchenware, 214 East 52nd Street, New York, New York 10022.

The filling should be made first.

FILLING

1½ cups granulated sugar
½ cup water
7 ounces (1¾ sticks) unsalted butter, cut into
    pieces, at room temperature
1 cup less 2 tablespoons milk
⅓ cup honey
12 ounces (3½ cups) walnuts, cut into small
    pieces (the nuts must be in small pieces,
    but they must not be ground, see Notes)

In a 2½- to 3-quart saucepan, cook the sugar and water over moderate heat, stirring with a wooden spatula, until the sugar is dissolved and the mixture comes to a boil. Wash down any sugar crystals clinging to the sides of the pan with a pastry brush dipped in cold water. Increase the heat to high and let boil without stirring. When the mixture starts to color, swirl the pan occasionally, until the syrup caramelizes to a rich butterscotch color. It will take about 7 or 8 minutes of hard boiling.

Remove the pan from the heat for a moment and add the butter and milk—it will give off a lot of steam and it will bubble hard—be careful. With a long-handled wooden spatula stir to mix, and adjust the heat so the mixture just barely simmers for 15 minutes; stir it occasionally. If the mixture appears to be curdled, beat it briskly with a medium-size wire whisk; it might not smooth out completely—O.K. (the curdled look will disappear when the tart is baked). After the 15 minutes, stir in the honey and then the nuts.

Pour the mixture into a large bowl and stir occasionally until cooled to room temperature. (If this is made a day ahead, it may be refrigerated. If so, let it stand at room temperature for at least an hour and stir it to soften before using.)

PASTRY

3 egg yolks

⅓ cup ice water

4 cups sifted all-purpose flour (as with all the recipes in this book that call for sifted flour, sift it before measuring even if the package says presifted)

¼ cup granulated sugar

¼ teaspoon salt

9 ounces (2¼ sticks) unsalted butter, cold and firm, cut into small pieces (the pieces should be no larger than ¼ to ½ inch square; cut the butter ahead of time and refrigerate it)

The pastry can be mixed in an electric mixer, or by hand, or in a food processor. Whichever method you use, first stir the yolks and water with a fork in a small bowl just to mix and then refrigerate.

In a mixer: Place the flour, sugar, salt, and butter in the large bowl of an electric mixer. Beat on lowest speed. If you are using a wide, flat-bottomed bowl, continually push the ingredients in toward the beaters with a rubber spatula (a cone-shaped bowl does it by itself). When the mixer has cut the butter into such small pieces that the mixture resembles coarse oatmeal (which takes about 5 minutes), add the egg-yolk and water mixture and beat for only a few seconds, scraping the bowl with the spatula, until well mixed but not until the mixture holds together.

By hand: Place the dry ingredients in a large bowl and use a pastry blender to cut in the butter until the particles are fine. Then use a large fork to stir in the egg-yolk mixture. It will be dry and crumbly.

In a food processor: This quantity is too much for the original-size processor. If you have one of the larger models, it can be used, following the same procedure as above.

To use the regular-size food processor, not the extra-large one, I have used the following procedure with excellent results. Place half of the flour, sugar, salt, and butter in the processor bowl. Process with 12 to 15 quick on-and-off pulses (12 to 15 seconds) until the butter particles are fine. Transfer to a large bowl. Repeat with the remaining ingredients. Stir the two processed mixtures together. Then use a large fork to stir in the egg-yolk mixture.

Turn the dough out onto a work surface, squeeze it between your hands and knead it until the dough holds together. (Do not handle so much that the butter melts.) Form the dough into a fat sausage shape about 6 inches long with flat ends. Score it lightly into thirds. Then cut it into two pieces—the one piece, for the bottom crust, should be a scant two-thirds (about 3½ inches long), and the other, for the top, should be a generous one-third (about 2½ inches long).

Form both pieces into smooth round balls, flour them lightly, and flatten them a bit into rounds with smooth edges. Wrap each piece in plastic wrap and let stand at room temperature for 20 to 30 minutes, or if the room is very warm, refrigerate the dough for 20 to 30 minutes but no longer or it will crack when it is rolled.

Adjust a rack one-third up from the bottom of the oven. Preheat the oven to 475 degrees. Have ready an 11 × 1-inch loose-bottomed blue or black steel quiche pan; do not butter it, and do not place it on a cookie sheet. If you have a cake-decorating turntable, place the quiche pan on it.

On a floured pastry cloth with a floured rolling pin, roll the larger piece of dough into a 14-inch circle (when it is in place in the pan it must extend a generous ½ inch above the sides of the pan). Loosely drape the pastry over the rolling pin and unroll it over the pan, centering it carefully. Press it into place in the pan. Trim the edges with scissors, leaving a generous ½ inch of pastry standing up above the sides of the pan.

On the floured pastry cloth with the floured rolling pin, roll the remaining piece of dough into a circle a little wider than the quiche pan. Let it stand.

Spoon the filling over the bottom crust and gently smooth it—it must not be mounded in the middle.

Flour your fingers lightly and press the raised rim of dough that extends above the pan (I use my thumb and the side of my folded-under index finger) to make it thinner (that section will be a double thickness when the top is in place; if it is too thick, it will not bake through).

Now, carefully fold down the pressed-thin rim, folding it in to cover the outside edge of the filling all the way around. With a brush, brush that folded-down section with water.

Drape the rolled-out top crust over the rolling pin and unroll it over the filling, centering it carefully. With your fingers press down on the rim to cut off excess pastry; then, with the back of fork tines (floured if necessary), press all around carefully to insure that the crusts are pasted together. It is best to hold the fork so the handle is over the center of the tart and the end of the prongs touch the inside of the rim of the pan. With a small, sharp knife, pierce the top in two or three places near the center.

Bake for 20 minutes until the top is golden brown. Watch it carefully and constantly; if it bubbles up anywhere, make a small slit with a sharp paring knife to release trapped air, and, if necessary, press down on the bubble with a metal spatula to flatten it. Remove from the oven. If the top is uneven, place a lightweight board or baking sheet on it for a few minutes to flatten it a bit as it cools.

Let stand in the pan until completely cool. Then cover the tart with a large, flat serving platter or board and *very carefully* turn over the platter and the tart. Remove the sides and bottom of the quiche pan.

Cut six strips of wax paper about 8 × 3 inches. Carefully lift the edges of the tart (with a wide metal spatula, or with your fingers) just enough to allow you to slide the edges of the wax papers under the tart to protect the platter while you ice the tart.

If you have a cake-decorating turntable or a lazy Susan, place the platter on it.

ICING

> 9 ounces semisweet chocolate (I have used
> Maillard's Eagle Sweet, Tobler Tradition,
> Lindt Excellence—all wonderful—but use
> any semisweet you like)
> 3½ ounces (1 stick minus 1 tablespoon)
> unsalted butter, cut into small pieces, at
> room temperature
> 16 perfect walnut halves (for decoration)

Break up or chop the chocolate into small pieces and place it and the butter in the top of a large double boiler over hot water on moderate heat. Cover for a few minutes until partly melted. Then uncover and stir until completely melted and smooth. If it is not perfectly smooth, whisk it with a small wire whisk. Remove from the hot water and let stand for about 10 minutes.

Pour all of the icing over the top of the tart.

With a long, narrow metal spatula, smooth the icing over the top, spreading it so that a bit runs down on the sides—and the top is very smooth. With a small, narrow metal spatula, smooth the icing over the sides to cover them completely and smoothly. Or better yet, instead of spreading the icing on the sides, when you spread the icing on the top, do it so that enough of it runs down on the sides to completely cover the sides.

Place the walnut halves in a rim around the top.

Do not allow the icing to dry before the paper strips are removed. Carefully remove the wax-paper strips by pulling each one out toward a narrow end.

This may be refrigerated for a week or two when it is firm (refrigerate and then cover it with plastic wrap). But bring it to room temperature before unwrapping, or it may be frozen (wrap after the icing is frozen firm, and thaw before unwrapping). Just remember to bring it to room temperature before serving.

NOTES: 1. *The nuts must be chopped but not ground. If the pieces are not small enough, it is difficult to serve the tart, and more difficult to eat it. I cut the nuts one at a time with a small paring knife. But I'm a nut; you could do them all at once on a board with a long, heavy French chef's knife. Try for pieces or slices about ⅛ inch thick. Prepare the nuts before you start the recipe—even days before if you wish.*

2. At Ma Maison this was served with a small mountain of whipped cream and a mound of fresh raspberries. Both of which make this even more divine. (Try flavoring the whipped cream with kirsch or framboise. For each cup of cream use 2 tablespoons of granulated or confectioners sugar and 1 tablespoon of kirsch or framboise.)

3. If you have any leftover scraps of pastry, use them to make sugar cookies. Press the scraps together, roll them out to about ⅛-inch thickness, cut with a cookie cutter, place on unbuttered cookie sheet, brush the tops with milk, and sprinkle them generously with granulated sugar. Bake them high in the oven at 425 degrees until the cookies are lightly browned on the bottoms and around the rims. Then place them briefly under the broiler to melt the sugar; broil until the sugar is bubbly, and slightly colored.

4. The big difference in Mr. Cofacci's recipe from the other three is the egg yolks in the pastry; the others didn't have any. And the others used less flour and less butter.

Paris-Brest

8 PORTIONS

This is extra special! It is dramatically beautiful and wonderfully delicious—you will love it. This is for a party, and although it is not difficult, it is not one I recommend for a beginner. It is a monster éclair shaped like a doughnut for the Jolly Green Giant filled with a luscious pastry cream (the best!) and with a layer of whipped cream.

And although that should be enough to make the cover of Life, you can, if you wish, fill the center with a mound of fresh strawberries. I did, when

I made this as a birthday cake and placed a ring of candles all around the top. Wow!

This is a classic French dessert. In the late nineteenth century there was a famous bicycle race from Paris to Brest and back to Paris; this was created to commemorate the race—it had to do with the shape of the race-track—or was it the shape of the bicycle wheels?

I have made the whole thing from start to finish in about 1½ hours, a record time. But, if you wish, both the cream puff and the pastry cream can be made a day ahead. Or the empty cream puff can be frozen. It takes only a few minutes to whip the cream and put it all together. Plan to put it together as close to serving time as is possible and comfortable; but it will be O.K. refrigerated for a few hours if necessary.

There are many ways of shaping the pastry into a large ring. I have the best results with a pastry bag and a plain round giant-size tube, 1¼ inches in diameter. But that size tube is too hard to find, so you can simply use the bag itself without any tube. The pastry bag should be about 16 inches long and must be made of plastic-coated canvas (made by Ateco) because you will cut the opening to make it larger and that type bag does not have to be hemmed. With scissors cut the small opening in the bag to make it 2 inches in diameter. Later on, you will also need a smaller bag with a star-shaped tube for applying the whipped cream.

CREAM PUFF PASTRY (Pâte à Choux)

3 ounces (¾ stick) unsalted butter, cut into
    small pieces, at room temperature
1 cup boiling water
1 teaspoon granulated sugar
Pinch of salt
1 cup sifted all-purpose flour
4 eggs (graded large), at room temperature
    (the size of the eggs is important: to be
    extra sure, the 4 eggs, in their shells, should
    weigh 8 ounces)

Adjust an oven rack one-third up from the bottom of the oven and preheat the oven to 425 degrees. Butter a cookie sheet and dust it all over with flour; invert and tap to shake off excess flour. With the tip of a knife, lightly trace around a 9-inch cake pan or plate on the center of the cookie sheet, and set it aside.

Off the heat, place the butter, boiling water, sugar, and salt in a heavy saucepan with a 2- to 3-quart capacity. Stir until the butter melts. Then place it on high heat and let stand only until the mixture comes to a full boil. (Do not boil unnecessarily or too much water will evaporate.)

Remove from the heat and immediately add the flour all at once and beat vigorously with a wooden spatula or wooden spoon until the mixture forms a ball and comes away from the sides of the pan. Then return to low heat and cook, stirring, for 30 seconds.

Turn the mixture into the large bowl of an electric mixer. On low-medium speed add the eggs one at a time and beat only until completely mixed after each addition. That's it.

Fold down a deep cuff on the outside of the prepared large pastry bag and transfer the warm mixture to the bag. Be careful not to let the mixture drip out of the bottom opening. Unfold the cuff and gently twist the top of the bag closed. (See Note.)

(It is easier to work with a pastry bag at table height than at counter height.) Place the prepared cookie sheet on a table. Hold the pastry bag at a right angle to the sheet with the opening very close to the sheet, and centered over the guideline. Press from the top of the bag so the pastry comes out slowly and thickly, forming a wide band of pastry. The ends should overlap slightly. Any pastry remaining in the bag may be pressed out in a thinner band on top of the heavy one, or it may be used to build up a low spot if there is one. Then, with the back of a spoon, smooth over any uneven areas. The band of pastry should be a generous 1½ inches wide and a scant 1 inch high. (If the shape is slightly uneven don't worry, but if it is terrible, scrape it all back into the pastry bag, wash/butter/flour the sheet, and try again.)

TOPPING

1 egg yolk
1 teaspoon water
¼ cup slivered (julienne) blanched almonds

Stir the egg yolk and water to mix. With a soft pastry brush, brush it over the top only of the pastry. (Do not let it run down on the sides or it may keep the pastry from rising.) Sprinkle the almonds on top.

Bake for 20 minutes. Then reduce the temperature to 350 degrees and bake for 40 minutes more (total baking time is 1 hour). The ring will rise to gargantuan proportions and it will become beautifully browned; don't worry if the almonds seem too dark—they are O.K. About 10 minutes before the baking is finished, reach into the oven and with a small, sharp paring knife cut about a dozen small slits all over the ring to allow steam to escape.

Transfer the baked pastry to a cake-decorating turntable or to a counter top or cutting board.

(In order to be able to replace the top in the correct spot over the bottom, place two toothpicks in the side, one above the line where you will cut, and one below it.)

Then, without waiting, while the pastry is very hot, cut it as follows: Use a serrated knife (preferably the small one called a tomato knife). Do not cut in the middle, but cut about one-third down from the top, in order to make the bottom deep enough to hold the filling. Carefully remove the top. Either with your fingers or with a fork, remove most of the excess moist dough from both the bottom and the top.

Let the ring stand at room temperature until you are ready to fill it. If it is going to wait overnight, only cover it loosely with plastic wrap; if you wrap it airtight it might soften. Or wrap and freeze it; to thaw, place the frozen halves cut sides up on two cookie sheets, on two racks, in a 425-degree oven for about 5 minutes (that should do both things: thaw and recrisp them).

PASTRY CREAM (Crème Pâtissière)

2 cups milk
4 egg yolks
⅔ cup sugar
⅛ teaspoon salt
¼ cup cornstarch
2 tablespoons unsalted butter, cold and firm,
    cut into 6 or 8 pieces
1¼ teaspoons vanilla extract

Place 1½ cups (reserve ½ cup) of the milk in a saucepan over moderate heat and cook, uncovered, until it is scalded.

Meanwhile, place the egg yolks in a mixing bowl, stir to mix with a small wire whisk, then gradually add the sugar, whisking constantly and briskly. (If you add the sugar all at once, it might granulate the yolks.) Add the salt and continue to whisk for about a minute.

Place the remaining ½ cup milk and the cornstarch in a small bowl and stir to dissolve the cornstarch.

When the milk in the saucepan forms tiny bubbles on the edge or a thin skin on the top, add it, very gradually at first, to the yolks, whisking constantly.

Slowly add the cornstarch mixture to the warm milk mixture, stirring constantly.

Transfer the mixture to a heavy 2- to 2½-quart saucepan. (If you do not have a large enough pan that is heavy, use any large pan placed over shallow hot water in a larger pan, thereby making a double boiler.)

Cook over moderate heat, scraping the bottom constantly with a rubber spatula. As you do, add the butter, one piece at a time. Continue to cook, continuing to scrape the bottom of the pan, until the mixture thickens. It will thicken faster on the bottom of the pan, so keep it all moving. As it starts to thicken on the bottom, reduce the heat slightly.

The pastry cream should cook until it thickens to the consistency of a heavy mayonnaise. (It might take about 8 minutes.) It should just barely start to bubble but it will not actually boil. Reduce the heat to lowest and continue to stir gently for about 2 minutes more.

Remove from the heat and transfer to a wide mixing bowl. Stir in the vanilla. If the cream is lumpy, whisk it very briefly for only a few seconds (actually beating it hard now could thin it).

Stir gently occasionally as it cools to prevent a skin from forming and to release steam. (You can speed up the cooling by placing the bowl of pastry cream in a larger bowl of ice and water.)

The pastry cream can be used now or it can be refrigerated overnight. (If you refrigerate it, cover the top of the bowl or container with a paper towel—above but not touching the pastry cream—to absorb the moisture and then cover with foil, plastic wrap, or the top of the container.)

WHIPPED CREAM

1½ cups heavy cream
2 tablespoons confectioners sugar
¾ teaspoon vanilla extract

In a chilled bowl with chilled beaters, whip the above ingredients until the cream holds a firm shape. Fit a 12- to 14-inch pastry bag with a #7 star-shaped tube. Fold down a deep cuff on the outside of the bag. Transfer the cream to the bag and unfold the cuff.

To assemble the Paris-Brest, place the bottom half of the puff on a large, flat serving plate. Spoon the pastry cream into the shell and smooth it.

Now, the thing to remember about putting the whipped cream over the pastry cream is that the outside edge of it will show and should look pretty. I make reversed "C" shapes, each one about 1½ inches long (or half-moon shapes with the horns facing in). Use any remaining whipped cream to form rosettes over the middle of the filling; they will help to keep the top slightly raised.

Replace the top of the cream puff, allowing the whipped cream to show slightly around the edge.

Refrigerate.

Before serving, sprinkle the top generously with confectioners sugar, sprinkled through a fine strainer held over the top.

When you cut this into portions be careful not to squash it; use a serrated knife (preferably the small one called a tomato knife).

NOTE: *Whenever you use a pastry bag, after filling it, unfold the cuff, twist the top closed, and, holding the bag with the point upright, twist the wide part of the bag to force out air and to force the mixture right up to but not out of the opening.*

VARIATION: *Make the cream puff as in Paris-Brest, cool, and split. Fill it with small scoops of ice cream in a variety of flavors and colors, put the top on, wrap in plastic wrap, and freeze. This wonderful dessert can be made any time and kept in the freezer—no last-minute work.*

This may be served with any kind of fruit—fresh, canned, frozen and thawed, raw or stewed, plain or brandied. And/or with Rum Sauce (see page 454)—double the amount of the sauce for this recipe. Or with the following World's Best Hot Fudge Sauce from my chocolate book.

THE WORLD'S BEST
HOT FUDGE SAUCE (1 CUP)

This is very thick, coal black, as shiny as wet tar, and not too sweet. It will turn chewy and even thicker when it is served over cold ice cream—great! It may be served hot or warm, but at room temperature or chilled it will be too thick. It may be refrigerated for a week or two before serving.

½ cup heavy cream
3 tablespoons unsalted butter, cut into
    small pieces
⅓ cup granulated sugar
⅓ cup dark brown sugar, firmly packed
Pinch of salt

½ cup strained Dutch-process cocoa powder
(it must be Dutch process to have the
right color and flavor. Droste and Wilbur's
are both popular brands)

Place the cream and butter in a heavy 1-quart saucepan over moderate heat. Stir with a small wooden spatula until the butter is melted and the cream just comes to a low boil. Add both sugars and stir for a few minutes until they are dissolved. (The surest test is to taste; cook and taste carefully without getting burned until you do not feel any undissolved granules in your mouth.)

Reduce the heat. Add the salt and cocoa and stir briskly with a small wire whisk until smooth. (If the sauce is not smooth—if there are any small lumps of undissolved cocoa—press against them, and stir well, with a rubber spatula.) Remove from the heat.

Serve immediately or cool and reheat slowly in the top of a double boiler over hot water, or in a heavy saucepan over the lowest heat.

This should be thick, but when it is reheated it may be too thick. If so, stir in a bit of hot water, adding very little at a time.

NOTE: *If you plan to store the sauce in the refrigerator, use a straight-sided jar or a container that flares out at the top. The sauce will become too firm when it is chilled to be spooned out of a jar. It is best to place the jar or container in hot water until the block of sauce melts on the outside and can be poured out of the container. Pour it into the top of a small double boiler over hot water, or in a small, heavy saucepan over the lowest heat. Stir and cut into pieces with a wooden spatula until completely melted.*

Zuger Kirsch-torte

12 TO 16 PORTIONS

Kirsch is German for cherries. Kirschwasser (kirsch, abv.) is a brandy made from cherries. A Kirschtorte can be almost any cake that contains kirsch or cherries. But a Zuger Kirschtorte, from the town of Zug in Switzerland, is something special. It is a world-famous, old-world, gorgeous and elegant dessert cake that is probably Switzerland's best-known cake. It is a big production to make. And worth every minute it takes. Once you make this you can be mighty proud. This is seldom mentioned in cookbooks for nonprofessionals, and is seldom found in bakeries or restaurants.

To describe it, from the bottom up: There is a layer of crisp almond meringue, a layer of kirsch buttercream, a 2-inch-thick, divine, light, buttery sponge cake soaked in a generous amount of kirsch syrup, then more of the buttercream, another layer of the meringue, and still more of the butter-cream. The sides are covered with buttercream and toasted slivered almonds and the top has a simple crosshatch design in the buttercream. Classy and beautiful!

If you wish, the layer of cake and the two layers of meringue can be made a day before completing the cake (store the meringues in the turned-off oven). The finished cake may be refrigerated for a day or two before it is served.

CAKE LAYER

½ cup sifted all-purpose flour
6 tablespoons sifted cornstarch
2½ ounces (5 tablespoons) unsalted butter
4 eggs plus 2 egg yolks (graded large or extra-
    large; the whites will be used for
    the meringue)
¾ cup granulated sugar

Adjust a rack one-third up from the bottom of the oven and preheat oven to 350 degrees. Butter a 9 × 2- or 3-inch spring-form pan. Line the bottom with a round of wax paper or baking-pan liner paper cut to fit. Butter the paper and dust all over with flour. Tap lightly over a piece of paper to shake out excess flour. Set the pan aside.

Sift together the flour and cornstarch and set aside.

Cut the butter into small pieces and place it in a small pan over low heat to melt slowly. Then set it aside to cool to tepid or room temperature, but not long enough for it to harden.

Meanwhile, place the eggs and yolks in the small bowl of an electric mixer, or if you don't have that kind of electric mixer, use a 7-cup-capacity bowl. Add the sugar and beat at high speed for about 5 minutes until the mixture increases in volume and reaches the top of the bowl. Transfer it to the large bowl of the mixer and continue to beat for 3 to 5 minutes more (about 8 to 10 minutes of beating altogether) until the mixture is very pale and thick and has tripled in volume.

Remove the bowl from the mixer.

Place the flour and cornstarch mixture in the sifter (over a piece of paper). Sift about one-third of the mixture over the egg mixture and, with a large rubber spatula, fold it in. Repeat, sifting about one-third at a time over the eggs, and folding gently and carefully to incorporate.

Now, in about four or five additions, add the melted and cooled butter, gently folding it in. Do not fold or handle a bit more than necessary. (With the first few additions, do not fold in the butter completely.)

Turn into the prepared pan. Bake for about 35 minutes until the cake barely begins to come away from the sides of the pan.

Let the cake cool in the pan for 5 minutes. Then, with a small, sharp knife, gently and carefully cut around the sides to release. Remove the sides of the pan. Cover the cake with a rack. Invert the cake and the rack. Remove the bottom of the pan; do not remove the paper lining. Leave the cake upside down to cool.

MERINGUE JAPONAISE

A meringue Japonaise has ground nuts folded into the egg-white mixture.

⅓ cup blanched almonds
1 cup granulated sugar
½ tablespoon all-purpose flour
4 egg whites (you will have 2 whites left over from the cake layer, and 4 from the buttercream; use any of those, or you can use whites that were left over from another recipe, frozen, and then thawed)

Adjust two racks to divide the oven into thirds and preheat oven to 275 degrees. Line two cookie sheets with baking-pan liner paper or aluminum foil. With a pencil, trace a 9-inch circle on each piece of paper or foil. Spread butter within the circle and about ¼ inch beyond. (It is not necessary to flour the buttered section. Curiously, in my experience, the meringue sticks to buttered and floured wax paper.)

The nuts must be finely ground. They can be ground in a processor, blender, or nut grinder (if you grind them in a processor or blender, add a bit of the sugar to keep them from lumping)—they must be fine, dry, and powdery. In a small bowl, stir the ground nuts with ⅓ cup (reserve remaining ⅔ cup) of the sugar and the flour. Set aside.

In the small bowl of an electric mixer, beat the whites until they hold a soft shape. Reduce the speed to moderate and gradually, 2 tablespoons at a time, add the reserved ⅔ cup of sugar beating for 10 to 15 seconds between additions. Then increase the speed to high and continue to beat until the sugar is dissolved (rub a bit between your fingers to be sure) and the meringue is very stiff—do not underbeat. Remove from the mixer.

In two additions, carefully fold the almond mixture into the meringue. Do not handle any more than necessary but be sure that the almond mixture is evenly incorporated.

To keep the baking-pan liner paper or foil in place while you work on it, use a bit of the meringue as a paste on each corner of the cookie sheet under the paper or foil.

To shape the meringue with a pastry bag, fold down a deep cuff on the outside of a large (about 15-inch) pastry bag. Fit it with a #6 (½ inch) plain round tube. To make it easy to fill the bag, stand it upright in a tall, narrow glass or jar. Transfer the meringue to the bag. Unfold and close the top of the bag.

Pressing on the top of the bag, press the mixture out, starting with a spot directly in the middle of the circle, and then pressing the meringue out into a long, continuous spiral like a coiled rope until the traced circle is filled in (the lines of meringue should just barely touch each other); however, the meringue will spread slightly in baking, and the meringue layers and the cake layer should have the same diameter—therefore, stop the meringue a scant ¼ inch inside the traced circle. (But if the layers become too wide it can be corrected later.)

After shaping both meringue layers, use a long, narrow metal spatula to smooth the tops and fill in any empty spots.

If you prefer, you can shape the meringue without the pastry bag by just spreading it. But it is much easier to form even layers if you use the bag.

Bake the layers for about 30 minutes. Then reverse them top to bottom and back to front and continue to bake for 30 minutes more (total baking time is 1 hour) until the meringues are crisp and dry and slightly browned. Turn off the oven heat and allow the meringues to remain in the oven until completely cool.

BUTTERCREAM

1 cup granulated sugar
¾ cup water
4 egg yolks (from eggs graded large or
    extra-large)
1 cup sifted confectioners sugar
8 ounces (2 sticks) unsalted butter
1 tablespoon kirsch

Place the sugar and water in a small, narrow saucepan over moderate heat. Stir with a small wooden spatula until the sugar is dissolved and the mixture comes to a boil. Insert a candy thermometer, raise the heat to high, and continue to boil without stirring until the thermometer registers 234 degrees (soft-ball stage).

Meanwhile, place the egg yolks and the confectioners sugar in the small bowl of an electric mixer. Stir slightly just to mix.

When the syrup is ready, start the mixer at high speed, hold the saucepan of syrup about 10 or 12 inches above the mixing bowl, and very gradually, in a thin stream, add the hot syrup to the yolks. When it is all added, continue to beat until cool.

In another bowl (if you do not have another small bowl for the mixer, you can do this in the large bowl) beat the butter (you can use the same beaters without washing) until it is soft. Add the kirsch and beat to mix. Then gradually add the softened butter to the egg-yolk mixture, beating until smooth. Set aside at room temperature.

KIRSCH SYRUP

⅓ cup water
3 tablespoons granulated sugar
⅓ cup kirsch

Place the water and sugar in a small saucepan over moderate heat. Stir with a small wooden spatula until the sugar is dissolved and the mixture comes to a boil. Set aside to cool to room temperature. Stir the kirsch into the cooled syrup.

To assemble the cake, place four strips of wax paper around the outer edges of a flat serving plate. If you have a cake-decorating turntable or a lazy Susan, place the plate on it.

Place a generous teaspoonful of the buttercream right in the middle of the plate to keep the cake from sliding while you ice it and also while you serve it.

Place one of the meringue layers, right side up, on the plate. Cover with a thin layer (about ¼ inch thick) of the buttercream.

Remove the round of wax paper or baking-pan liner paper from the bottom of the cake layer. Place the cake upside down on top of the buttercream.

With a pastry brush, brush the kirsch syrup, a little at a time, slowly over the cake until it is all absorbed. The cake will absorb it all.

Cover with another thin layer (¼ inch thick) of the buttercream.

On top of that, place the remaining meringue layer upside down (flat side up). If the meringue layers extend out beyond the cake layer, it is easy to trim them with scissors (especially if the meringues are as crisp and dry as they should be).

Now, cover the sides and then the top with the remaining buttercream, spreading the buttercream as smoothly as you can.

DECORATION

3½ ounces (1 cup) blanched almonds,
    thinly sliced
Confectioners sugar

The almonds can and should be toasted ahead of time (they should not be warm when you use them). To toast, place them on a jelly-roll pan in the center of a 350-degree oven, stirring occasionally, for about 15 minutes until they are lightly colored.

With your fingers, pick up some of the cooled toasted almonds and place them on the buttercream around the sides of the cake, placing the almonds more heavily along the top of the sides than the bottom. Continue until you have used all of the almonds and the top of the sides is well covered. As you do this, quite a few of the almonds will fall onto the wax-paper strips on the plate. With a long, narrow metal spatula, lift some of the fallen almonds and turn the spatula blade sideways to put the almonds on the buttercream around the bottom of the sides, so that the sides are covered evenly.

Strain a few spoonfuls of confectioners sugar through a fine strainer over the top of the cake—there should be a rather generous coating of the sugar.

Remove the wax-paper strips by slowly pulling each one out toward a narrow end.

Refrigerate the cake for about half an hour.

Then, score a design of diamonds on the top as follows: Use a long, sharp knife, and press the length of the blade gently into the buttercream to make a line. Repeat, placing the lines about ⅓ or ¼ inch apart, parallel with one another, all over the top. Whenever some of the buttercream sticks to the blade, wipe the blade clean to keep the lines neat. Then repeat, this time making the lines at an angle to the first ones, so you have a pattern of small diamonds all over the cake.

Refrigerate for a day or two. Serve cold.

Jalousies

6 PORTIONS

This is one of my favorite recipes. It is the Counterfeit Puff Pastry from my first dessert book shaped into a chic, classy, classic French pastry like the ones you see only in the most elegant French bakeries.

This should be served while it is very fresh—the fresher the better—but the pastry must be made ahead of time, and it really does not take long to put the Jalousie together.

This recipe can be doubled.

COUNTERFEIT PUFF PASTE

8 ounces (2 sticks) unsalted butter
1½ cups unsifted all-purpose flour
½ cup sour cream

The butter should be cold and firm, and cut into very small squares; cut each stick into lengthwise quarters and then slice each strip into pieces about ½ inch wide. It is best to cut it ahead of time and refrigerate it for a while before you use it.

The first step may be done by hand or in a processor. *By hand:* Place the flour in a wide mixing bowl. With a pastry blender cut the butter into the flour until the mixture resembles coarse crumbs; some of the pieces of butter may remain the size of small dried peas. Do not work it any more; it should not be a smooth mixture.

In a food processor: Fit the processor with the metal blade. Place the flour and butter in the bowl of the processor. Process on-and-off (quick "pulses") for only about 10 seconds. Be careful not to overprocess; the mixture should not be homogenous—you should see little pieces of butter in it. Then transfer the mixture to a large mixing bowl.

After cutting in the butter, either by hand or by machine, add the sour cream and stir briefly. Do not handle too much. Turn the mixture out onto a work surface and knead only until it holds together. Flour your hands, form the mixture into an oblong about 3 × 5 inches, flour it lightly, wrap it in plastic wrap and refrigerate for at least 2 hours, or overnight, or longer—or freeze it. (Thaw in the refrigerator overnight.)

You will need a 10½ × 15½-inch (or larger) jelly-roll pan. (This must be baked on a pan with sides, because so much butter runs out during baking.) Do not butter the pan.

With a strong and sharp knife cut the dough into two different-size oblongs—cutting lengthwise—one piece should be one-third of the dough and the other should be two-thirds. Replace the larger piece in the refrigerator.

Flour a pastry board or work surface, and a heavy rolling pin. Place the smaller piece of dough on the floured surface. If it is too hard to be rolled, pound it firmly with the rolling pin, but do not pound it out of shape. Then carefully roll the dough into an oblong 15 inches long, 5 inches wide, and ⅛ inch thick. While rolling, keep the shape as even as you can, although the edges will be trimmed later.

If the kitchen is warm, work quickly.

While you are rolling the dough you will see that the pieces of butter form a marbleized effect. That is how it should be, and how it will be if you did not handle the dough too much while mixing it.

Fold the dough over so that the short ends meet but be careful not to press down on the fold. With your hands, carefully transfer the folded dough to the unbuttered jelly-roll pan, placing the folded edge in the middle of the pan. Then unfold the dough. The short ends should just reach the short ends of the pan.

FILLING

⅓ cup thick apricot, currant, or other
thick preserves

Stir the preserves lightly to soften.

Wet a pastry brush with cold water and then shake it out well (the brush should not be dripping); with the brush (re-wet it as necessary) wet a 1-inch border around the dough.

Then spread the preserves on the dough, excluding the wet border.

If the kitchen is warm, place the pan in the refrigerator.

Now roll the larger piece of dough into the same shape and size as the other; this piece will be thicker than the first piece.

Quickly fold this piece, but not the way the other was folded—fold this one in half the long way. Now, to cut slits that will give a jalousie effect, use a small, sharp knife and cut through the folded edge (at a right angle to the fold), making cuts 1 inch apart and 1 inch long (when you unfold this, each cut will be 2 inches long).

Unfold, and then in order to make it easier to transfer, fold the strip in the opposite direction (both short ends meeting) and center it over the bottom layer. Unfold. Then, with the sides of your hands and with your fingertips, press gently to seal the edges, but keep away from the very outside edge (if you press directly on the edge it will prevent the cake from rising properly on the edge); press but do not squash the 1-inch border. Do this carefully and thoroughly or the filling will run out.

Now the four sides must be cut even. I find it easiest to do this with a pizza cutter. Or use a small, sharp knife. (The pastry will rise better if the edges are cut neat and sharp—again, be careful not to squash them together.) You can cut as much as ¼ inch off each side if it is necessary to straighten the edges.

GLAZE

1 egg (see Glaze Note)

Beat the egg lightly just to mix. The glaze will be brushed over the top to give the Jalousie a beautiful golden color. However, if it drips down on the cut sides, it will prevent the dough from rising properly. Therefore, if you have a small, soft artist's water-color brush, that is the best. However, whatever brush you use, it should not be so wet that the egg runs and drips. With a brush that is only slightly wet, brush the top. Brush it again if you wish.

Place the Jalousie in the refrigerator for about half an hour or more (it should be very cold when it goes into the oven).

Adjust a rack one-quarter or one-third down from the top of the oven. (If this is baked any lower the bottom will burn.) Preheat the oven to 400 degrees.

Place the cold Jalousie in the oven and immediately reduce the temperature to 350 degrees. Bake for 40 minutes until well colored. You must be very careful not to take this out of the oven too soon. If it is not baked enough it will have wet dough inside.

GLAZE NOTE: *If you use a glaze of only egg yolk mixed with ½ teaspoon of water instead of the whole egg, it will make a darker and shinier crust. I like it better. But I am writing it this way in order to warn you, do not let it fool you—you must bake the crust the full time in spite of the dark color.*

Prepare the icing a few minutes before the baking is finished.

ICING

¾ cup sifted confectioners sugar
Boiling water

Place the sugar in a small bowl and add only about 1 tablespoon of the water. Stir to mix. The mixture should be thick but fluid. If necessary, add more water, but only a few drops at a time. If it gets too thin, add more sugar.

As soon as the cake comes out of the oven, immediately, with a pastry brush, brush the icing over the hot cake, including the openings where the jelly shows. It does not have to be a solid coating—it can be drizzled. The heat of the cake will melt the icing and make a shiny and almost transparent coating.

Let stand for about 10 minutes. Then, carefully, use a firm and wide metal spatula under the cake to make sure it is not stuck anywhere. And then use a flat-sided cookie sheet or two wide spatulas to transfer the Jalousie to a rack to cool.

When it is completely cool, if you have a chocolate-roll board, slide the cake onto it. Or transfer it to a long and narrow platter. This is extremely light/flaky/fragile/delicate, so handle with care.

Cut the cake with a very sharp knife into slices 1 inch wide, and serve 2 to a portion.

NOTE: *Any leftover scraps of the dough may be used for making delicious sugar cookies.*

Press them together, wrap, and chill. Then roll the dough in granulated sugar instead of flour, sugaring both sides generously. Roll the dough to ⅛- or ¼-inch thickness. Cut into strips, long or short, wide or thin; 3 × 1½ inches is a happy medium.

Turn one end of the strip to twist it in the middle (like a corkscrew) and place on an unbuttered jelly-roll pan. Sprinkle with a bit more sugar. Chill. Bake one-third of the way down in a 350-degree oven until thoroughly dry, crisp, and golden brown. Do not underbake; they are better if the sugar caramelizes a little.

Haleakala Cake

12 GENEROUS PORTIONS

In Hawaii, Haleakala is "house of the sun." Here, it is a two-layer cake originally from the Royal Hawaiian Hotel in Waikiki Beach. The layers, which are so easy you will think there is a mistake, are moist and delicious. The thick pineapple filling goes both between the layers and also on top, under the icing, a recipe from my chocolate book. The best high, white, fluffy 7-minute or marshmallow-type icing I know. And the cake is covered all over with a thick layer of shredded coconut.

This is a big, dramatic cake to make for a special occasion. For a lot of people. For a happy celebration. For a birthday—or any party.

(And to top all this joy is the fact that both the cake and the icing call for only egg whites—no yolks. If you did not know what you were saving those whites for in the freezer, this could be it.)

If you wish, the layers can be frozen, and the filling can be refrigerated for a few days. But the icing should be made and the cake should be assembled the day it is served.

PINEAPPLE FILLING

This can be made a day or two ahead and refrigerated until you are ready for it.

2 1-pound, 4-ounce cans (each 2½ cups)
    crushed pineapple (packed in natural juice)
2 tablespoons fresh lemon juice
2 tablespoons plus 1½ teaspoons cornstarch,
    firmly pressed into the measuring spoon
2 tablespoons granulated sugar
⅛ teaspoon salt
Yellow food coloring
1 teaspoon vanilla extract

Pour the pineapple into a large strainer set over a large bowl. Press firmly on the pineapple with a large spoon or spatula to press out all the juice. Set the pineapple aside and measure the juice—you should have 2 cups of juice. Add the lemon juice.

In a heavy 6- to 8-cup saucepan stir together the cornstarch, sugar, and salt. Mix thoroughly. Then, very gradually at first, stir in the pineapple juice. The mixture should be smooth.

Place over moderate heat and cook, stirring and scraping the bottom and sides with a rubber spatula, until the mixture thickens and comes to a boil. Reduce the heat and simmer, stirring gently, for 1½ minutes.

Remove from the heat. Stir in 6 or 7 drops of yellow food coloring and the vanilla. Then stir in the drained pineapple. Cool, stirring occasionally, and then refrigerate for at least a few hours or up to a few days.

HAWAIIAN CAKE

2 cups sifted all-purpose flour
3½ teaspoons double-acting baking powder
1 teaspoon salt
4 ounces (1 stick) unsalted butter
1 teaspoon vanilla extract
1½ cups granulated sugar
1 cup milk
4 egg whites (about ½ cup; they may be whites
    that were left over from another recipe,
    frozen, and then thawed)

Adjust a rack one-third up from the bottom of the oven and preheat oven to 350 degrees. Cut baking-pan liner paper or wax paper to fit the bottoms of two 9 × 1½-inch layer-cake pans. Butter the sides of the pans and one side of the papers. Place the papers in the pans, buttered sides up. Then dust the pans with flour and tap the pans lightly over a piece of paper to shake out excess flour. Set aside.

Sift together the flour, baking powder, and salt and set aside.

In the large bowl of an electric mixer, beat the butter until it is soft and smooth. Add the vanilla and then gradually add the sugar and beat well, scraping the sides occasionally and beating until thoroughly mixed. On low speed alternately add the sifted dry ingredients in three additions with the milk in two additions, scraping the bowl and beating after each addition until it is incorporated. Beat on high speed for 10 to 15 seconds. Then add the unbeaten egg whites (yes, *unbeaten*) and beat on high speed for 2 more minutes. The mixture will look slightly curdled—O.K.

Pour half of the batter (a somewhat generous 2 cupfuls) into each pan. Tilt the pans slightly to level the batter. Then, to make them more level, hold a pan with both hands 6 or 8 inches above the work surface and drop it onto the work surface two or three times. That levels it—about as level as it can get.

Bake for 30 to 35 minutes until the tops are nicely browned, the layers have come away from the sides of the pans, and the tops barely spring back when they are lightly and gently pressed with a fingertip.

As soon as you remove the cakes from the oven, cut around them with a table knife. Then let them stand for 5 minutes. Cover each pan with a rack, turn it over, remove pan and carefully and slowly peel off the paper lining, removing a small part at a time; cover with another rack and turn over again, leaving the cakes right side up to cool.

Before you start the icing, prepare a large, flat cake plate or a serving board by placing four strips of wax paper around the outer edge. Place one cooled cake layer on the plate, placing the cake upside down. Check to be sure that the wax paper touches the cake all around. Then, if you have a cake-decorating turntable, place the cake plate on it.

MARSHMALLOW ICING

This should be used as soon as it is made. Cakes with this icing should not be frozen. You will need a candy thermometer.

> 1½ cups granulated sugar
> ⅔ teaspoon cream of tartar (see Note)
> ⅔ cup water
> ⅛ teaspoon salt
> ⅔ cup egg whites (from 4 to 5 eggs; they may
>   be whites that were left over from another
>   recipe, frozen, and then thawed)
> 1¼ teaspoons vanilla extract

Place the sugar, cream of tartar, and water in a 6-cup saucepan (preferably one that is tall and narrow—in a wide one the mixture will be too low to reach the bulb of the candy thermometer). With a wooden spatula, stir over moderate heat until the sugar is dissolved and the mixture begins to boil. Cover the saucepan so that it is airtight (if the pan has a spout, cover it securely with foil or a pot holder) and let boil for 3 minutes. (This keeps the steam in the pot and dissolves any sugar granules that stick to the sides.)

Uncover and insert a candy thermometer. Raise the heat to high and let boil without stirring until the thermometer registers 242 degrees.

Shortly before the sugar syrup is done (or when the thermometer registers about 236 degrees: soft-ball stage) add the salt to the egg whites in the large bowl of an electric mixer and beat on high speed until the whites are stiff. (If the sugar syrup is not ready when the whites are, turn the beater to the lowest speed and let beat slowly until the syrup is ready. Or you can let the whites stand but no longer than necessary. If it looks as though the syrup might be done before the whites are ready, lower the heat to slow the cooking slightly.)

When the syrup is ready (242 degrees: medium-ball stage), with the mixer on high speed very gradually add the syrup in a thin, threadlike stream, holding the pan about 12 inches above the top of the bowl of whites. Then beat at high speed for about 5 minutes more until the icing is like a thick marshmallow mixture. Mix in the vanilla. The icing may still be—probably will be—warm when it is used.

Spread half of the pineapple filling on the bottom cake layer. Place the other cake layer over the filling, right side up (both bottoms meet in the middle).

Spread the reserved filling on top.

Now you have a mountain of gorgeous icing to cover it all with. First, with a small metal spatula, spread a thin layer of the icing on the sides of the cake to seal any loose crumbs. Then build up more and more icing on the sides until it is ½ to ¾ inch thick. Smooth the sides. Then gradually, carefully, place the remaining icing all over the top and smooth it. With the back of a spoon form swirls and peaks on the sides only.

COCONUT TOPPING

Use about ½ cup of shredded coconut and sprinkle it generously in a thick layer all over the top.

Then carefully remove the wax-paper strips by pulling each one out slowly toward a narrow end.

Let the cake stand uncovered at room temperature.

NOTE: *To measure ⅔ teaspoon: Measure 1 teaspoon and, with a small metal spatula or with a table knife, mark it into thirds. Then cut away ⅓ and return it to the box.*

Black-and-White Layer Cake

This is a high, six-layer, loaf-shaped cake composed of alternate chocolate and white sponge layers (made from two separate recipes) with chocolate buttercream between the layers and as an icing. It is elaborate, fancy, special, dramatic, gorgeous, and delicious. Make it for a party, and make it ahead of time if you wish; it freezes perfectly.

This is not quick and easy—but it is not difficult; it is exciting to make and a thrill to serve.

10 TO 12 PORTIONS

WHITE SPONGE SHEET

5 eggs (graded large or extra-large), separated
⅓ cup granulated sugar
1 teaspoon vanilla extract
¼ cup sifted all-purpose flour
Pinch of salt
Pinch of cream of tartar

Adjust a rack to the middle of the oven. Preheat the oven to 350 degrees. You will need a 10½ × 15½ × 1-inch jelly-roll pan. To line the pan with foil, turn the pan over, cover it with a piece of foil a few inches longer than the pan, press down the sides and the corners to shape the foil, remove the foil, turn the pan right side up, place the foil in the pan, and carefully press it into place. To butter the foil, place a piece of butter in the pan and place the pan in the oven to melt the butter, then brush it all over the foil. Set the pan aside. (Incidentally, I have recently found that buttered foil is the most successful method of preparing a pan for a sponge sheet—that goes for this recipe or any other sponge sheet.)

Place the yolks in the small bowl of an electric mixer. Add 3 tablespoons of the sugar (reserve the remaining sugar) and the vanilla and beat at high speed for a few minutes until pale (almost white) and thick. On low speed add the sifted flour, scraping the bowl with a rubber spatula, and beating only until smooth.

Transfer the mixture to a larger mixing bowl. (It is easier to fold-in in a large bowl.)

Use the small bowl of the electric mixer, or any other small bowl and an egg beater, or use a large bowl and a wire whisk (the bowl and beaters must be clean) to beat the egg whites with the salt and cream of tartar until they hold a soft shape. Gradually add the reserved sugar and beat until the whites hold a definite shape but not until they are stiff or dry.

Fold about a third of the whites into the yolks—do not be too thorough—and then fold the remaining whites into the yolks, folding carefully only until blended.

Transfer the mixture to the prepared pan. Spread it smooth (it will stay where you put it and will not run during baking).

Bake for 20 to 23 minutes until the top springs back when it is lightly pressed with a fingertip and the cake begins to come away from the sides of the pan.

Place a long piece of wax paper over the baked cake. Cover with a flat cookie sheet. Holding them firmly together, invert the cake pan and the cookie sheet. Remove the cake pan and carefully peel off the foil. Do not allow the cake to remain upside down any longer than necessary or the top (which is now on the bottom) will stick to the paper. Quickly cover the cake with another cookie sheet and turn over again, remove the wax paper, and leave the cake right side up to cool.

CHOCOLATE SPONGE SHEET

6 ounces semisweet chocolate (see Note)
1 teaspoon instant coffee (powdered
     or granular)
¼ cup boiling water
4 eggs (graded large), separated
⅓ cup granulated sugar
1 teaspoon vanilla extract
⅓ cup sifted all-purpose flour
Pinch of salt
Pinch of cream of tartar

Prepare the oven and the jelly-roll pan as in the above directions for the White Sponge Sheet.

Break up or coarsely chop the chocolate and place it in the top of a small double boiler over hot water on moderate heat. Dissolve the coffee in the water and add to the chocolate. Stir occasionally until the chocolate is melted. Remove the top of the double boiler and set it aside to cool slightly.

In the small bowl of an electric mixer, beat the yolks with 3 tablespoons of the sugar (reserve the remaining sugar) and the vanilla. Beat for a few minutes until the mixture is thick and pale.

On low speed add the tepid chocolate, scraping the bowl with a rubber spatula and beating only until mixed. Then mix in the flour. Remove from the mixer and transfer to a larger bowl.

Use the small bowl of the electric mixer, or any other small bowl and an egg beater, or use a large bowl and a wire whisk (the bowl and beaters must be clean) to beat the egg whites with the salt and cream of tartar until they hold a soft shape. Gradually add the reserved sugar and continue to beat until the whites hold a definite shape but not until they are stiff or dry.

Fold about one-third of the whites into the chocolate mixture—do not be too thorough—and then fold in the remaining whites, folding carefully only until blended; do not handle any more than necessary.

Turn the batter into the prepared jelly-roll pan and spread it smooth.

Bake at 350 degrees for 15 minutes or until it feels set and firm when lightly pressed with a fingertip.

Cover the cake with a long piece of wax paper, cover the paper with a flat cookie sheet, and invert the pan and the sheet. Remove the pan and gently peel off the foil; quickly cover with another cookie sheet and turn over again, remove the wax paper, and leave the cake right side up to cool.

CHOCOLATE BUTTERCREAM

6 ounces semisweet chocolate (see Note)
2 tablespoons heavy cream
8 ounces (2 sticks) plus 1 tablespoon
    unsalted butter
7 egg yolks
1 cup strained confectioners sugar
Pinch of salt
1 teaspoon vanilla extract

Break up or coarsely chop the chocolate and place it in the top of a small double boiler over hot water on low heat. Add the heavy cream and 1 tablespoon of the butter (reserve the remaining 2 sticks at room temperature). Stir until smooth.

Meanwhile, in the small bowl of an electric mixer, beat the egg yolks at high speed for a few minutes until pale and thick. On low speed gradually add the warm chocolate mixture, scraping the bowl constantly with a rubber spatula.

Transfer the mixture to the top of the double boiler (the one the chocolate was melted in) over hot water on *low* heat and cook for 5 minutes, scraping the bottom and sides constantly with a rubber spatula. The mixture must never get really hot.

Now transfer the chocolate mixture to a mixing bowl. Place some ice and water in a larger mixing bowl. Then place the bowl of chocolate into the bowl of ice water and stir gently until the chocolate cools to tepid.

Meanwhile, in the large bowl of an electric mixer, beat the reserved 2 sticks of butter with the confectioners sugar, salt, and vanilla until soft and smooth. Then add the chocolate mixture and continue to beat for just a minute or two until smooth, creamy, and gorgeous.

You will need a long, narrow, flat serving tray—a chocolate-roll board (measuring about 5 × 18 inches) is perfect.

Use a ruler and toothpicks to mark the cakes, the long way, into thirds (you will have three strips 15½ × 3½ inches). It is important to mark and cut them carefully—they must all be the same width. Use a long, thin, sharp knife to cut the cakes.

Carefully place a strip of white cake on the serving tray or board. Spread a thin layer of buttercream over the cake; the buttercream should completely cover the cake, but keep it thin or you will not have enough.

Now place a chocolate layer on top. (The chocolate cake is fragile and if it does not want to cooperate, here's how to do it. Cut the chocolate strip crosswise into two or three even pieces, and transfer each piece separately, using a metal pancake turner to transfer with. You should not have any trouble this way and it will not show that the strips were patched.)

Spread more buttercream over the chocolate layer. Continue to alternate white and chocolate layers with buttercream between them.

Do not ice the top and sides yet. Reserve the remaining buttercream at room temperature.

Make room for the cake in the freezer or refrigerator. Cover the top of the cake with a piece of plastic wrap. To flatten the cake slightly—and to level the top—place a tray or a cookie sheet or another chocolate-roll board (or anything flat) on top of the cake. If you have used another chocolate-roll board on top it will be heavy enough to flatten the cake, but if you have used something lighter, place a few weights (small cans or whatever) evenly distributed over the top. But be careful that whatever is on top is not so heavy it squashes the cake. Place in the freezer for about half an hour or in the refrigerator for a little longer.

Just before you are ready to finish icing the cake, beat the reserved buttercream well with the mixer.

Then spread it to coat the top and sides completely. It may be smooth (that's how I do it) or it may be in peaks. If you make it smooth, try to reserve about ½ cup or so of the buttercream to use as decoration. Place the ½ cup buttercream in a pastry bag fitted with a star-shaped tube (the tube should be #2 or #3, that is, a moderately small size) and form a row of small rosettes touching each other on each long edge of the top.

Wow—gorgeous!

Refrigerate the cake and serve it cold. Or freeze it (freeze until firm before wrapping); to thaw, place the wrapped cake in the refrigerator for a few hours, then unwrap and serve.

NOTE: *I use Lindt Excellence chocolate for this recipe. Use any sweet, semi-sweet, or bittersweet, but use the best you can get.*

Coffee Cream Sponge Cake

This is a light, delicate cake to make as dessert for a dinner or for a tea party. It is a two-layer, coffee-flavored sponge cake, filled and iced with coffee and chocolate-flavored whipped cream. The layers may be made ahead of time and frozen if you wish; it is best if the whipped cream is made and put on the cake the day you serve it, but it may be done in the morning for that night.

8 PORTIONS

1 cup sifted all-purpose flour
1 teaspoon double-acting baking powder
1 tablespoon instant coffee
¼ cup boiling water
3 eggs (graded large or extra-large), separated
1 cup granulated sugar
½ teaspoon vanilla extract
¼ teaspoon salt

Adjust a rack to the middle of the oven and preheat oven to 350 degrees. Butter two round 9-inch layer-cake pans, line the bottoms with baking-pan liner paper or wax paper cut to fit, butter the paper, dust with flour, then, over a piece of paper, tap to shake out excess.

Sift together the flour and baking powder and set aside. Dissolve the coffee in the water and set aside. In the small bowl of an electric mixer beat the yolks with ¾ cup of the sugar (reserve the remaining ¼ cup of sugar), beating for several minutes until the mixture is pale and thick. On low speed, mix in a few tablespoons of the sifted dry ingredients. Then add the vanilla and liquid coffee, scraping the bowl with a rubber spatula and beating only until smooth. Add the remaining dry ingredients and beat, still on low speed, only until incorporated.

In a clean, small bowl with clean beaters, beat the egg whites and the salt until they hold a soft shape. Gradually add the reserved ¼ cup of sugar and continue to beat until the whites hold a definite shape but not until they are stiff or dry.

Fold a few spoonfuls of the whites into the yolks. Then, in a larger bowl, fold the yolks and the remaining whites until they are blended. Do not handle any more than necessary.

Divide the mixture between the prepared pans and smooth the tops.

Bake for 20 to 25 minutes until the tops spring back when lightly pressed with a fingertip.

Cool the layers in the pans for 2 or 3 minutes. Then, to release them, very carefully cut around the sides with a small, sharp knife—be careful not to tear or cut the cakes. Cover each layer with a rack, turn over the pan and the rack, remove the pan (do not remove the paper lining now), cover with another rack and turn over again, leaving the layers right side up. When the cakes have cooled, cover each one with a rack, invert, peel off the paper lining, cover with another rack and turn over again, leaving the cakes right side up.

Prepare a flat cake plate by lining the sides with four strips of wax paper (see page 19). Place a cake layer upside down on the plate and check to see that the cake touches the paper all around. If you have a cake-decorating turntable, place the cake plate on it.

COFFEE-CHOCOLATE WHIPPED CREAM

1 ounce semisweet chocolate
1 tablespoon instant coffee
1 tablespoon boiling water
2 cups heavy cream
1 teaspoon vanilla extract
1½ tablespoons granulated sugar

Chop the chocolate very fine and place it in the top of a small double boiler over hot water on moderate heat. Dissolve the coffee in the boiling water and pour it over the chocolate. Stir until smooth and then remove from over the hot water and set aside to cool.

When it is completely cool, gradually add 2 or 3 tablespoons of the cream to the chocolate mixture, stirring until smooth and liquid.

In a small, chilled bowl with chilled beaters, whip the remaining cream with the vanilla and sugar until it holds a soft shape. Then, while beating, add the chocolate mixture and continue to beat until the cream is stiff enough to hold its shape as an icing. It is nicer if it is not too stiff; you must watch it very carefully—it stiffens more quickly than plain whipped cream.

Cover the bottom layer with a ½-inch-thick layer of the cream. Then place the top layer on right side up (both bottoms meet in the center) and use the remaining cream to cover the sides and the top of the cake. Spread it smoothly or swirl it into curlicues.

Refrigerate for a few hours or all day.

OPTIONAL DECORATION: *If you wish, decorate the top with a few chocolate shavings, a sprinkling of grated chocolate, or a rim of hulled fresh strawberries standing point up on the top of the cake (strawberries and cream with coffee and chocolate are a wonderful combination). But the cake is lovely with or without any decoration.*

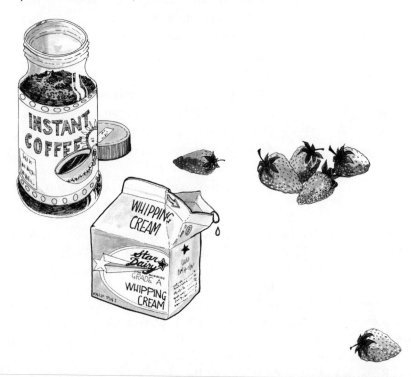

Spicy Sponge Roll

8 PORTIONS

This is a light sponge roll made with a delicious blend of spices and filled with chocolate/Cognac-flavored whipped cream. The spices make it a wonderful winter dessert; consider it for Christmas or Thanksgiving. It may be made the day before it is served, or it may be frozen (even for a few weeks) and sliced and served directly from the freezer (it will not be too stiff).

1 cup sifted confectioners sugar
3 tablespoons sifted all-purpose flour
¼ teaspoon salt
¼ teaspoon finely ground black pepper
1½ tablespoons powdered instant espresso or other powdered (not granular) instant coffee
1½ teaspoons ginger
1 teaspoon allspice
1 teaspoon cinnamon
1 teaspoon nutmeg
1 teaspoon cardamom
⅛ teaspoon cloves
1 tablespoon unsweetened cocoa powder
5 eggs (graded large), separated
½ teaspoon cream of tartar
Additional confectioners sugar (for turning the cake out of the pan)
Additional cocoa (for sprinkling on top)

Adjust a rack to the center of the oven and preheat oven to 350 degrees. Butter a 10½ × 15½ × 1-inch jelly-roll pan. Line the pan with aluminum foil as follows: Turn the pan upside down, cover it with a piece of foil about 19 inches long, fold down the sides and the corners to shape the foil, remove the foil, turn the pan right side up, place the foil in the pan and press it into place. To butter the foil, place a piece of butter in the pan, place the pan in the oven to melt the butter, then spread it with a brush or with crumpled wax paper to coat the foil.

Remove and set aside ½ cup of the sugar.

Sift the remaining ½ cup of sugar with the flour, salt, pepper, coffee, ginger, allspice, cinnamon, nutmeg, cardamom, cloves, and cocoa. Resift twice more (even if it is a triple sifter) and set aside.

In the small bowl of an electric mixer, beat the egg yolks at high speed for several minutes until they are pale lemon-colored. On low speed add the sifted flour mixture, scraping the bowl as necessary with a rubber spatula and beating only until incorporated. Set aside.

In the large bowl of the electric mixer, with clean beaters, beat the egg whites with the cream of tartar until they hold a soft shape when the beaters are raised. Gradually add the reserved ½ cup of confectioners sugar and continue to beat until the whites hold a firm shape, but don't let them become stiff or dry.

In about three additions, carefully fold three-quarters of the whites into the yolks, and then fold the yolks into the remaining whites. Do not handle any more than necessary.

Turn the mixture into the lined pan, and spread it smooth.

Bake for 15 minutes until the cake barely springs back when it is gently pressed with a fingertip.

While the cake is baking, spread out a smooth cotton towel. Sprinkle the additional confectioners sugar on the towel (enough to coat it, to keep the cake from sticking).

Immediately turn the cake out onto the towel and remove the pan and the foil. Starting at a narrow end, roll the hot cake and the towel together, making a firm roll but not squashing the cake any more than necessary.

Transfer the cake in the towel to a rack and let stand until cool.

FILLING

1½ cups heavy cream
¼ cup sifted confectioners sugar
1 tablespoon unsweetened cocoa powder
½ teaspoon unflavored gelatin
2 teaspoons cold water
2 tablespoons Cognac or brandy

In the small bowl of an electric mixer, mix the cream, sugar, and cocoa; do not beat, just mix. Refrigerate until you are ready to use it.

In a small heatproof cup, sprinkle the gelatin over the cold water and let stand for a few minutes.

Then place the cup in a small pan containing a little hot water over low heat. Let stand for a minute or so until the gelatin is dissolved. Set aside, but only briefly—do not let it cool completely.

Beat the cream-cocoa mixture until it holds a soft shape. Stir the Cognac into the gelatin and quickly, while beating, add it to the softly whipped cream and continue to beat until the cream holds a firm shape.

Unroll the cooled sponge roll. Spread the cream over the cake, leaving about 1½ inches uncovered at one short end. Carefully roll the cake, rolling it toward the end where the cream stops short. Place it, seam down, on a chocolate-roll board or on any long and narrow serving platter.

Refrigerate for at least 3 hours. Or cover well with plastic wrap and freeze.

Just before serving, sprinkle the top with unsweetened cocoa through a small strainer held over the cake.

NOTE: *Although this is delicious as it is, it is also wonderful served with The World's Best Hot Fudge Sauce (see page 54). The sauce should be tepid, at room temperature, not really hot or cold. Ladle or pour a generous ribbon of it over each portion. If you are serving eight people, double the amount of sauce called for in the recipe.*

Fruitcakes, Cakes with Fruit, and Nut Cakes

All of the cakes in this section will slice more neatly and easily if they are refrigerated so that they are cold when they are sliced.

Pearl's South-ampton Fruitcake

16 TO 18 POUNDS OF
CAKE IN 4, 5, OR
6 CAKES

This recipe came about when I wanted to send a gift to my dear friend Pearl Borinstein. Pearl is the most generous and fabulous hostess I know—her parties are legendary. She was on a round-the-world cruise on the luxury liner Queen Elizabeth II. After several conversations with the post office, it was decided that there might be a better chance that she would receive it if I mailed it to Southampton, England, than to any of the other ports. And since I planned to send it weeks before she would arrive there, I decided on a fruit-cake; it would surely last a long time. (I have heard of 25-year-old fruitcakes that were still wonderful—the liquor preserves them.)

Many people have said about this cake, "It's perfectly wonderful—I'm crazy about it, and I don't even like fruitcake." O.K. But I was happier when an English gentleman who came to visit us said that it was as good as the one he makes and that one, he said, is the best there is.

This recipe makes 4 large cakes, each in a 9 or 10 × 1½- or 2-inch layer-cake pan, or 6 cakes if made in 8-inch pans. It is typically Olde English: dark, extravagant, luxurious, powerful, loaded with fruits and liquors. But I doubt that you will find this recipe in any book, English or otherwise; the recipe evolved because I had just received a large order of candied and dried fruits and I wanted to use some of each one.

The variety of fruits can be changed if certain ones are not available. Instead of buying the ones that are already cut into small pieces and packed in little plastic containers, I buy whole candied fruits by the pound and cut them up myself (see Note). I think it makes a world of difference. I also think the cake is better if the fruit is not cut too small.

Making this takes a lot of time. The fruit must marinate for a week or more, and the baking time is 5 hours. But it is worth every minute.

FRUIT PREPARATION

In the absence of any of the following fruits, you may substitute others; just use about the same volume. The fruit can be prepared weeks ahead of time if you would like; I suggest a minimum of a week—it takes at least that long for the fruit to absorb all the liquor.

1 pound (generous 3 cups) raisins
1 pound (generous 3 cups) currants
1 pound (2 packed cups) pitted dates, each
    date cut into 2 or 3 pieces
½ pound (1½ firmly packed cups) dried
    apricots, each apricot half cut into
    2 or 3 pieces
½ pound (1½ firmly packed cups) dried brown
    figs, cut into ½-inch pieces
6 ounces (1 cup) candied ginger, cut into
    ¼-inch pieces
½ pound (2 cups) candied lemon rind, cut
    into ½-inch pieces
½ pound (2 cups) candied orange rind, cut
    into ½-inch pieces
½ pound (1½ cups) candied cherries, cut
    into halves
½ pound (1½ cups) candied pineapple, cut
    into ½-inch pieces
½ pound (1½ cups) candied citron, cut into
    ½-inch pieces
1 cup Cognac
½ cup Grand Marnier

Place all of the above ingredients in a large bowl. Stir to mix well. Then transfer to a large jar with a tight cover, or divide among two or three jars. Cover tightly. Let stand for a week or more, turning the jars from side to side and from top to bottom occasionally to marinate the fruit thoroughly. (It is best to do this on a tray of some kind in case a jar leaks.)

2½ cups sifted all-purpose flour
1 teaspoon double-acting baking powder
3 tablespoons unsweetened cocoa powder
1 teaspoon powdered cloves

1 teaspoon cinnamon

1 teaspoon mace

2 teaspoons powdered (not granular) instant
   coffee or instant espresso

1 pound (4 sticks) unsalted butter

1 pound (2¼ firmly packed cups) dark
   brown sugar

9 eggs (graded medium or large) or 8 eggs
   (graded extra-large or jumbo)

1¼ cups dark molasses

1½ pounds (7 cups) pecan halves

1½ pounds (7 cups) walnut halves or
   large pieces

Additional Cognac and/or Grand Marnier
   (to be used after the cakes are baked)

Adjust two racks to divide the oven into thirds and preheat oven to 225 degrees (check the temperature with a portable mercury thermometer; if it is any hotter the cakes will burn). Butter the sides only of four 9- or 10-inch layer-cake pans. (They may be 1½ or 2 inches deep. If they are only 1½ inches deep you might have enough batter for an additional small cake.) Cut baking-pan liner paper or aluminum foil to fit the bottoms of the pans, butter one side of the paper or foil, and place them buttered side up in the pans. Set aside.

Sift together the flour, baking powder, cocoa, cloves, cinnamon, mace, and powdered instant coffee, and set aside.

In the large bowl of an electric mixer, cream the butter. Add the sugar and beat well until light in color. Add the eggs one at a time, beating well after each addition. (The mixture will appear curdled—it is O.K.)

On low speed add the sifted dry ingredients in three additions alternating with the molasses in two additions. (It might still look curdled—O.K.)

In a very large mixing bowl (or any very large container) mix the fruit into the batter—include any liquor that has not been absorbed. Finally, mix in the nuts. Either use a large and heavy wooden spoon or spatula, or use your hands.

Divide the batter evenly among the prepared pans; it is all right if they fill the pans all the way to the tops. Pat the tops well to make them smooth and level and to make the batter compact, with no air spaces.

Bake for 5 hours, checking the temperature occasionally with a portable mercury thermometer. Once or twice during the baking reverse the positions of the pans, top to bottom and front to back, to ensure even baking.

Remove from the oven and cool for half an hour in the pans on racks. Carefully, with a small, sharp knife, cut around the sides to release. Then cover each pan with a rack, turn over the pan and rack, remove the pan and the paper lining, cover with another rack and turn over again, leaving the cakes right side up.

When the cakes have cooled—or while they are cooling—brush them with a conservative amount of additional Cognac and/or Grand Marnier (I use a mixture of both). Then carefully wrap the cakes airtight in plastic wrap. (Until they are chilled handle them carefully—they are fragile.)

Store the cakes for at least a week in the refrigerator, brushing them once or twice again with more Cognac and/or Grand Marnier. Then they may remain in the refrigerator or they may be frozen. They may be brushed occasionally with additional liquor; however, if they are frozen, let them stand at room temperature for about an hour before brushing them with more liquor—they absorb more when they are not frozen.

When I give this cake as a gift, I include the following note: "Refrigerate or freeze. Cake should be very cold when it is sliced. Use a very sharp, heavy knife. Cut small portions, this is RICH."

NOTE: *All of these candied fruits are available (in large pieces—the way I like them) at Paprikas Weiss, 1546 Second Avenue, New York, New York 10028, or H. Roth & Son, 1577 First Avenue, New York, New York 10028.*

Light Fruit-cake

6½ POUNDS
(1 TREMENDOUS CAKE)

Merry Christmas! This is a high, wide, and hand-some cake especially appropriate for the holidays— it is marvelous for a very large party. It should be made weeks or even months ahead (although I once served it 5 days after making it and it was great) and wrapped in a cloth kept wet with Cognac, or brushed with Cognac while it ages. This recipe calls for long, slow baking.

5 ounces (1 cup) light raisins
½ cup Cognac or brandy
8 ounces (1½ cups) candied citron, cut into slices or small squares

5 ounces (1 cup) candied pineapple or candied
     ginger, cut into ¼-inch slices
4 ounces (1 cup) candied red or green cherries,
     cut into halves
4 ounces (1 cup) candied orange rind, cut into
     slices or small squares
4 cups sifted all-purpose flour
8 ounces (2 cups) slivered (julienne)
     blanched almonds
4 ounces (generous 1 cup) pecan halves or
     large pieces
12 ounces (3 sticks) unsalted butter
1 teaspoon vanilla extract
2 cups granulated sugar
6 eggs (graded large), separated
½ teaspoon mace
¼ teaspoon salt
½ cup milk
Finely grated rind of 2 or 3 lemons (some of
     the juice will be used for Icing)
1 teaspoon cream of tartar
Additional Cognac or brandy (for brushing on
     the baked cake)

Mix the raisins and Cognac or brandy in an airtight jar. Let stand, turning the jar occasionally, for at least an hour or overnight.

Adjust a rack to the middle of the oven (even though it is a high cake, if you bake it lower in the oven, the top will remain too light because of the low temperature). Preheat the oven to 275 degrees. You will need a 10 × 4-inch tube pan which may be in one piece or it may be a two-piece pan (the sides separate from the bottom and tube); and it may be either nonstick or otherwise. Whichever you use, butter the pan even if it is a nonstick pan (including the tube in the middle), line the bottom with a round (with a hole in the middle) of baking-pan liner paper or brown wrapping paper (in the absence of baking-pan liner paper, brown wrapping paper is better than wax paper for this cake), butter the paper, and dust the pan all over with fine, dry bread crumbs (including the tube—sprinkle the crumbs on the tube with your fingertips). Be especially careful not to miss even a small spot; check the center tube carefully. Then, turn the pan upside down over a piece of paper, tap to shake out excess crumbs.

Place the citron, pineapple, cherries, and orange rind in a large, wide mixing bowl (use one larger than you think you will need, or you will not be able to flour the fruit well—and it should be large enough to add all the remaining ingredients). Add ½ cup of the sifted flour (reserve 3½ cups). With your fingers, toss the fruit and flour so each piece of fruit is thoroughly separated and floured. Then add the nuts and toss again. Set aside.

In the large bowl of an electric mixer, cream the butter until it is soft and smooth. Beat in the vanilla and 1⅔ cups (reserve the remaining ⅓ cup) of sugar. Add the yolks 2 or 3 at a time, scraping the bowl with a rubber spatula and beating until thoroughly incorporated after each addition.

Sift the reserved 3½ cups of sifted flour with the mace and salt. Then, on low speed, add one-third of the sifted dry ingredients to the butter mixture, and mix only to blend. Beat in the milk, then another third of the dry ingredients, then the Cognac-soaked raisins along with any Cognac the raisins did not absorb, and finally beat in the remaining dry ingredients.

Remove from the mixer and stir in the lemon rind.

In the small bowl of an electric mixer, with clean beaters, beat the whites until they are barely foamy. Add the cream of tartar and continue to beat until the whites hold a soft shape. Reduce the speed to moderate and gradually add the reserved ⅓ cup of sugar. Then, on high speed again, beat until the whites hold a definite shape but not until they are stiff or dry.

Add the butter-sugar-flour mixture and the beaten whites to the floured fruits and, with a large wooden spatula (rubber is too soft for this thick mixture), fold the three mixtures together only until thoroughly incorporated.

Spoon into the prepared pan and smooth the top.

Bake for 3¼ hours until a cake tester gently inserted all the way to the bottom comes out clean and dry. During baking, if the top of the cake begins to darken too much, cover it loosely with foil.

As soon as you remove the cake from the oven, brush the top with a few tablespoons of the additional Cognac or brandy. (It will soften the crust caused by the long baking.)

Then remove the cake from the oven and let it stand in the pan on a rack for at least an hour or a bit longer until it is tepid.

Cover with a rack, turn over the pan and the rack, remove the pan (do not remove the paper lining yet), cover with another rack and turn over again, leaving the cake right side up to finish cooling. When it is completely cool, turn the cake carefully over again just for a moment and peel off the paper lining. Leave it right side up.

The traditional way to age this cake is to sprinkle a cheesecloth or a thin towel with Cognac or brandy and wrap the cake with it, then place it in a large plastic bag or wrap it in foil. About once every week or two, moisten the cheesecloth or towel with more Cognac or brandy. Or, untraditionally, omit the cheesecloth and just brush the Cognac on the cake (an easier procedure, I think); keep the cake wrapped in wide plastic wrap or in a large plastic bag.

They say that fruitcakes can be kept at room temperature for a year or more; however, I store mine in the refrigerator or freezer.

The icing is optional. If you do use it, it may be applied either a few hours before serving or the day before.

FRUITCAKE ICING

1 cup plus 2 tablespoons sifted
    confectioners sugar
2 tablespoons unsalted butter, melted
1 tablespoon milk
2 teaspoons lemon juice

In a small bowl, stir together all the ingredients until smooth. The icing should be a thick but flowing mixture, and may be adjusted as necessary with additional sugar, milk, or lemon juice. It will be a very smooth icing with a pale yellow color (from the butter), and it should be used immediately.

Place the cake on a serving plate and spoon or pour the icing over the top of the cake. With a long, narrow metal spatula spread it to make a thin and even layer over the top only. If the consistency is exactly right, it may run down the sides slightly in a few spots—just leave it—do not spread the icing on the sides.

After several hours the icing will dry, and although it will not become hard, it will not be sticky.

Transfer the cake to a serving plate.

If possible, refrigerate the iced cake before serving; all such cakes slice best when they are cold. Serve in thin slices, two or three slices to a portion. (Use a very sharp, strong knife.)

NOTE: *Although I love the old-fashioned simplicity of this cake without any decoration on the icing, you can, if you wish, make a design (plain or fancy) with cut-up candied fruits or whole candied cherries or large pecan halves, or any combination of fruits and nuts.*

All of the candied fruits called for are available (in large pieces—the way I like them) at Paprikas Weiss, 1546 Second Avenue, New York, New York 10028, or H. Roth & Son, 1577 First Avenue, New York, New York 10028.

The Original Kentucky Whiskey Cake

24 OR MORE
PORTIONS

This is an heirloom recipe for an extravagant and marvelous raisin/nut/bourbon fruitcake. It is a cake traditionally served for Thanksgiving and Christmas, but it is wonderful any time. It lasts well and makes a magnificent gift. It is 5½ pounds of deliciousness. Make it at least several days before serving, or make it whenever and freeze it. Prepare the raisins at least a day before baking.

You will need an extra-large mixing bowl for folding in the beaten egg whites.

1½ pounds (4½ cups) dark and light (or all dark) raisins
1 cup bourbon
2 cups sifted all-purpose flour
1 teaspoon double-acting baking powder
½ teaspoon salt
8 ounces (2 sticks) unsalted butter
1 nutmeg, freshly grated, or 2 teaspoons powdered nutmeg
2 cups granulated sugar
6 eggs (graded large), separated
1 pound (5 cups) pecan halves or large pieces

At least a day before baking (or a week before) place the raisins in a jar with a tight-fitting top. Add the bourbon. Turn occasionally from top to bottom. (If the jar might leak when it is upside down, place it in a bowl.)

Adjust a rack one-third up from the bottom of the oven. You will need a 10 × 4-inch tube pan, which may have a separate bottom or may be all in one piece, and it may have a nonstick lining or not. Butter the pan (even if it is nonstick), line the bottom with baking-pan liner paper or brown wrapping paper cut to fit, butter the paper, and dust with fine, dry bread crumbs (with your fingertips, sprinkle the crumbs on the tube). Then, over a piece of paper, tap to shake out excess crumbs.

Sift together the flour, baking powder, and ¼ teaspoon of the salt (reserve ¼ teaspoon of salt). Set aside.

In the large bowl of an electric mixer, beat the butter until it is softened. Add the nutmeg and 1¾ cups of the sugar (reserve the remaining ¼ cup) and beat for 5 minutes until the mixture is very creamy. Add the egg yolks (it is O.K. to add them all at once) and beat for a few minutes, scraping the bowl as necessary with a rubber spatula. On low speed add about one-third of the sifted dry ingredients and beat only to mix. Then mix in about half of the raisins along with any bourbon that was not absorbed. Then add another third of the dry ingredients, the remaining raisins and bourbon, and finally the remaining dry ingredients, scraping the bowl as necessary with a large rubber spatula and beating only until incorporated after each addition.

Remove from the mixer and stir in the nuts. Now transfer the mixture to a larger bowl in order to have room to fold in the beaten whites. Set aside.

In the small bowl of an electric mixer, with clean beaters, beat the whites and the reserved ¼ teaspoon of salt until the whites hold a soft shape. Reduce the speed to moderate and gradually add the remaining ¼ cup of sugar. Then increase the speed to high and beat briefly only until the whites hold a definite shape but not until they are stiff or dry.

With a large rubber spatula stir one-quarter of the whites into the cake batter. Then fold in the remaining whites.

Turn the mixture into the prepared pan. Smooth the top.

Bake for 2½ hours until a cake tester inserted into the middle of the cake comes out clean and dry. If the top of the cake begins to darken too much during baking, cover it loosely with foil.

Remove from the oven and let stand for 30 minutes. (The top of the cake will be 1 inch below the top of the pan.)

Cover the pan with a rack, carefully turn over the pan and the rack, remove the pan, peel off the paper lining, cover with another rack and turn over again, leaving the cake right side up.

When the cake has cooled, wrap it airtight and refrigerate it for a few days before serving, or freeze it.

The cake should be cold when it is cut. Use a very sharp, firm knife and make the slices thin.

NOTE: *If you wish, you can wrap the cake in a napkin that has been soaked with bourbon or you can just stuff the center hole with a piece of cheesecloth that has been soaked with bourbon, and then wrap the cake with plastic wrap or foil and let it age that way at room temperature for at least a few days—it is a fine cake either way, with or without the additional bourbon, but it is possibly a little more fine with it.*

Irish Whiskey Cake

This is an old recipe for a deliciously flavored small fruitcake with less fruit than the usual. The caraway seeds do something wonderful. It is marvelous with tea or coffee, or with wine. It keeps well and is great to give as a gift.

1 9-INCH LOAF CAKE

2 cups sifted all-purpose flour
1 teaspoon double-acting baking powder
¼ teaspoon mace
¼ teaspoon salt
Finely grated rind of 2 lemons
1 tablespoon plus 1 teaspoon lemon juice
5 ounces (1¼ sticks) unsalted butter
1 teaspoon vanilla extract
1 cup light brown sugar, firmly packed
2 eggs (graded large or extra-large), separated
½ cup Irish whiskey (or any Scotch, whiskey, bourbon, or blend)
½ cup diced candied orange peel
½ cup light raisins
1 tablespoon caraway seeds
¾ cup pecans, cut into medium-size pieces
About 1 tablespoon additional butter, at room temperature (to be used after the cake is baked)

Adjust a rack one-third up from the bottom of the oven and preheat oven to 350 degrees. Butter a loaf pan that measures 8½ × 4½ × 2¾ inches and has a 6-cup capacity. Dust it with fine, dry bread crumbs, then, over a piece of paper, tap to shake out excess crumbs.

Sift together the flour, baking powder, mace, and salt and set aside.

Mix the lemon rind and juice and set aside.

In the large bowl of an electric mixer, cream the butter. Add the vanilla and then the sugar and beat to mix well. Add the yolks and beat well.

On low speed add the sifted dry ingredients in three additions, alternating with the whiskey in two additions, scraping the bowl as necessary with a rubber spatula and beating only until incorporated after each addition.

Remove from the mixer. Stir in the lemon rind and juice, candied orange peel, raisins, caraway seeds, and pecans.

In a small bowl beat the egg whites until they hold a definite shape but not until they are stiff and dry, and fold them into the batter.

Turn into the prepared pan and smooth the top. Then, with the spatula or with a spoon, form a shallow trench lengthwise down the middle of the cake. (That makes a more level top, less of a mound, when baked.)

Bake for 1¼ hours (or longer) until a cake tester inserted into the middle comes out clean and dry. While the cake is baking, if it begins to darken too much, cover it loosely with foil. Test this carefully and be sure that you do not underbake.

As soon as you remove the cake from the oven, spread the softened butter over the top. The top of the cake will have formed a deep crack—it is O.K.

Let the cake stand in the pan on a rack for about 20 minutes. Then cover it with another rack, turn over the pan and the rack, remove the pan, and carefully turn the cake right side up to cool on the rack.

It is best to wrap and refrigerate this for at least a few hours—preferably overnight or longer—or freeze it before slicing. It slices best when it is cold.

If the top has a crisp crust (delicious), slice it with a serrated bread knife.

Florida Rum Cake

16 PORTIONS

This is made in a fancy-shaped tube pan; it is a buttermilk walnut cake with a generous amount of lemon, orange, and rum glaze—the combination is divine. It is a pretty cake and may be made for a party dessert, or it may be served as a coffee cake. It should be made at least a day before serving; it may be frozen.

You will need a one-piece tube pan that has a design and an 8- to 10-cup capacity.

2½ cups sifted all-purpose flour
2 teaspoons double-acting baking powder
1 teaspoon baking soda
½ teaspoon salt
8 ounces (2 sticks) unsalted butter
1 cup granulated sugar
2 eggs (graded large or extra-large)
1 cup buttermilk
Finely grated rind of 1 large fresh lemon
Finely grated rind of 2 large, deep-colored oranges
} (juice of lemon and oranges will be used for the Glaze)
4 ounces (generous 1 cup) walnuts, chopped into small pieces (⅛- to ¼-inch pieces)

Adjust a rack one-third up from the bottom of the oven and preheat oven to 350 degrees. Butter a one-piece kugelhopf or Bundt-type tube pan that has an 8- to 10-cup capacity; it is best to use soft (not melted) butter and a pastry brush. Dust the pan all over with fine, dry bread crumbs, then, over a piece of paper, tap to shake out excess crumbs. Set aside.

Sift together the flour, baking powder, baking soda, and salt, and set aside.

Beat the butter in the large bowl of an electric mixer until it is soft. Add the sugar and beat to mix well. Add the eggs, one at a time, and beat to mix after each addition. Then, on low speed, add the sifted dry ingredients in three additions alternately with the buttermilk in two additions, scraping the bowl as necessary with a rubber spatula and beating only until smooth after each addition.

Remove from the mixer. Stir in the grated rinds and then the nuts.

Turn into the prepared pan and smooth the top.

Bake for 55 to 60 minutes, until the top springs back sharply when it is lightly pressed with a fingertip.

Meanwhile, prepare the glaze.

GLAZE

3 tablespoons fresh lemon juice
½ cup fresh orange juice
1 cup granulated sugar
5 tablespoons dark rum

Place both juices and the sugar in a small saucepan and set aside.

When the cake is done, remove it from the oven, set it on a rack, and, at the same time, place the saucepan over moderate or high heat and stir with a small wooden spatula until the sugar is dissolved and the mixture just comes to a low boil. Remove it from the heat and stir in the rum.

Pierce all over the top of the cake with a cake tester. Then, gradually spoon the hot glaze over the hot cake (still in the pan), spooning only about a tablespoonful at a time (or a little more at the beginning). When about half of the glaze has been added, and some of it remains around the rim of the cake pan (instead of being absorbed immediately), use a small, narrow metal spatula or a table knife and gently ease the edges of the cake (around the tube also) just a bit away from the pan, allowing the glaze to run down the sides. Continue adding the glaze (and releasing the sides occasionally) until it is all absorbed. (Toward the end you will wonder, but the cake *will* absorb it all.)

Let stand for about 10 minutes, until the bottom of the pan is not too hot to touch. Then cover the pan with a cake plate, hold the pan and plate firmly together, and turn them over. Remove the pan. If it does not come away easily, bang both the pan and the plate against the work surface; once should be enough. Remove the pan. Brush away any loose crumbs on the plate.

Let stand for a few hours and then cover airtight with plastic wrap. Let stand overnight (if possible).

Serve this in thick slices.

NOTE: *When you cut the cake you will see that it has absorbed the glaze on the outer edges, not all the way through to the middle.*

Mrs. O'Shaugh-nessy's Cake

This is an Irish loaf cake with a generous amount of currants that don't sink. It bakes with a richly browned crust, a nicely rounded top, and a mild lemon-orange flavor. It is delicious, easy to make, keeps well, and is lovely to wrap as a gift.

1 8½- or 9-INCH
LOAF CAKE

5 ounces (1 cup) currants
Boiling water
1¾ cups sifted all-purpose flour
1 teaspoon double-acting baking powder
¼ teaspoon salt
½ teaspoon mace
4 ounces (1 stick) unsalted butter
1 teaspoon vanilla extract
1 cup minus 2 tablespoons granulated sugar
2 eggs (graded large or extra-large)
½ cup milk
Finely grated rind of 2 lemons
Finely grated rind of 1 large, deep-
colored orange
½ teaspoon caraway seeds

Adjust a rack one-third up from the bottom of the oven and preheat oven to 350 degrees. You can use either an 8½ × 4½ × 2½-inch loaf pan or a 9 × 5 × 3-inch loaf pan (the batter will not fill a 9 × 5 × 3-inch pan, but it will be an attractive loaf anyhow). Butter the pan and dust it with fine, dry bread crumbs, then, over a piece of paper, tap to shake out excess crumbs.

Cover the currants with boiling water and let stand for 5 minutes. Drain in a strainer and turn out onto several thicknesses of paper towels. Fold the paper over the currants and press to absorb excess water. Let stand.

Sift together the flour, baking powder, salt, and mace and set aside.

In the large bowl of an electric mixer, beat the butter until it is soft. Add the vanilla and then the sugar and beat to mix well. Add the eggs one at a time, beating until thoroughly mixed after each addition. On low speed add about one-third of the dry ingredients, scraping the bowl as necessary with a rubber spatula and beating only until incorporated. Gradually add the milk and beat until smooth. Then add the remaining dry ingredients and beat only until smooth.

Remove from the mixer and stir in the grated rinds. Turn into the prepared pan, smooth the top, and then, with a rubber spatula or with the bottom of a spoon, form a slight trench (about ½ inch deep) down the length of the loaf. That will keep it from rising too high in the middle.

Sprinkle the caraway seeds all over the top.

Bake about 1 hour until a cake tester gently inserted into the middle comes out clean and dry.

Let the cake stand in the pan on a rack for about 10 minutes, then cover it with a rack, turn over the pan and the rack, remove the pan, and gently turn the loaf right side up to cool on the rack.

If you can wait, wrap this and refrigerate it overnight or freeze it for about an hour before serving. It is best to cut this with a serrated French bread knife.

Cuban Coconut Pound Cake

16 PORTIONS

This cake has a fine-grained, compact texture. It keeps well, slices well, freezes well, and is quick and easy to make. It has a generous amount of coconut and some sliced almonds. The original Cuban version uses freshly grated coconut, which is wonderful. If you buy the coconut already shredded, you may use either the sweetened or un-sweetened—the cake is superspecial with either. Everyone who has tasted this raves about it and I recommend it mucho!

8 ounces (2 sticks) unsalted butter
1 teaspoon vanilla extract
½ teaspoon almond extract
½ teaspoon salt
2 cups granulated sugar
5 eggs (graded large)
3 cups sifted all-purpose flour
1 cup milk
7 ounces (2⅔ loosely packed cups) shredded coconut
3 ounces (1 cup) unblanched almonds, thinly sliced (see Note)

Adjust a rack one-third up from the bottom of the oven and preheat oven to 325 degrees.

You will need a 10-inch tube pan (a plain pan with no design). The baked cake will be 2½ inches high, but if the pan is deeper it is all right. I have used a 10 × 4-inch tube pan and the cake was beautiful. The pan can be in one piece or two (the sides being a separate piece from the bottom and tube); it can be nonstick or not. If it is nonstick it does not have to be buttered, but it does have to be lined with a round of baking-pan liner paper or buttered wax paper (buttered side up) cut to fit. If the pan is not nonstick, butter the bottom and sides, line it with a round of baking-pan liner paper or wax paper cut to fit, butter the paper, and dust the pan all over with fine, dry bread crumbs, then, over a piece of paper, tap to shake out excess crumbs.

In the large bowl of an electric mixer, cream the butter until it is soft and smooth. Add the vanilla and almond extracts, the salt, and the sugar and beat to mix. Add the eggs one at a time, beating until incorporated after each addition (the mixture will appear curdled—it is O.K.). On low speed alternately add the flour in three additions with the milk in two additions, scraping the bowl with a rubber spatula and beating only until incorporated.

Remove from the mixer and fold in the coconut and the nuts.

Turn into the prepared pan and smooth the top.

Bake for 1½ hours until the top is golden brown and a cake tester inserted into the cake (all the way to the bottom) comes out clean.

Let stand on a rack for 15 minutes. Then cover with a rack, turn the rack and the cake pan over, remove the pan (do not remove the paper yet), cover with another rack and invert again, leaving the cake right side up. Let stand until cool.

When the cake is cool, carefully peel off the paper lining.

Wrap the cool cake in plastic wrap. If possible, refrigerate it overnight before serving. Or place it in the freezer for about 45 minutes. It must be cold when it is sliced or it will crumble.

Serve two or three thin slices to a portion.

NOTE: *Although the original Cuban version of this cake was made with unblanched almonds, if you cannot get them, use the blanched ones.*

Survival Cake

16 LARGE SLICES

This recipe is from friends in Colorado who always make it to take on river-rafting or mountain-climbing and camping trips. Make it for a picnic, or for lunch boxes, or just for surviving whatever. It is wonderfully satisfying, not too sweet, and it keeps well and travels well. It is made in a shallow, square pan and is cut into slices for serving.

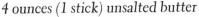

4 ounces (1 stick) unsalted butter
½ cup dark or light brown sugar, firmly packed
½ cup dark or light molasses
¾ cup prepared black coffee, water, or apple juice
5 ounces (1 cup) raisins
12 ounces (1½ cups) pitted dates, cut into large pieces
2 cups strained or sifted all-purpose whole-wheat flour (see Note)
½ teaspoon salt
1 teaspoon baking soda
1 teaspoon double-acting baking powder
2 teaspoons cinnamon
½ teaspoon mace
½ teaspoon cloves
¼ teaspoon ginger
¼ teaspoon finely ground black pepper
3 eggs (any size)
½ cup wheat germ, toasted or untoasted
5½ ounces (1½ cups) walnuts, cut or broken into medium-size pieces

Adjust a rack to the center of the oven and preheat oven to 350 degrees. Prepare a 9-inch square cake pan (1¾ to 2 inches deep) as follows: Center a 12-inch square of aluminum foil over an overturned pan, fold down the sides and the corners to shape the foil, then remove the foil, turn the pan right side up, place the foil in the pan, and press carefully into place. To butter the foil, place the pan in the oven with a piece of butter in it to melt as the oven heats. Then spread the melted butter with a brush or with crumpled wax paper.

Place the 4 ounces of butter in a heavy 2-quart saucepan over moderate heat to melt. Add the brown sugar, molasses, coffee (or water or apple juice), raisins, and dates. Stir occasionally until the mixture comes to a boil. Remove from the heat, pour into a large mixing bowl, and stir occasionally until the mixture cools to room temperature.

Meanwhile, sift together the flour, salt, baking soda, baking powder, cinnamon, mace, cloves, ginger, and black pepper.

When the hot mixture has cooled, add the eggs and stir with a wooden spatula to mix. Then stir in the wheat germ, then the sifted dry ingredients, and finally the nuts.

Turn into the prepared pan and smooth the top.

Bake for about 40 minutes until the cake feels firm when lightly pressed with a fingertip.

Cool in the pan for 10 or 15 minutes. Then cover with a rack, turn over the pan and the rack, remove the pan, peel off the foil, cover with another rack and turn over again, leaving the cake right side up to cool.

When completely cool and firm enough to slice (placing it in the freezer for about half an hour or so will make the slicing easier), transfer the cake to a board. With a long, thin, sharp knife cut the cake in half. Then cut each half into 8 slices.

To preserve the freshness and make it generally stronger for packing and for surviving, wrap each slice individually in clear cellophane, wax paper, or foil.

NOTE: *Any whole-wheat flour that did not go through the strainer or sifter should be stirred back into the part that did go through.*

Whole-Wheat Walnut Cake

This is a large, compact cake, somewhat like a pound cake full of nuts, somewhat like a fruitcake with nuts only. It is beautiful and delicious, every bite full of large chunks of walnuts. It is 5 pounds of cake, an impressive gift. Serve it as a coffee cake or with wine. Or serve it with ice cream. It calls for both whole-wheat and white flour, and long, slow baking.

16 TO 18 PORTIONS

12 ounces (3 sticks) unsalted butter
½ teaspoon salt
½ teaspoon finely ground black pepper
1 teaspoon vanilla extract

½ teaspoon almond extract

1 teaspoon powdered ginger

1 teaspoon powdered (not granular)
   instant coffee

½ teaspoon allspice

2 cups granulated sugar

6 eggs (graded large), separated

2 cups sifted all-purpose white flour

⅔ cup milk

1½ cups sifted all-purpose whole-wheat flour

⅓ cup Cognac, brandy, or whiskey

1 pound (4 generous cups) walnut halves or
   large pieces

1 teaspoon cream of tartar

Adjust a rack one-third up from the bottom of the oven and preheat oven to 275 degrees. You will need a 10 × 4-inch tube pan (a plain pan with no design); it can be either a one-piece pan, or the sides can be separate from the bottom and tube; it can be plain metal or it can have a nonstick finish. Butter the pan (even if it is nonstick), line the bottom with a round of wax paper or baking-pan liner paper cut to fit, butter the paper, dust all over with fine, dry bread crumbs, then, over a piece of paper, tap out excess.

Place the butter, salt, and pepper in the large bowl of an electric mixer and beat until soft. Add the vanilla and almond extracts, the ginger, powdered instant coffee, and allspice, and then 1½ cups of the sugar (reserve the remaining ½ cup of sugar). Beat well for about 3 minutes, scraping the bowl as necessary with a large rubber spatula. Add the egg yolks all at once and continue to beat for about 5 minutes more.

On low speed, add about half the white flour and beat only to mix. Then add half the milk, beat only to mix, then the second half of the white flour, and then the balance of the milk. Next, add half the whole-wheat flour, then the Cognac, and finally the balance of the whole-wheat flour, continuously scraping the bowl with the rubber spatula and beating only until incorporated.

Transfer the mixture to a mixing bowl larger than the large bowl of the mixer. Stir in the nuts.

If you do not have an additional large bowl and an additional set of beaters for the mixer, wash the ones you have just used. Place the egg whites in the large bowl, add the cream of tartar, and beat until the whites hold a soft shape. On moderate speed gradually add the reserved ½ cup of sugar. Increase the speed to high and beat until the whites have a thick, marshmallowlike consistency.

Add about one-third of the whites to the walnut mixture (which will be quite thick) and fold or stir until incorporated. Then add all of the remaining whites and fold together until incorporated. Be patient; it will seem to take a long time.

Turn the mixture into the pan and smooth the top.

Bake for 2¾ to 3 hours until a cake tester gently inserted into the cake, all the way to the bottom, comes out clean.

Remove from the oven. Let the cake stand in the pan for about half an hour. The top of the cake will be about 1 inch below the top of the pan.

Cover with a rack, turn over the pan and the rack, remove the pan (but not the paper lining), cover with another rack and turn over again, leaving the cake right side up to cool. Do not remove the paper lining until the cake has cooled completely.

Wrap the cooled cake in plastic wrap or in a plastic bag and refrigerate overnight or longer, or freeze.

Cut into very thin slices, and serve two or three slices to a portion.

NOTE: *If some of the whole-wheat flour did not go through the sifter, it should be stirred into the part that did go through.*

Raisin Cake with Apples

10 PORTIONS

This is an old, traditional Swedish coffee cake. Or, if you serve it with ice cream, it becomes a dessert cake. It is an easy cake made with sliced raw apples that are rolled in cinnamon-sugar and placed into the top of the cake before it is baked. It is delicious and best the day it is made.

You will need a spring-form pan 9 inches in diameter; it may be either 2 or 3 inches deep (if you have both sizes, use the 2-inch).

1¾ cups sifted all-purpose flour
1 teaspoon double-acting baking powder
½ teaspoon salt
5 ounces (1¼ sticks) unsalted butter
1 teaspoon vanilla extract
1¼ cups granulated sugar

3 eggs (graded large or extra-large)
Finely grated rind of 1 large lemon
2½ ounces (½ cup) light raisins (dark raisins
    may be substituted but the light are
    traditional in this cake)

Adjust a rack to the center of the oven and preheat oven to 350 degrees. Butter a 9-inch spring form (see introduction to recipe) and set it aside.

Sift together the flour, baking powder, and salt and set aside.

In the large bowl of an electric mixer, beat the butter until it is soft and smooth. Add the vanilla and then the sugar and beat to mix very well. Add the eggs one at a time and beat until thoroughly incorporated after each addition. Beat for 1 minute after the last addition. On low speed gradually add the sifted dry ingredients, scraping the bowl with a rubber spatula as necessary and beating only until incorporated. Remove from the mixer.

Stir in the lemon rind and then the raisins.

Turn into the prepared pan and smooth the top. Let stand while you prepare the topping.

TOPPING

2 large firm and tart apples (about 1 pound;
    Granny Smith or Red or Golden Delicious
    are good for this)
2 teaspoons cinnamon
1 tablespoon plus 2 teaspoons granulated sugar
Confectioners sugar (to be sprinkled on top
    before serving)

Peel, quarter, and core the apples. Cut each section into lengthwise slices about ⅓-inch wide at the outside edge.

In a small bowl stir the cinnamon and granulated sugar together.

One at a time, turn an apple slice in the cinnamon-sugar and then place it into the cake, placing it at an angle, pointed edge down, deep into the dough (just the outside of the apple should remain above). The slices should be placed at a right angle to the rim to form a ring around the edge of the pan. They should be as close to each other as possible. Remaining slices should be cut into smaller pieces to fill in the middle and empty spaces around the edge.

Bake for 1 to 1¼ hours until a toothpick gently inserted in the middle comes out dry.

Let the cake cool in the pan for 15 minutes. Remove the sides of the pan. Cover the cake with a rack, turn over the cake and the rack, remove the bottom of the pan, cover the cake with another rack and turn over again, leaving the cake right side up.

This may be served while it is still slightly warm. Or let it stand to cool completely.

Just before serving cover the top generously with confectioners sugar, sprinkling it through a fine strainer; sprinkle it heavily in the center but not around the rim.

Kathy's Cranberry Loaf

12 TO 16 PORTIONS

My friend Kathy Fleegler of Cleveland, Ohio, is a cateress and cooking teacher. This is one of her favorite recipes to cater, to teach, and to make for her family and friends. It is a moist loaf with a texture somewhat like a moist fruitcake. Loaded with nuts and whole cranberries, the combination is gorgeous—crunchy and cranberry-sour. And the loaf is brushed with a generous amount of orange glaze that soaks into the cake. It should be made at least a day ahead, but it freezes wonderfully and may be made way ahead.

The loaf is made with either fresh cranberries or with frozen whole cranberries. Kathy says to buy extra cranberries when they are in season and freeze them. (To freeze: Do not wash before freezing [because if they are not thoroughly dry before freezing, they become mushy]; in a plastic bag, they will keep for a year. To use: Just pour out as many as you need, rinse quickly, drain well, and use them frozen. Do not thaw.)

Serve this as a dessert or as a tea or coffee cake.

2 cups whole cranberries
2½ cups sifted all-purpose flour
¼ teaspoon salt
1 teaspoon double-acting baking powder
1 cup granulated sugar
7 ounces (2 cups) walnut halves or
    large pieces
2 eggs (graded large or extra-large)
1 cup buttermilk

¾ cup tasteless salad oil
Finely grated rind of 1 or 2 deep-colored
oranges (juice will be used for the Glaze)

Adjust a rack to the center of the oven (if it is lower the loaves will be too pale on top) and preheat oven to 350 degrees. You will need two loaf pans measuring 8½ × 4½ × 2½ inches or slightly smaller (they should each have a 5- or 6-cup capacity). Butter the pans, dust them with fine, dry bread crumbs, then, over a piece of paper, tap out excess crumbs. Set aside.

If you are using fresh cranberries, pick over them, rinse, drain, and spread out on a towel to dry. If you are using frozen berries, they should wait in the freezer until you are ready for them, then rinse and drain quickly and use them frozen.

Sift together, in a large bowl, the flour, salt, baking powder, and sugar. Then stir in the nuts and the cranberries.

In a bowl beat the eggs to mix; beat in the buttermilk and salad oil, and then stir in the orange rind.

Pour the liquids over the dry ingredients and stir to mix.

Spoon half of the mixture into each of the prepared pans and smooth the tops; the pans should be half or three-quarters filled.

Bake for about 1 hour or until a cake tester gently inserted into the middle comes out clean and dry.

About 15 minutes before the baking time is finished, if the tops look too pale, raise the racks to a higher position. (A crack will form down the length of each loaf while it is baking—it is O.K.) The loaves will not reach the tops of the pans, they will be only about 2 inches high. Remove from the oven and let stand for 10 minutes. Meanwhile, prepare the glaze.

ORANGE GLAZE

1 cup granulated sugar
1 cup orange juice

Stir the sugar and orange juice in a small saucepan over moderate heat until the sugar is dissolved.

(The loaves will be transferred to two plates or platters or trays, or one plate or platter or tray large enough to hold both, or to anything with a rim to keep the glaze from running over.)

Cover each loaf with a rack, turn over the pan and the rack, remove the pan, cover with another rack and turn over again, leaving the loaf right side up. Now, with your hands, gently transfer each loaf to the rimmed plate, platter, tray, or what-have-you. Pierce the tops gently in many places with a cake tester.

With a pastry brush, brush the hot glaze generously over the tops and sides of the loaves. When much of the glaze has run down off the loaves, use a wide metal spatula and gently raise one end of the loaf, at the same time tilting the plate, to let the glaze run under the bottom of the loaf. Continue to brush on the glaze from the plate. After a while you will think that there is too much glaze and that the loaves simply will not absorb all of it. You are about right, there will probably be a little left on the plate. Refrigerate the loaves uncovered. The remaining syrup will become thicker and syrupy as it chills; spread it over the loaves with a spoon or spatula.

Refrigerate the loaves, uncovered, for several hours or overnight before serving. Or, if you are going to freeze them, first place each loaf on wax paper or foil on a tray and freeze uncovered. Then transfer to a large piece of plastic wrap and wrap airtight. The outsides of the loaves will be sticky (yummy) but when you unwrap them only a very little will cling to the wrapping, and the loaves will look shiny/gorgeous.

To serve after freezing, the loaves should be unwrapped while they are frozen (so the glaze does not stick too much to the wrapping), transferred to a plate, and refrigerated uncovered for a few hours or left at room temperature to thaw.

Cut with a very sharp knife. Serve two slices (about ½ inch thick) to a portion. Each loaf should serve 6 or 8.

NOTE: *You might like to try this with vanilla ice cream—the combination of the sour berries with the sweet ice cream is wonderful.*

Oatmeal Cake

This cake is extremely popular all around the country, and it has been for a long, long time. It is made in a shallow oblong pan and is cut into squares; it may be left in the pan for picnics or occasions when it is important to carry a cake in the pan. It is unusually and wonderfully moist, mildly spiced, and has a butterscotch-candylike crunchy topping. It keeps well; it can be frozen. Serve plain as a coffee cake, or with ice cream as a dessert.

16 SQUARES

1 cup quick (not instant) rolled oats (I have been using Shiloh Farms oats from health-food stores)
1¼ cups boiling water
1½ cups sifted all-purpose flour
1 teaspoon baking soda
1 teaspoon cinnamon
¼ teaspoon nutmeg
½ teaspoon salt
4 ounces (1 stick) unsalted butter
1 teaspoon vanilla extract
1 cup granulated sugar
1 cup dark or light brown sugar, firmly packed
2 eggs (graded large or extra-large)

Adjust a rack to the center of the oven. Preheat oven to 350 degrees. Butter a 9 × 13 × 2-inch metal cake pan. Dust it all over with rolled oats (in addition to those called for in the recipe), then, over a piece of paper, tap out excess. Set aside.

Place the cup of oats in a bowl, stir in the boiling water to mix, and let stand for 20 minutes.

Sift together the flour, baking soda, cinnamon, nutmeg, and salt, and set aside.

In the large bowl of an electric mixer, cream the butter. Beat in the vanilla. Add both sugars and beat well. Then add the eggs and beat well. Beat in the rolled oats. On low speed add the sifted dry ingredients, scraping the bowl with a rubber spatula and beating only until incorporated.

Turn into the pan and smooth the top.

Bake for about 40 minutes until the cake begins to come away from the sides of the pan and until it springs back when lightly pressed with a fingertip.

While the cake is baking, prepare the following topping.

NUT-COCONUT TOPPING

5 ounces (1¼ sticks) unsalted butter
⅔ cup dark or light brown sugar, firmly packed
¼ cup light cream
⅔ cup walnuts or pecans, cut into
    medium-size pieces
3 ounces (1 packed cup) shredded coconut

Cream the butter. Add the sugar and then the cream, mixing well. Stir in the nuts and coconut.

Use two teaspoons, one for picking up and one for pushing off, and place the topping all over the top of the hot cake, covering the cake as thoroughly as you can.

This should now be placed about 12 inches below a preheated broiler until it bubbles well all over. Watch carefully—it takes only a few minutes. (If the topping is not level, it is easy to spread with the back of a spoon as soon as it is removed from the broiler.)

Cool in the pan.

This is such a moist cake that it will not cut evenly or neatly, but it really doesn't matter. But if you put it in the freezer for about an hour it will cut beautifully.

Sour-Cream Coffee Cake

12 SQUARES

Extra scrumptious! This is an easy-to-make, deliciously moist sour-cream raisin cake with a crunchy, nutty topping that sinks into the cake in places and is too good! It is baked in an oblong shallow pan and is great for a picnic or whenever you want to carry the cake with you right in the pan. Or make it for a fancy coffee or tea party, or Sunday brunch, or for any other time. But make it.

TOPPING

1 tablespoon sifted all-purpose flour
1¼ teaspoons cinnamon
¾ cup dark or light brown sugar, firmly packed
2 tablespoons firm unsalted butter, cut into
    ½-inch squares
3½ ounces (1 cup) pecans, cut into medium-
    small pieces, about ¼ inch in diameter
    (walnuts may be substituted)

Adjust a rack to the center of the oven and preheat oven to 350 degrees. Generously butter a 13 × 9 × 2-inch metal baking pan. Or use an oven-proof glass pan and a 325-degree temperature (see Note).

Stir the flour, cinnamon, and sugar together in a bowl. Add the butter and with a pastry blender cut it into the dry ingredients until the mixture resembles coarse meal—do not overmix, a few slightly larger pieces of butter will not hurt. Stir in the nuts. Set aside at room temperature unless the room is very warm, in which case, refrigerate.

CAKE

2 cups sifted all-purpose flour
1 teaspoon double-acting baking powder
1 teaspoon baking soda
Scant ¼ teaspoon salt
4 ounces (1 stick) unsalted butter
1 cup granulated sugar
3 eggs (graded large)
1 cup sour cream
2½ ounces (½ cup) light raisins

Sift together the flour, baking powder, baking soda, and salt and set aside.

In the large bowl of an electric mixer, cream the butter until it is soft. Add the sugar and beat to mix well. Add the eggs one at a time, scraping the bowl with a rubber spatula and beating until thoroughly incorporated after each addition. On low speed add the sifted dry ingredients in three additions alternating with the sour cream in two additions, beating only until incorporated after each addition.

Remove from the mixer and fold in the raisins.

Turn into the prepared pan and smooth the top. Sprinkle the prepared topping loosely and evenly all over the cake.

Bake for 30 to 35 minutes until a toothpick or a cake tester gently inserted in the middle comes out clean and dry. The cake might take a little longer to bake in a glass pan.

This may be served warm or after it has cooled to room temperature.

NOTE: *The pan may be buttered as directed and then the cake may be cut into squares directly in the pan and removed with a wide metal spatula. If you plan to carry the cake in the pan to a picnic—or if you simply like a cake that you can leave in the pan until you cut portions—that is definitely the way to handle it.*

But I prefer to remove the cake from the pan in one piece, and cut the portions with a long knife (which can only be done if the cake has been removed from the pan). If you want to do it this way, here's how. First line the pan with foil as follows: Turn the pan over and cover the bottom with a 16- or 17-inch length of foil, fold down the sides and the corners of the foil to shape it, remove the foil, turn the pan right side up, place the foil in the pan, and press it into place in the pan. To butter the foil, place a piece of butter in the pan and put the pan in the oven, so the butter melts. Then brush it with a pastry brush or spread it with crumpled wax paper.

To remove the baked cake from the foil-lined pan, let the cake cool for about 10 or 15 minutes in the pan. Then, to keep the crumb topping from falling off, cover the cake securely with foil, cover that with a cookie sheet, turn over the cake pan and the cookie sheet (pressing them firmly together), remove the pan, peel off the foil lining, cover the cake with a serving platter, a board, or another cookie sheet, and turn over again, leaving the cake right side up.

Blueberry-Nut Loaf Cake

This is a delicate orange-flavored loaf, loaded with fresh blueberries and walnuts. It is delicious as a dessert or as a coffee cake. When you cut into it you will see the darker purple and magenta berries against a lighter, glowing orange background of cake. Gorgeous! Remember this cake in blueberry season.

ABOUT 10 PORTIONS

1¼ cups fresh blueberries
2 cups sifted all-purpose flour
½ teaspoon salt
⅔ cup granulated sugar
1½ teaspoons double-acting baking powder
½ teaspoon baking soda
1 egg (graded large or extra-large)
2 tablespoons unsalted butter, melted
¾ cup orange juice (grate the rinds of 2 oranges before squeezing the juice)
Finely grated rind of 2 large, deep-colored oranges
5 ounces (1¼ cups) walnut or pecan halves or large pieces

Adjust a rack one-third up from the bottom of the oven and preheat oven to 350 degrees. Butter a 10½ × 4 × 3-inch or 9 × 5 × 3-inch loaf pan. Dust it all with fine, dry bread crumbs, then, over a piece of paper, tap to shake out excess crumbs. Set the pan aside.

Wash the berries in a large bowl of cold water. Then spread them out in a single layer on a towel. Pat the tops lightly with paper towels and let stand until dry—the berries must be completely dry.

Place the dry berries in a bowl. Measure out the flour, then remove 1 teaspoon and toss the teaspoon of flour very gently with the berries. Set aside.

Sift together the remaining flour, salt, sugar, baking powder, and baking soda. Set aside.

In the large bowl of an electric mixer, beat the egg just to mix. Mix in the butter and orange juice. Then, on low speed, add the sifted dry ingredients and beat only to mix. Remove from the mixer.

Stir in the grated rind and then the nuts.

Spread about one-quarter of the mixture in the prepared pan—it will be a very thin layer.

Gently and carefully (without squashing) fold the floured berries into the remaining batter. Place over the thin layer of batter in the pan. Smooth the top.

Bake for about 70 minutes until a cake tester gently inserted into the middle comes out clean and dry. (The cake will form a crack on the top during baking—it is supposed to. It looks beautiful.)

Let the cake cool in the pan on a rack for about 10 minutes—but no longer, or it will steam and the bottom crust will be wet.

This is a tender and fragile cake—be extremely careful when you remove it from the pan. If any of the berries run out to the sides of the cake they might stick and it could be necessary to cut around the sides with a small, sharp knife or with a small, narrow metal spatula to release the cake.

Cover the cake with a rack. Gently turn the cake pan and the rack over. Remove the pan, cover with another rack, and very carefully turn over again, leaving the cake right side up to cool.

Pineapple Upside-Down Cake

This pretty cake is quick and easy, light and delicious, and although it is very old-fashioned, it never goes out of style. It makes a lovely dessert cake but is also wonderful as a coffee cake to serve at breakfast, brunch, or a kaffeeklatsch. Serve it while it is fresh; it is extra good while it is still hot and for several hours after it is baked.

6 TO 8 PORTIONS

TOPPING

Pam, or any other nonstick cooking spray
2⅓ ounces (5⅓ tablespoons) unsalted butter
½ cup light brown sugar, firmly packed
1 20-ounce can or 2 8¼-ounce cans
    sliced pineapple (packed in natural juice)
Optional: pecan halves, canned black Bing
    cherries, stewed prunes, candied cherries,
    or maraschino cherries

You will need a frying pan with a heatproof handle or a pie plate with an 8-cup capacity. (The average deep 10-inch frying pan or 12-inch pie plate will be the right size, but measure the capacity to be sure.)

Adjust a rack to the center of the oven and preheat oven to 350 degrees. Spray the pan or plate with Pam—this recipe works better with a nonstick spray than it does with a buttered pan.

Place the butter in a small pan over moderate heat to melt.

Pour the melted butter evenly over the bottom of the sprayed pan or plate. Sprinkle the sugar evenly all over the butter, then, with your fingers, pat the sugar to press it into an even layer, making sure it is all moistened with the melted butter.

Drain the pineapple, reserve the juice for the cake batter, and place the slices on paper towels to dry.

Now, with the pineapple rings, make a pretty design around the outside of the plate on top of the sugar. And, if there is room, place one ring in the middle. If there is not room for a whole ring in the middle, you can use one half of a ring. Cut it into quarters and form a design with the pieces.

You will probably not use all of the pineapple slices.

Traditionally, pecan halves are arranged flat side up in a pattern in the spaces between the pineapple rings. And a black Bing cherry, a piece of stewed prune, or a pitted fresh cherry or a candied cherry is put in the middle of each ring.

Either arrange the fruit as described or make up your own pattern. My favorite design is as follows: Place one pineapple ring directly in the center. Cut the other rings in half, making two half circles from each ring. Place the half circles, touching each other (and touching the ring in the center) and fitting one against the other, all facing the same way—the cut sides of one against the round side of another, all around the pan.

Set the pan aside and prepare the batter.

CAKE BATTER

1 cup sifted all-purpose flour
⅓ teaspoon double-acting baking powder
    (measure 1 level teaspoon, mark it into
    thirds, return ⅔ to the box and use the
    remaining ⅓)
¼ teaspoon salt
2 eggs
⅔ cup sugar
1 teaspoon vanilla extract
6 tablespoons drained pineapple juice from the
    canned rings

Sift together the flour, baking powder, and salt and set aside. In the small bowl of an electric mixer, beat the eggs at high speed for about a minute. Gradually add the sugar while beating and continue to beat (total beating time about 5 minutes) until the mixture is thick and pale. Add the vanilla and the pineapple juice and beat on low speed, scraping the bowl with a rubber spatula, beating only until smooth. Still on low speed, add the sifted dry ingredients, scraping the bowl and beating only until smooth.

Pour the batter evenly over the fruit.

Bake for 45 to 50 minutes until the top just barely springs back when it is lightly pressed with a fingertip and a toothpick gently inserted into the middle comes out clean and dry. (The cake might begin to come away from the sides of the pan—another sign that it is done.)

While it is baking, prepare the glaze (see below).

The very second that the cake comes out of the oven it must be removed from the pan. Cover the cake with a serving plate or board. If you have baked the cake in a frying pan, the handle might be in the way; use good pot holders and be careful. Center the plate carefully, and immediately turn over the plate and the frying pan or pie plate—hold it all firmly to prevent the cake plate from slipping. Having turned everything over, *do not* remove the frying pan or pie plate immediately; wait a minute or so to allow all of the butter/sugar topping to settle onto the cake. Remove the pan or pie plate carefully. If any nuts have slipped out of place on the cake, rearrange them.

APRICOT GLAZE

½ cup apricot preserves

The preserves should be bubbling hot and ready to be used as soon as the frying pan or pie plate is removed. Therefore, 5 or 10 minutes before the cake is done, melt the preserves in a small pan over moderate heat. Force them through a strainer. Return to the pan and bring to a boil.

With a pastry brush, brush the hot preserves generously over the top and sides of the hot cake.

Serve the cake hot or cooled.

Use a serrated knife for slicing, preferably the small one called a tomato knife.

California Carrot Cake

Dense, moist, rich, solid, tantalizing, loaded with goodies, and as pretty as a picture (made in a fancy tube pan). You will love this. Make it as a dessert, a coffee cake, or as a wonderful gift.

16 PORTIONS

1½ cups unsifted all-purpose whole-wheat flour
½ cup unsifted all-purpose white flour
2 teaspoons baking soda
2 teaspoons cinnamon
¾ teaspoon nutmeg
½ teaspoon allspice
½ teaspoon cloves
½ teaspoon salt
¾ pound carrots (to make 2 cups shredded)
3 eggs (graded large or extra-large)
¾ cup tasteless salad oil
¾ cup buttermilk
1½ cups honey
1 8-ounce can (1 cup) crushed pineapple
    (packed in natural juice)
5 ounces (1 cup) raisins
4 ounces (generous 1 cup) walnuts, cut or
    broken into medium-size pieces
Optional: confectioners sugar

Adjust a rack one-third up in the oven and preheat the oven to 375 degrees. Butter a fancy-shaped tube pan with a 12-cup capacity (I use the 10-inch Bundt pan)—butter it even if it has a nonstick finish—and dust it all over with fine, dry bread crumbs. Invert over a piece of paper and tap to shake out excess crumbs. Set aside.

Sift together the whole-wheat and white flours, baking soda, cinnamon, nutmeg, allspice, cloves, and salt. Set aside.

Wash the carrots (do not peel them) and cut off the ends. Shred the carrots with a fine shredder—you can use a manual grater (on a 4-sided metal grater use the small round openings) or a food processor (use the fine shredding disk). You should have 2 cups, firmly packed. Set aside.

In a really large mixing bowl, beat or whisk the eggs just to mix. Gradually beat in the oil, buttermilk, and honey. Then stir in the carrots, pineapple (with its juice), raisins, and nuts.

Add the sifted dry ingredients all at once and stir/mix only until the dry ingredients are moistened. (Do not overmix; if the bowl is large enough and if you stir with a large rubber spatula, you will not overmix.) It will be a very liquid (thin) mixture.

Turn into the prepared pan and rotate the pan a bit to smooth the top.

Bake for 45 to 50 minutes until a cake tester inserted in the middle comes out clean.

Let the cake cool in the pan for about 15 minutes. Then cover it with a rack, hold the pan and rack firmly together, and invert. Remove the pan and let the cake stand until it is completely cool.

Carefully, with two wide metal spatulas, transfer the cake to a plate.

Before serving, sprinkle the top generously with the optional confectioners sugar, shaking it through a fine strainer held over the top of the cake.

Plain Cakes

The Best Damn Lemon Cake

8 TO 10 PORTIONS

I served this recently to friends who have eaten their way through all of my books. The first thing they said became the name. And then they added, "My favorite of all. . . . If someone went into business making and selling this they would get very rich."

You will need lemon extract as well as fresh lemons. The surprise in the recipe is that it contains ground almonds.

This is better when it is not too fresh—it is still wonderful after several days.

½ cup blanched almonds
1½ cups sifted all-purpose flour
1 teaspoon double-acting baking powder
¾ teaspoon salt
¼ pound (1 stick) unsalted butter
1 cup granulated sugar
2 eggs (graded large)
½ cup milk
1 ounce (4 tablespoons) lemon extract
Finely grated rind of 2 extra-large or 3 medium-size lemons (juice will be used for Glaze)

Adjust a rack one-third up from the bottom of the oven and preheat the oven to 350 degrees. Butter an 8½ × 4½ × 2¾-inch loaf pan with a 6-cup capacity (see Note). Dust it all with fine, dry bread crumbs, invert over a piece of paper, and tap firmly to shake out excess. Set the pan aside.

The almonds must be ground very fine. It can be done in a food processor, a blender, or a nut grinder. Then set them aside.

Sift together the flour, baking powder, and salt and set aside.

In a small, heavy saucepan over low heat, melt the butter.

Transfer it to the large bowl of an electric mixer. Add the sugar and beat a bit to mix. On low speed, beat in the eggs one at a time, beating only to mix well. Then, on low speed, add the sifted dry ingredients in three additions alternating with the milk in two additions, scraping the bowl with a rubber spatula and beating until mixed after each addition. Mix in the lemon extract.

Remove from the mixer. Stir in the grated rind and then the ground almonds.

It will be a rather thin mixture. Turn it into the prepared pan.

Bake for 65 to 75 minutes, until a cake tester carefully inserted into the center of the cake, all the way to the bottom, comes out just barely clean and dry. (If the pan is long and narrow the cake will bake in less time than if it is short and wide. During baking, the cake will form a large crack or two on the top; the crack, or cracks, will remain light in color—it is O.K.)

Two or 3 minutes before the cake is done, prepare the glaze.

GLAZE

⅓ cup plus 2 tablespoons granulated sugar
⅓ cup fresh lemon juice

Stir the sugar and juice in a small, heavy saucepan over moderate heat only until the sugar is just dissolved; do not boil the mixture.

When the cake is removed from the oven, let it stand for 2 or 3 minutes. Then, with a brush, brush the hot glaze very gradually over the hot cake; the glaze should not be applied quickly—it should take about 5 minutes to apply it all.

Let stand until tepid, not quite completely cool. Then, gently invert the cake onto a rack. (If the cake sticks in the pan, cover it loosely with foil or wax paper, turn it upside down onto your right hand, tap the bottom of the pan with your left hand, and the cake will slide out.) Turn the cake right side up.

When the cake is completely cool, wrap it in plastic wrap or foil and let stand for 12 to 24 hours before serving. Or place it in the freezer for about 2 hours, or in the refrigerator for about 4 hours, before serving.

NOTE: *For this cake, do not use a nonstick pan, or a black metal pan, or a glass pan; it should be aluminum, preferably heavy weight. And do not double the recipe and bake it in one larger pan, it is not as good—it is better to make two or more cakes in the specified 6-cup loaf pan.*

Lemon Buttermilk Cake #2

12 TO 15 PORTIONS

Shortly after my first dessert book was published, I received several calls and letters from people who said there was something wrong with the Lemon Buttermilk Cake.

I said it couldn't be. I had made the cake many times. I had taught it. My daughter made it often.

I compared the recipe in the book with my original copy and they looked the same (with a minor change in wording). Then I made the cake from the book and there was indeed something wrong. The cake sank and was like a wet pudding. I tried everything I could think of but I simply could not correct it. In desperation I had to delete the recipe from later editions of the book. (I wanted to ask my publisher to recall all of the books. I wanted to say, "General Motors does it, why can't we?")

We live about two miles from Isaac Singer. When Mr. Singer won the Nobel Prize for literature I heard him speak on television. He explained that his biggest problems in writing were caused by demons, who, he said, frequented the Singer home and created disasters.

Then I knew what happened to the Lemon Cake. Demons!

Anyone who has spent much time baking knows that demons are never far away.

Recently I rewrote the recipe completely. It is #2. This works.

Finely grated rind of 2 or 3 large lemons (juice will be used below and for Glaze)
3 tablespoons lemon juice
3 cups sifted all-purpose flour
½ teaspoon baking soda
½ teaspoon salt
½ pound (2 sticks) unsalted butter
2 cups granulated sugar
3 eggs (graded large or extra-large)
1 cup buttermilk

Adjust a rack one-third up from the bottom of the oven and preheat oven to 350 degrees. You will need a tube pan with a 10-cup capacity (that is generally 9 inches in diameter); it can be a pan with a design or a 9 × 3½-inch tube pan without a design. If you use a pan with a design, butter it (even if it is nonstick) and then dust it all over with fine, dry bread crumbs. If you use the plain 9 × 3½-inch tube pan, butter it, line the bottom with baking-pan liner paper or wax paper cut to fit, butter the paper, and dust all over with crumbs. With either pan, tap to shake out excess crumbs over a piece of paper. Set aside.

Place the lemon rind and juice in a small cup and set aside.

Sift together the flour, baking soda, and salt, and set aside.

In the large bowl of an electric mixer, beat the butter until it is slightly soft. Add the sugar and beat until well mixed. Add the eggs one at a time, beating well after each addition. On low speed add the sifted dry ingredients in three additions, alternating with the buttermilk in two additions, scraping the bowl with a rubber spatula, and beating only until smooth after each addition.

Remove from the mixer and stir in the lemon rind and juice.

Turn into the prepared pan and smooth the top.

Bake for 1 hour to 1 hour and 15 minutes or until a cake tester gently inserted into the middle comes out clean and dry.

As soon as the cake is put in the oven, mix the glaze.

GLAZE

½ cup fresh lemon juice
⅓ cup granulated sugar

Mix the juice and sugar and let stand, stirring occasionally, while the cake is baking.

Remove the cake from the oven and let it stand in the pan for 5 minutes. Then cover it with a rack and very carefully turn over the pan and the rack and place it over a large piece of foil. Remove the pan. If you have used a paper lining, peel it off now.

With a pastry brush, brush the glaze all over the top, sides, and tube of the hot cake.

Let stand until completely cool.

Buttermilk Loaf Cake

This is perfectly plain/beautiful/delicious, and is easy to make.

3 cups sifted all-purpose flour
½ teaspoon double-acting baking powder
½ teaspoon baking soda
¾ teaspoon salt
8 ounces (2 sticks) unsalted butter
1½ teaspoons vanilla extract
2 cups granulated sugar
4 eggs (graded large)
1 cup buttermilk
Finely grated rind of 2 or 3 lemons

Adjust a rack one-third up from the bottom of the oven and preheat oven to 325 degrees. Butter a 10 × 5 × 3-inch loaf pan, or any other loaf pan with a 10-cup capacity (or two smaller pans), dust all over with fine, dry bread crumbs, and tap to shake out excess crumbs over a piece of paper.

Sift together the flour, baking powder, baking soda, and salt, and set aside.

In the large bowl of an electric mixer, cream the butter. Beat in the vanilla. Add the sugar and beat only until well mixed, scraping the bowl as necessary with a rubber spatula. Add the eggs one at a time, beating only until incorporated after each addition. Beat for about 1 minute after the last addition. On low speed, alternately add the sifted dry ingredients in three additions with the buttermilk in two additions, scraping the bowl as necessary and beating only until incorporated after each addition.

Remove from the mixer and stir in the grated rind.

Turn the batter into the prepared pan and shake the pan a bit to level it.

Bake for 1 hour and 30 to 35 minutes (less time in smaller pans) until a cake tester gently inserted into the middle of the cake comes out clean. The top will be richly browned and only slightly mounded.

Let cool in the pan for 10 or 15 minutes. Cover with a rack and turn the pan and the rack over, remove the pan, cover with another rack and turn over again, leaving the cake right side up to cool.

This can be served either side up.

If you can wait, wrap and refrigerate the cooled cake at least overnight, or freeze it for about an hour before serving.

Poppy Seed Cake

12 PORTIONS

"I left my heart in San Francisco . . ." When my husband and I were there on a tour for the chocolate book, Cocolat, the divine French pastry and chocolate specialty shop, baked an array of chocolate goodies for us that were *magnifique! Sheila Linderman* was the chef in charge of the affair. And, to top it off, she gave me this nonchocolate recipe that she says is "my absolute favorite cake— number one on my list and everyone else's." It is a delicious plain cake that is like a cross between a sponge cake and a pound cake. It is baked in a tube pan and has no icing. The poppy seeds give an interesting appearance and a mild, nutty flavor and slightly crunchy texture. The cake lasts remarkably well.

2 cups unsifted all-purpose flour
1 teaspoon baking soda
½ teaspoon double-acting baking powder
8 ounces (2 sticks) unsalted butter
1½ cups granulated sugar
5 eggs (graded large), separated, plus 1 additional white (or you can use 4 eggs— graded extra-large—plus 1 additional white)
1 cup sour cream
¼ cup poppy seeds
1½ teaspoons vanilla extract
Pinch of salt
¼ teaspoon cream of tartar

Adjust a rack one-third up from the bottom of the oven and preheat oven to 350 degrees. You will need a plain (no design), loose-bottomed (bottom and tube in one piece—sides in a separate piece) tube pan (angel-food pan) with a 12-cup capacity that will be 10 inches in diameter and 4 inches in depth; it should be an aluminum pan—it must not have a nonstick finish. Do not butter or line the pan.

Sift together the flour, baking soda, and baking powder and set aside.

In the large bowl of an electric mixer, cream the butter. Add 1¼ cups sugar to the butter, reserving the remaining ¼ cup of sugar, and beat well for several minutes until light and creamy. Add the yolks all at once and beat for 2 or 3 minutes, scraping the bowl as necessary with a rubber spatula.

In a small bowl stir the sour cream, poppy seeds, and vanilla together to mix.

On low speed beat about one-third of the dry ingredients into the butter mixture. Then add the sour-cream mixture, scraping the bowl as necessary with a rubber spatula and beating only until incorporated. Add the remaining dry ingredients and beat only until smooth. Remove from the mixer and set aside.

Place the egg whites in the small bowl of an electric mixer, add the salt, and, with clean beaters, beat until foamy. Add the cream of tartar and beat until the whites hold soft peaks when the beaters are raised. Gradually add the reserved ¼ cup of sugar and beat until the whites hold definite peaks, but not until they are really stiff or dry.

Fold one-quarter of the whites into the batter; do not be completely thorough at this stage. Fold in another quarter. Then add the batter to the remaining whites and fold together only until blended.

Turn into the pan and rotate the pan briskly first in one direction, then the other, to level the batter.

Bake for about 50 to 55 minutes until a cake tester gently inserted into the cake comes out clean and dry. There will be a crack in the top of the cake—O.K. The cake will not come to the top of the pan—also O.K.

Remove from the oven and immediately turn the pan over and let the cake stand upside down in the pan until it is completely cool.

To freeze the cake: It is best to freeze the cake before cutting it out of the pan. Wrap with aluminum foil and freeze.

To remove the cake from the pan: You will need a sharp knife with a firm blade (it *must* be firm) about 6 inches long. Insert the blade at one side of the pan between the cake and the pan, inserting the blade until its tip touches the bottom of the pan. Press the blade firmly against the pan in order not to cut into the sides of the cake. With short up-and-down motions saw all around the cake, continuing to press the blade against the pan. Then saw around the tube—if you have a knife with a narrow blade (such as a boning knife) use it to cut around the tube.

Remove the sides of the pan. Then carefully, again pressing the blade against the pan, cut the bottom of the cake away from the pan.

Cover the cake with a flat cake plate and turn the cake and the plate over. Remove the bottom of the pan, leaving the cake upside down.

Orange Chiffon Cake

16 PORTIONS OR MORE

In 1927, Henry Baker, a 64-year-old California insurance salesman who liked to bake, invented a cake. It was as light as angel food and as rich as a butter cake. The recipe was a closely guarded secret for 20 years. Baker often made the cake for famous Hollywood restaurants and for celebrities, and both he and his cake became famous.

Eventually, Mr. Baker sold his secret to Betty Crocker. The details of the deal were kept as secret as the recipe had been, but Betty Crocker and General Mills wound up with the recipe and in 1948, when they introduced it to America as Chiffon Cake, it was hailed as "the cake discovery of the century." The mystery ingredient, new to cake-making, was salad oil.

It is a large cake that will make many portions. It keeps well. It may be baked a day before serving, or it may be served as soon as it is cool, or it may be frozen. It is easy to make.

2 cups sifted all-purpose flour
1½ cups granulated sugar
3 teaspoons double-acting baking powder
1 teaspoon salt
½ cup tasteless vegetable oil (i.e., Mazola, Wesson, or safflower)
7 eggs (graded large), separated
Finely grated rind of 2 lemons
Finely grated rind of 3 deep-colored oranges
¾ cup orange juice
½ teaspoon cream of tartar
Optional: confectioners sugar

Adjust a rack one-third up from the bottom of the oven and preheat oven to 325 degrees. You will need a 10 × 4-inch tube pan (angel-food cake pan). It must not be a nonstick pan. And it must be the kind that is made in two pieces, the bottom and tube in one piece and the sides in a separate piece. Do not butter the pan.

Into a large mixing bowl, sift together the flour, sugar, baking powder, and salt.

Make a wide well in the middle of the dry ingredients. Add in the following order, without mixing, the oil, egg yolks (reserve the whites), the lemon and orange rinds, and the orange juice. With a large or medium-size strong wire whisk, beat until smooth. Set aside.

In the large bowl of an electric mixer, beat the egg whites with the cream of tartar until they hold a stiff peak when the beaters are raised. For this recipe they must be stiffer than usual; when they hold a stiff (or firm) peak, beat for 1 minute more. That should make them just right; they should not be beaten until they are dry.

In three additions, fold about three-quarters of the yolk mixture into the whites. Then fold the whites into the remaining yolk mixture. Do not handle any more than necessary. (The yolk mixture is heavier; it will sink in the whites. To incorporate the two mixtures without additional folding, it may be necessary to gently pour the mixture from one bowl to another once or twice.)

Gently pour the batter into the cake pan.

Bake for 55 minutes at 325 degrees. Then increase the temperature to 350 degrees and bake for an additional 10 or 15 minutes, until the top springs back when it is lightly pressed with a fingertip.

Immediately hang the pan upside down over the point of a funnel or over the neck of a narrow bottle (see Notes). Let the cake hang in the pan until it is completely cool.

To freeze the cake: It is best to freeze it in the pan before cutting it out of the pan. Wrap in aluminum foil and freeze.

To remove the cake from the pan: You will need a sharp knife with a firm blade (it *must* be firm) about 6 inches long. Insert the blade at one side of the pan between the cake and the pan, inserting the blade all the way down to the bottom of the pan and pressing it firmly against the pan in order not to cut into the sides of the cake. With short up-and-down motions, saw all around the cake, continuing to press the blade against the pan. Then cut around the tube (I use a knife with a very thin blade for cutting around the tube; a wider blade will cut into the cake slightly).

Remove the sides of the pan. Then carefully, again pressing the blade against the pan, cut the bottom of the cake away from the pan.

Cover the cake with a flat cake plate and turn the cake and the plate over. Remove the bottom of the pan and leave the cake upside down.

Sprinkle with the optional confectioners sugar, sprinkling it through a strainer—make it a generous coating.

NOTES: 1. *Do not decide to use lemon juice in place of the orange juice. When I tried it several times, some kind of a chemical reaction took place and the cakes fell.*

2. *Many angel-food cake pans have little feet to raise the inverted pan, but often they do not raise the cake enough and it is necessary to hang the*

cake on a funnel or the neck of a bottle. But there are some new pans now that have a raised extension on the center tube, and that usually does raise the cake enough, so it is not necessary to use the funnel or bottle. The cake should be at least one inch above the counter.

CHOCOLATE WHIPPED CREAM

This cream is frequently served with the Orange Chiffon Cake; however, it is optional.

2 cups heavy cream
1 cup strained confectioners sugar
½ cup unsweetened cocoa powder (preferably
　　Dutch process)
Pinch of salt
½ teaspoon vanilla extract

In a chilled bowl with chilled beaters, whip all the ingredients together until the cream is stiff enough to hold a shape. Spread it all over the cake shortly before serving. Or serve it separately as a sauce, and spoon it over each portion.

A beautiful presentation is made by covering the cake with the chocolate whipped cream and surrounding it all with a generous ring of huge fresh strawberries, unhulled. It is a picture!

Sand Torte

12 PORTIONS

Don't let the name scare you. This is a plain, firm, fine-grained, dense and compact pound cake. The texture is a little sandy, but deliciously so.

Sand Torte is an old classic cake that is extremely popular in many European countries. I was told about an enterprising young taxi driver in Denmark who displayed the sign "Sandkage" in the rear of his cab—his wife baked them and he sold as many as she could produce to the people who rode in his cab.

Serve this with coffee, tea, or wine, or with ice cream, fruit, or custard.

You will need a tube pan with an 8- to 10-cup capacity. It really should be one with a fancy design (although this can be made in a pan without a design). I have been making it lately in a black iron kugelhopf pan made by Le Creuset people under the name "Cousances," available at many kitchen shops, including Cooktique, 9 Railroad Avenue, Tenafly, New Jersey 07670. It bakes into a gorgeous shape and has a beautiful color.

It is best to make this a day before serving; it should stand for 24 hours, preferably in the refrigerator, before it is sliced.

Finely grated rind of 1 large lemon
2 tablespoons lemon juice
1 cup sifted all-purpose flour
1 cup unsifted cornstarch
1¾ teaspoons double-acting baking powder
8 ounces (2 sticks) unsalted butter
1 cup granulated sugar
6 eggs (graded large), separated
¼ teaspoon salt
Optional: confectioners sugar (to be sprinkled over the cake)

Adjust a rack one-third up in the oven. Preheat the oven to 350 degrees. Butter an 8- to 10-cup-capacity tube pan with a fancy design. The best way is to use soft but not melted butter and a pastry brush, brushing in all directions to be sure the pan is all coated. Then dust with fine, dry bread crumbs. Tap over paper to shake out excess.

Mix the lemon rind and juice and set aside.

Sift together the flour, cornstarch, and baking powder and set aside.

In the large bowl of an electric mixer, beat the butter until it is soft. Add ¾ cup of the sugar, reserving the remaining ¼ cup, and beat for at least 2 or 3 minutes. Then add the egg yolks (all at once is O.K.) and beat at high speed for at least 5 minutes, scraping the bowl as necessary with a rubber spatula. The mixture should be beaten until it is very pale, silky smooth, and almost liquid.

On low speed add about half of the sifted dry ingredients and beat only to mix. Remove from the mixer.

Add the rind and juice mixture and stir until incorporated. Then add the remaining sifted dry ingredients and stir with a rubber spatula until the mixture is perfectly smooth.

You will need the large mixer bowl again now for beating the whites. If you do not have an additional large bowl for your mixer, transfer the egg-yolk mixture to any other large mixing bowl.

The bowl and beaters must be absolutely clean and grease-free. Add the salt to the egg whites and beat until they hold a soft shape. Reduce the speed to moderate and gradually add the reserved ¼ cup of sugar. Then increase the speed again and beat only until the whites hold a definite shape but not until they are stiff or dry.

Add about one-quarter of the beaten whites to the yolk mixture and stir it in. Then add another quarter and fold it in—do not fold completely until the end. Then fold in another quarter. Finally, fold in the remainder, handling lightly and as little as possible to blend the mixtures.

Turn the batter into the prepared pan and smooth the top.

Bake for 45 to 55 minutes (the timing will vary with different pans) until the top is richly colored and springs back when lightly pressed with a fingertip, and until a cake tester gently inserted into the middle of the cake comes out clean and dry. Do not overbake or the cake will become dry and crumbly.

Remove the pan from the oven but do not remove the cake from the pan until it has cooled to room temperature. Then cover the pan with a plate, turn the pan and the plate over, remove the pan, and leave the cake upside down.

Refrigerate the cake until it is firm enough to handle. Then wrap it in plastic wrap or in a plastic bag and refrigerate overnight.

Before serving, the top may be covered with confectioners sugar sprinkled through a fine strainer held over the cake.

Cut into thin slices, two or three to a portion.

English Madeira Cake

1 SMALL LOAF

This is an old English recipe for a cake that does not contain Madeira; it has this name because it was for many years, and still is, served with Madeira—or with sherry. It is a plain, plain loaf, with an especially fine texture and an extra-light, almost white, color inside. It is like a very light, tender, delicate, marvelous pound cake. It keeps well. It slices beautifully. It makes a very nice gift and/or it is great to have on hand as a coffee or tea cake. And it is easy to make.

2 cups sifted all-purpose flour
2 teaspoons double-acting baking powder
¼ teaspoon salt
6 ounces (1½ sticks) unsalted butter
1 teaspoon vanilla extract
¾ cup granulated sugar
3 eggs (graded large)
½ cup milk
Finely grated rind of 1 large or 2 small lemons

Adjust a rack to the center of the oven (if you bake this lower the top will be too pale). Preheat the oven to 350 degrees. You will need a loaf pan with at least a 4-cup capacity; that could be 8 × 4 × 2½ inches. It is possible to bake this in a larger pan, but if you do the cake will not be as high and as beautiful. Butter the pan and dust it all over with fine, dry bread crumbs. (I use bought bread crumbs and because this is such a fine-grained cake, I grind the crumbs a bit more in the processor—just enough to make them slightly finer but not long enough to grind them to a powder.) Then turn the pan upside down over a piece of paper and tap lightly to shake out excess.

Sift together the flour, baking powder, and salt and set aside.

In the small bowl of an electric mixer (it must be the small bowl; in a large bowl the beaters will not reach enough of the mixture) beat the butter briefly until it is soft. Add the vanilla and granulated sugar and beat at high speed for 5 minutes until the mixture is pale and soft. Scrape the sides occasionally with a rubber spatula. Add the eggs one at a time, beating until each addition is incorporated. Then beat again at high speed for 5 minutes more until the mixture is a very pale cream color and almost liquid.

Transfer to the large bowl of the electric mixer. On low speed, add the sifted dry ingredients in three additions alternately with the milk in two additions.

Remove from the mixer, stir in the grated rind, and turn into the prepared pan. Smooth the top. The batter will be only about half an inch below the top—O.K.

Bake for 1 hour and 10 minutes or until a cake tester gently inserted into the middle of the cake comes out clean and dry. If you have baked it in a larger pan, the cake will be shallower and will therefore bake in less time. (In a 10-inch loaf pan it bakes in 45 minutes.)

Let the cake cool in the pan on a rack for 20 to 25 minutes. Then gently, turn it out onto a rack. And, with your hands, gently turn it right side up. Let stand to cool.

It is best to wrap the cooled cake and refrigerate it for a few hours or overnight before serving.

NOTE: *This will rise in the middle and form a crack in the center; the crack will be paler than the rest of the cake. That is as it should be.*

Jelly Roll

6 TO 8 PORTIONS

This little fat-bellied jelly roll is quick, easy, simple, plain, homey, old-fashioned, and very, very good. Serve a slice with tea or coffee. Or the jelly roll can be the beginning of many fancy desserts, i.e., serve a slice on each plate with a generous pile of fresh strawberries or raspberries mounded on top with soft whipped cream over it all. Or jelly roll, ice cream, and chocolate sauce. Et cetera.

The cake itself is soft enough to roll easily without cracking, and yet it is firm enough to hold up and be delicious.

4 eggs (graded large), at room temperature
¾ teaspoon double-acting baking powder
½ teaspoon salt
¾ cup granulated sugar
1 teaspoon vanilla extract
¾ cup sifted cake flour (do not substitute all-purpose flour)
Generous ¾ cup firm, tart jelly (currant is good)
Additional granulated sugar for sprinkling on the cake

Adjust a rack to the center of the oven and preheat oven to 400 degrees. Prepare a 15½ × 10½ × 1-inch jelly-roll pan as follows. Invert the pan, cover it with a piece of foil several inches longer than the pan, fold down the sides and the corners of the foil to shape it, then remove the foil, turn the pan right side up, and place the shaped foil in the pan. Press it into place. Place some butter in the pan (for buttering the foil), place it in the oven just until the butter is melted, and then brush or spread the butter all over the foil. Set aside.

Place the eggs, baking powder, and salt in the small bowl of an electric mixer. Beat at high speed for about 3 minutes until very fluffy. Reduce the speed slightly and gradually add the ¾ cup granulated sugar. Increase the speed to high again and beat for 10 to 12 minutes more (total beating time is 13 to 15 minutes) until the mixture is quite thick and falls in a wide and heavy ribbon when the beaters are raised.

Transfer to the large bowl of the mixer. Beat in the vanilla. Then sift the flour over the batter (sift it even though you sifted it before measuring it) and beat on low speed, scraping the bowl with a rubber spatula *only until incorporated*—do not overbeat.

Instead of dumping the whole mixture into the middle of the prepared pan, it is better to pour it in a thick ribbon down the length of one side of the pan and then the other side. Then with a rubber spatula spread the mixture to make it even—do not handle any more than necessary.

Bake for 13 minutes until the top springs back when lightly pressed with a fingertip and the foil begins to come away from the sides of the pan.

While the cake is baking, place the jelly in a small bowl and stir it well with a fork or a wire whisk just to soften it. Have ready a few spoonfuls of granulated sugar, a smooth cotton towel, and a flat cookie sheet.

As soon as the cake is done, sprinkle the top with granulated sugar, cover the cake with a smooth cotton towel (a tea towel), and cover the towel with a flat cookie sheet. Invert the cake pan and the cookie sheet. Remove the cake pan. Peel off the foil (it will come off beautifully without sticking). Pour the jelly over the cake and spread it with a rubber spatula to make a thin layer; cover all but about half an inch at one narrow end.

Roll the cake from the narrow end opposite the one where the jelly stops short. Use the towel to help start the roll. Roll tightly but gently.

Transfer the cake, seam down, to a flat platter or a board.

Serve at room temperature or refrigerated. Serve two or three thin slices, overlapping, for each portion.

Pies and Tarts

Tarts

Pies

A *plain American pie is a work of art. If you are not an experienced pie-maker, there is a whole world of challenge and satisfaction ahead of you. When it turns out right, you have accomplished a major work of which you and your family and friends should be extremely proud. And I would like to add my compliments to the chef.*

If you have not made fruit tarts, some of which look like magnificent pieces of jewelry, others simply like sweet, ripe, juicy, mouth-watering fruit, and some like both, you are going to have such fun with these recipes I wish I could be there to see the results and hear the raves.

Pie Pastry

This recipe is from my chocolate book. These amounts are for a 9-inch crust; for a 10-inch crust, see Notes. I recommend using an ovenproof glass pie plate.

1 cup sifted all-purpose flour
Scant ½ teaspoon salt
3 tablespoons vegetable shortening (such as Crisco), cold and firm
3 tablespoons unsalted butter, cold and firm, cut into small pieces
About 3 tablespoons ice water

(If the room is warm, it is a good idea to chill the mixing bowl and even the flour beforehand. Some pie pro's store their flour in the freezer or refrigerator so it will be cold and ready.)

Place the flour and salt in a large mixing bowl. Add the shortening and butter. With a pastry blender cut in the shortening and butter until the mixture resembles coarse crumbs—when partly cut in, raise the bowl with both hands, quickly move it away from you, up, and then toward you in a jerky motion to toss the bottom ingredients to the top. Search for any large pieces of butter or shortening and cut them individually with a knife. It is all right to leave a few pieces about the size of small peas.

Sprinkle 1 tablespoon of the ice water by small drops all over the surface. Mix and toss with a fork. Continue adding the water only until the flour is barely moistened. (Too much water makes the pastry sticky/soggy/tough.) Do not ever dump a lot of the water in any one spot. (I know one cook who uses a laundry-sprinkling container and another who uses a salt shaker to add the water; that way they distribute it in a fine spray all over.) When the water is partly added, with both hands raise the bowl, quickly move it away from you, up, and then toward you in a jerky motion to toss the dry flour to the top. If you add the water too quickly—if you don't stir/mix enough while you are adding it—you might be convinced that you need more water. But maybe you don't, maybe you just need to add the water more slowly and stir/mix more.

When adequate water has been added, the mixture will still be lumpy, but with practice you will know by the look of it that it will form a ball when pressed together. I have occasionally had to add a little more water, but very little—only 1 to 2 teaspoons. Often, if it looks too dry, additional stirring with the fork will bring the mixture to the right stage, and it will not be necessary to add more water.

The shortening and the butter must not melt (they should remain in little flour-coated flakes), so do not handle now any more than necessary. Turn the mixture out onto a large board or work surface and, with your hands, just push the mixture together to form a ball. (My mother never touched the dough with her hands at this stage—she turned it out onto a piece of plastic wrap, brought up the sides of the plastic, and squeezed them firmly together at the top, pressing from the outside and letting the mixture form a ball without actually touching it.) If the dough is too dry to hold together do not knead it, but replace it in the bowl and use a knife to cut it into small pieces again, then add a few more drops of water and stir again.

Lightly flour your hands, round the ball of dough, then flatten it slightly and smooth the edges. Wrap the dough in plastic wrap and refrigerate for about an hour. (I don't always have the time or patience to wait for the dough to chill. I have found that if it was not handled too much in the mixing, if the room is not too warm, and if I work with a light touch, the results are perfectly satisfactory without the chilling.)

Baked Pie Shell

Rolling out the dough is easiest if you work on a pastry cloth. Flour the cloth by rubbing in as much flour as the cloth will absorb, then lightly brush off any loose excess flour. Rub flour on the rolling pin. (I use a French-style rolling pin that is long and narrow and tapered at both ends. It is too long and too narrow for the stockinette cover that is sold with pastry cloths; just keep it lightly floured while you roll with it.)

Place the flattened ball of dough on the cloth. If the dough is very firm, pound/whack it sharply in all directions with the rolling pin to flatten it into a circle about 7 inches in diameter. If it is not too firm, just press down on it gently in all directions with the rolling pin to form a 7-inch round. With your fingers, smooth and pinch together any small cracks at the edges.

Now start to roll, always from the center out. Do not roll back and forth and do not turn the dough over during rolling. Roll first in one direction and then another, trying to keep the shape round. If the edges crack slightly, pinch them together. If the dough cracks anywhere other than the edges, or if the circle is terribly uneven, do not reroll the dough; simply cut off uneven edges and use the scraps as patches. The piece used as a patch should be turned over when it is put in place; then roll over that area lightly to seal.

It may be necessary to reflour the pin occasionally. It should not be necessary to reflour the cloth, but if there is any hint that the dough might stick, reflour it very lightly. The less flour you use the better—too much flour toughens pastry.

Roll the dough into a circle 13 inches in diameter for a 9-inch pie plate; 14 inches for a 10-inch plate—the dough should be a scant ⅛ inch thick. It is important that the rolled-out pastry be exactly the same thickness all over so it will brown evenly.

Incidentally, I use Pyrex pie plates, and until they make a black steel pie plate (which makes the crust brown better) I like glass better than metal ones.

To transfer the pastry, drape the pastry over the rolling pin. To do this, hold the pin over the left side of the pastry, raise the left side of the pastry cloth to turn the dough over the rolling pin, roll it up loosely and then unroll it over the pie plate centering it evenly. With your fingers, ease the sides of the dough down into the plate—it is important not to stretch the dough or it will shrink during baking.

The dough must touch the plate all around—press the bottom where it meets the sides, then press gently against the sides. If your fingernails are in the way, cut a small portion of the dough from an uneven edge, form it into a small ball, flour it lightly, and use it as a tamping tool to press the dough into place.

Now, if you have a cake-decorating turntable or a lazy Susan to place the pie plate on, you will find it much easier to trim and shape the crust.

With scissors, cut the edge of the crust, leaving about a ½- to ¾-inch overhang beyond the outside edge of the pie plate. With floured fingertips fold the edge to the outside, down, and back on itself, forming a hem that extends about ½ inch up over the rim. Press the hem lightly together between your floured thumb and the side of your bent-under fore-finger, making it stand upright. As you do this, press it a bit thinner. (While you are handling the edges, if the kitchen is warm and the pastry becomes sticky, refrigerate it briefly.)

See the directions on the following page for forming an extra-deep pastry.

Now, with lightly floured fingertips, form a decorative edge on the shell. There are many ways of doing this; here's one. You will be moving clockwise around the rim, starting at three o'clock. Point your left fore-finger and place it at a right angle across the rim of the pastry. Your left hand will be over the inside of the plate with your finger sticking over to the outside. Move your right arm so the elbow is up, then with your right hand grip the pastry rim using the thumb and side of the bent-under fore-finger. Grip slightly ahead (clockwise) of your left finger, and twist the pastry edge toward the center of the plate. Remove both hands and then replace your left forefinger just ahead (clockwise again) of the twist you have just formed. This will be at about four o'clock on the rim. Repeat the twists all around the edge. Check and reshape any uneven spots.

Then, with your fingertips, press the sides of the pastry firmly against the sides of the plate.

With a fork, carefully prick the bottom all over at ¼- to ½-inch intervals.

Place the shell in the freezer for 15 minutes or more until it is frozen firm. (This helps prevent shrinkage.) Wrapped airtight, it may be frozen for months if you wish.

About 15 or 20 minutes before you bake this, adjust an oven rack one-third up from the bottom and preheat the oven to 450 degrees.

In order to keep the pastry shell in place during baking, cut a 12-inch square of aluminum foil. Place the foil ("shiny side down" is my own fetish; foil manufacturers say it doesn't matter) in the frozen shell. Press it into place all over; if your fingernails are in the way, place a pot holder or a folded dish towel against the foil while you press it. Do not fold the edges of the foil over the rim of the crust; let the corners of the foil stand up. Fill the foil at least three-quarters full with dried beans or with the

aluminum pellets that are made for this purpose. (If you use beans, reserve them to use again for the same purpose.) Aluminum pellets are
available by mail from Williams-Sonoma, P.O. Box 3792, San Francisco,
California 94119, and in New York from Bridge Kitchenware, 214 East
52nd Street, New York, New York 10022.

Bake the frozen shell for 12 to 13 minutes until it is set and lightly
colored around the edges. Remove it from the oven. Reduce the heat to
400 degrees. Gently remove the foil and beans by lifting the four corners of
the foil. Replace the shell in the oven and continue to bake about 7 or 8
minutes more, or longer if necessary. Watch it almost constantly; if it starts
to puff up anywhere, reach into the oven and pierce the puff with a cake
tester to release trapped air. Bake until the edges are richly colored—a too-
pale crust is not as attractive as one with a good color. The bottom will
remain paler than the edges. (During baking, if the crust is not browning
evenly reverse the position of the pan.)

Place on a rack and cool to room temperature.

NOTES: 1. *For a 10-inch crust, increase the amounts to 1¼ cups flour, generous ½ teaspoon salt, 3¾ tablespoons vegetable shortening, 3¾ tablespoons butter, and 3¾ tablespoons ice water.*

*2. The ingredients for the crust may easily be doubled for two shells
or for a pie with both a bottom and a top crust.*

*3. I think it is a great luxury to have an unbaked pie shell in the
freezer. I try to keep one, frozen in the pie plate, all ready for the oven.
I wrap it in plastic wrap or in a freezer bag. Then I only have to line it with
foil and fill it with the dried beans when I am ready to bake. (I think it is
better that way than to freeze it baked.)*

TO FORM AN EXTRA-DEEP PIE SHELL

Follow the above directions (rolling the dough ½ inch wider than previous
directions) up to folding the hem of the pastry. When you fold, fold a
¾-inch rather than a ½-inch hem or border, and do it so that you have a
raised ¾-inch hem standing straight up all around the rim (the very outside
edge of the pastry that was folded back over itself should actually rest on
the rim of the plate). Form it into a straight and even wall all around.
Then, to flute it, leaving it upright, use the thumb and index finger of
your right hand. Flour them lightly, and pinch from the outside so the
outer edge of the raised wall of pastry forms a horizontal "v" (or a "v"
that has the point facing the outside). It seems easiest to me to start
at the right side (three o'clock) of the plate, and use the index finger
of your left hand to support the inside of the crust while you pinch it.

Pinch again 1 inch away from the first. Continue to pinch and form "v's" all around the outside of the rim 1 inch apart. Then do the same from the inside of the rim, this time starting at the left side (nine o'clock) of the plate, pinching between two out-pointing "v's" on the outside, and forming a nice, neat zigzag pattern all around, with the crust standing up ½ inch.

French Tart Pastry

1¾ cups unsifted all-purpose flour (stir to aerate before measuring)
2 tablespoons granulated sugar
¼ teaspoon salt
4 ounces (1 stick) unsalted butter, cold and firm, cut into small pieces (see Notes)
1 egg (graded large)
1 tablespoon ice water

The pastry can be prepared in a processor, a mixer, or by hand.

In a food processor: Fit the bowl with the metal blade. Place the flour, sugar, salt, and butter in the bowl. Process on-and-off for 10 seconds (ten 1-second pulses) until the mixture resembles coarse meal. Place the egg and water in a small bowl and beat to mix. Then, through the feed tube, add the egg and water and continue to process briefly (about 20 seconds) only until the mixture barely (but not completely) holds together.

In an electric mixer: The same procedure can be followed, using the large bowl of the mixer and low speed; use a rubber spatula to keep pushing the butter pieces into the beaters.

By hand: Place the dry ingredients in a mound on a large board or work surface, form a well in the middle, place the pieces of butter with the egg and water in the well. With the fingertips of your right hand work the center wet ingredients together, gradually incorporating the dry ingredients until the two mixtures are all mixed. It helps to use a dough scraper or wide metal spatula to push the dry ingredients in toward the center as necessary.

However you have arrived at this stage of the pastry, now turn the mixture out onto a large unfloured board or smooth work surface. Knead briefly (only a few seconds) until the mixture is smooth and holds together and press the mixture together to form a ball. Smooth the sides and flour it lightly. Unless the kitchen is terribly hot, or unless you have handled the mixture too much (enough to melt the butter), it is not necessary to refrigerate this before using. If you must, refrigerate it for only about an hour. If it is refrigerated too long it will crack when you roll it out.

NOTES: 1. *Cut the stick of butter lengthwise, then cut each half lengthwise again, and slice all four quarters into ½-inch slices. It is best to cut and refrigerate the butter ahead of time.*

2. *After shaping this pastry, if you have any leftover scraps, make cookies. Press the scraps together, roll on a floured pastry cloth with a floured rolling pin to about ¼-inch thickness, cut with cookie cutters, sprinkle with granulated sugar, and bake at 350 degrees only until the cookies are slightly colored. They are delicious.*

Directions for a Crumb Crust

(*This is from my first dessert book.*)

Although the crumb mixture may be pressed into place directly in the pie plate, I line the plate with foil first and then remove the foil before filling the crust. This guarantees easy serving—the crust *cannot* stick to the plate. It is a bit more work (or play) but I think well worth it.

For a 9-inch pie plate (I use a glass one), use a 12-inch square of foil. Place the plate upside down on a work surface. Place the foil over the plate and, with your hands, press down on the sides of the foil, pressing it firmly against the plate all around. Remove the foil. Turn the plate right side up. Place the shaped foil in the plate. Now, to press the foil firmly into place in the plate, use a pot holder or a folded towel to press with, making sure that the foil touches all parts of the plate. Fold the edges of the foil down over the rim of the plate.

Turn the crumb-crust mixture into the foil-lined plate. Using your fingertips, distribute the mixture evenly and loosely over the sides first and then the bottom. Then press the crust firmly and evenly on the sides, pushing it up from the bottom to form a rim slightly raised over the edge of the plate. Be careful that the top of the crust is not too thin. To shape a firm edge, use the fingertips of your right hand against the inside and press down against it with the thumb of your left hand. After firmly pressing the sides and the top edge, press the remaining crumbs evenly and firmly over the bottom. There should be no loose crumbs.

Bake in the center of a preheated 375-degree oven for 8 minutes, or until very lightly browned on the edges.

Cool to room temperature.

Freeze for at least 1 hour, overnight if possible. It must be frozen solid.

Remove from the freezer. Raise the edges of the foil and carefully lift the foil (with the crust) from the plate. Gently peel away the foil as follows: Support the bottom of the crust with your left hand and peel the foil, a bit at a time (do not tear the foil), with your right hand. As you do so, rotate the crust gently on your left hand.

Supporting the bottom of the crust with a small metal spatula or a knife, ease it back into the plate very gently in order not to crack it. It will not crack or break if it has been frozen long enough.

Mom's Apple Pie

6 GENEROUS PORTIONS

This is my mother's Florida version of the classic apple pie. It has both top and bottom crusts with a thick filling of apple slices poached before they are put into the pie, and held together with a delicious cinnamon-nutmeg-orange syrup that is not so thin that it runs and not too thick so it still oozes slightly as it should and is perfectly delicious.

PIE CRUST

Prepare a double amount of Pie Crust (see page 131), cut it in half, gently shape each half into a ball, flour them lightly and flatten them slightly, wrap in plastic wrap and refrigerate while you prepare the filling.

FILLING

2 tablespoons fine, dry bread crumbs
8 apples (3¼ pounds; see Note)
¾ cup orange juice
½ cup water
1 cup granulated sugar
2 tablespoons plus 1 teaspoon unsifted
    all-purpose flour
Pinch of salt

1 teaspoon cinnamon
1 teaspoon nutmeg
1 teaspoon vanilla extract
1½ tablespoons unsalted butter

Peel the apples and cut them into quarters. Remove the cores, then cut each quarter into about four lengthwise slices, each about ½ inch thick at the outside edge. There should be 10 to 11 cups.

You will need a large, preferably shallow, pan (a frying pan or a sauté pan) that has a tight cover. Place ½ cup of the orange juice (reserve the remaining ¼ cup) in the pan. Add the water and sugar. Place over moderate heat, stirring occasionally until the syrup comes to a low boil. Add the apples, cover the pan, and cook gently, stirring the apples occasionally, until they are barely tender but still hold their shape. As the apples finish cooking, remove them from the pan (a slotted spoon is easiest) and place them in a large colander or strainer set over a large plate.

Measure the remaining syrup—you need 1 cup. If there is more, boil it down; if there is less, add water.

Place the reserved ¼ cup orange juice in a small mixing bowl with the flour, salt, cinnamon, and nutmeg. Beat with a small wire whisk until smooth. Add the 1 cup of syrup, transfer to a small saucepan over moderate heat and cook, stirring constantly with a rubber or wooden spatula, until the mixture thickens. It should be about as thick as a thick cream sauce. Then reduce the heat to lowest and cook, stirring occasionally, for 2 minutes more. Remove from the heat, stir in the vanilla and the butter, and set aside. Stir occasionally until the syrup cools.

TO MAKE THE PIE

Adjust an oven rack one-third up from the bottom of the oven and preheat the oven to 425 degrees.

Use one piece of the pastry as follows to line a 9-inch glass pie plate (which should not be buttered).

Flour a pastry cloth and a rolling pin. Place the pastry on the cloth. Press down on it gently with the rolling pin to flatten it without rolling until it is a circle 6 to 7 inches wide. Then, rolling gently from the center out toward the rim, in all directions, roll the pastry out to a 12-inch circle. (If the edge begins to crack while you are rolling it, pinch the cracks together before they become large.)

Either fold the rolled-out pastry in half and lift it, or drape it over the rolling pin and lift it—whichever feels best to you—and place it evenly in the plate. Press the sides into the plate without stretching the dough. With scissors, cut the rim even with the outside edge of the plate. Sprinkle the bread crumbs on the bottom and set aside.

Roll out the other half of the dough, rolling it out to a 12-inch circle (the same as the first half).

Fold it in half. Then, for steam to escape, use the tip of a teaspoon to make a half-moon-shaped cut about ½ inch in from the fold and an equal distance from both top and bottom of the semicircle of dough. Cut through both layers. Then make two more cuts, one an inch above the first and another an inch below. Let stand.

Place the cooked, cooled, drained apple slices in the bottom crust. Pour the cooled syrup evenly over the apples.

Then, wet the top rim of the bottom crust; either use a small, soft brush dipped into water, or use your fingertips dipped into water.

Place the folded pastry over the apples, carefully centering the fold; then unfold it to cover the whole pie.

Now cut the edge of the top pastry with scissors leaving an overhang ½ inch wider than the bottom crust. Then, with your fingers, fold that extra ½ inch over and under the rim of the bottom crust (not the plate). Flour your fingertips and press the rim together to seal the top and bottom crusts, and also to make the edge a little thinner. Then, with floured fingers, flute the crust into an attractive design (see page 134). It should be a high, standing-up rim.

GLAZE

1 egg yolk
1 teaspoon water

Mix the yolk and water and brush the mixture on the crust, including the fluted rim.

Bake for 30 to 35 minutes until the pie is richly colored—do not underbake.

Place on a rack.

Serve while warm or at room temperature.

NOTE: *Use any apples that are firm, crisp, tart, and delicious. The better the apples are, the better the pie will be. My favorites are Granny Smith. But apple pie experts also recommend Cortland (tart and snowy), Rhode Island Greening (for sour apple pie), Green Newton Pippin (sharp), and Golden Delicious (dry and sweet).*

Colorado High Pie

6 TO 8 PORTIONS

This has a crumb crust, a layer of sautéed apples, a mountainous topping of especially light and airy rum Bavarian, and a thin layer of whipped cream —divine! The crust can and should be made ahead of time and frozen; the apple filling can be made a day or two ahead; the topping should be made 3 to 10 hours before serving.

CRUMB CRUST

1¼ cups graham-cracker crumbs
¼ cup granulated sugar
Scant ¼ teaspoon nutmeg
2 ounces (½ stick) unsalted butter, melted

Adjust a rack to the center of the oven and preheat the oven to 375 degrees.

Mix the above ingredients. Use a 9-inch pie plate and follow the Directions for a Crumb Crust (see page 137) to prepare, bake, and cool the crust.

APPLE FILLING

2 pounds firm and tart apples (3 to 4 large
    apples; Granny Smith are very good)
2 tablespoons unsalted butter
3 tablespoons granulated sugar

Peel, quarter, and core the apples. Cut each piece in half the long way, and then cut crossways into slices ½ to ¾ inch wide.

Melt the butter in a frying pan with a tight cover. Add the apples and sugar, stir to mix, cover tightly, and cook over moderate heat for a few minutes until the apples have given off their juice. Then uncover and stir over high heat until the apples are tender and all of the liquid has evaporated. The mixture should be like a chunky applesauce. If the liquid evaporates before the apples are tender, cover the pan again, reduce the heat a bit, and let the apples steam, then uncover and stir over high heat again to dry a bit if necessary. Do not overcook.

Set aside the pan and let the apples cool or spread them in a thin layer on a large plate to cool. The apples can be used soon or they can be transferred to any container and refrigerated until you are ready for them.

RUM CHIFFON BAVARIAN

1 envelope unflavored gelatin

¼ cup cold tap water

¾ cup milk

3 eggs (graded large or extra-large), separated,
   plus 1 additional egg white (the white
   may be one that was left over from another
   recipe, frozen and then thawed)

½ cup granulated sugar

1 teaspoon vanilla extract

¼ cup dark rum

1 cup heavy cream

Pinch of salt

Sprinkle the gelatin over the water in a small cup and let stand. Heat the milk, uncovered, over moderate heat until scalded. In the top of a double boiler, off the heat, stir the yolks just to mix. When the milk has formed a slightly wrinkled skin on its surface, gradually add it to the yolks, stirring as you do. Then stir in ¼ cup of the sugar (reserve remaining ¼ cup).

Place the top of the double boiler over hot water and cook the custard on moderately high heat, scraping the bottom and sides continuously with a rubber spatula, until the mixture thickens enough to coat a spoon; that will be 180 degrees on a candy thermometer. Add the softened gelatin and stir to dissolve.

Transfer the mixture to a medium-size mixing bowl and stir in the vanilla and rum. Place the bowl of hot custard into a larger bowl of ice and water.

Using a rubber spatula, scrape the bottom and sides constantly until the mixture has cooled—test it on your wrist—do not let it start to thicken. Remove from the ice water (but reserve the ice water) and set aside.

In a chilled bowl with chilled beaters, whip the cream until it holds a definite shape but not until it is really stiff, and set aside.

In the small bowl of the electric mixer, beat the 4 egg whites with the salt until they hold a soft shape. Reduce the speed to moderate, gradually add the reserved ¼ cup of sugar, increase the speed to high again and continue to beat only until the whites hold a definite shape, but be careful not to overbeat or they will be too stiff to be folded in. Set aside.

Now, return the custard mixture to the ice water and stir constantly until it barely begins to thicken. Then gradually fold it (about one-third at a time) into the whipped cream; fold this mixture and the whites together. (It is best to do this last folding in a larger bowl. However, do not handle any more than necessary—keep it light and airy.)

To assemble the pie, begin by spreading the apples in the crust.

It will look as though you have more Bavarian than the crust will hold. Indeed you do. Here's how to make it fit. Create some temporary room for the pie in the freezer. Pour about half of the Bavarian (or as much as the crust will hold) over the apples. Place the pie in the freezer for about 5 minutes, just until the Bavarian is slightly set. (Reserve the remaining Bavarian at room temperature.) Then, after about 5 minutes, when the Bavarian on the pie is slightly set, pour or spoon on about one-quarter or one-third of the remaining Bavarian, or as much as it will hold without running over. Replace in the freezer. Continue until all the Bavarian is safely mounded on the pie. Do not allow it to freeze; it will only take a few minutes in the freezer each time.

Refrigerate for at least a few hours.

WHIPPED CREAM TOPPING

1 cup heavy cream
½ teaspoon vanilla extract
2 tablespoons confectioners or granulated sugar
Optional: a bit of shaved semisweet chocolate

A few hours before serving, place the cream, vanilla, and sugar in a chilled bowl and, with chilled beaters, whip only until the cream is stiff enough to hold a shape—be careful not to whip it any more than necessary.

Place the cream by spoonfuls over the top, starting at the edges. Then use the back of the spoon to shape the cream into swirls and peaks.

Sprinkle the middle of the top with the optional bit of shaved chocolate.

Tart Tatin

(Upside-Down
Apple Pie)

6 GENEROUS PORTIONS

Technically, a tart is considered a sort of pie with an undercrust only—no crust covering the filling. While this tart is baking it has a top crust only, then it is turned over, making a bottom crust only.

There is a theory that this recipe originated when a waitress dropped a pie. When she returned the damaged upside-down pie to the kitchen, it inspired someone there to perfect this. And then there is another story: Tart Tatin was not the result of an accident but was carefully planned in order to eliminate a wet or soggy bottom crust. It is generally believed that the recipe was originally from the Hotel Tatin run by the two Tatin sisters in the town of Lamotte-Beuvron in France. But some historians recall that the Tatin sisters did not really create this. They say it was an easy, inexpensive peasant dessert and that everyone in the locality was making it. However, when word of this recipe spread to other areas, it was the Tatin version that they spoke about.

When I had this at Maxim's in Paris it looked like a pizza, very large and very thin. I make it in a 10-inch Pyrex pie plate that is 1¾ inches deep, and makes a Tart Tatin that is deeper than the usual. You can use any shallow round baking dish or tart pan that measures about 10 inches in diameter. And if it is shallower than the pie plate, simply use fewer apples, and you will have a thinner tart.

For many years, before I ever made this, I heard dire warnings about the difficulty of getting it all out of the inverted plate without some of the apples sticking to the plate. I was gun-shy before trying it. So I lined the plate with aluminum foil. And it worked like a charm. I have done it that way ever since.

I have successfully prepared this early in the day and refrigerated it. But this is best if it is baked about 3 or 4 hours before serving. Don't turn it out onto the plate, however, until just before you serve it. (See Note.)

Pastry for pie crust (see page 131)
5 medium-size tart cooking apples (I like Granny Smith)
4 ounces (1 stick) unsalted butter, at room temperature
¾ cup granulated sugar
1 tablespoon cinnamon (this is not traditional but it is wonderful)

If you wish, the crust may be prepared ahead of time and refrigerated. Or it can be mixed immediately before using. Adjust a rack one-third up from the bottom of the oven and preheat oven to 400 degrees. Prepare a 10 × 1¾-inch pie plate as follows: Turn the plate over, center a 12-inch square of foil over the plate, fold down the sides of the foil to shape it to the plate, and then remove the foil and turn the plate right side up. Place the foil in the plate, pressing it carefully into place. Smooth over the foil with your fingers, a pot holder, or a folded towel. Fold the corners (and extending edges, if there are any) back over the rim of the plate. Butter the sides only, with additional butter, melted, using a pastry brush or wax paper.

Peel the apples. Cut them into quarters and remove the cores. Cut each quarter into four lengthwise slices and set aside.

Place 3 tablespoons of the butter and ⅓ cup of the sugar in a small pan over moderate heat to melt the butter. Set aside.

Mix 3 tablespoons of the sugar with the cinnamon and set aside.

Place the remaining 5 tablespoons butter (it must be soft but not melted) in the bottom of the foil-lined plate. With the back of a teaspoon spread it carefully to cover the bottom. Sprinkle the remaining sugar evenly over the butter.

Now place some of the apple slices neatly and carefully overlapping each other, first around the outer edge and then in the center. Sprinkle with about half of the cinnamon sugar. Cover with the remaining apple slices and the remaining cinnamon sugar. Then pour the melted butter and sugar mixture over the surface.

Cover the top with a piece of wax paper and, with your hands, press down on the paper to press the apples into a compact, rather smooth layer. Remove the wax paper.

Now, on a floured pastry cloth with a floured rolling pin, roll the dough into a circle as wide as the plate. Use something the size of the plate as a pattern and trim the pastry with a pizza cutter, a pastry wheel, or a small, sharp knife.

Carefully fold the pastry in half, then lift it, center it over the apples, unfold it, and that is all. Do not press it down on the edge of the plate.

Bake for about 35 minutes until the crust is a nice golden color.

Let stand in the pan on a rack for 2 or 3 hours until the bottom of the pan has cooled.

You will need a cake plate with a slight rim to turn this out onto. Cover the tart with the cake plate. There may be a considerable amount of juice; therefore it is important to invert the pie plate quickly before the juice runs all over. If you are quick, none will run out, but just in case, hold it over the sink while you quickly turn the cake plate and the pie plate over, carefully holding them firmly together.

If the juice runs onto the plate, use paper towels to absorb it and leave the plate clean.

GLAZE

Apply the glaze as close to serving time as is comfortable.

Melt about ½ cup of apricot preserves in a small saucepan or frying pan over moderate heat, stirring with a wooden spatula. Press it through a strainer. Return to the pan and bring to a boil; let boil for about half a minute. Then brush it all over the top of the apples.

In France this is served alone, or with Crème Fraîche (see page 386) or whipped cream. If you serve the whipped cream, use 1 cup heavy cream, 2 tablespoons sugar, and ½ teaspoon vanilla extract. In a chilled bowl with chilled beaters, whip only until the cream holds a soft shape but not until it is stiff. If you whip the cream ahead of time, refrigerate it. It will probably separate slightly while standing. Just beat it a bit with a small wire whisk right before using. Serve the cream separately, ladling a spoonful over the side of each portion.

Or serve it with ice cream.

NOTE: *Some wonderful restaurants where Tart Tatin is a spécialité prepare it ahead of time, but bake it to order and serve it* HOT, *right out of the oven. It is delicious.*

Blueberry Pie #1

(single crust)

6 GENEROUS PORTIONS

This can have either a baked pie crust or a crumb crust. Either way, the crust is baked empty, and part of the filling is cooked in a saucepan on top of the stove. Then, when both the crust and the filling have cooled, the filling is mixed with more whole, uncooked berries, poured into the crust and refrigerated until serving time. The pie needs at least 3 hours in the refrigerator before it is served, but it can wait for most of the day if you wish.

1 9-inch baked pie shell (see page 131) or
crumb crust (follow recipe for crumb crust
in Colorado High Pie, see page 141)

2 small boxes (2 pounds) blueberries (each
    box will measure about 3 cups, even though
    it is generally called 1 pint)
¼ cup cornstarch
¼ cup cold tap water
¾ cup boiling water
1 cup granulated sugar
¼ teaspoon salt
1½ tablespoons fresh lemon juice
1 tablespoon unsalted butter

Place the berries in a large bowl of cold water. Let the water run off between your fingers as you scoop up the berries and place them on paper towels to drain. As you do so, pick over them carefully to remove any unripe berries, loose stems, etc.

In a small bowl, stir the cornstarch in the cold water until it dissolves. Then add the boiling water and stir until smooth. Place in a 1-quart saucepan. Add the sugar, salt, and ½ cup (reserve the remaining 5½ cups) of the berries. Place over low-medium heat and stir constantly. While cooking and stirring, press the berries against the sides of the pan to crush them. Cook until the mixture comes to a low boil, then thickens and becomes somewhat clear. It should take about 10 minutes. Then reduce the heat to low and cook very gently for about 3 or 4 minutes more.

Stir in the lemon juice and butter. Then, in a large bowl, gently mix the reserved berries with the warm sauce. Stir occasionally until cool.

Pour the cooled mixture into the prepared crust.

Refrigerate for at least 3 hours.

WHIPPED CREAM

Whipped cream and this pie go wonderfully well together. Be prepared with plenty of it.

2 cups heavy cream
3 tablespoons granulated or confectioners sugar
3 tablespoons kirsch or cassis, or ¾ teaspoon
    vanilla extract

Place all of the ingredients in a chilled bowl and beat with chilled beaters only until the cream holds a soft shape. It should not be stiff. (If you whip the cream more than an hour or so ahead of time, refrigerate it. It will probably separate slightly while it stands. Just beat it a bit with a small wire whisk right before using.)

Serve the cream separately, ladling a generous amount over the side of each portion.

Blueberry Pie #2

(double crust)

6 TO 8 PORTIONS

This is the classic, traditional blueberry pie than which there is none more delicious or delectable, none to be prouder of, none to serve with more fanfare, and none to enjoy more.

The crust can be prepared a day or two ahead and it can be ready to roll out. The berries can be washed and drained and ready to use. Then the actual "making the pie" is not too much work.

PIE CRUST

Prepare a double amount of Pie Crust (see page 131), divide it in half, gently shape each half into a ball, flour them lightly, wrap in plastic wrap, and refrigerate for an hour or longer. (Although if you handle it carefully, the crust can be used without first being refrigerated.)

FILLING

2 small boxes (2 pounds) fresh blueberries
6 tablespoons unsifted all-purpose flour
1 cup granulated sugar
¼ teaspoon salt

¼ teaspoon mace
Finely grated rind of 1 lemon

Fill a large bowl with cold water. Place the berries in the bowl and, with your hands, fingers slightly spread, transfer the berries to a towel to drain and dry.

Sift together the flour, sugar, salt, and mace and set aside.

When you are ready to bake, adjust a rack one-quarter or one-third up from the bottom of the oven (according to how many rack settings your oven has—lower is better). Preheat the oven to 450 degrees. You will need a 9-inch Pyrex pie plate.

Flour a pastry cloth and a rolling pin. Work with one piece of the dough at a time. Place the dough on the cloth, press down on it with the rolling pin (flattening it without rolling) until it is a circle 6 to 7 inches wide. Then, rolling gently from the center out toward the rim, roll the pastry out to a 12-inch circle.

Either fold the rolled-out pastry in half and lift it, or drape it over the rolling pin and lift it, placing it evenly in the plate. Press the sides into the pan without stretching the dough. With scissors, cut the edge even with the outside rim of the plate. Sprinkle 3 tablespoons of the sifted flour mixture evenly over the bottom of the pastry. Refrigerate.

Roll the remaining half of the pastry out to another 12-inch circle. Let it stand briefly on the pastry cloth.

Place the berries in a large bowl. Add the grated rind and toss gently with a rubber spatula. Add about half of the remaining sifted dry ingredients and toss gently, just a bit, with the rubber spatula.

Place half of the berries in the crust. Sprinkle with half of the now-remaining sifted dry ingredients. Cover with the remaining berries, mounding them high in the middle, and then sprinkle with the last of the dry ingredients. With your fingers, press down gently to flatten the mound slightly without spreading any berries toward the rim.

Have a small dish of cold water handy. Wet your three middle fingers and, with your fingers, generously wet the rim of the lower crust.

Fold the rolled-out pastry in half. Carefully lift it and place it with the fold across the middle, over the berries. Unfold and carefully arrange the top crust to touch the bottom crust around the sides. With scissors, cut the top crust, leaving a ½-inch border beyond the bottom crust.

Starting at a spot on the edge of the crust away from you, use your left hand to raise the rim of the bottom crust, and use your right hand to fold the border of the upper crust over, around, and then under the bottom crust—not the plate. Flour your fingertips as necessary. Continue all around the plate. As you do this you can at the same time press against the two edges to seal the top and bottom crusts together well.

Now, to finish the edge, stand it all upright around the rim, forming a little wall to control any juices that bubble out. Then, with your fingertips, flute the edge (see page 134).

EGG WASH

1 egg

Beat the egg just to mix and brush it gently with a soft brush all over the top of the crust, including the rim. You will use only a small amount of the egg wash to brush on the pie. (I have made it a rule never to write a recipe that is different from the way I make it. And I never have—until now. But I will explain and then leave it up to you. I use only the yolk and 1 teaspoon of water mixed together. That makes a much darker glaze. I think pies are more beautiful and more appetizing with a dark crust. However, I am afraid that if you see how dark the crust becomes after only 20 minutes of baking you will get worried and possibly take the pie out of the oven before it has baked enough.)

Now, one last thing before this beauty goes into the oven. You must cut air vents for steam to escape. Use a small, sharp paring knife. Cut 6 or 7 sunburst or fan lines radiating out from the center directly on top, leaving a 1- to 2-inch space in the middle (the cuts should not get too close to the outside edge or too much juice will bubble out). Each cut should be about 1½ inches long. Cut each one twice to open the cut a little.

That's it.

Bake at 450 degrees for 20 minutes. Then reduce the temperature to 375 degrees and bake for 40 minutes longer. (Total baking time is 1 hour.)

Cool on a rack.

Refrigerate until cold and serve cold. (The filling might be too runny until it is chilled.)

This is even better with vanilla ice cream.

Kirsch Strawberry Pie

Kirsch and strawberries are sensational, especially topped with whipped cream. This pie is beautiful, easy, and unusual. It is a gelatin pie, must be refrigerated until served, and is best the day it is made.

6 TO 8 PORTIONS

1 9-inch baked pie shell (see page 131) or
    baked crumb crust (see page 141)
2 pint boxes (2 pounds) fresh strawberries
1 envelope plus 1½ teaspoons
    unflavored gelatin
¼ cup cold water
¾ cup warm water
1 cup granulated sugar
Red food coloring
¼ cup kirsch
1 tablespoon Grand Marnier, Cointreau,
    or brandy

Wash the berries quickly, remove the hulls, and let drain on paper towels. Slice the berries, cutting each one into three or four lengthwise slices.

In a processor or a blender, purée enough of the berries to make 1 cup. (Or you can mash them to a pulp with a fork.) Chill the remaining sliced berries in the refrigerator.

In a small cup, sprinkle the gelatin over the cold water and let stand.

Place the 1 cup of berry pulp in a 6- to 8-cup saucepan. Add the ¾ cup warm water. Stir occasionally over moderate heat until the mixture comes to a boil. Add the sugar and stir to dissolve. Remove from the heat.

Add the softened gelatin and stir to dissolve.

Add enough red food coloring to give the mixture a nice rich color. Strain through a large but rather fine-meshed strainer to remove the seeds.

Place the bowl of the gelatin mixture in a larger bowl partly filled with ice and water and stir occasionally until the mixture thickens and becomes syrupy (this might take longer than you expect).

When the mixture thickens, stir in the kirsch and Grand Marnier, and then the refrigerated berries. Mix well but gently and turn into the prepared pie shell or crumb crust.

Refrigerate from 4 to about 10 hours.

WHIPPED CREAM

The whipped cream may be put on the pie an hour or two before serving; it is best if it does not stand longer.

> 1 cup heavy cream
> 2 tablespoons granulated or confectioners sugar
> ½ teaspoon vanilla extract
> Optional: a few toasted slivered almonds

In a chilled bowl with chilled beaters, whip the cream with the sugar and vanilla until the cream holds a definite shape. Either spread it over the firm filling or, with a pastry bag fitted with a star-shaped tube, form a border of swirls around the outside edge; let the red show in the middle.

Sprinkle the cream lightly with the optional almonds.

NOTE: *If you wish, you can also add a few fresh blueberries when you fold in the refrigerated sliced strawberries.*

Individual Deep-Dish Strawberry-Rhubarb Pies

6 INDIVIDUAL PIES

Strawberries and rhubarb are a fantastic combination and they make a wonderful pie. However, since they are both extremely juicy, it is best not to use a bottom crust which would get wet. And since serving this is something like serving soup, I make it in individual bowls; that solves all the problems and it is attractive!

You will need six ovenproof bowls, each with a 10-ounce capacity. Pyrex makes bowls that measure 4½ inches across the top and are called "10-ounce deep pie cups." Or use onion soup bowls.

> Double the amount of pastry for pie crust
> (see page 131)
> 1 pint box (1 pound) fresh strawberries
> Generous 3 cups (about 1 pound) fresh
> rhubarb, cut into ½-inch pieces

Finely grated rind of 1 large, deep-
colored orange
1½ tablespoons orange juice
1½ cups granulated sugar
4½ tablespoons unsifted all-purpose flour
⅛ teaspoon salt
Milk (to brush on the crust)
Additional granulated sugar (to sprinkle over
the tops)

Adjust a rack to the center of the oven and preheat oven to 400 degrees. Lightly butter the bottoms of six 10-ounce individual ovenproof bowls.

Wash, hull, and drain the berries. If they are very large, cut them in half. The rhubarb should be washed, not peeled, and cut into pieces. Place the berries and rhubarb in a large bowl. Mix the rind and juice and sprinkle it over the fruit. Toss gently to mix.

In a bowl, mix together the sugar, flour, and salt. Then sift the mixture over the fruits and stir gently with a rubber spatula. Set aside.

Now the pie crust. Lightly flour a pastry cloth and rolling pin, work with half of the dough at a time, and roll it until it is ⅛ inch thick (thin). Do not worry too much about the shape, but make it an even thickness.

To cut rounds of the dough: You will need a plate or something to use as a pattern that measures 1 to 1¼ inches more in diameter than the tops of the bowls. Set the plate, or the pattern, on the rolled-out dough, placing it against an edge. With a pizza cutter, a pastry cutter, or a small, sharp knife, cut around the plate or pattern. Cut two more rounds (three from each half of the dough). Then, with a wide metal spatula, carefully transfer the rounds to a piece of wax paper until you are ready to use them. (See Note about leftover scraps of dough.) Roll out the other half of the dough and cut three more rounds. Let the rounds wait a moment.

With a large spoon, divide the floured and sugared fruits evenly among the six buttered bowls, mounding them slightly, and letting most of the dry ingredients remain in the mixing bowl. Then spoon the dry ingredients remaining in the bowl evenly over the fruit.

Wet your fingertips with water and wet the rim of one of the bowls. Pick up a round of pastry and place it over the fruit but do not press it onto the wet rim. To form a thick edge on the pastry, flour your finger-tips and fold a hem, folding under a scant ½ inch of the pastry. The hem should be wide enough—or narrow enough—so the pastry extends about ¼ inch beyond the rim of the bowl.

Now, with your fingertips, press down on the doubled rim to seal it to the bowl. To be sure it is well sealed, press all around with the back of the tines of a fork, flouring the tines as necessary.

Repeat to prepare all six pies.

With a pastry brush, brush some milk over the tops, and then sprinkle with granulated sugar.

Place all the pies on a jelly-roll pan (the pan must have sides).

With a small, sharp knife, cut a slit about ¾ inch long in the very center of each pie crust. It is important to make sure that the slits are open and that they do not close; flour the knife blade and recut the slits, pushing the sides slightly apart. (The slits serve two purposes: One, they allow steam to escape; and two, they serve as receptacles for "pastry handles"—see Note.)

Bake for 30 minutes until the tops are nicely colored. Do not underbake; these should not be pale (dark is better). If the baking time is almost up and the tops are still pale, raise the rack (the top of the oven is hotter). And if the pies in the back of the oven are darker, reverse the pan front to back.

The filling should bubble and it may bubble over—O.K.

Cool to room temperature. (If you have baked these in glass, as they cool you will see that the filling sinks about an inch below the crust—O.K.)

Refrigerate for at least 4 hours, or up to 10 or 12 hours, before serving.

Serve a spoon with each pie.

NOTE: *To decorate these pies, cut the dough that remains after the rounds are cut, cutting six handle-shaped pieces. They can be cut freehand; they do not all have to be exactly the same. Or, if you are more comfortable with a pattern, cut one out of paper. What you want is an elongated tear-drop shape, about 4 inches long, 1¼ inches wide at the top, and ½ inch wide at the bottom (the bottom does not come to a point like a real tear-drop). Cut the "handles" with a pizza cutter, a pastry cutter, or a small, sharp knife. Then you will need something to cut a small round hole out of the wide part of each handle—use a ½- to ¾-inch cookie cutter, pastry-bag tube, or a thimble. Place the handles on an unbuttered cookie sheet, brush them lightly with milk, sprinkle with sugar, and bake at 400 degrees until they are nicely colored and extra crisp.*

Let the handles wait until serving time. Immediately before serving, place a handle, narrow end down, into the slit of each pie.

While making these handles recently, I discovered something. I still had some scraps of dough after the handles were all cut. Very carefully, I placed the scraps on top of each other in layers. Then, without straightening or smoothing the edges, I rolled the dough with a rolling pin until it was about ⅛ inch thick. I used a small, round, scalloped cookie cutter and cut out rounds, placed them on a cookie sheet, brushed with milk and sprinkled with sugar, and baked them. They were marvelous, puffed-up, light, flaky, crisp, delicious cookies.

Strawberry Chiffon Pie

This has a light, delicate, creamy, dreamy filling made with mashed berries and gelatin, and a topping of whipped cream and more berries. It is as pretty as a picture and as delicious as it looks. It is best if the filling is made the same day the pie is served, but it must chill for at least 3 hours.

6 TO 8 PORTIONS

1 9- or 10-inch extra-deep baked pie shell (see page 135)
1 pint box (1 pound) fresh strawberries
1 envelope unflavored gelatin
¼ cup cold water
3 eggs (graded large), separated
1 tablespoon fresh lemon juice
¾ cup granulated sugar
Scant ¼ teaspoon salt
½ teaspoon cream of tartar

Wash the berries quickly, remove the stems and hulls, and drain them well on paper towels. Then cut the berries into very small dice or mash them coarsely with a potato masher or with a large fork, or process them briefly in a food processor. (If the berries are large they should be halved or quartered, and then processed only 2 cups at a time—process with three or four on/off pulses, but not so long that they liquify.) There should be 2 generous cups of diced/mashed berries. Set the berries aside.

Sprinkle the gelatin over the water in a small cup and let stand.

In the small bowl of an electric mixer, beat the yolks until they are pale colored. Then beat in the lemon juice and ¼ cup of the sugar (reserve the remaining ½ cup).

Transfer the mixture to the top of a large double boiler over hot water on moderate heat. Stir constantly with a rubber spatula, scraping the bottom and the sides, until the sugar dissolves and the mixture thickens to the consistency of a medium cream sauce.

Then add the softened gelatin and stir to dissolve. Add the prepared berries and stir to mix well.

Remove the top of the double boiler and transfer the mixture to a large bowl. Place the large bowl into a larger bowl partly filled with ice and water. Stir frequently with a rubber spatula until the mixture barely (only barely) starts to thicken. Remove it from the ice temporarily.

In the small bowl of the electric mixer, beat the egg whites with the salt and cream of tartar until the whites thicken and hold a definite shape but not until they are stiff and dry. Reduce the speed to moderate and gradually add the reserved ½ cup of sugar. Increase the speed to high again and continue to beat until the whites are glossy and resemble a thick marshmallow cream.

Replace the bowl of strawberry mixture over the ice again for a few moments. Stir constantly with a rubber spatula until the mixture thickens enough to form a slight mound when some of it is dropped back onto itself off the spatula. (If possible, it should be the same thickness as the beaten whites.)

Gradually fold about half of the strawberry mixture into the beaten egg whites. Then fold the whites into the remaining strawberry mixture.

Pour the mixture into the baked pie shell. If you have made a 9-inch crust you might have more filling than the crust will hold. That's O.K. Pour in as much filling as the shell holds—up to the rim—then place the filled crust in the freezer for about 10 minutes until the filling sets a bit. Meanwhile, reserve the excess filling at room temperature. Then add a bit of the remaining filling to the top of the pie, place it in the freezer again very briefly, and then add the rest of the filling.

Refrigerate.

There are many ways you can decorate and present this. Whipped cream can be spread over the top, or it can be applied with a pastry bag fitted with a star-shaped tube. If you would like to take care of the whipped cream early in the day and not worry about the cream standing too long, here's the way to do it.

WHIPPED CREAM (with gelatin)

½ teaspoon unflavored gelatin
1 tablespoon cold water
1 cup heavy cream

1 tablespoon granulated or confectioners sugar
½ teaspoon vanilla extract

Sprinkle the gelatin over the water in a small heatproof custard cup. Let stand for 5 minutes to soften.

Place all but about 2 tablespoons of the cream in a small chilled bowl of the electric mixer. Add the sugar and vanilla. With chilled beaters, beat until the cream holds a very soft shape. Let stand briefly while you melt the gelatin.

Place the cup of gelatin in a little hot water in a small pan over low heat and let stand until the gelatin dissolves.

Remove the dissolved gelatin from the hot water. Start the mixer again, quickly stir the reserved 2 tablespoons of cream into the warm gelatin and immediately, while beating, add it to the whipped cream and continue to beat until the cream is stiff enough. Do not overbeat. (This small amount of gelatin will only keep the cream from separating or running; it is not enough to actually set the cream.)

Place the cream over the top of the filling and either smooth it or form it into swirls and peaks. Or fit a pastry bag with a large star-shaped tube, fill the bag with the cream, and form a wreath of whipped cream (by making a series of small, touching, S-shaped turns) or form six or eight large rosettes around the outer edge.

STRAWBERRY TOPPING (optional)

You will need about 2 cups of berries, washed, hulled, drained, and cut into halves or quarters if they are the very large ones. Mound them in the space left inside the whipped cream. Or, if you have covered the top with whipped cream, do not cut the berries; place them whole, standing point up, all over the top.

A few sprigs of fresh mint in the center look lovely.

Pumpkin Pie

This has a smooth, light, creamy, custardy filling with a delicious, flavored, delicate blend of spices.

This is easy to prepare, and although it is traditional for Thanksgiving and Christmas, it is equally appreciated all year.

8 PORTIONS

To eat this at its very most delicious, make it a few hours or less before serving. But with the unbaked crust waiting in the pie plate in the freezer, it takes only a few minutes to put the filling together. (When the pie stands overnight the filling is still fine but the crust loses its fresh flaky quality.)

> 1 extra-deep 9-inch pie shell (see page 135), frozen unbaked
> 1¾ cups light cream (or 1 cup heavy cream and ¾ cup milk)
> 3 eggs (graded large or extra-large)
> ½ teaspoon vanilla extract
> ¾ cup light brown sugar, firmly packed
> ½ teaspoon salt
> ¼ teaspoon finely ground black pepper
> ½ teaspoon ginger
> ¼ teaspoon mace
> ¼ teaspoon nutmeg
> 1 pound (2 cups) canned pumpkin (buy the kind labeled "solid pack," not "pumpkin-pie filling," or to use fresh pumpkin, see Notes)

Adjust a rack one-third up from the bottom of the oven and preheat oven to 450 degrees.

Have the prepared unbaked crust in the freezer. It must be in the freezer at least 20 or 30 minutes, although of course it can be there longer.

Place the cream (or heavy cream and milk) in a small saucepan, uncovered, on moderate heat. Let stand until a slightly wrinkled skin forms on top or tiny bubbles appear around the edge.

Meanwhile, in the large bowl of an electric mixer or any large bowl with a wire whisk, beat the eggs lightly just to mix. Beat in the vanilla, sugar, salt, and spices. Then add the pumpkin and mix well. (If you have been using a whisk, it will be better to mix in the pumpkin with a rubber or wooden spatula.) Gradually stir in the hot cream.

Do not remove the pie crust from the freezer until you are ready to bake it. Pour the pumpkin mixture into the frozen crust.

Bake for 10 minutes at 450 degrees, then reduce the oven temperature to 350 degrees and bake for 30 to 40 minutes longer (total baking time 40 to 50 minutes) until a small, sharp knife gently inserted into the middle of the pie comes out clean. (Every time you test the pie with the knife it will leave a scar which will increase in size as the pie cools. Do not cut more than necessary. Having made this many times, I know that in my oven it takes a total of 45 minutes to bake—I don't test.)

Place the baked pie on a rack.

Serve while still barely warm or at room temperature.

WHIPPED CREAM

2 cups heavy cream
¼ cup granulated or confectioners sugar
1 teaspoon vanilla extract

In a chilled bowl with chilled beaters, whip together all the ingredients.

If the pie is still slightly warm when you serve it, it is best to serve the whipped cream separately (the heat of the pie would melt the cream). Whip the cream until it is not too stiff; it should barely hold a shape and should be more like a thick sauce. But if the pie has cooled to room temperature, the cream can be whipped until it holds a definite shape, and can be spread over the top of the pie. Either way, the cream can be whipped a few hours ahead, refrigerated, and then whisked a bit with a small wire whisk just before using.

NOTES: 1. *If you are serving the pie while it is still slightly warm, place the whipped cream in the freezer for about 20 minutes before you serve it. The slightly warm, spicy pie and the icy cold, bland cream are a wonderful combination.*

2. To use fresh pumpkin: With a large, heavy knife, cut the pumpkin into chunks. With a small paring knife, cut away the rind and the seeds and the membranes. Cut the meat into pieces 2 or 3 inches in diameter. Place in a heavy saucepan with 1 inch of boiling water. Cover and simmer until the pumpkin is tender when tested with a small, sharp knife. Drain the pieces on a towel. Purée through a food mill or (a few pieces at a time) in a food processor. (The puréed pumpkin should be smooth, but do not process long enough to liquify it.) This may be frozen.

Honey Yam Pie

This is an old Creole recipe from New Orleans. The pie is delicate, light, more like custard than potatoes—but you will know it is sweet potatoes you are eating. It is not too rich or too sweet, and is easily made with canned yams (or sweet potatoes).

8 PORTIONS

1 extra-deep 9-inch baked pie shell
  (see page 135)
2 tablespoons apricot preserves
1 1-pound, 1-ounce can yams or sweet potatoes,
  in syrup
4 eggs (graded large or extra-large)
⅓ cup honey
⅓ cup orange juice
⅔ cup heavy cream
⅛ teaspoon salt
1 teaspoon vanilla extract
¼ teaspoon nutmeg

While the crust is baking, heat the preserves and strain them. As soon as the crust is done brush the hot preserves on the hot crust, and return to the oven to bake 2 minutes more to set the preserves. Set aside to cool.

Leave the oven on. The rack should be one-third up from the bottom of the oven and the temperature should be 450 degrees.

Drain the yams and reserve the liquid. Purée the yams in a food processor or a blender, adding a spoonful (or a bit more) of the reserved liquid (you will not need the remaining liquid), just enough to moisten the yams sufficiently to make a purée.

In a bowl beat the eggs lightly just to mix. Mix in the honey, orange juice, cream, salt, and vanilla.

Gradually stir the egg mixture into the yams. Then strain through a large strainer set over a large bowl.

Now, very slowly pour the filling into the crust, pouring against the rim rather than in the center (a safety precaution to keep the apricot glaze unbroken—the glaze protects the bottom crust so it doesn't become wet or limp). Either grate the nutmeg over the top or sprinkle it on.

Carefully place the pie in the oven and immediately reduce the temperature to 350 degrees.

Bake for 40 minutes or until the filling is just set. You can test it by tapping the rim of the plate; when the filling barely moves, but does not shake, it is done.

Cool completely.

WHIPPED CREAM

1⅓ cups heavy cream
2 tablespoons honey
½ teaspoon vanilla extract
Optional: 2 tablespoons bourbon, rum,
   or brandy

In a chilled bowl with chilled beaters, whip together all the ingredients until the cream holds a definite shape. It is best not to place the cream on top of the pie much ahead of time. If you whip it ahead of time, refrigerate it. Whisk it briefly with a small wire whisk just before using.

Shortly before serving, either spread the cream all over the top or, with a pastry bag and a star-shaped tube or with a teaspoon, form a border of whipped cream and leave the center uncovered.

Or serve the whipped cream separately, spooning it over individual portions.

Refrigerate the pie and serve it cold.

Lemon Tartlets

20 TARTLETS

These are tiny, bite-size pastries with a light and flaky buttery crust and a tart, creamy lemon filling. They are fancy, classy, elegant; make them for your most important occasions. They should be refrigerated or frozen until they are served; serve them like cookies—they are finger food. Both the pastry and the filling recipes may be doubled. You will need small, round tartlet pans that measure 2¾ inches in diameter and are ½ inch deep, and a cookie cutter that fits them (3 1/16 inches).

PASTRY

1 cup unsifted all-purpose flour
2 tablespoons granulated sugar
¼ teaspoon salt
4 ounces (1 stick) unsalted butter, cold and
    firm, cut into small pieces
1 egg (graded large), slightly beaten just to mix

This can be made in a food processor or an electric mixer.

In a processor: Fit the bowl with the metal blade and place the flour, sugar, salt, and butter in the bowl. Process on-and-off for a few seconds until the mixture resembles coarse meal. Then add the egg and process only until the mixture barely holds together—be careful not to process any longer.

In an electric mixer: Follow the same procedure, using the large bowl of the mixer and low speed—do not overmix. (It takes longer in a mixer.)

Turn the mixture out onto a board or work surface and press it together with your hands. Divide the dough in half and form it into two balls, flatten them slightly, wrap in plastic wrap, and refrigerate for an hour or so.

To bake, adjust a rack one-third up from the bottom of the oven and preheat the oven to 350 degrees.

Lightly flour a pastry cloth and a rolling pin. Roll one piece of the pastry at a time, rolling until it is a scant 1/16 inch thick (very thin!); it is more delicate/crisp/flaky if it is thin.

Cut the rolled-out pastry with a plain or scalloped round cutter that is 3 1/16 inches in diameter. With a small metal spatula or with a table knife transfer each round of pastry into a tartlet pan. With your fingers press the pastry into place in the pans. (If you don't have enough pans, just do as many as you can at a time.) Place the lined pans in the freezer for a few minutes or longer.

Cut small squares of aluminum foil about 3¼ inches on a side. When the pastry is firm, press a square of foil into each tartlet. Place them on a cookie sheet. Fill with dried beans or with aluminum pellets to keep the pastry in place.

The pastry should be cold or frozen when it is baked. Bake for 13 minutes. Remove from the oven and quickly and carefully remove the foil and beans or pellets. Then return the pastry shells to the oven and continue to bake for a few minutes longer until the pastry is a light golden color; it should not be too pale—it looks and tastes better when it has some color.

Let the tartlet forms stand for a moment or so until you can remove the baked shells from the pans. Set aside to cool.

(If these are made ahead of time, wrap them airtight and freeze until you are ready to fill them.)

You will need 20 baked shells of the size indicated for the following amount of filling.

(If you have leftover pastry, roll it out, cut it into shapes, sprinkle with sugar, and bake thin cookies.)

LEMON FILLING

This is an English recipe, called lemon curd or lemon cheese. It is used like a jam or jelly as a spread for toast or muffins, or as a filling for a layer cake or a sponge roll. It keeps for several weeks in the refrigerator. It is very easy to make a jar of this as a lovely gift.

This is not as temperamental as the usual egg custard. The large amount of sugar (or is it the lemon juice?) seems to protect the eggs from curdling. Stir frequently, but don't worry.

> 3 eggs (graded large or extra-large) plus
> 1 egg yolk
> 1 cup granulated sugar
> ¼ pound (1 stick) unsalted butter, cut
> into pieces
> Finely grated rind of 2 large lemons
> 6 tablespoons fresh lemon juice

Place the eggs and the yolk in the top of a large double boiler. Add the sugar and whisk or beat lightly to mix. Add the butter, rind, and juice.

Place over hot water on moderate heat. Cook, uncovered, stirring frequently with a rubber spatula, for 20 to 25 minutes or until the mixture is as thick as a heavy cream sauce. Strain into a wide-topped pitcher.

Place 20 baked tartlet shells on a tray. Pour the warm filling into the shells, carefully filling each one almost to the top. The filling will set as it cools.

OPTIONAL DECORATION: *These may be left completely plain. Or they may be topped while the filling is still soft with a light sprinkling of finely chopped, unsalted, green pistachio nuts, or a bit of crumbled, toasted, sliced almonds, or a sliver of preserved kumquat. Whatever, keep it small and simple. Or wait until shortly before serving and top each one with a rosette of whipped cream, or with a border of small rosettes of whipped cream.*

Refrigerate or freeze until serving time—they may be eaten frozen. Refrigerated, they are tender and delicate; frozen, they are almost the texture of a semifirm cheese.

To freeze, pack the tartlets in a single layer in a box that is shallow but deep enough so the cover does not touch the filling. Freezer paper or plastic wrap will stick to the filling unless the tarts are frozen firm before they are covered.

NOTE: *If your pans are a different size from mine, the cookie cutter must be large enough to cut rounds of pastry that will reach just to the rims of the pans, or a tiny bit above the rim; the pastry may shrink slightly in baking.*

Lemon Meringue Pie

This is heaven—pie-in-the-sky heaven. The crust is crisp, bland, flaky; the filling is slightly runny but not too runny and not wet, with a sharp, sour flavor to make you squeal; and the meringue is a sweet cloud on your plate.

This should be baked the day it is served.

6 TO 8 PORTIONS

1 9-inch baked pie shell (see page 131)
Finely grated rind of 3 lemons
¼ cup fresh lemon juice

4 egg yolks (from eggs graded large; you will
   use the whites for the meringue)
⅓ cup cornstarch (it is not necessary to sift
   the cornstarch)
1½ cups granulated sugar
¼ teaspoon salt
1½ cups warm tap water
2 tablespoons unsalted butter, cut into pieces,
   at room temperature

Adjust a rack to the center of the oven and preheat oven to 400 degrees.

Mix the rind and juice and set aside. Place the yolks in a small mixing bowl and set aside.

Place the cornstarch, sugar, and salt in a heavy 2-quart saucepan and stir to mix. Gradually add the water, stirring with a rubber spatula until smooth. Place over medium heat and stir gently and constantly until the mixture comes to a low boil. Boil gently, stirring with the rubber spatula, for 1½ minutes.

Add the butter and stir briefly to melt.

Remove from the heat. Add a few large spoonfuls of the hot cornstarch mixture to the yolks, stirring well to mix thoroughly. Then pour the yolk mixture into the cornstarch mixture, stirring gently. Also stir in the lemon rind and juice.

Return to moderate heat and stir gently until the mixture comes to a boil again. Boil, stirring gently, for 1 minute.

Immediately pour the hot mixture into the pie crust and begin to make the meringue (the filling should not be completely cool when you cover it with the meringue).

MERINGUE

4 egg whites (left from the filling)
Pinch of salt
¼ teaspoon cream of tartar
½ cup granulated sugar

Place the whites, salt, and cream of tartar in the small bowl of an electric mixer and beat at high speed until the whites hold a soft point when the beaters are raised. Reduce the speed to moderate and gradually add the sugar, adding 2 tablespoons at a time and beating about 20 seconds between additions. Then increase the speed to high again and beat only until the mixture holds a firm point when the beaters are raised—it should be stiff but do not overbeat.

It is essential that the meringue touch the crust all around the plate or the meringue will shrink away from the crust when it is baked. The filling should still be quite warm when you put the meringue on. Place the meringue by teaspoonfuls (use two spoons, one to pick up the meringue and one to push it off) all around the edge, sealing the meringue to the crust. Then gradually place the remaining meringue over the center. First spread it smooth and then, with the back of a teaspoon, pull up the meringue, forming peaks and swirls. It is more attractive if the peaks are few and large rather than many and small.

Bake the pie immediately but only until the meringue is lightly colored on the peaks; it will take 7 to 9 minutes.

Have a draft-free spot ready to cool the pie—a draft could make the meringue fall or weep. (I clear a spot in a dish cabinet.) Place the pie on a rack and let it cool completely.

Serve immediately or refrigerate. The filling becomes firmer when refrigerated; delicious both ways, but I like it best refrigerated.

Mrs. Foster's Lime Pie

8 PORTIONS

For years I had heard raves about a certain pie that was served at a lovely, small, family-style restaurant in New York City. The restaurant was called Mr. and Mrs. Foster's Place. I just heard that unfortunately the restaurant is no longer in business. The pie is a frozen chiffon dream. It tastes somewhat like an extra-sour, fluffy ice cream. I was thrilled when I met Mrs. Foster and she gave me the recipe. It is one that she created years ago—as good as can be, and easy. It can be frozen up to 2 or 3 weeks, and is served directly from the freezer.

CRUMB CRUST

1¼ cups graham-cracker crumbs (I use the
    bought ones)
¼ cup granulated sugar
2 ounces (½ stick) unsalted butter, melted

Adjust a rack one-third up from the bottom of the oven and preheat oven to 350 degrees.

In a bowl, mix the crumbs with the sugar. Then add the butter and stir with a rubber spatula until the butter is evenly distributed; the mixture will not hold together.

Turn the mixture into a 9-inch ovenproof glass pie plate. With your fingertips loosely distribute the crumbs evenly over the bottom and sides of the plate. Then press firmly, first on the sides and then on the bottom, to form a compact crust.

Bake for 10 minutes and then cool to room temperature. While the crust cools, prepare the filling.

FILLING

5 eggs (graded large), separated
¾ cup granulated sugar
⅔ cup fresh lime juice (grate the rind of
    2 limes before squeezing, to use below;
    see Notes)
Finely grated rind of 2 limes
⅛ teaspoon salt

Adjust rack one-third up and preheat the oven to 350 degrees.

In the small bowl of an electric mixer beat the yolks with ½ cup of the sugar, reserving remaining ¼ cup of sugar, at high speed for 5 minutes until the mixture is very pale and thick.

On low speed gradually add the lime juice, scraping the bowl with a rubber spatula and beating only until mixed.

Remove from the mixer and stir in the grated rind.

Turn the mixture into the top of a large double boiler over shallow hot water on moderate heat (the water should simmer gently). Cook, scraping the sides and bottom constantly for 6 or 7 minutes or until the mixture thickens enough to coat a wooden spoon. When it is just done, a candy thermometer will register 175 to 180 degrees.

Remove the top of the double boiler immediately and pour the mixture into a large mixing bowl. Stir occasionally until it cools.

In the large bowl of an electric mixer, add the salt to the egg whites and beat until they hold a soft shape. Reduce the speed to moderate and gradually add the reserved ¼ cup of sugar. Increase the speed again and continue to beat until the mixture holds a definite point, but not until it is actually stiff or dry.

Gradually, in three additions, fold the yolk mixture into the whites, handling very little and very carefully. It is not necessary to fold the first and second additions thoroughly.

Turn the mixture into the crust. It will look like there is too much filling, but it is all right, just mound it high. (It will be about 4 inches high in the middle.)

Bake for 15 minutes until the top is lightly browned.

Cool on a rack to room temperature. (The pie will shrink slightly as it cools—O.K.) Then freeze the pie. When it is frozen, cover it with plastic wrap. The pie may be kept frozen for up to 3 weeks. Serve it frozen.

WHIPPED CREAM

1½ cups heavy cream
3 tablespoons granulated sugar
1 teaspoon vanilla extract

In a chilled bowl with chilled beaters whip the above ingredients until the cream holds a soft shape. (It is better if it is not too stiff.)

The whipped cream may be spread over the top of the pie just before serving. Or, if you do not plan to serve the entire pie at once, the cream may be spooned over each portion individually.

Use a very firm and heavy, sharp knife for serving.

NOTES: 1. *This is indeed sour. Wonderfully sour! For a sweeter pie, Mrs. Foster suggests cutting down the lime juice to ½ cup. But Mrs. Foster and Nancy Nicholas, my editor, and I all love the full amount.*

2. This is very nice with fresh strawberries put on top just before serving.

Key Lime Pie

6 TO 8 PORTIONS

People who don't live in South Florida often ask if I have a recipe for Key Lime Pie. They are surprised when I tell them that you need a certain kind of lime called a Key lime (Citrus aurantifolia). They are small, round, and yellow, with a different taste from green Persian limes. These limes grow in the Florida Keys and in the

Miami area—and Mexico and the West Indies. They are seldom sold commercially. They were originally planted by the Spaniards for seamen because citrus wards off scurvy.

The original Key Lime Pie was made with a baked crust because it was created before graham crackers were manufactured. And it was topped with baked meringue, never ever with whipped cream, since the recipe, made with canned milk, came about because of a lack of both refrigeration and grazing land for milk cows in the Florida Keys.

But there are endless variations now: crumb crust or baked crust; 2, 3, 4, or 5 eggs; egg whites folded into the filling, or as meringue on top, or not at all; whole eggs used in the filling; whipped cream on top or not; baked or unbaked filling; frozen or unfrozen pie, etc., etc., etc.

Nellie and Joe have been bottling and selling local lime juice for about 20 years now. There is a company in Key West that sells Nellie and Joe's Lime Juice by the bottle. There is a question about whether or not it is actually Key lime juice, although it is the juice of limes from South Florida and the West Indies. The juice is not reconstituted, and it is indeed the very same juice that is used by most if not all of the South Florida restaurants for what they call Key Lime Pie. (And it is great for limeade, or seviche.) You can order it by mail from Mrs. Biddle's Candy Store, 528 Front Street, Key West, Florida 33040.

This is the most popular version of all the Key Lime Pies. It is so easy (no cooking) you will think something is missing. It must be made the day before serving or it will be too runny.

This recipe can be made with green limes or with lemons, but then it is not a Key Lime Pie. Although it is close. The grated rind of Key limes is bitter and should not be used in the pie. However, if you make this recipe with green limes or with lemons, it will be better if you include the grated rind of 1 or 2 limes or lemons.

CRUMB CRUST

1½ cups graham-cracker crumbs
¼ cup granulated sugar
½ teaspoon cinnamon
¼ teaspoon nutmeg
2 ounces (½ stick) unsalted butter, melted

Mix the above ingredients and follow the Directions for a Crumb Crust (see page 137).

FILLING

4 egg yolks
1 14-ounce can sweetened condensed milk
½ cup Key lime juice

You can use an electric mixer, an egg beater, or a wire whisk. Beat the yolks lightly to mix. Add the condensed milk and mix. Gradually mix in the lime juice.

Pour into the crumb crust. It will make a thin layer; the color will be pale lemon—not green. (It will be fluid now, but after it stands it will become about as firm as a baked custard and will slice beautifully.)

Refrigerate overnight.

Whipped cream is optional on this, natives do not use it—restaurants do. (I do.)

WHIPPED CREAM

2 cups heavy cream
¼ cup confectioners or granulated sugar
1 teaspoon vanilla extract

In a chilled bowl with chilled beaters whip the ingredients until the cream holds a shape and is firm enough to spread over the pie. If you whip the cream ahead of time, refrigerate it. It will separate slightly as it stands; just whisk it a bit with a wire whisk when you are ready to use it.

Spread the whipped cream over the filling.

OPTIONAL: *Fresh strawberries and Key Lime Pie are a divine combination. Either form a border of them standing up around the rim, or serve them separately.*

Frozen Key Lime Pie

6 TO 8 PORTIONS

A variation of Key Lime Pie. This does not freeze too hard and is delicious served right from the freezer. It will resemble sherbet. I have frozen this pie for weeks and even months and then when I served it, it was perfect.

Follow the preceding recipe with these changes. Use 2 whole eggs, separated (instead of 4 yolks).

In a small bowl beat the yolks until they are pale. Gradually add the condensed milk, beating only to mix. Then on low speed beat in the lime juice. Set aside.

Beat the egg whites with a pinch of salt until they hold a point when the beaters are raised, but not until they are stiff or dry.

Fold about one-third of the whites into the lime juice mixture and then, in a large bowl, fold together the lime juice mixture and the remaining beaten whites. Do not handle any more than necessary.

Turn into the prepared crumb crust and smooth the top.

Freeze for about an hour and then wrap airtight with plastic wrap. Continue to freeze the pie.

Orange Angel Pie

6 TO 8 PORTIONS

This is a famous Florida recipe. Many years ago it won first prize and best-in-show in a Florida cooking contest. Famous Southern hostesses have since made it their own specialty. It has a meringue shell, an orange-custard and cream filling, and a whipped-cream and fresh-orange topping. Luscious!

The meringue shell and the filling should both be made a day before serving (the meringue is too sticky to serve when it is fresh). The topping should be put on shortly before serving.

You will need a 10-inch ovenproof glass pie plate.

MERINGUE SHELL

4 egg whites (from eggs graded large or extra-
    large; you will use the yolks for the filling)
¼ teaspoon salt
¼ teaspoon cream of tartar
1 cup granulated sugar
1 teaspoon vanilla extract

Adjust a rack one-third up from the bottom of the oven and preheat oven to 275 degrees. Butter a 10-inch ovenproof glass pie plate and set it aside.

In the small bowl of an electric mixer at moderate speed, beat the egg whites for a few seconds until they are foamy. Add the salt and cream of tartar, and beat until the whites hold a soft shape but not until they are stiff. Continue to beat at moderate speed and start to add the sugar, adding 1 rounded tablespoonful at a time. Beat for about half a minute between additions. When about half of the sugar has been added, add the vanilla and then continue to add the remaining sugar as before. When all of the sugar has been added, increase the speed to high and beat for 7 or 8 minutes more until the sugar is dissolved—test it by rubbing a bit between your fingers. If it feels grainy, beat some more. The meringue will be very stiff and beautifully shiny. (Total beating time from start to finish is 15 to 18 minutes.)

The meringue will be sticky and hard to handle. Use a tablespoon to pick it up with and a rubber spatula to push it off. Place well-rounded tablespoonfuls of the meringue, touching one another, around the side of the plate. (While placing each spoonful around the sides, try to make it form a high peak as you scrape it off the spoon; and remember—the less you fool with it the better it will look.) Then place the remaining meringue over the bottom of the plate. Spread it to form a shell about 1 inch thick, and extending about 1 inch above the sides of the plate. Be careful not to spread the meringue over the edge of the plate; the meringue rises and spreads out during baking and if it has been spread over the edge it might run over the sides and be difficult to serve. (I use the back of a teaspoon along the inside of the rim to bring the meringue up in high peaks, forming a high shell without letting it spread over the rim.)

Bake for 1¼ to 1½ hours until the meringue is a pale sandy color. It should dry out in the oven as much as possible, but the color should not become darker than pale, pale gold.

Turn off the heat, open the oven door slightly, and let the meringue cool in the oven. It will crack as it cools—don't worry—it is all right.

FILLING

2 seedless oranges
5 egg yolks
½ cup granulated sugar
Finely grated rind of 1 lemon
2 tablespoons lemon juice
⅛ teaspoon salt
1 cup heavy cream

Grate the rind of the oranges fine (you can grate the lemon rind at the same time if you wish) and set aside. Peel and section the oranges (see page 19). Cut each orange section crossways in half and place the pieces of orange in a strainer set over a bowl. Let them stand to drain well. (The recipe will not use the drained-off juice.)

Place the yolks in the top of a small double boiler off the heat. Beat them with a small wire whisk to mix well. Stir in the sugar, grated orange and lemon rinds, lemon juice, and salt. Place over hot water on moderate heat and cook, stirring and scraping the bottom and sides constantly with a rubber spatula, until the mixture thickens to the consistency of a soft mayonnaise; it should take 8 to 10 minutes.

Remove the top of the double boiler, stir in the well-drained, cut-up oranges, and let stand until cool. Then refrigerate briefly to chill slightly.

Meanwhile, in a small chilled bowl with chilled beaters, whip the cream until it is quite firm. Fold a large spoonful of the orange mixture into the cream, fold in another large spoonful, and then fold the remaining orange mixture and the cream together, handling as little as possible—they do not have to be completely blended.

Spoon this filling into the cooled meringue shell.

Refrigerate overnight. After an hour or so, cover the top loosely with plastic wrap.

Before serving, prepare the topping. (If you want to section the oranges for the topping when you make the shell and filling, refrigerate them overnight in their juice, then drain them well in a strainer before using.)

TOPPING

3 seedless oranges
1 cup heavy cream
½ teaspoon vanilla extract
2 tablespoons confectioners sugar

Peel and section the oranges (see page 19) and place them in a strainer set over a bowl to drain. If you have room in the refrigerator, place the oranges in the strainer in the refrigerator to chill for half an hour or more before serving.

In a small chilled bowl with chilled beaters, whip the cream with the vanilla and sugar until it just barely holds a shape, but not until it is really stiff. Refrigerate it until you are ready to assemble the pie. (If it stands too long it will separate slightly; just beat it or stir it a bit right before using.)

Shortly before serving (either right before or an hour or two before) place large spoonfuls of the whipped cream around the outer edge of the filling, and cover the center space with a mound of the orange sections.

(This should be easy to serve. But if you have any trouble cutting it, dip the knife in hot water before making each cut.)

VARIATIONS: *I have had this pie with a generous sprinkling of shredded coconut all over the whipped cream. And I have heard of it being made with about ¼ cup finely cut-up pecans folded into the meringue just before it is placed in the pie plate. A cateress I know, who says that this pie is her most popular item, uses drained, crushed pineapple on top instead of the sectioned oranges. It lends itself to many of your own ideas.*

Florida Cream-Cheese Pie

6 TO 8 PORTIONS

This delicious pie is adapted from Jane Nickerson's Florida Cookbook *(University of Florida Press, 1973). Mrs. Nickerson was food editor for* The New York Times *for many years and she is now food editor for many Florida newspapers.*

The pie is filled with a light and fluffy cream-cheese/gelatin mixture that is full of fresh orange sections; biting through the bland/sweet cheese mixture and at the same time the sweet/tart/juicy orange is a taste thrill.

This makes a lovely dessert, even after a large meal. It can be served a few hours after it is made or it can wait overnight.

1 9-inch extra-deep baked pie shell
    (see page 135)
1½ cups orange sections (see page 19; you
    will need 4 or 5 large seedless oranges)
½ cup fresh orange juice (may be drained
    from the oranges or may be additional)
1 envelope unflavored gelatin
8 ounces cream cheese, at room temperature
½ cup granulated sugar
½ cup milk
1 cup heavy cream

Drain the orange sections in a large strainer set over a large bowl and set aside. Place the ½ cup of juice in a small custard cup. Sprinkle the gelatin over it and let stand for 3 to 5 minutes. Then place the cup in a little hot water in a small pan over low heat. Let stand for a few minutes until the gelatin is dissolved. Then remove it from the water and set aside briefly.

Meanwhile, place the cheese in the large bowl of an electric mixer and beat until smooth and soft. Add the sugar and then the milk and beat well. Then stir the gelatin mixture and gradually add it to the cheese mixture, scraping the bowl with a rubber spatula, and beating until perfectly smooth.

In a small chilled bowl with chilled beaters whip the cream until it holds a definite shape when the beaters are raised but not until it is really stiff. Set aside.

Put some ice and water in a large bowl, filling it about one-quarter full. Place the bowl of cream-cheese mixture in the ice and water. Stir with a rubber spatula until the mixture thickens just so that it barely mounds when dropped from the spatula. Remove from the ice water, saving the ice water.

Immediately fold about half of the cheese mixture into the whipped cream. Then fold the whipped cream into the remaining cheese mixture.

Replace the bowl of cheese mixture in the larger bowl of ice and water. Stir very gently until the mixture begins to hold a shape. Then gently fold in the drained orange sections and turn it all into the pie crust, mounding it high in the middle.

Refrigerate.

NOTE: *Mrs. Nickerson also makes this in a graham-cracker crust. It is delicious, but since a crumb crust is not as deep as a baked crust, there is always some filling left over. If you use a crumb crust, pour the extra filling into one or two wine glasses or custard cups to serve separately.*

Creamy Coconut Cream-Cheese Pie

This easy pie, in a spicy crumb crust, is filled with a mixture of coconut, cream cheese, whipped cream, and Cognac and crème de cacao, which makes it a sort of a Brandy Alexander Cheese Pie (if you use gin in place of the Cognac you will have a Gin Alexander Pie). It has an optional chocolate sauce. All in all, it is a delicious and unusual dessert.

8 PORTIONS

CRUMB CRUST

1¼ cups graham-cracker crumbs
1 tablespoon granulated sugar
1 teaspoon ginger
1 teaspoon cinnamon
2 ounces (½ stick) unsalted butter, melted

Adjust a rack to the center of the oven and preheat oven to 375 degrees.

Mix the above ingredients. Use a 9-inch pie plate and follow the Directions for Crumb Crust (see page 137) to prepare, bake, and cool the crust.

FILLING

6 ounces cream cheese, at room temperature
2 tablespoons granulated sugar
¼ cup milk
3⅓ ounces (1 to 1⅓ cups) shredded coconut
2 tablespoons Cognac or brandy
2 tablespoons crème de cacao
1 envelope unflavored gelatin
¼ cup cold tap water
2 cups heavy cream

Place the cream cheese, sugar, milk, coconut, Cognac, and crème de cacao in the bowl of a food processor or in the jar of a blender. Process or blend for 30 seconds. The mixture should be thoroughly mixed and the coconut shreds should be cut into smaller pieces, but should not be too fine. Transfer this mixture to a large mixing bowl.

Sprinkle the gelatin over the water in a small heatproof cup. Let stand for about 5 minutes to soften. Then place the cup in a little hot water in a small saucepan or frying pan over low heat. Let stand only until the gelatin is dissolved. Then remove from the hot water and set aside for a moment.

Meanwhile, as the gelatin is dissolving, remove and set aside about 2 tablespoons of the heavy cream. In a chilled bowl with chilled beaters (it can be the small bowl of the electric mixer if you wish), whip the remaining cream only until it holds a very soft shape. Quickly stir the reserved 2 tablespoons of cream into the gelatin and quickly, while beating, add the gelatin all at once to the partially whipped cream, and continue to beat until the cream holds a definite shape, but not until it is really stiff.

Fold the whipped cream mixture and the cheese mixture together. If the mixture is runny, place some ice and water in a large bowl, place the bowl of filling in the ice water, and stir/fold very gently only until the mixture thickens enough so it can be slightly mounded in the crust.

Pour the filling into the crust, mounding it slightly.

Refrigerate for 4 to 10 hours.

Serve just as it is, or with the following sauce.

BIMINI CHOCOLATE SAUCE

½ cup heavy cream
6 ounces semisweet chocolate, coarsely
    chopped or broken (see Note)
2 tablespoons unsalted butter

Place all the ingredients in a small, heavy saucepan over low heat. Stir occasionally until the chocolate is melted. Then stir the sauce briskly with a small wire whisk until it is as smooth as honey.

The sauce should be served at room temperature, poured or spooned over the top of the pie. (If you serve this sauce with ice cream, it may be served cool or warm.)

If the sauce thickens too much while it stands, stir it with a wire whisk to soften, or, if necessary, stir over hot water to soften.

NOTE: *I use Tobler or Lindt extra-bittersweet, or Tobler Tradition, or Lindt Excellence (both semisweet)—you can use any semisweet.*

Old-Fashioned Butterscotch Pie

This old Southern recipe makes a velvety smooth and creamy pie with a rich butterscotch flavor. Make this early in the day to serve that night. (If you wish, the pie crust may be made ahead of time and may be frozen, unbaked, in the pie plate.)

1 9-inch baked pie shell (see page 131)

6 TO 8 PORTIONS

Optional: 2 ounces (½ cup) pecans, cut or broken into medium-small pieces

3 egg yolks
3 ounces (¾ stick) unsalted butter
1 cup dark brown sugar, firmly packed
1 cup boiling water
2 tablespoons unsifted all-purpose flour
3 tablespoons cornstarch
Scant ½ teaspoon salt
1⅔ cups milk
1¼ teaspoons vanilla extract

Sprinkle the optional nuts over the bottom of the baked pie shell and set aside.

Place the yolks in a medium-size mixing bowl and set aside.

Place the butter in a 10- to 12-inch frying pan over moderate heat to melt and begin to brown slightly. (The browned butter adds more flavor.) Add the brown sugar, stir to mix, and bring to a boil, stirring occasionally. After bubbles form all over the surface, continue to boil for 3 minutes, stirring occasionally with a wooden spatula.

Now, be careful with this next step. Have ready a long-handled wooden spoon or spatula. Add the boiling water to the boiling sugar mixture; it will all bubble up furiously and give off steam. Stir to mix. Remove from the heat and set aside.

Sift together the flour, cornstarch, and salt into a 3-quart saucepan. Gradually stir in the milk. If there are any lumps in the mixture press on them with a rubber spatula to dissolve them. When the mixture is smooth, stir in the hot brown sugar mixture.

Place over low-medium heat and cook, scraping the bottom and sides of the pan constantly with a rubber spatula, until the mixture comes to a boil. Then continue to scrape the pan and let the mixture boil for 1 minute.

Remove from the heat and add a few large spoonfuls of the hot mixture to the egg yolks, mixing well with a small wire whisk. Whisk in a few more spoonfuls. Then pour the yolk mixture into the remaining hot milk mixture, stirring well.

Place over low heat and cook, stirring, until the mixture comes to a low boil. Continue to stir and scrape the pan, and let simmer for 1 minute.

Remove from the heat. Stir in the vanilla. Pour into a large mixing bowl. Stir frequently, very gently, folding the mixture to allow steam to escape, until the mixture is cool.

Turn into the prepared pie shell and refrigerate for several hours.

WHIPPED CREAM

1 cup heavy cream
2 tablespoons confectioners or
    granulated sugar
½ teaspoon vanilla extract

In a chilled bowl with chilled beaters, whip the ingredients until the cream holds a firm shape. Place the whipped cream by spoonfuls all over the top of the pie, placing the spoonfuls around the rim first and then on the center. If you have a cake-decorating turntable place the pie plate on it. With a long, narrow metal spatula smooth the whipped cream. Then, if you wish, use the back of a spoon to form a few large swirls in the cream.

Coconut Cream Pie

8 PORTIONS

This is a very old-fashioned, traditional Southern pie that is creamy-thick and full of coconut. When it has been refrigerated enough, the filling will be just barely thick enough to hold its shape (that is the way it should be); it must be refrigerated at least 5 to 6 hours before it is served.

1 9-inch baked pie shell (see page 131)
6 tablespoons unsifted all-purpose flour
½ cup granulated sugar
¼ teaspoon salt
2 cups milk
1 cup shredded coconut
2 egg yolks
1 tablespoon unsalted butter
¾ teaspoon vanilla extract
Scant ¼ teaspoon almond extract

Sift the flour, sugar, and salt together into the top of a large double boiler off the heat. Add the milk very gradually at first, whisking it in with a small wire whisk, until the mixture is smooth. With a rubber spatula stir in the coconut.

Put a little hot water in the bottom of the double boiler, place the top over it, and cook on moderate heat. (It is all right if the water boils.) Stir and scrape the bottom and sides frequently with the spatula for about 10 minutes until the mixture thickens. Then continue to cook, stirring occasionally, for 10 minutes more.

Place the egg yolks in a mixing bowl. Add a bit of the hot coconut mixture, stirring well as you do. Continue, gradually mixing in about half of the coconut mixture. Then stir the yolk mixture into the remaining coconut mixture.

Replace over the hot water on moderate heat and cook, stirring, for 2 minutes more.

Remove from heat. Add the butter, vanilla and almond extracts, and mix gently.

Transfer to a wide bowl to cool, occasionally stirring gently.

Pour the cooled coconut mixture into the pie shell.

TOPPING

1 cup heavy cream
2 tablespoons granulated or confectioners sugar
½ teaspoon vanilla extract
About ½ cup shredded coconut

In a chilled bowl with chilled beaters, whip the cream, sugar, and vanilla until the cream holds a definite shape. Spoon the cream over the top of the filling and spread it smoothly or form it into swirls and peaks. Sprinkle generously with the coconut.

Refrigerate for at least 5 or 6 hours. (It is a good idea to set the refrigerator control to coldest for a few hours before serving the pie.)

Coffee and Cognac Cream Pie

6 PORTIONS

This is positively wonderful! It is a small pie (made in an 8-inch plate) with a wonderfully crunchy crust of crumbled Amaretti and butter . . . with a smooth, creamy, dreamy, barely set filling of coffee, Cognac, and whipped cream . . . topped with more whipped cream and chocolate shavings or grated chocolate.

Although it can be cut into six small portions, it is not too much for four. Or maybe two.

The crust can be made way ahead and frozen, or it can be made about 2 hours before you use it. The filling is best if you make it the day you serve it, but it can be made early. And I suggest that you put the whipped cream on top no earlier than necessary, but a few hours ahead is O.K.

Get ready for a treat.

CRUST

4 to 5 ounces Amaretti (to make 1 cup of
    crumbs, see Note)
3 ounces (¾ stick) unsalted butter, melted

Prepare an 8-inch glass pie plate as follows: Turn the plate upside down, cover it with a large square of aluminum foil, press down on the sides of the foil to shape it, then remove the foil, turn the plate right side up, and place the foil in the plate. Press it smoothly into place and fold the corners and the edge of the foil back over the rim of the plate.

In a bowl mix the crumbs and butter.

Turn the crust mixture into the plate. With your fingertips distribute it loosely over the bottom and then the sides of the plate. Press it firmly into place (it must be firm), first pressing the sides and then the bottom. (This crust does not get baked.)

Place the crust in the freezer for at least an hour or two, or as much longer as you wish. (If you leave it longer, wrap it in plastic wrap.)

When you are ready to use the crust (or anytime after it is frozen) remove the foil as follows: Turn the edges of the foil up. Carefully lift the foil and the frozen crust. Slowly and carefully peel the foil away, holding the crust upright on your left hand as you peel with your right hand. When the foil is removed, gently replace the crust in the plate, holding a knife or a small spatula under the crust to ease it in slowly.

Now the crust can wait at room temperature or in the refrigerator while you prepare the filling.

FILLING

1½ teaspoons unflavored gelatin

2 tablespoons water

1½ tablespoons instant espresso or other instant coffee

2 tablespoons boiling water

3 egg yolks

½ cup granulated sugar

¼ teaspoon salt

½ teaspoon vanilla extract

¼ cup Cognac

1 cup heavy cream

In a small heatproof cup sprinkle the gelatin over the water. Dissolve the coffee in the boiling water. Set aside.

In the small bowl of an electric mixer, beat the yolks with the sugar at high speed for about 5 minutes until the mixture is thick and almost white. Mix in the salt and vanilla.

Place the cup of gelatin in a little hot water in a small pan over low heat, until the gelatin is dissolved.

Then mix the gelatin with the coffee and Cognac and, gradually, on very slow speed, add the mixture to the yolks, scraping the bowl with a rubber spatula and beating only until smooth. Set aside.

In a small chilled bowl with chilled beaters whip the cream only until it holds a shape, not until it is really stiff. Let the whipped cream stand now until you are ready for it.

Place the bowl containing the egg-yolk mixture into a larger bowl half filled with ice and water, and scrape the yolks' bowl constantly with a rubber spatula until the mixture thickens to the consistency of a heavy cream sauce.

Fold about half of the egg-yolk mixture into the whipped cream and then fold the cream into the remaining yolk mixture.

Very carefully pour the filling into the prepared crust. Watch the edges to be sure it doesn't run over. There will probably be more filling than the crust will hold. If so, do not use it all at once. Place the filled crust in the freezer or the refrigerator briefly only until the filling begins to set. Then add the remaining filling, pouring it carefully onto the center of the pie.

Refrigerate for at least 2 hours.

TOPPING

1 cup heavy cream
1 tablespoon plus 1 teaspoon granulated sugar
½ teaspoon vanilla extract
Chocolate shavings or grated chocolate

In a chilled bowl with chilled beaters whip the cream with the sugar and vanilla only until the cream holds a shape but not until it is really stiff.

Fit a pastry bag with a large star-shaped tube. Fold down a deep cuff on the outside of the bag. Transfer the whipped cream to the bag. Close the top and press from the top forming large rosettes of cream in a border around the rim of the pie. Sprinkle the chocolate shavings or grated chocolate on the filling in the middle. Or, if you prefer, simply spread the cream all over the top.

Refrigerate.

NOTE: *Amaretti are Italian macaroons—extra dry and crunchy with a very special taste and texture. They are made in two sizes: The large size comes wrapped two together in tissue paper; the small size is called Amarettini. (They are available at specialty food stores including Manganaro Foods, 488 Ninth Avenue, New York, New York 10018, or Williams-Sonoma, P.O. Box 3792, San Francisco, California 94119.) To make 1 cup of crumbs you will need about 8 tissue-paper packages, or a scant 4 ounces. To crumble them, place the packages on a board or work surface, whack them with a heavy cleaver, then unwrap the papers and grind the Amaretti in a food processor or a blender until the crumbs are fine. The Amarettini do not have to be crumbled before they are processed or blended. Or you* can place them in a bag and crush them with a rolling pin. Either way, they must be fine crumbs.

Amaretti do make an extraordinary crust, but the pie can be delicious even if you don't have Amaretti. Any other kind of crumbs may be substituted—either graham crackers, chocolate wafers, zwieback, or Oreo cookies (crumble the Oreo cookies and the filling together), etc.

Tarts

ABOUT QUICHE PANS AND FLAN RINGS

The following group of recipes calls for a variety of sizes of shallow, loose-bottomed metal quiche pans or narrow flan rings (not china one-piece quiche pans). I use them interchangeably, but if I have a choice I recommend the quiche pans, because occasionally the butter in the pastry runs out under the flan ring. And if the ring itself and the cookie sheet it is on are not absolutely flat, the pastry itself runs out. However, even that can be coped with. Just cut it away with a small, sharp knife as soon as the pastry is removed from the oven.

If you have never used either the quiche pans or flan rings for making dessert tarts, please do. It is a wonderful baking experience, and the results are especially gorgeous. (And many people have told me that they find these recipes easier than regular pies.)

Look for black steel quiche pans; they will make the bottom crust brown better than shiny metal pans.

The pans and rings are more and more popular lately and are generally available at kitchen equipment shops. They can be bought at, or ordered by mail from, Bridge Kitchenware, 214 East 52nd Street, New York, New York 10022.

Apricot Tart

8 TO 10 PORTIONS

This is a favorite dessert that I taught in many cities around the country where I gave cooking classes. And, when Food & Wine Magazine *asked me for a recipe for their cover, this was it. It is a wonderful tart made of the best pastry I know. It can be beautifully plain, or creative and artistic with a design on top made of some of the pastry.*

It is great fun to make and you will be proud to serve it. Plan it for a party (or a magazine cover).

The filling can be made days or weeks ahead—the apricots soak overnight, but if you are in a rush, they need not be soaked, just simmer them longer to soften them. The pastry is best made right before using it.

In cooking classes I served this warm, even hot. I have also frozen it for weeks and thawed it to serve. Or I have made it several hours ahead of time and let it cool to room temperature. Any of these ways is fine.

You will need a plain flan ring measuring 9½ inches in diameter and ¾ inch in depth (see Notes).

The filling should be made first.

FILLING

12 ounces dried apricots (see Notes)
2 cups water
1¼ cups granulated sugar
½ teaspoon vanilla extract
¼ teaspoon almond extract
Optional: 1 tablespoon rum, Cognac, or kirsch
Optional: about 2 tablespoons thinly sliced
    toasted almonds

Soak the apricots overnight in water.

Then place the apricots and water in a heavy saucepan. Add the sugar and stir to mix. Place over moderately high heat and stir until the mixture comes to a boil. Reduce the heat slightly, cover, and simmer for about 10 minutes—stir occasionally to be sure it is not sticking or burning. Then uncover, raise the heat to moderately high again, and stir almost constantly until the apricots are very tender and are beginning to fall apart and the liquid has thickened—reduce the heat if necessary to avoid spattering—and remember that the mixture will thicken more as it cools; do not cook until it becomes too dry. It usually takes about 8 to 10 minutes, but apricots vary considerably and some may take longer. You can help them along by cutting the apricots with the side of a wooden spoon as you stir them. Do not purée them—you should have thick, chunky apricot preserves.

Remove from the heat. Cool a bit and then stir in the vanilla and almond extracts and the optional liquor. If you wish, stir in a few thinly sliced toasted almonds.

This can be used as soon as it has cooled, or it can be refrigerated for weeks. (Many of the people who came to the cooking classes told me they liked this apricot preserve so much that they made it to serve with toast—I agree.)

RICH FLAN PASTRY (pâte sablée)

2½ cups unsifted all-purpose flour
Scant ½ teaspoon salt
½ cup granulated sugar
8 ounces (2 sticks) unsalted butter, cold and
    firm, cut into ½-inch pieces (it is best to
    cut the butter ahead of time and
    refrigerate it)
1 egg plus 2 additional yolks (graded large)
Finely grated rind of 1 lemon
2 teaspoons lemon juice

This may be put together in a food processor or, traditionally, on a board.

In a food processor: Fit the processor with the steel blade. Place the flour, salt, and sugar in the bowl of the processor. Add the butter and process on-and-off (like pulse beats) for about 10 seconds until the mixture resembles coarse meal.

In a small bowl mix the egg, yolks, rind, and juice. Then, with the processor going, add these mixed ingredients through the feed tube and process only briefly (just a few seconds) until mixed, not until it all holds together—it should be dry and crumbly.

Traditional method: Place the flour on a large board, marble, or smooth countertop. Form a well in the center and add all the remaining ingredients. With the fingertips of your right hand, work the center ingredients together. Then gradually incorporate the flour, using a dough scraper or a pancake turner in your left hand to help move the flour in toward the center. When all of the flour has been absorbed, knead briefly only until the dough holds together.

For either method: Turn the pastry out onto a large board, marble, or counter top. Press together to form a ball. Then "break" the dough as follows. Start at the further end of the ball of dough and, using the heel of your hand, push off a small piece (it should be a few tablespoonfuls), pushing it against the work surface and away from you. Continue until all the dough has been pushed off.

Form the dough into a ball again, cut it in half, and then form into two balls. Lightly flour the balls of dough. With your hands, flatten them slightly into rounds 6 to 8 inches in diameter. Wrap them in plastic wrap and let them stand at room temperature for 20 to 30 minutes. (If the room is very warm, or if the pastry was handled too much, it may be refrigerated for about 10 minutes, but no longer. If it is cold when it is rolled out it will form small cracks on the surface and the filling might run out.)

To shape and bake: Place two racks in the oven, one one-third up from the bottom and one in the center, and preheat the oven to 375 degrees. Butter the inside of a 9½ × ¾-inch flan ring and place it on an unbuttered flat cookie sheet (the sheet should have at least one flat edge so you can slide the baked tart off the sheet).

Flour a pastry cloth and a rolling pin. Place one round of the dough on the cloth and roll it into a 12-inch circle.

Drape the dough over the rolling pin and transfer it to the flan ring, centering it carefully as you unroll it.

With your fingertips carefully press the dough into place without stretching it. The dough will stand about ½ inch above the ring on the sides. If necessary, straighten it with scissors, leaving ½ inch of dough above the rim.

If the dough cracks or tears while you are working with it, it can be patched with a little additional dough.

Spoon the cold apricot filling into the shell and smooth the top of it—it should be flat, not mounded.

Flour the fingers of your right hand. Hold a spot on the rim of the dough, holding it with your thumb and the side of your bent-under index finger. Press on the raised edge of the dough to flatten it and make it thinner. Work all the way around. Then fold the thinner rim of dough down over the filling, pulling it in toward the center a bit in order to keep it slightly away from the flan ring.

Roll the remaining half of the dough until it is a scant ¼ inch thick, then trim it to a circle about 10 or 10½ inches in diameter (use anything that size as a pattern and cut around it with a pizza cutter, a pastry wheel, or a small, sharp knife).

With a pastry brush dipped in water, or with your fingertips, wet the rim of the bottom dough that is folded over the filling. Now, to transfer the top crust, drape it loosely over the rolling pin and unroll it over the filling.

With your fingertips press down on the edges to seal both crusts together. Then cut around the rim with a table knife to remove excess
dough; the edge of the dough must not extend over the flan ring or the
dough might stick and it will be difficult to raise and remove the ring
after the tart is baked. Then press around the edge of the pastry with the
back of tines of a fork to seal it. Again, keep the upper edge of the pastry
slightly away from the flan ring.

GLAZE

1 egg yolk
1 teaspoon water

Beat the yolk and water just to mix and strain it through a strainer. Brush
it over the top of the tart but be careful not to let it run down the sides—
that could make it stick to the flan ring. With the back of a table knife,
score a diamond pattern in the dough, being very careful not to score the
dough deeply; make shallow lines about ½ inch apart, first in one direction
and then, on an angle, in the opposite direction.

To make a design on the top, press together all left-over scraps of the
dough and roll them out on the pastry cloth with the rolling pin. Roll
this a little thinner than the crusts. Cut with a long, sharp knife or a pastry
wheel into ½-inch-wide strips. Place them on the tart in a bow design.
Then cut the remaining dough with a small scalloped or plain round cutter, or with a heart-shaped cutter, and place these around and on top of
the bow.

(When *Food & Wine Magazine* made this, it was for their Valentine
Day issue. They cut out the additional dough with large heart-shaped
cutters, and placed one heart in the middle and six in a circle around it.
It was gorgeous!)

Brush it all well with the egg wash.

With the tip of a small, sharp knife, cut a few small slits (air vents),
cutting right up against the bow or other design so the cuts do not show.

Bake low in the oven for about 30 minutes. Then reduce the oven
temperature to 350 degrees, raise the tart to the center of the oven, and
bake for 20 to 30 minutes more (total baking time is 50 to 60 minutes)
until the top is beautifully browned.

When the tart is removed from the oven, if any of the pastry has run
out under the flan ring, use a small, sharp knife to trim and remove it.

It is easiest to remove the flan ring if you do it immediately, while
the pastry is hot, before it cools and becomes crisper. Use pot holders that

are not too thick and bulky (or use a folded towel or napkin) and, very gently, slowly, and carefully, raise the ring to remove it.

(If you have trouble removing the ring, let it stand until the tart is cool. Then slide the tart [still in the flan ring] onto an inverted 8- or 9-inch round cake pan. The ring will then slide down, and the tart can be transferred to a serving plate. All of these directions are "HANDLE WITH CARE.")

If you were able to lift the flan ring up off the hot tart, then let the tart cool completely on the cookie sheet.

When cool, use a flat-sided cookie sheet as a spatula, and carefully transfer the tart to a flat serving plate. Or carefully loosen the tart by sliding a long, narrow metal spatula under it and, if it moves easily, just use your hands to slide it off the flat side of the cookie sheet. But don't force it; if it feels as though the tart might crack, use something large and flat (i.e., the bottom of a loose-bottomed quiche pan) to transfer it.

APRICOT GLAZE

¼ cup apricot preserves
2 teaspoons water

In a small pan over moderate heat, stir the preserves and water until the mixture comes to a boil. Strain through a strainer, then brush the glaze carefully all over the top of the tart. (If you plan to freeze the baked tart, do not glaze the top until the tart is thawed—glaze it shortly before serving.)

This tart is delicious as it is, but it is still better with vanilla ice cream; the slightly sour taste of the apricots with the smooth, sweet ice cream is gorgeous!

NOTES: 1. *This can be made in a 9-inch loose-bottomed cake pan in place of the flan ring. Even though the cake pan is deeper, you can make a tart only ¾ inch deep in it.*

2. *I use plain supermarket apricots; they have a nice tart flavor and they generally work better for this recipe than some of the fancier, more expensive apricots. (Some of the more expensive ones do not fall apart as they should, even after long cooking.)*

Grape Tart

This has a marvelous crust made of a rich ground-almond butter-cookie dough that resembles Linzer Torte. You press it into the pan with your fingertips; it is baked empty and then filled with concentric rings of grapes in a variety of colors, and kirsch-flavored apricot preserves. It is a most delicious dessert, and gorgeous. It is festive and partyish; serve it any time you can get beautiful grapes and you want to make a big impression. Have you seen the candles that look like French fruit tarts? That's what this tart looks like.

The crust may be prepared ahead of time and frozen if you wish. Finish the tart from 4 to 12 hours before serving.

The seeds must be removed from the grapes, a slow process. If you like detail work, you will enjoy doing it. I do. Otherwise, it would be good to have someone help. (This can be made with seedless grapes; it won't be as dramatic all in one color, but it will still be an exciting dessert.)

You will need an 11- or 12-inch loose-bottomed quiche pan that must not be more than 1 inch deep.

ALMOND CRUST

7½ ounces (1½ cups) blanched almonds
1 cup unsifted all-purpose flour
¼ teaspoon salt
¾ teaspoon cinnamon
Pinch of cloves and/or ginger
½ cup granulated sugar
5 ounces (1¼ sticks) unsalted butter
2 egg yolks

To prepare the pan, place the rim of an 11 or 12 × 1-inch loose-bottomed quiche pan in the freezer. Melt 2 or 3 tablespoons of butter (in addition to the butter in ingredients—this is for buttering the pan). With a pastry brush, brush it all over the inside of the chilled rim (the cold pan will set the butter and keep it from running). Then butter the bottom of the pan and put it into place in the rim. Use a generous amount of fine, dry bread crumbs to sprinkle all over the bottom and the sides. Then, carefully, holding the bottom in place with your fingertips, shake out excess crumbs over paper. (If the pan is not buttered and crumbed, the crust will stick; do it thoroughly.) Set aside.

The almonds must be ground to a fine powder. This can be done in a processor or a blender (in a processor or blender, adding a spoon or two of the sugar will prevent the almonds from lumping), or a nut grinder. If you use a processor, leave them in the processor bowl and finish the crust as follows: Add the flour, salt, cinnamon, cloves and/or ginger, and sugar and process briefly only to mix. Cut the butter into pieces, add, and process to mix very well. Then, through the feed tube, add the yolks and process until the mixture holds together. Turn it out onto a board and work it a bit between your hands until it is thoroughly mixed.

Without a processor, cream the butter, add the sugar, and beat to mix. Mix in the yolks and then the remaining dry ingredients. Mix or knead until thoroughly mixed.

Here's the best way to line the pan with this nut mixture. Take about 2 or 3 tablespoons of the dough and roll it between your hands into a short and fat cigar shape. Press it against the rim of the pan. Continue, overlapping the pieces slightly, all around the rim. Then divide the remaining dough into three or four pieces, flatten them slightly between your hands, and press into the bottom of the pan. Be sure that wherever the pieces meet all seams are pressed together well. Smooth the top of the rim; it must not be higher than the rim of the pan. Press the bottom firmly to make a smooth and compact layer. The bottom crust will be about ⅓ inch; the sides may be a bit thicker. Bend your index finger and press your knuckle into the angle where the sides and bottom meet—that section should not be too thick.

To decorate the rim, press the back of the blade of a table knife slightly at an angle across the top of the rim to score it. Repeat at ¼-inch intervals all around the rim.

Place the crust in the freezer until it is firm.

To bake, adjust a rack one-third up from the bottom of the oven and preheat oven to 350 degrees. Tear off a 12-inch square of aluminum foil. Brush one side of it with butter (it is not usually necessary to butter the foil for lining a crust, but it is advisable in this recipe) and place it, buttered side down, in the frozen crust. Press firmly into place. Fill with dried beans or pie pellets.

Bake for 35 minutes. Remove the crust from the oven and carefully remove the foil and beans by lifting the corners of the foil.

Continue to bake the crust. If the bottom puffs up, flatten it very gently and slightly with the back of a wide metal spatula. Bake for 15 to 20 minutes more until the crust is brown on the edges and done (although it will be soft to the touch) on the bottom.

Set aside to cool. When the crust has cooled to tepid or room temperature, remove the sides of the pan by placing the pan over a bowl that is narrower than the base of the quiche pan. The sides of the pan will slide down. You can either leave the pastry on the bottom of the pan or you can transfer it to a flat serving platter or a board. To transfer it, let it cool completely. Then, gently and carefully, transfer it with two wide metal spatulas, or use a flat cookie sheet or the bottom of a quiche pan as a spatula. If it seems too fragile to move, freeze it first. Either way, be careful.

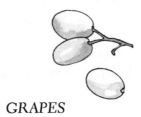

GRAPES

You will need about 3 pounds (9 cups) of grapes. If you can get red, green, and black grapes, it will make a stunning tart. But if you can get only one or two colors, it is O.K. It will look best if the grapes are large. Remove the grapes from the stems and wash them in a bowl of cold water. Drain them in a strainer. Now, with a small, sharp knife cut a grape in half from top to bottom, cutting through the stem end. With your fingernail remove the seeds. Then place the two halves next to each other, cut sides down, on paper towels. Continue with all the grapes, keeping the halves in matched pairs.

APRICOT GLAZE

18 ounces (1½ cups) apricot preserves
1 envelope unflavored gelatin
¼ cup kirsch

Stir the preserves in a saucepan over moderate heat until they melt. Meanwhile, sprinkle the gelatin over the kirsch in a small custard cup and let stand for 5 minutes. When the preserves have melted, pour them through a strainer set over a bowl; press on them with the back of a spoon to force them through the strainer. Return the strained preserves to the saucepan. Stir over heat, bring to a boil, add the softened gelatin, stir to dissolve, and then simmer gently for 3 minutes. Remove from heat.

Now, to assemble the tart, brush the hot glaze generously over the bottom and sides of the crust, and lightly over the top of the rim. The glaze will act as a glue for the grapes. Start by making a row of one kind of grape around the rim, placing the two halves together (it should look like the grapes were never cut), and placing each grape standing up, resting on its stem end or at a slight angle. Complete one circle of grapes and brush it generously with the glaze. Then make the next row, using another kind of grape (unless you have only one kind), fitting them compactly and brushing them generously with the glaze. With large grapes, I make five rows and fill in the center with more grapes. It will depend on the size of the grapes and how compactly you place them.

If the glaze starts to thicken while you are working with it, replace it over heat to melt again. When you have filled the tart with grapes, pour all the remaining glaze evenly over everything.

Refrigerate for 4 to 12 hours.

You will need a strong, heavy, sharp knife for serving.

French Apple Tart

8 PORTIONS

This recipe is from a French pastry-chef friend who made it at some of the leading restaurants in France—he made it for years at the Plaza Athenée in Paris—and here in the States. This is exactly the way he does it; some of the steps may seem unconventional, but the results are divine.

It has a prebaked pastry crust made in a flan ring, a thick filling of stewed apples, a topping of broiled, very thinly sliced apples, and a coating of apricot glaze. It is gorgeous!

This involves several steps and takes quite a while. But if you don't want to do it all at once, the crust can be made ahead of time and frozen (it is best to freeze it before it is baked rather than after) and the filling can be refrigerated for a few days. It is best to complete it all the day it is to be served.

You will need a 9½ × ¾-inch flan ring.

FLAN PASTRY

1 cup unsifted all-purpose flour
1 tablespoon granulated sugar
⅛ teaspoon salt
4 ounces (1 stick) unsalted butter, cold and
    firm, cut into ½-inch pieces (it is best to cut
    it ahead of time and refrigerate it; cut

it into lengthwise quarters, and then
into ½-inch dice)
1 egg yolk
1 teaspoon ice water
Finely grated rind of 1 lemon (the juice will
be used for the Filling)

The pastry can be put together in a food processor or by hand.

In a food processor: Fit the processor with the metal blade. Place the flour, sugar, salt, and butter in the bowl of the processor and process on-and-off (like pulse beats) 8 to 10 times, or for 8 to 10 seconds, only until the mixture resembles coarse meal. In a small cup mix the yolk, water, and rind. Then, with the processor going, add this mixture all at once through the feed tube and process only briefly until mixed—but not until the mixture holds together; it will be crumbly.

Turn it out onto a large board or work surface, knead briefly until the dough holds together, and then press it together to form a ball. Flour it lightly and, with your hands, flatten it into a circle about 6 inches in diameter. If the edges crack, pinch them together.

Traditional method: Place the flour on a large board or work surface. Form a well in the middle and add all the remaining ingredients. With the fingertips of your right hand, work the center ingredients together. Then gradually incorporate the flour, using a dough scraper or a pancake turner in your left hand to help move the flour in toward the center. When all the flour has been absorbed, knead briefly only until the dough holds together. Then press it into a ball, flour it very lightly, and then, with your hands, flatten it into a circle about 6 inches in diameter.

The dough should not be refrigerated before it is rolled out, unless the kitchen is very warm, or unless you have handled it so much that the butter has started to melt. If so, it should be wrapped and refrigerated for only about half an hour.

To shape and bake: Adjust a rack to the center of the oven and preheat the oven to 375 degrees. Place a 9½ × ¾-inch flan ring on a cookie sheet.

Lightly flour a pastry cloth and a rolling pin. Carefully roll the dough into a circle 12 to 12½ inches in diameter.

To transfer the pastry: Drape the pastry over the rolling pin. To do this, hold the pin over the left side of the pastry, raise a left corner of the pastry cloth to turn the pastry over the rolling pin, roll it up loosely, and then unroll it over the pie plate centering it evenly.

If you have a cake-decorating turntable, place the cookie sheet with the pastry on the turntable; you will find it much easier to trim and finish the pastry.

With your fingertips carefully press the dough into place without stretching it, just ease it down. Then, with scissors, trim the edge, leaving an even ½- to ¾-inch border standing up above the flan ring. Fold a small hem in toward the center, leaving a very small amount of the dough (only a scant ¼ inch) extending up above the top of the flan ring. (If the top cracks slightly while you are turning it over to form a hem, that is to be expected. Just smooth it a bit.) The pastry must not extend out beyond the sides of the flan ring or it will not be possible to slip the ring up to remove it after the crust is baked.

To decorate the top edge of the rim, you may either score it with the back of the blade of a table knife (forming lines at an angle, ¼ inch apart), or crimp it with a dough crimper (a tool that resembles wide tweezers and has a zigzag pattern on the tips—the secret of using this tool is to do so with a very light touch; if you squeeze it hard, or until it is closed, it breaks off pieces of the dough—it is only supposed to decorate it, not break it off).

With a fork, prick holes in the bottom crust at ¼- to ½-inch intervals.

Place the pastry, on the sheet, in the freezer for a few minutes until it is firm. (It may be wrapped, but leave it on the cookie sheet, and it may be frozen for weeks if you wish.)

To keep the pastry in place, lightly butter a 12-inch square of aluminum foil and place it, buttered side down, over the pastry. Press it carefully into place; do not fold the foil down on the sides. Fill it with dried beans or rice or with the aluminum pie weights that are made for this purpose.

Bake for about 25 minutes. Remove the sheet from the oven. Be extremely gentle or the sides of the crust might crack—it is fragile. Slowly and carefully remove the foil and the beans by lifting the corners of the foil. Then continue to bake for 5 or 10 minutes more. After removing the foil lining, the bottom of the crust might puff up; watch it carefully and use a cake tester to pierce it as often as necessary. (If it still puffs up, place a pot holder directly on the pastry over the puff to hold it down. Bake for about 5 minutes and then remove the pot holder.)

As it bakes, the crust will shrink in diameter. When it does, remove it from the oven for a moment and carefully lift off the flan ring.

Bake the shell for a total of 30 to 35 minutes. When done, it will be completely dry, the bottom will be a pale sandy color, and the edges will be darker.

Remove from the oven and let stand to cool.

(My mother used to say, "Care befull," and somehow it made me listen more than if she said it correctly. I say it to you now.) This beautiful pastry shell is DELICATE/TENDER/FRAGILE—EXTREMELY BREAKABLE. Do not try to pick it up to transfer it. Use a flat-sided cookie sheet or the bottom of a loose-bottomed quiche pan (spatulas are not wide enough) and transfer the shell to a large, flat serving platter.

FILLING

2½ pounds firm and tart apples
    (about 5 apples)
⅔ cup granulated sugar
½ cup water
½ teaspoon cinnamon
¼ teaspoon mace or nutmeg
2 teaspoons lemon juice
1 teaspoon vanilla extract

Peel, quarter, and core the apples. Cut each quarter into four chunks to make applesauce. Place the apples, sugar, and water in a large, heavy saucepan. Cook, covered, for about 5 minutes. Uncover and stir in the cinnamon, mace or nutmeg, and lemon juice. Stir constantly until the apples are tender. They should begin to get mushy and fall apart; however, some apples do not fall apart even after they have cooked. If your apples don't fall apart, mash them with a potato masher. If the juice evaporates before the apples are tender, add a bit more water. Do not overcook. The mixture will thicken more as it cools, and it should not be too dry.

When done, stir in the vanilla and set the pan aside, or transfer the mixture to a large plate to cool. You will have 4 cups of thick, chunky applesauce. (If you wish, you may refrigerate this for days.)

APPLE TOPPING

3 to 4 apples (a generous 1½ pounds)
3 ounces (¾ stick) unsalted butter, melted
Granulated sugar

Peel, quarter, and core the apples. Then cut each quarter the long way into very thin slices—the thinner the better (within reason). I cut each quarter into 8 to 10 slices; however 6 to 8 slices would be quite acceptable. (This step takes patience.)

Line a large jelly-roll pan with aluminum foil. Brush it with some of the melted butter. Place the apple slices next to each other in rows on the buttered foil. If you cut the apples very thin, you will have to do this in two batches. With a pastry brush, brush the slices lightly with the melted butter or, with the brush, pat the butter on in order not to move the slices out of place (you may not have to use all of the butter) and sprinkle them generously with granulated sugar to help them brown.

Preheat the broiler. Place the pan in the position closest to the broiler, and broil until the slices are cooked and lightly browned on the edges (it is all right if some of the slices remain pale). Watch carefully. It might become necessary to reduce the heat slightly if your broiler has a heat control or to lower the position of the pan slightly. As the slices become done, use a wide metal spatula and transfer them to a large platter or to wax paper or foil to cool. (If you let them cool on the foil on which they were broiled, they may stick in the caramelized sugar.)

APRICOT GLAZE

12 ounces (1 cup) apricot preserves

Place the preserves in a small saucepan over moderate heat and stir until melted. Then press through a strainer, return to the pan, bring to a boil, and boil for 1 minute.

With a pastry brush, brush a thin layer of the hot glaze on the bottom of the crust and also on the top of the rim. (Reserve the remaining glaze.)

Then place the apple filling in the shell. Spread it out and smooth the top. If you have enough, mound it slightly in a low dome shape.

Use the broiled apple slices to form two circles of slices, one next to the rim, and another inside of that, completely covering the filling. Use your fingers to place the slices very carefully. The slices should be at a right angle to the rim. They should deeply overlap each other. The more closely these are placed, the more attractive, so take your time and be patient. Right in the middle of the tart the slices should form a pointed mound.

Reheat the remaining apricot glaze and, with a pastry brush, brush it all over the apple slices—it will seem to be more than you need, but use it all—make it heaviest in the center.

Refrigerate, and serve cold.

To serve, use a sharp and heavy knife, and cut slowly, in order to keep the apple slices in place and to avoid cracking the crust, which is crisp and fragile.

VARIATION: *Orange Apple Tart. In place of the broiled sliced apple topping, cover the apple filling with slightly overlapping slices of peeled seedless oranges (these do not get broiled). They should be sliced crossways, and should be no thicker than ¼ inch, thinner is better. Then brush the hot apricot glaze over the oranges. The apples and oranges must both be delicious to begin with. If they are, this is terrific.*

Orange Tart

8 PORTIONS

This consists of a shallow pastry shell brushed with apricot preserves, filled with fresh orange sections, and covered with a thickened orange-juice mixture. It is light, tart, wonderfully refreshing, but should only be made when the oranges are delicious. It is best the day it is made, but the crust can be prepared ahead of time and placed in the freezer unbaked until you are ready for it. And, if you wish, the oranges can be sectioned a day ahead. Then there is not too much left to do to put it all together.

You will need a 9-inch flan ring only ½ or ¾ inch deep (a pie plate is too deep).

PASTRY

1 cup unsifted all-purpose flour
2 tablespoons granulated sugar
¼ teaspoon salt
4 ounces (1 stick) unsalted butter, cold and
  firm, cut into small pieces
1 egg (graded large), beaten lightly just to mix

This can be made in a food processor or an electric mixer.

In a food processor: Fit the bowl with the metal blade and place the flour, sugar, salt, and butter in the bowl. Process on-and-off for only a few seconds until the mixture resembles coarse meal. Then add the egg and process only until the mixture barely holds together—be careful not to process any longer.

In a mixer: The same procedure may be followed, using the large bowl of the mixer and low speed. The "coarse-meal" stage will take longer to arrive at in the mixer than in the processor; while you are mixing, use a rubber spatula to push the ingredients in toward the beaters.

Turn the mixture out onto a lightly floured board. Flour your hands, squeeze the pastry together, form it into a ball, flour the ball lightly, flatten it to a 6- or 7-inch circle, and put it on a floured pastry cloth. With a floured rolling pin roll the pastry into a 12-inch circle.

Place a 9 × ½ or ¾-inch flan ring on a cookie sheet. Roll the pastry loosely on the rolling pin, and unroll it over the flan ring, centering it carefully. With your fingers, press it into place. With scissors, trim excess, allowing ½- to ¾-inch overlap. Fold excess inside to form a double thickness on the rim and press together firmly. The rim should be upright a scant ¼ inch above the flan ring. If you wish, form a design on the folded edge by pressing the back of a knife blade at an angle across the top of the rim, at ¼-inch intervals all around the edge, or crimp it with a dough crimper.

Place the pastry shell on the cookie sheet in the freezer at least until it is frozen or longer if you wish (if you do leave it in the freezer longer, cover it well with plastic wrap or foil after it is frozen).

When you are ready to bake, adjust a rack to the center of the oven and preheat the oven to 375 degrees. Line the frozen shell with aluminum foil and fill it with dried beans or pie weights (aluminum pellets made for that purpose) to keep the shell in place.

Bake for 30 minutes. Remove from the oven and carefully remove the foil and beans by lifting the four corners of the foil. Return the shell to the oven and continue to bake for about 10 minutes more until the shell is thoroughly dry and lightly browned; after removing the foil keep an eye on the pastry—if it puffs up, prick it with a cake tester.

Remove the shell from the oven and let stand until completely cool. Remove the flan ring by lifting it off.

ORANGE FILLING

About 10 seedless oranges
⅔ cup sugar
Water, kirsch, rum, or Cognac (if needed)
2 tablespoons cornstarch
Pinch of salt
2 teaspoons kirsch, rum, or Cognac, or
*   1 teaspoon lemon juice*
¼ cup apricot preserves
Optional: seedless green grapes
Optional: additional apricot preserves

Peel and section the oranges (see page 19), placing the sections and the juice in a bowl. Add the sugar and stir gently to mix without breaking the fruit. Let stand about 15 minutes.

Then pour it all into a large strainer set over a large bowl, and let drain for about 15 minutes.

Measure the juice. You need 1 cup; if there is less, add water, kirsch, rum, or Cognac to make 1 cup.

In a small, heavy saucepan stir the 1 cup of liquid with the cornstarch and salt until smoothly blended. Place over moderate heat and stir gently until the mixture comes to a low boil, thickens, and becomes clear (it will take about 5 minutes). Then reduce the heat to low and stir gently for a minute or two. Add the 2 teaspoons kirsch, rum, or Cognac, or the 1 teaspoon lemon juice and mix gently. Set aside and let stand, stirring occasionally, until cool.

Meanwhile, *very carefully* transfer the pastry shell (the safest way is to use a flat-sided cookie sheet or the bottom of a quiche pan as a spatula) to a large, flat cake plate or a board and make room for it in the refrigerator.

In a small pan over moderate heat stir the preserves until they come to a boil. Turn the hot preserves into the pastry shell and brush or spread them to cover the bottom.

Then place the drained orange sections over the preserves in a neat pattern as follows: Place 1 slice at a right angle to the rim on the right-hand side of the shell (three o'clock), with the thick (curved) side facing the top (twelve o'clock). Place another slice closer to you, slightly overlapping the first. Continue to form a circle of orange sections all around the shell, overlapping each other slightly more toward the center of the pie than on the outside, rather like a fan pattern. Then form another similar circle inside the first. Fill in the space in the center by placing the slices any way they fit, or by cutting them into smaller pieces if that seems easier.

Carefully spoon the cornstarch mixture all over the oranges.

This should be refrigerated for at least 2 or 3 hours, or as long as 10 hours (but after that the cornstarch mixture begins to dry out).

Before serving this may be decorated with a few seedless green grapes, either mounded in the center or in a ring around the outside. And, if you wish, the grapes can be brushed with a bit of additional melted apricot preserves.

Straw-berry Tart

8 PORTIONS

This crisp, cookielike shell, baked in a flan ring or a quiche pan, is filled with strawberries and generously covered with a glaze made of puréed strawberries. It is a picture. And very delicious.

If you wish, the pastry shell may be shaped in the flan ring and frozen for days or weeks. It is best to bake it when you are ready to use it; that should be the day you serve it.

You will need a 9- or 10-inch flan ring, ¾ or 1 inch deep. Or a similar-size, loose-bottomed quiche pan.

Prepare the pastry as in the recipe for Orange Tart (see page 200), but if you use a 10-inch flan ring or quiche pan, roll the pastry out to a 12½- to 13-inch circle.

FILLING

2 or 3 pint boxes (2 or 3 pounds) fresh straw-
    berries, depending on the size of the berries
    and the size of the flan ring (if you use

the berries whole you will need a large
number; but if they are very large, you
can cut them in half, and use only half
as many)
1 cup granulated sugar
⅛ teaspoon salt
2 teaspoons unflavored gelatin
½ cup plus 1 tablespoon water
1 tablespoon lemon juice
3 tablespoons cornstarch

Place the berries in a large bowl of cold water, agitate them briefly, and then immediately remove them from the water. The sand will settle to the bottom—do not disturb it while you remove the berries. Pick off the stems and hulls and drain on towels.

In a blender or a food processor, purée 1 box of the berries to make 2 cups purée. Strain the purée through a large strainer set over a large bowl. Place the strained purée in a heavy 2-quart saucepan and add the sugar and salt.

In a small custard cup, sprinkle the gelatin over 2 tablespoons of the water, and let stand.

Place the remaining ½ cup minus 1 tablespoon of water and the lemon juice in a small bowl with the cornstarch and stir to dissolve. Add the cornstarch mixture to the strained berries.

Place over moderate heat. Stir constantly but gently with a rubber spatula for about 6 or 7 minutes until the mixture comes to a low boil, thickens, and becomes rather clear. Then reduce the heat to low, add the softened gelatin, and stir to dissolve. Continue to cook and stir gently for 3 minutes more.

Remove from the heat and gently transfer to a wide bowl to cool.

While the cornstarch mixture cools, place the berries in the baked shell. They may stand upright, in a pattern of concentric circles. Or, if they are large, they may be cut in half and placed on their cut sides, overlapping one another in concentric circles. Either way, they should completely fill the shell.

With a teaspoon, gently spoon the cooled gelatin mixture evenly all over the berries and the spaces between. If the berries were halved and are overlapping, it may be necessary to raise some of them a bit to allow the mixture to run under and around them, and to fill up all the space.

Refrigerate the tart for at least a few hours.

If the tart was made in a quiche pan, place it over a bowl that has a narrower diameter than the opening in the bottom of the pan. The sides of the pan will slide down away from the tart. Now, either serve the tart on the bottom of the pan on a large serving plate, or remove it from the bottom by using a flat-sided cookie sheet, or the bottom of another quiche pan, or two wide spatulas, and carefully transfer it to a serving plate or board.

OPTIONAL DECORATION: *Just before serving, peel a kiwi fruit (with a vegetable parer), slice it crossways in very, very thin circles, and place them, overlapping, in a ring around the top. If there are not enough slices, cut them in half and use half slices.*

WHIPPED CREAM

2 cups heavy cream
¼ cup granulated or confectioners sugar
1 teaspoon vanilla extract

In a chilled bowl with chilled beaters, whip all the ingredients until the cream holds a soft shape but not until it is stiff.

Serve the cream separately, placing a generous spoonful alongside each portion.

Straw-berry and Blueberry Tart

6 TO 10 PORTIONS (DEPENDING ON THE SIZE OF THE TART SHELL)

This is a 4-star red, white, and blue production for the 4th of July, or whenever both strawberries and blueberries are in season. It has a crisp pastry shell baked in a shallow flan ring and a layer of cream cheese that is covered with a beautiful pattern of strawberries and blueberries all coated with currant jelly. The crust may be frozen, if you wish, before it is baked. The crust should be baked and the tart should be assembled from 2 to 10 hours before serving.

You will need a flan ring no more than ¾ or 1 inch deep, and 9, 10, or 11 inches wide. If you have a choice, use the largest size—you will have room for more filling—but the ring must be shallow.

Prepare the pastry as in the recipe for Orange Tart (see page 200), but if you use a 10- or 11-inch flan ring, roll the pastry 3 to 3½ inches wider than the ring. The baked but empty pastry shell will be fragile—if you freeze it for at least half an hour it will be safer to transfer. Transfer it to a flat cake plate or a serving board.

FILLING

8 ounces cream cheese, at room temperature
2 tablespoons granulated sugar
¼ cup heavy cream

Beat the cheese until it is soft and smooth. Add the sugar and cream and mix thoroughly.

Spread the filling in a smooth layer over the bottom of the crust. Refrigerate.

TOPPING

12 ounces (1 cup) seedless red currant preserves
1 pint box (1 pound) fresh strawberries,
    washed, hulled, and drained
1 pint box (1 pound) fresh blueberries, washed
    and drained

Place the preserves in a small, heavy saucepan over low heat and stir until they are smoothly melted and come to a boil. Set aside.

If the strawberries are small, place a circle of them standing upright around the outer edge of the tart. If they are very large, cut them in half lengthwise and make a circle of halves, cut side down, each half over-lapping the previous one.

With a teaspoon spoon a thin layer of the preserves over the berries to coat them completely.

Now, depending on the size of your pastry shell, you will use all or only part of the blueberries. Start by placing about half of them in a bowl with about half of the melted preserves. Mix gently with a rubber spatula. With a teaspoon, spoon the berries into the space left in the middle of the tart. If you have room for more (they may be mounded a bit but not too high or it will be difficult to serve) mix as many as you want with more of the preserves and mound them. Then spoon a few teaspoons of the melted preserves over the top of the blueberries.

How about that!

O.K. Right into the refrigerator for at least 2 hours, preferably not more than 10.

NOTE: *You will see that this is not an exactly precise recipe as far as just how much fruit or preserves you will use. You may not have room to use it all. If so, use only as much as looks good, and save the rest for something else.*

Pear and Almond Tart

10 GENEROUS PORTIONS

This is festive and gorgeous and should be photographed for the cover of a food magazine. It is wonderful for Thanksgiving, Christmas dinner, or a New Year's Eve party. Or any time you can get good pears. (They are generally best in the fall and winter. Three favorite varieties are Comice, Anjou, and Bartlett.)

You will need a 12½ × 1-inch metal quiche pan with a loose bottom.

The pastry can be made and shaped in the pan days or weeks ahead (freeze it) but it should be baked and the tart should be finished the day it will be served.

FRENCH TART PASTRY (see page 136)

Prepare the pastry and place the ball of dough on a lightly floured pastry cloth. With your hands, flatten it into a round about 7 inches in diameter with smooth edges; pinch together if necessary to seal any cracks on the edges. Then, with a floured rolling pin, roll the dough out to a circle 15½ to 16 inches in diameter.

This is such a wide circle of tender and delicate pastry that it might crack or tear while you transfer it to the quiche pan. If so, don't get upset. You can patch it. Or you can press it all together and reroll it.

Fold the rolled-out dough in half and then in half again, forming a triangle. Very quickly, very carefully, place it in the pan with the point of the triangle in the center of the pan. Quickly and carefully unfold the dough and press it into place. If it is too large anywhere, and too small somewhere else, remove the excess and place it where you need it. When you patch the dough it is best to wet the edges with a bit of water and be sure to press it securely.

With scissors trim excess allowing ½- to ¾-inch overlap. Fold excess inside to form a double thickness on the rim and press together securely. The rim should be upright only about ⅛ inch above the pan. If you wish, form a design on the folded edge by pressing the back of a knife blade at an angle across the top of the rim at ¼-inch intervals all around the edge, or crimp it with a dough crimper.

Place the pastry shell in the freezer until it is firm. Or if you wish, this can be frozen for weeks.

When you are ready to bake, adjust a rack one-third up from the bottom of the oven and preheat the oven to 375 degrees.

Line the pastry shell with aluminum foil; the regular 12-inch foil is too narrow, but that is the kind to use—the wider one is too stiff. Use one long piece, and then another, crossing the first piece, at a right angle to it. Press the foil into place in the frozen shell. The ends of the foil should extend a few inches above the rim of the pastry.

Fill the foil with dried beans or pie weights (aluminum pellets made for this purpose).

Do not place the quiche pan on a cookie sheet—it keeps the bottom from browning. Bake for 20 minutes. Then remove the pan from the oven and carefully remove the foil and beans by lifting the bottom piece of foil from opposite sides, and return the pastry to the oven to bake 10 to 15 minutes longer until the pastry is lightly colored on the edges and slightly colored on the bottom.

While the pastry is baking (or after it has been baked, if you prefer) prepare the filling.

ALMOND FILLING

5 ounces (1 cup) blanched almonds
1 egg (graded large) plus 1 egg yolk
¼ teaspoon almond extract
1 tablespoon dark rum, Cognac, or bourbon
½ cup granulated sugar
2 ounces (½ stick) unsalted butter, melted

The almonds must be ground to a fine powder; it can be done in a food processor or a blender (in a processor or a blender it is best to add a spoonful or two of the sugar to keep the nuts from lumping) or a nut grinder, but make them fine. Set aside.

In a small bowl beat the egg and yolk just to mix. Stir in the almond extract, rum, sugar, melted butter, and the ground almonds.

Set the filling aside and prepare the pears.

PEAR FILLING

6 to 7 medium-size firm pears (about 3¼
     pounds)—the pears must not be soft
     or overripe
Juice of 1 large lemon
¼ cup granulated sugar

With a vegetable parer, peel the pears, then cut each one in half the long way, and with the tip of a small paring knife cut out the cores and seeds and remove the stems. After each pear is ready, brush it all with lemon juice and set it aside on a large plate.

When the pastry shell is baked, remove it from the oven. Raise the oven temperature to 400 degrees. Let the shell stand for about 10 minutes (but it will not hurt if it cools completely).

Spread the almond filling in an even layer over the bottom of the shell.

Place about 10 pear halves, flat sides down and pointed ends in toward the middle, touching one another around the outer edge of the tart. (If the pears are too wide, trim a small slice off the sides.)

Now, to fill the center space with pears: Cut 2 halves the long way making 4 pieces. Then cut each quarter the long way into 4 or 5 thin slices.

Place these slices in a fanlike pattern, overlapping one another, to fill in the center. The slices will overlap more in the middle and fan out at the outside. You will probably still have a small empty spot in the middle; cut a piece of pear into a square shape to fill that in.

Brush and sprinkle any remaining lemon juice over the pears. Sprinkle the sugar over all.

Bake one-third up from the bottom in the preheated 400-degree oven for 50 minutes.

While the tart is baking, prepare the glaze.

GLAZE

1 cup apricot preserves
1 tablespoon dark rum, Cognac, or bourbon

Stir the preserves and liquor over moderate heat until melted. Force through a strainer set over a bowl. Return to the saucepan.

About 8 to 10 minutes before the tart is finished baking, bring the preserves to a boil and let them simmer slowly for about 5 minutes.

Remove the baked tart from the oven. Brush the hot preserves over the hot tart (if you are careful not to allow it to run down the sides, you can brush it over the top edge of the pastry). It will be a generous amount of glaze. After you have covered everything well, pour the remaining glaze, drizzling it slowly, over all the fruit.

Immediately return the glazed tart to the hot oven for 3 minutes—it sets the glaze.

Remove from the oven and cool to room temperature.

Place the cooled quiche pan over a bowl that is narrower than the diameter of the rim of the pan. The sides of the pan will slip down. Then, either serve the tart on the bottom of the pan, or transfer it to a large, flat serving plate or board. Use a flat-sided cookie sheet or the bottom of a quiche pan like a spatula to transfer the tart.

Refrigerate until serving time.

Purple Plum and Almond Tart

10 TO 12 PORTIONS

This is a large, colorful, mouth-watering, French fruit tart. You will need an 11 × 1-inch metal quiche pan with a separate bottom, or an 11 × 1-inch flan ring placed on a cookie sheet. The pan will be lined with pastry, prebaked, then covered with a ground almond filling and then with purple plum halves. It will all be baked together and then brushed with apricot preserves. The purple juices from the plums run over the almond filling and, if they are juicy, a bit might run over the rim of the pastry, making a gorgeous picture.

This should be served within 6 hours after it is made; after that it loses its fresh look.

FRENCH TART PASTRY (see page 136)

Prepare the pastry and place the ball of dough on a lightly floured pastry cloth. With your hands, flatten it into a round about 7 inches in diameter with smooth edges. Then, with a floured rolling pin, roll the dough into a circle 14 to 14½ inches in diameter.

Drape the pastry over the rolling pin and unroll it over the quiche pan or the flan ring on a cookie sheet. Ease the pastry down on the sides to fit into the pan where the sides and bottom meet. With scissors trim excess allowing ½- to ¾-inch overlap. Fold excess inside to form a double thickness on the rim and press together. The rim should extend only about ⅛ inch above the pan or ring.

If you wish, score a design on the edge by pressing the back of a table knife at an angle at ¼-inch intervals across the rim all around.

Place the pastry shell in the freezer until it is firm. Or, if you wish, this can be frozen for weeks.

When you are ready to bake, adjust a rack one-third up from the bottom of the oven and preheat oven to 375 degrees. Line the frozen pastry with a 12-inch square of aluminum foil. Let the corners of the foil stand up, do not fold them over the sides of the pastry. Fill the foil with dried beans or with pie weights.

Bake for 20 minutes, then remove the pastry from the oven, carefully remove the foil and beans by lifting the four corners and return the pastry to the oven to bake for 10 to 15 minutes more. During this time keep an eye on the bottom of the pastry; if it puffs up, prick it carefully with a cake tester. (The pastry will shrink away from the sides of the pan.)

The filling can be made while the pastry is baking or after it has been removed from the oven.

ALMOND AND PLUM FILLING

5 ounces (1 cup) blanched almonds
1 egg (graded large) plus 1 egg yolk
¼ teaspoon almond extract
1 tablespoon Cognac or brandy
¾ cup granulated sugar
2 ounces (½ stick) unsalted butter, melted
10 medium-size or large plums (about 2½
    pounds; I do not use the small blue
    plums for this)
1 tablespoon kirsch, Cognac, or brandy

The almonds must be ground to a fine powder; this can be done in a food processor, a blender (if you use a processor or a blender, add a large spoonful of the sugar to keep the nuts from lumping), or a nut grinder, but grind them fine. Set aside.

In the small bowl of an electric mixer, beat the egg and the yolk with the almond extract, Cognac, and ½ cup of the sugar (reserve remaining ¼ cup). Mix in the melted butter and the ground almonds.

If you have just baked the pastry shell, let it stand for about 10 minutes (it does not have to cool completely but it can if you wish). Raise the oven rack to one-third down from the top. The oven should be preheated to 375 degrees.

Cut the plums in half and remove the pits.

Spread the almond filling in an even layer over the bottom of the pastry shell. Cover the filling with the plums, placing them cut side down. Start with a circle of 12 halves on the outside (more or less, depending on the size of the plums), touching each other. Then, inside them, a circle of 6 halves (again, more or less, depending on the size), touching each other. And 1 half in the middle. With medium-size plums there will be 1 half of a plum left over.

Sprinkle with the reserved ¼ cup sugar. Drizzle with the 1 tablespoon kirsch or Cognac.

It is generally best not to place a quiche pan on a cookie sheet (it might prevent the bottom from browning). In this recipe the plum juice may run over; therefore, place a cookie sheet or a jelly-roll pan on a rack below to catch any overflow.

Bake for 30 to 45 minutes, depending on the ripeness of the fruit. It should be tender but not too soft. Test it with a cake tester.

While the tart is baking, prepare the glaze.

GLAZE

½ cup apricot preserves

Stir the preserves in a small pan over low heat until they are completely melted and come to a boil. Force them through a strainer. Return to the pan. Just before you remove the tart from the oven, bring the glaze to a boil again.

When the tart is removed from the oven it should stand for 2 or 3 minutes (no more) before the glaze is applied. (The fruit will be a little wrinkled now, but unless the tart was overbaked it won't be too shriveled.)

With a pastry brush, brush the hot glaze all over the fruit and over the space between the fruit and on the rim.

Return the tart to the oven for 2 or 3 minutes. (It helps to set the glaze.)

If some of the juice ran over the pastry it might make it difficult to remove the sides of the quiche pan or the flan ring after the tart has cooled. Therefore, do not wait until it cools. After about 5 minutes, remove the tart as follows.

Place the pan over a bowl that is smaller in diameter than the opening in the bottom of the pan. As you do, the sides of the pan should slide down. If it needs a little help, easy does it. Use a cookie sheet as a spatula to transfer the tart very carefully from the bottom of the pan to a serving platter. If it is stuck to the bottom, release it gently with a knife or a long, narrow spatula.

To remove the tart from a flan ring, lift the ring to remove it, and use a flat-sided cookie sheet as a spatula to transfer the tart very carefully to a serving platter.

Peach and Almond Tart

10 TO 12 PORTIONS

This variation of the previous Purple Plum and Almond Tart should be prepared only when peaches are at the height of their season. The pastry with its almond filling can be baked a day ahead if you wish and the peaches can be poached a day ahead if you wish. But an hour or two before serving, the peaches should be drained, placed on the tart, and glazed—it will take only about 10 minutes. And will be gorgeous.

FRENCH TART PASTRY (see page 136)

Follow the recipe for the Purple Plum and Almond Tart through the directions to place the almond filling in the partially baked tart shell. Bake on the center rack of a preheated 375-degree oven for 25 minutes until the filling is golden brown and barely firm to the touch. Set aside to cool.

PEACH TOPPING

5 large freestone peaches, ripe but firm
½ cup granulated sugar
¼ cup water
½ teaspoon vanilla extract
2 tablespoons kirsch, rum, or Cognac
½ cup apricot preserves

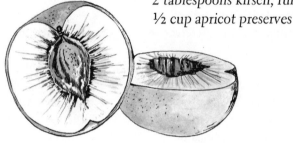

Blanch the peaches and peel them (see Stewed Peaches, page 404). Cut them in half, separate the halves, remove the pits, and cut each half into 6 even lengthwise slices.

Place the sugar, water, vanilla, and kirsch in a large, wide frying pan that has a tight cover. Stir over moderate heat until the sugar melts and the mixture comes to a boil.

Add the sliced peaches, reduce the heat to low, cover, and simmer gently, stirring the peaches very carefully a few times with a rubber spatula. Cook for only 3 to 5 minutes, more or less, depending on the ripeness of the peaches. They must not be overcooked or become limp. When they are just barely tender, use a slotted spoon and transfer them to a large, flat dish. (If you prepare the peaches a day ahead, cover the plate with plastic wrap and refrigerate overnight. Then continue with the next step.)

When the peaches are cool, place them carefully on several thicknesses of paper towels to drain well.

Meanwhile, remove the flan ring or the sides of the quiche pan.

Boil the syrup remaining in the pan for a few minutes over high heat until it thickens to a thick jelly. Watch it carefully and stir it occasionally with a wooden spatula.

Place the apricot preserves in a small, heavy saucepan over moderate heat. Add a scant tablespoon of the reduced peach syrup (see Note), stir occasionally until the preserves are melted, and then force through a strainer. Return the preserves to the saucepan, bring to a boil, then reduce the heat to low and keep the preserves warm.

Place the drained peaches on top of the almond filling as follows: Place 1 slice at a right angle to the rim on the right side of the tart (three o'clock) with the thick (curved) side facing up (twelve o'clock). Place another slice closer to you, slightly overlapping the first. Continue to form a circle of slices all around the tart, overlapping each other slightly more toward the center of the tart than on the outside, rather like a fan pattern. Then form another similar circle inside of the first. And continue until there is just a small space left in the center; it might be easiest to fill that if you dice a few of the slices. Or, if the peaches are really large, there might not be any space left in the center.

Brush the warm strained apricot preserves over the top to cover the peaches completely.

Transfer the tart, using a flat-sided cookie sheet or the bottom of a quiche pan as a spatula, to a large, flat serving plate or a board. Or, if you have baked this in a quiche pan, it may be served on the bottom of the pan if you wish.

It is best to serve this within an hour or two. The beautiful glaze on the peaches begins to fade.

NOTE: *The little bit of thick jelly that remains in the pan after boiling down the peach syrup may be scraped out and used as a jelly on toast.*

Lemon and Almond Tart

12 TO 16 PORTIONS

This has a prebaked pastry crust and two fillings: one almond (like marzipan) and one lemon (with juice, grated rind, and pieces of diced fresh lemon). Both fillings are poured into the baked crust and it is all baked together. The lemon and almond fillings run together and bake into a creamy, semifirm, custardy mixture.

Although this is still delicious after standing all day (and even overnight), here's how to serve it at its freshest, and yet not have any last-minute fuss. The pastry can be made way ahead of time and frozen, unbaked, in the pan. Then, it can be baked early in the day for that night. And, at the same time, the two fillings can be prepared (this does not take long). Cover the fillings and let the empty baked crust and the two fillings stand at room temperature until 3 or 4 hours (more or less) before serving. Then put it all together (it takes only a minute or two) to bake.

You will need a 12½ × 1-inch fluted metal quiche pan with a separate bottom, or a 12½ × 1-inch flan ring. And be prepared with a large enough flat serving platter or a serving board. Or, if you have used a quiche pan, serve the tart right on the bottom of the pan (placed on a tray or a board or whatever you have that is large enough).

FRENCH TART PASTRY (see page 136)

Prepare the pastry and place it on a lightly floured pastry cloth. With your hands, flatten it into a circle about 7 inches in diameter with smooth edges. Then, with a floured rolling pin, roll it out to a circle 15½ to 16 inches in diameter. If you are using a flan ring place it on a cookie sheet. (Do not place a quiche pan on a cookie sheet—it might keep the bottom from browning.)

Now, caution: This is such a wide circle of pastry that if you drape it over a rolling pin to transfer it, the weight of the pastry is very likely to cause it to come apart. It is safer to fold this loosely in half and then in half again to make a triangle and, with your hands, put it in the pan, placing it carefully to cover only one-quarter of the pan with the point in the middle. Then, carefully (try to keep your fingernails away), unfold and press it into place. If it is too large anywhere, and too small somewhere else, remove the excess and place it wherever you need it. If you patch the pastry, wet the ends a bit with water and be sure to press it securely; the patch must not open during baking. If you have a disaster while placing the pastry in the pan, either patch it or form it into a ball again and reroll (it might even behave better if it is rolled twice).

With scissors trim excess allowing a generous ½-inch overlap. Fold excess inside to form a double thickness on the rim, press together to form a strong rim that stands ⅛ to ¼ inch above the pan or ring. There must not be any low spots.

Place the pastry shell in the freezer until it is firm. Or, if you wish, this can be frozen for weeks. (Wrap after it becomes firm.)

When you are ready to bake, adjust a rack one-third up from the bottom of the oven and preheat the oven to 375 degrees.

Since the regular 12-inch aluminum foil will not be wide enough to line this pan, and the wider foil is too heavy to work with comfortably, use two pieces of the 12-inch foil, each about 17 inches long. Place them in the pastry, crossing each other at right angles. Press the foil into place in the pastry.

Fill the foil with dried beans or with the aluminum pellets that are made for that purpose.

Bake in the preheated oven for 20 minutes. Remove from the oven for a moment, carefully remove the foil and beans by lifting the bottom piece of foil (lift from opposite sides), and return the pastry to the oven to bake 10 to 15 minutes longer until it is lightly colored on the edges. Total baking time, 30 to 35 minutes. (The pastry will shrink away from the sides of the pan.) After removing the foil, keep an eye on the pastry; if the bottom puffs up, prick it immediately and gently with a cake tester.

While the pastry crust is baking, or after it has baked, prepare both fillings.

You will use the same oven rack position and oven temperature to bake this tart with the filling, therefore do not turn off the oven after baking the crust.

ALMOND FILLING

5 ounces (1 cup) blanched almonds
1 egg (graded large) plus 1 egg yolk
¼ teaspoon almond extract
1 tablespoon Cognac or kirsch
½ cup granulated sugar
2 ounces (½ stick) unsalted butter, melted

The almonds must be ground to a fine powder; this can be done in a food processor, a blender (when you grind nuts in a processor or a blender, adding a spoonful of the sugar will keep the nuts from lumping), or a nut grinder—but they must be ground fine. In the small bowl of an electric mixer, beat the egg and the yolk with the almond extract and Cognac or kirsch. Add the sugar and beat until it is pale. Mix in the melted butter and the ground almonds. Set aside.

LEMON FILLING

2 extra-large or 3 medium-size lemons
1 cup granulated sugar
2 teaspoons unsifted all-purpose flour

4 eggs (graded large)
1 cup light corn syrup
1½ tablespoons unsalted butter, melted

Grate fine the rind of 1 extra-large or 2 medium-size lemons. Squeeze the juice of 1 extra-large or 1½ medium-size lemons to make 3 tablespoons juice. Mix the juice with the rind. Set them aside. With a small, sharp paring knife, peel 1 extra-large or 1½ medium-size lemons. Carefully and completely remove every bit of white. Section the lemons by cutting down on either side of the membrane to loosen the sections. Remove all the pits. Place the wedge-shaped sections on a flat plate or a board and cut them lengthwise and then crosswise, making pieces about ¼ to ⅓ inch in diameter. However, if the lemons are small it will not be necessary to cut the wedges lengthwise—just crosswise. You should have approximately 3 tablespoons of pieces. (Use more or larger pieces if you wish.) Mix the pieces with the juice and rind.

In a small bowl stir the sugar and flour to mix.

In the small bowl of an electric mixer, or in any bowl with an egg beater or a wire whisk, beat the eggs just to mix. Beat in the sugar-flour mixture just to mix. Then mix in the corn syrup and the melted butter. With a rubber spatula stir in the lemon juice mixture.

Now pour the almond filling into the prebaked crust and smooth it with a rubber spatula or the back of a spoon. It will be a very thin layer.

Place the tart on a rack one-third up from the bottom in the preheated 375-degree oven.

With a ladle, gently ladle the lemon filling over the almond filling. It will not stay in separate layers; the lemon will run down into the almond —it is O.K. CAUTION! Be extremely careful when you pour the lemon filling into the tart; if any of it runs over the sides of the crust it will cause the tart to stick to the pan as though it were the strongest glue in the world—you will probably break the tart in trying to remove it from the pan. (Guess how I know?)

Bake for 35 to 40 minutes until a small, sharp knife inserted into the middle comes out clean. The top will become brown. Do not cover it with foil during baking (it would stick).

If it looks as though some filling might have run over, it is best to remove the tart immediately while everything is hot, before it cools and hardens. Carefully remove the sides of the quiche pan (by placing the pan on a bowl that is narrower than the opening in the bottom of the pan) or if you have used a flan ring, raise it gently with your fingers. If the bottom is stuck, use a long, sharp knife to release it. Then use a flat-sided cookie sheet, or the bottom of a quiche pan, to transfer the tart to a flat serving plate.

If it does not look as though some filling has run over, let the tart cool before removing it to a serving plate.

Let the tart stand for at least a few hours. Serve at room temperature.

SUGAR TOPPING

Sprinkle the top generously with confectioners sugar through a fine strainer held over the tart.

Yeast Cakes

ABOUT USING YEAST

All of these recipes are written for active dry yeast that comes in little packages, three packages fastened together. The expiration date is printed on the back; be sure to check it.

Dissolving

The liquid that the yeast is dissolved in should be from 105 to 115 degrees F when tested with a thermometer—I use a candy thermometer. To test it without a thermometer, sprinkle a bit of it on the inside of your wrist; it should feel comfortably warm.

Rising

Yeast doughs rise best at a temperature of about 85 to 90 degrees F. If the outdoor temperature or room temperature is close to that, simply cover the bowl or pan as directed and pick a draft-free spot. Or, if you have to create the right temperature, here's how: Place a large shallow pan of hot water on the bottom rack of the oven. And, if your oven has one, turn on the light (this adds heat). Place a room thermometer in the middle of the oven (mine does not stand so I hang it from an oven rack adjusted to the top position). Watch the thermometer; you will be able to maintain a steady temperature by adding additional hot water, or by opening the oven door a bit when necessary.

In many gas ovens, the pilot light gives off enough heat to maintain the correct temperature. And then, once the yeast has started to grow and the dough has started to rise, the dough itself gives off heat. Therefore it is not always necessary to use the pan of hot water.

If you want to delay the rising process, place the dough, at any stage during its rising, in the refrigerator. The cold will slow down the rising. Then, when it is placed in a warm temperature again, it will resume rising.

If a yeast dough has been shaped or poured into the pan, and has been rising in an 85-degree oven, it may be removed from the oven and may stand at room temperature while the oven is heating to the temperature specified for baking. But before you turn the oven on, don't forget to remove the room thermometer.

Kneading

Flour the dough lightly and shape it into a ball. Place it on a large board or roomy work surface. Push the heel of your right hand down into the dough and push hard, pushing away from you. Then, with your left hand, fold the further edge of the dough toward you and over the center, and at the same time give the dough a quarter turn to the right. Repeat pushing, folding, and turning the dough with a smooth rhythm. Keep extra flour handy as you knead; if the dough becomes sticky, flour the dough and the work surface as necessary. And keep a dough scraper handy to use if the dough sticks to the work surface.

The Embassy's Nut Crescents

48 CRESCENTS

These are from the Austrian Embassy in Washington, where they are the talk of the town. They are one of the very best pastries I ever ate; the lightest, tenderest, most delicate, most delicious, and most irresistible. This recipe can make your reputation as a pastry chef. And they are easy and fun to make, although they do take time.

There is a theory that crescents (croissants) of various doughs were first made in Vienna around 1683, at the time when the Turks were besieging Vienna. The crescent moon was the Turkish symbol. In a gesture of defiance the Viennese pastry chefs made bread and pastry in the crescent shape, implying "we can break you up and crumble you and eat you and there won't be anything left of you."

Serve these with afternoon tea or coffee, with breakfast, brunch, or a light luncheon, or, since they are so good, serve them anytime at all with or without anything at all.

The dough must be frozen for 1½ hours or refrigerated overnight before the pastries are shaped. Then they must rise for 2 hours before they are baked. Then you will be in heaven.

3 eggs (graded large or extra-large)
½ cup sour cream
8 ounces (2 sticks) unsalted butter,
    cold and firm

½ cup granulated sugar
5 cups plus 2 tablespoons sifted
    all-purpose flour
¾ teaspoon salt
¼ cup warm water (105 to 115 degrees,
    see Dissolving, page 221)
2 packages active dry yeast
Finely grated rind of 1 large or
    2 small lemons
1 egg white (to be used just before baking for
    brushing on top)

In a small bowl, with a beater or a whisk, beat the eggs to mix. Add the sour cream and beat to blend. Set aside.

On a board or flat plate, cut the butter into small pieces; cut each stick lengthwise into quarters and then cut across into small dice. Set aside.

Remove and reserve about ½ teaspoon of the sugar. Into a large mixing bowl sift the remaining sugar with the flour and salt. (See Notes for mixing in a food processor.) Add the butter. With a pastry blender cut the butter into the sifted dry ingredients until the mixture resembles coarse meal. Set aside.

Warm a 1-cup glass measuring cup by filling it with warm water. Let stand for a few minutes. Empty it, and then pour in the ¼ cup warm water. Add the reserved ½ teaspoon of sugar. Sprinkle the yeast on top. Stir with a table knife to mix. Let stand for a few minutes until the mixture rises up to near the top of the cup.

Then stir the yeast mixture, the egg mixture, and the grated lemon rind into the butter and flour mixture. Mix thoroughly with a heavy wooden spatula.

Spread out a long piece of wax paper (about 20 inches long). You will use it after the dough is kneaded.

Turn the dough out onto a large board or work surface. It will be sticky. To knead it, hold a dough scraper or a wide metal spatula in your left hand and, with the scraper or spatula, lift the mass of dough, turn it over, and with the palm of your right hand push off the dough and then spread it away from you, pushing it against the work surface. Continue for 5 minutes. The dough will still be sticky. (But kneading it is not a bad experience; actually, you can really just handle it roughly any way that is comfortable for you.)

Then, with the scraper or spatula, transfer the dough to the spread-out wax paper. Fold the paper over the top and, with your hands, form the dough into a flat, round shape about 8 inches in diameter.

Without spoiling the shape, slide the dough in the wax paper into a plastic bag, or wrap it loosely in foil.

Freeze for 1½ hours (or longer) or refrigerate overnight. (If the dough is frozen much longer, or for a few days, it must be refrigerated overnight or it will be too stiff to handle.)

FILLING

> 5 ounces (1¼ cups) walnuts
> 2½ ounces (½ cup) currants
> 1 cup granulated sugar
> 3 ounces (¾ stick) unsalted butter, melted
> ¼ cup heavy cream
> 1 teaspoon vanilla extract

Chop the walnuts very fine. In a bowl, mix the nuts with the currants and sugar. Then stir in the butter. Mix the cream and vanilla, and add to the mixture. Refrigerate.

Before shaping the crescents, lightly butter cookie sheets, or have ready nonstick sheets or jelly-roll pans.

To shape the crescents, cut the cold dough into 8 equal pie-shaped wedges. Work with one piece at a time, keep the others refrigerated or frozen.

Flour your hands and press the piece of dough into a ball. Flatten it a bit. Then, on a lightly floured board, with a floured rolling pin, roll the dough out to form a 9-inch round. The shape does not have to be perfectly even.

With a pastry cutter or a pizza wheel, or with a long, sharp knife, cut the dough into 6 pie-shaped wedges.

Place a slightly rounded teaspoonful of the filling close to the wider base of each wedge; do not spread it out. Starting at the base, roll the wedge toward the point, enclosing the filling. (It is not necessary to fuss with the ends, or to pinch any seams together, because when the dough rises and bakes it will meld together and will form one mass of dough with the filling in the middle.)

Place each roll, as you roll it up, on the prepared sheet, with the point underneath. Turn the horns down to shape into short, fat crescents. Place the crescents 2 inches apart.

Cover loosely with a thin, lightweight cotton towel or linen or cotton napkin or with loose plastic wrap or wax paper and let rise (see Rising, page 221) for 2 hours until double in size.

About 15 or 20 minutes before the crescents have finished rising, adjust two racks to divide the oven into thirds (if you bake only one sheet at a time bake it in the center of the oven) and preheat the oven to 350 degrees.

Beat the egg white only until it is barely foamy. With a soft brush, gently brush the white over the top of the crescents.

Bake for 15 minutes until nicely browned. If you bake two sheets at once, reverse them top to bottom and front to back after 10 minutes to ensure even browning. If you bake only one sheet at a time and if the crescents in the back are browning sooner than those in front, turn the sheet front to back.

A little bit of the filling might run out of a few of these—it will not be much—don't worry about it.

With a wide metal spatula (or a plastic spatula if you are using a nonstick pan) transfer the crescents to racks to cool.

After only a few minutes, eat a crescent while it is still quite warm. These are sensational warm or cold, but please do taste one warm.

Two or three crescents should be an adequate portion, but I saw an entire batch disappear when a few friends stopped in unexpectedly while I was baking.

NOTES: 1. *To use a food processor for cutting the butter into the dry ingredients, fit the processor with the metal blade. Then, unless you have an extra-large processor, do it in two batches, placing half of the dry ingredients in the bowl and adding half of the cut-up butter in each batch. Process for about 10 seconds with quick on-and-off pulses until the mixture resembles coarse meal. Transfer both batches to a large mixing bowl and stir in the remaining ingredients.*

2. *It is not necessary to bake these all at once. The dough may be stored for a few days in the freezer or refrigerator, and the crescents may be baked only 6 at a time.*

3. *The baked crescents may be frozen. Place them in a single layer on a tray and cover airtight with plastic wrap. Or, package them two together, bottoms together, in plastic sandwich bags, and place all the bags in a strong box. Handle them as carefully as you possibly can.*

Miniature Schnecken

This has to be one of the most exciting and most gratifying of all my kitchen activities.

If you have never used yeast before, don't be afraid to make these. They are easy, but they do take time. And they must be started a day ahead, as the dough must be refrigerated overnight. But if they had to be started a month ahead, I would make arrangements; they are that good.

"Schnecken" is the German word for snails. They are made of a rich dough, rolled around a filling of sugar, cinnamon, nuts, and currants and baked in pans lined with sugar, butter, and pecans. When the Schnecken are turned out of the pans, the sugar, butter, and pecans become a scrumptious topping.

Technically, these are bite-size coffee cakes. They are incredibly delicious, light, tender, delicate, gorgeous, and extremely popular.

The recipe is written for pans that make small muffins. I especially like one of my pans that came from a wholesale restaurant supply store. (But it is now available at many kitchen shops. It can be bought at, or ordered by mail from, Bobbi & Carole's Cookshop, 7251 S.W. 57th Court, Miami, Florida 33143.) It has 24 muffin forms, each one is 2 inches in diameter at the top and 1¼ inches in depth. That size is slightly larger than the forms for small muffins that are sold in retail hardware stores. Either size works well. It is best to use a pan that is not very shiny; a shiny pan prevents browning. This recipe makes 36 Schnecken; I use my pan that makes 24 plus a hardware store pan that makes 12. But they can be made larger or smaller depending on the size of your muffin pans. And I bake them in two ovens. But you can bake part of the recipe at a time. The dough can wait in the refrigerator for as long as 3 days if you wish. Or the shaped and risen dough can wait in the kitchen for about 20 minutes until you have room in the oven. To be sure that the bottoms are dark enough, it is best to bake these on only one rack at a time.

DOUGH

1 envelope (¼ ounce) active dry yeast
2 tablespoons warm water (see Dissolving, page 221)
¼ cup granulated sugar
3 ounces (¾ stick) unsalted butter, cut into small pieces, at room temperature
2 tablespoons milk, scalded

1 egg (graded large, extra-large, or jumbo),
    at room temperature
½ cup sour cream, at room temperature
½ teaspoon salt
About 2¾ cups unsifted all-purpose or
    bread flour

Sprinkle the yeast over the warm water in a small bowl, stir with a fork or a table knife to mix, and set aside.

Place the sugar and butter in a large mixing bowl (this may be mixed in an electric mixer or by hand with a wooden or rubber spatula). Add the hot milk and mix until the butter is melted. Add the egg and stir or beat to mix; mix in the sour cream, and then the yeast. Add the salt and 1¾ cups of the flour (reserve the remaining 1 cup of flour until the following day) and beat until the mixture is very smooth. (It will be thick and sticky.)

Lightly butter a 6-cup bowl (if you double the recipe, the bowl must be twice as large). Place the dough in the buttered bowl, cover airtight with plastic wrap or foil, and refrigerate overnight, or for as long as 3 days.

The refrigerated dough should rise to double in bulk, or to the top of the bowl. Use a wooden spatula and stir the dough briefly to deflate it.

When you are going to bake the Schnecken, prepare the pans as follows:

MIXTURE #1: TOPPING

8 ounces (2 sticks) unsalted butter
1 tablespoon plus 1 teaspoon light corn syrup
1 cup plus 3 tablespoons light brown sugar,
    firmly packed
3½ ounces (1 cup) pecan halves

Remove and set aside 5½ ounces (1 stick plus 3 tablespoons) of the butter. Melt the remaining 2½ ounces (5 tablespoons) of the butter.

Use part of the melted butter to prepare the muffin pans; brush it on generously with a pastry brush. Reserve the remaining melted butter to brush on the rolled-out dough.

Beat the reserved 5½ ounces of unmelted butter with the corn syrup to mix, add the sugar and beat until thoroughly mixed. Divide this mixture among the buttered muffin forms, placing a generous teaspoonful in the bottom of each form (it is not necessary to spread it around). Then place 2 or 3 of the pecan halves (depending on their size) in each form, placing them touching each other, flat side up, and pressing them deeply into the butter and sugar mixture. Set the prepared pans aside.

TO SHAPE THE SCHNECKEN

Place the 1 cup of flour reserved from the dough on a large board or work surface and spread it out slightly. Turn the chilled dough onto the board. Knead (see Kneading, page 222) for about 8 minutes, incorporating all of the flour. (At first it will look as though you have too much flour, but after a few minutes of kneading you will see that the dough will absorb all of it.) Form the dough into a ball, flour it lightly, cover it loosely with a kitchen towel, and let stand for 10 or 15 minutes.

Then form the dough into a cylinder about 15 inches long and 2½ inches in diameter (the shape must be even). With your fingers, flatten it slightly.

With additional flour, lightly flour a large board or work surface and a rolling pin. Roll the dough in both directions until it is about 25 inches long and 9 to 10 inches wide. While you are rolling, do try to keep the shape oblong and the edges even—at least as even as you can. If the dough seems rubbery and shrinks back after you roll it (and it probably will), let it stand for about 10 minutes and then roll again. It might be necessary to let it stand more than once while you are rolling it.

Brush the rolled-out dough with the remaining melted butter.

MIXTURE #2: FILLING

Boiling water
½ cup currants
½ cup granulated sugar
2½ teaspoons cinnamon
2½ ounces (generous ¾ cup) pecans, finely
    chopped (they should not be ground but
    they must be fine)
Finely grated rind of 2 large lemons

Pour boiling water over the currants to cover them and let stand for 1 minute (no longer—they lose their taste and texture if they soak too long), drain them in a strainer, and then turn them out onto several thicknesses of paper towels, fold the paper over the top, and press on it to remove excess water. Set aside.

Mix the sugar and cinnamon and with a large spoon sprinkle it over the buttered dough (sprinkle all the way to both narrow ends or the end Schnecken won't have any). Then with your fingers sprinkle with the currants, pecans, and grated rind (again all the way to both narrow ends but stop a bit short of one long side).

Now carefully roll like a jelly roll, rolling tightly from the long side where the filling reaches the edge. As you roll, watch the ends of the roll; pull out the dough a bit or push it in as necessary to keep the ends about the same thickness as the rest of the roll. Pinch the seam to seal it.

With your hands, stretch the rolled-up dough gently until it is 36 inches in length. (If your work area is not wide enough, the roll of dough may be cut in half, and each half handled separately.)

With a sharp knife carefully cut the roll into slices. (It is a good idea to mark the slices with a ruler in order to have them all the same size.) If the muffin forms measure 2 inches in width and 1¼ inches in depth, the slices should be a scant 1 inch in width. But if the forms are smaller, the slices should be only about ½ inch in width. (See Note.)

Place the slices, one cut side down, in the prepared pans.

With your fingers, press on each slice firmly to press it down into the pan. (The tops of the slices will come just about to the tops of the pans, but they may be a bit higher or lower.)

Cover each pan loosely with plastic wrap or with a lightweight kitchen towel or cloth napkin; it must not be tight—the dough needs room to rise. Place the pans in a warm spot (see Rising, page 221) and let stand for about 1½ to 1¾ hours until the dough is puffy and slightly risen. (It will feel light and airy if you touch it very gently, although it might not look actually doubled.) The Schnecken will rise a bit more while they are baking.

About 20 minutes before the Schnecken have finished rising, adjust a rack one-third up from the bottom of the oven. Preheat the oven to 375 degrees.

Bake the Schnecken for 20 to 25 minutes until they are richly colored. They should not be pale. If you have used one large pan, when the baking time is slightly more than half finished, reverse it front to back if necessary to ensure even browning.

You will need a flat cookie sheet or a jelly-roll pan to turn the baked Schnecken onto; the sheet or pan must be slightly larger than the pan of Schnecken.

As soon as they are removed from the oven, DON'T WAIT, immediately cover with a flat sheet, hold firmly with pot holders at both sides, and turn both the sheet and the pan over. Let stand for only about 10 or 15 seconds, then lift the pan an inch or so from the sheet and wait briefly for all the Schnecken to slip out.

Any caramelized sugar-butter mixture that runs off the Schnecken may be scooped up (with a table knife) and replaced on top of the Schnecken while they are still hot.

Now, if you can, wait about a minute (at least) before you gobble these up. Serve them warm. Or let them stand and serve them cool. Or freeze them; thaw before serving.

NOTE: *If the muffin forms are very small, and if you cut slices that are less than 1 inch thick, you will make more than 36 miniature Schnecken. If you have only a few extra, they may be baked in any small pans. I have used individual brioche pans and baba pans. Or you could use custard cups. Or you could place them close to each other in a small round or square pan that they fit. If you do not have any of the butter-sugar-corn syrup mixture left over, it is enough if you just butter the extra pans. Small pans or cups should be placed on a cake pan or on any small sheet to keep them from toppling over in the oven. They can wait at room temperature until you have room for them in the oven. Or, before you let them rise, they can be covered and refrigerated, to rise and bake some other time. (The rising time will naturally be longer if they are taken directly from the refrigerator.)*

Savarin

10 PORTIONS

According to culinary history, in the year 1609, Stanislaus Leszczynski, the king of Poland, was eating a piece of dry kugelhopf. He was inspired to pour some rum over the cake. It was genius; the rum-soaked cake was so delicious it became his favorite, and, incidentally, one of Stanislaus's main claims to fame. The king named the cake Ali Baba, the name of the hero in his favorite story from A Thousand and One Nights. *It became the rage in Paris at the beginning of the nineteenth century, and the name was then abbreviated to Baba. In the year 1840, a French pastry chef used the same recipe without the raisins and he named it after his hero, Brillat-Savarin. This too became famous, and the name was later shortened to Savarin. It is a light and airy Baba au Rhum without raisins.*

It is an easy yeast dough (no kneading and only 1 rising), made in a fancy pan, soaked, after baking, with a mild rum syrup and coated with a shiny apricot glaze. It is a dessert cake either just as it is or with whipped cream and brandied fruit.

Since this is such a de luxe dessert, and quite easy, consider it for your next party. Or, if you are like I am, make it immediately for yourself.

You will need a one-piece fancy tube pan or a deep ring mold with a 10-cup capacity.

The method for using yeast in this recipe is called the "sponge method." It was a more popular method in the days when yeast might have been stale when it was sold; this method assured that the yeast was alive and well before it was used.

SPONGE

½ cup warm milk (100 to 115 degrees,
    see Dissolving, page 221)
1 package active dry yeast
2 tablespoons granulated sugar
½ cup sifted all-purpose flour

To warm the large bowl of an electric mixer, place the bowl in the sink and run hot tap water into it for a minute, and then pour the water out. Pour the warm milk into the warm bowl. Sprinkle the yeast over the milk, let stand for 5 minutes, and then stir briefly with a fork. Add the sugar and stir. Add the flour and stir (or beat with the mixer) just to mix well. Cover with plastic wrap and let stand at a temperature of 80 to 90 degrees (see Rising, page 221) for about 30 minutes, or just until the mixture is bubbly. (Sugar and flour are the two foods that yeast needs in order to grow. It will bubble as it grows. And a warm temperature will make it grow quickly.)

While the yeast is proofing (or proving, as in "proving that it is O.K."), butter a 9-inch (10-cup) fancy tube pan or a plain ring mold and dust it all over lightly with fine, dry bread crumbs (butter and crumb the pan even if it has a nonstick finish), and tap to shake out excess crumbs over a piece of paper. Set aside.

DOUGH

2½ ounces (½ cup) blanched almonds
4 ounces (1 stick) unsalted butter
4 eggs (graded large), at room temperature
1½ cups sifted all-purpose flour
¼ teaspoon salt

The almonds may be prepared way ahead of time if you wish. First, they should be toasted. Place them in a shallow pan in a 350-degree oven and shake or stir occasionally until they become a pale, light gold color. Then they must be ground to a fine powder; this may be done in a food processor, a blender, or a nut grinder. Set the toasted and ground nuts aside.

The butter should be melted very slowly. Cut it into pieces and melt it over low heat; it should become only lukewarm. Set it aside briefly.

Now, beat the sponge mixture with the mixer only to deflate it. Add the almonds and beat only to mix. Then, on low speed, add the eggs alternately with the flour and salt, scraping the bowl with a rubber spatula and beating until smooth after each addition. Beat in the butter before the last addition of flour.

Then beat at medium-high speed for 10 minutes until the dough becomes elastic. (If it starts to crawl up on the beaters, reduce the speed as necessary.)

Pour into the prepared pan, smooth the top, and cover with plastic wrap. Let rise (see Rising, page 221). It will take about 50 minutes for the dough to double in bulk; at that time it will be about ½ inch below the sides of the pan, slightly higher in the middle.

About 15 or 20 minutes before the dough has finished rising, adjust a rack one-quarter or one-third up from the bottom of the oven and preheat the oven to 375 degrees.

Bake the cake for 20 minutes until it is light brown; the top will have risen almost another inch.

Cover the hot cake with a rack, turn over the cake pan and the rack, remove the pan (don't wash it—you are going to use it again), and let the cake stand fancy side up for about 15 minutes.

Meanwhile, prepare the syrup.

RUM SYRUP

2 cups water
1 cup granulated sugar
½ cup dark rum

Mix the sugar and water in a saucepan over moderately high heat stirring until the sugar is dissolved and the mixture comes to a boil. Simmer without stirring for 15 minutes. Remove from the heat and stir in the rum.

Carefully replace the pan that the cake was baked in over the cake. Turn the cake pan and the rack over, leaving the cake in the pan again. With a small, sharp knife cut many shallow slits in the crust on top of the cake (in order to make it easy for the cake to absorb the syrup).

Slowly pour the hot syrup over the cake. It will absorb it all and it will remain miraculously light. Let stand for 1 to 1½ hours in the pan.

Cover the cake with a flat cake plate. Turn the cake pan and the plate over and remove the pan again, leaving the cake flat side down on the plate.

Prepare the glaze.

APRICOT GLAZE

½ cup apricot preserves
2 tablespoons granulated sugar
2 tablespoons dark rum

In a small saucepan over moderate heat cook the preserves and sugar, stirring constantly, until the mixture comes to a boil. Boil slowly, stirring, for 5 minutes, or until the mixture registers 225 degrees on a candy thermometer.

Press the hot glaze through a strainer and stir in the rum.

With a pastry brush, brush the hot glaze all over the cake.

This can be served (deliciously) with sweetened and vanilla-flavored whipped cream (which may be served separately or heaped in the center of the cake) and brandied fruit (i.e., black Bing cherries, apricots, pears, peaches, or pineapple), or with any simply stewed fruit without the brandy. Or with fresh raspberries or strawberries.

NOTE: *The Savarin may be frozen, but it will look best if you freeze it without the syrup and glaze; apply the syrup and glaze the day it is served. The cake does not have to be hot when the syrup is applied, but it must be completely thawed.*

Babka

1 LARGE 9-INCH CAKE

This Polish cake is traditionally served at Easter time, but it is so popular that many bakeries in many countries make it all year. It is one of the most elegant coffee cakes: plain, but rich and buttery, generously studded with raisins, and golden colored from the many egg yolks. It is easily made without kneading, and has only one rising. This keeps well and is even better a day after it is baked. You will need a one-piece 9-inch kugelhopf pan or other fancy tube pan with a 10-cup capacity. But there is one hitch. If the cake is baked in a shiny metal pan, it will be too pale. It will be gorgeous if it is baked in a 10-cup, nonstick, Bundt pan (if you have one this size, treasure it—it seems that the manufacturer has stopped making it), or in a black iron kugelhopf pan made by Le Creuset under the name "Cousances" (available at many kitchen shops, including Cooktique, 9 Railroad Avenue, Tenafly, New Jersey 07670).

¼ cup very warm water (105 to 115 degrees, see Dissolving, page 221)
1 envelope active dry yeast
½ cup plus 1 teaspoon granulated sugar
6 ounces (1½ sticks) unsalted butter
6 egg yolks (from eggs graded large, extra-large, or jumbo)
3 cups unsifted all-purpose flour
½ teaspoon salt
¾ cup milk
Finely grated rind of 2 medium-size lemons
5 ounces (1 cup) raisins (they may be half dark and half light or all of either color)
Optional: confectioners sugar

Fill a small bowl with hot water to warm it; shake out the water but do not dry the bowl. Place the ¼ cup of warm water in the bowl, sprinkle the yeast over it, add 1 teaspoon of the sugar (reserve the remaining ½ cup of sugar), and stir with a fork or a knife to mix. Let stand at room temperature for about 10 minutes; the mixture will start to increase in bulk.

Meanwhile, in the large bowl of an electric mixer, beat the butter until it is soft. Add the reserved ½ cup of granulated sugar and mix well. Add the yolks, two or three at a time, and beat until the mixture lightens a bit in color. Add the yeast mixture, about half of the flour (reserve the remaining half), and the salt. Beat to mix.

Meanwhile, in a small saucepan, on low heat, warm the milk until it registers 105 to 115 degrees on a candy thermometer.

Gradually add the warm milk to the yeast mixture, and then add the reserved flour, and beat on low speed until smooth.

Continue to beat on low speed for 3 minutes, and then remove from the mixer.

Sprinkle the lemon rind over the batter (do not drop it on in one lump or it will stay that way) and stir with a heavy wooden or a large rubber spatula to mix well. Then mix in the raisins.

Butter a 10-cup, fancy-shaped tube pan (see above—butter the pan even if it is nonstick); it is best to do this with a pastry brush and soft (not melted) butter.

Pour the dough evenly into the pan. With the back of a spoon, smooth the top.

Cover with buttered plastic wrap (buttered side down). Let rise (see Rising, page 221) for about 2 hours or a little longer until the dough reaches the top of the pan; in the center, the dough should be just slightly above the top of the pan—on the edges, slightly below. However, before it is quite that high, remove the plastic wrap (the dough might stick to it even though it is buttered).

Before baking, adjust a rack one-third up from the bottom of the oven and preheat the oven to 400 degrees.

Bake the cake at 400 degrees for 5 minutes, then reduce the temperature to 350 degrees and bake for 30 minutes more (total baking time is 35 minutes). The top should be well browned, but if it seems to be too dark, cover it loosely with foil.

Remove from the oven and let the cake stand in the pan for 10 minutes. Then cover with a rack, carefully turn over pan and rack, and remove the pan. Let stand until completely cool.

Wrap the cooled cake and let it stand overnight, or for at least several hours. If you are in a hurry for it, refrigerate or freeze it briefly.

If you wish, sprinkle the top with confectioners sugar before serving.

NOTE: *You can keep this in the freezer and, for an unplanned occasion, you can slice it frozen—it will slice nicely. Then, the slices will thaw quickly. Or, for a special treat, toast them.*

Kugelhopf

1 LARGE CAKE THAT
MAKES ABOUT
16 PORTIONS

This is a plain but rich and buttery, slightly dry, not-too-sweet raisin-nut coffee cake made with an easy yeast dough. There is no kneading and only one rising. The traditional kugelhopf mold is a tube pan with a fluted design. The shape was said to have been inspired by the sultan's turban (the pan is also called a Turk's head) when the Turks were defeated at the gates of Vienna in 1683. *The Viennese bakers who helped defend their city during the siege created this as a victory cake.* (Although some history books say it was created in the year 1609 at Lemberg, Poland; see Savarin, page 230.)

You will need a one-piece fancy tube pan with a 12-cup capacity. Generally, a fancy tube pan with a 10-inch diameter across the top has a 12-cup capacity.

Start this ahead of time. It is best to marinate the raisins overnight, and I think the cake is best the day after it is baked, although many people like it fresh from the oven.

2½ ounces (½ cup) dark raisins
5 ounces (1 cup) light raisins
} or use 1½ cups dark raisins

⅓ cup kirsch or light rum
About 15 whole blanched almonds (to prepare the cake pan)
1 cup milk
2 packages active dry yeast
¾ cup granulated sugar
8 ounces (2 sticks) unsalted butter
1 tablespoon vanilla extract
¼ teaspoon ginger
¼ teaspoon nutmeg
5 eggs (graded large), at room temperature
4 cups unsifted all-purpose flour
1 teaspoon salt
Finely grated rind of 2 large lemons
2½ ounces (½ cup) blanched or unblanched almonds, thinly sliced
Optional: ½ cup diced candied citron or orange peel

Confectioners sugar *(to be sprinkled over the baked cake)*

Place both raisins and the kirsch or rum in a jar with a tight cover. Let stand for a few hours or overnight, turning the jar from side to side occasionally.

Prepare a 12-cup fancy tube pan by brushing soft (not melted) butter all over the pan. The 10-inch Bundt pan makes a gorgeous kugelhopf; butter and crumb the pan even if it has a nonstick lining. Dust it with fine, dry bread crumbs and then tap to shake out excess crumbs over a piece of paper. Place a whole blanched almond in the bottom of each flute in the design. Set the prepared pan aside.

Heat the milk until it reaches 105 to 115 degrees on a candy thermometer; when it is right it will feel comfortably warm if it is sprinkled on the inside of your wrist. Transfer to a small bowl to stop the cooking. Sprinkle the yeast over the milk. Add 1 teaspoon of the sugar (reserve the remaining sugar) and stir with a fork or a table knife until all the yeast is moistened. Set aside.

Place the butter in the large bowl of an electric mixer and beat until it is soft. Add the vanilla, ginger, nutmeg, and the reserved sugar and beat until very well mixed. Add the eggs one at a time, beating well after each addition. On low speed mix in about half (2 cups) of the flour, beat until smooth, gradually add the yeast mixture and beat until smooth, then add about 1 more cup of the flour. Beat at moderate speed for about 5 minutes. Add the remaining 1 cup of flour and the salt and beat for 2 or 3 minutes more. (If the batter climbs up on the beaters, use the lowest speed or beat with a wooden spatula.)

Remove from the mixer. Stir in the lemon rind, sliced almonds, optional citron or orange peel, and the marinated raisins (along with any unabsorbed kirsch or rum). Stir well to be sure that the nuts and fruits are evenly distributed.

Gently, in order not to disturb the almonds, pour into the prepared pan, with the back of a spoon smooth the top, and cover with buttered plastic wrap (buttered side down). Let rise at 80 to 90 degrees (see Rising, page 221) for about 1 hour until doubled in size; it will probably be ¼ inch below the top of the pan on the rim and even with the top, or slightly above, in the middle. (Don't worry if it rises a little higher. Traditionally, kugelhopf rises so high it looks as though the pan were too small.) While it is rising it will be necessary to remove the plastic wrap before the dough rises into it; it might stick even though the plastic is buttered. Then let it finish rising uncovered.

To prepare the oven for baking, adjust a rack to the lowest position.

(Remove any other racks—they will be in the way when you reach in to cover the pan with foil.) Preheat the oven to 400 degrees.

Bake the cake for 10 minutes (it will rise about another inch above the top of the pan during those 10 minutes, but then, during baking, it will settle down a bit). Then reduce the temperature to 350 degrees and continue to bake for another 20 minutes, then cover it loosely with foil to prevent the top from becoming too dark and continue to bake another 20 minutes (total baking time is about 50 minutes).

When the cake is done, a cake tester inserted into the middle will come out clean and dry and the cake will begin to come away slightly from the sides of the pan.

Cool in the pan for 10 minutes, then cover with a rack, turn over the pan and rack, remove the pan, and let the kugelhopf cool for several hours or overnight before serving. Sprinkle it with confectioners sugar (either plain or vanilla sugar; see page 4), straining the sugar through a fine strainer held over the cake.

Election Day Cake

4 8-INCH LOAVES

This is more than a recipe, it is a lesson in American history. More than a century ago this cake was a payoff that was given by politicians to men who voted a straight party ticket. I can't find out which political party it was; it might have been both parties. The custom started in Hartford, Connecticut, and spread through much of New England.

It is a light and airy, brandied and spiced, not-too-sweet raisin bread with white icing—plain and old-fashioned. Hostesses make it today to serve as a coffee cake at election parties while waiting for the returns to come in, or as a sweet bread for breakfast or brunch. Apart from its original payola purpose it is marvelous any time, and I cast my vote for it any day.

The fruit should be marinated overnight or for at least 6 hours before you mix the dough.

This recipe makes 4 loaves in 8 × 4 × 2½-inch pans. That size has a 5-cup capacity. If you must use slightly larger pans it will be all right, but if the pans are much larger the loaves will not be as high and pretty.

5 ounces (1 cup) light raisins

5 ounces (1 cup) dark raisins

½ cup diced citron (candied pineapple could
be substituted)

4 ounces (generous 1 cup) walnuts, cut or
broken into medium-size pieces

½ cup brandy

¾ cup warm water (105 to 115 degrees, see
Dissolving, page 221)

1 cup granulated sugar

4 envelopes active dry yeast

¾ cup milk

1¼ teaspoons salt

8 ounces (2 sticks) unsalted butter, cut into
small pieces, at room temperature

2 eggs, beaten

8 cups sifted all-purpose flour (you might need
a bit more for kneading)

½ teaspoon cinnamon

½ teaspoon nutmeg

½ teaspoon allspice

¼ teaspoon cloves

Place both kinds of raisins, citron, walnuts, and brandy in a jar with a tight cover (1-quart size is O.K. if you push the fruit down tightly). Cover the jar securely, place it in a bowl (in case it leaks), and turn it from side to side and from top to bottom occasionally and let stand overnight.

When the fruit is ready, proceed with the recipe.

Warm a bowl with about a 4-cup capacity by letting warm water run into it. Dry it quickly. Place the ¾ cup warm water in the warm bowl. Add 2 tablespoons of the sugar (reserve the remaining sugar) and sprinkle the yeast over the top. Stir with a table knife to mix. Set aside uncovered at room temperature to rise for about 10 minutes.

Meanwhile, place the milk, the reserved sugar, the salt, and the butter in a saucepan over moderate heat and stir until the mixture is warm (105 to 115 degrees). The butter will not all be melted but it should be soft.

Transfer the warm milk and butter mixture to a very large mixing bowl. Add the eggs and the yeast mixture. Stir to mix well. (If the butter is still in lumps, stir briefly with a strong wire whisk.)

Resift 1 cup of the flour with the cinnamon, nutmeg, allspice, and cloves, and stir it into the yeast mixture. Then, with a heavy wooden spatula, stir in 5 or 6 more cups of the flour, or as much as you can stir in.

Spread out the remaining flour on a large board or work surface. Turn the dough out on top of it. Knead to incorporate all of the flour. Then (see Kneading, page 222) knead the dough (if it is too sticky to knead, add only a few more spoonfuls of additional flour as necessary) for 5 minutes until it is beautifully smooth and elastic. (It is a wonderful dough to handle.)

You will need a large bowl for the dough to rise in. Mine has a 7-quart capacity. Butter the bowl. Place the dough in the bowl, turn it over to butter all sides, cover with plastic wrap, and let rise (see Rising, page 221) for 1 hour, in which time it will more than double in bulk (in a 7-quart bowl it will rise to about 1 inch from the top of the bowl).

Meanwhile, drain the marinated fruit in a strainer. If there is any brandy that has not been absorbed, do not use it for this recipe. Spread out several long thicknesses of paper towels, spread the fruit on the paper, and pat the top with more paper, to dry the fruit a bit.

When the dough has risen, make a fist and punch down the middle of the dough to deflate it. Then turn the sides in toward the middle.

Turn the dough out onto a lightly floured board or work surface. With a floured rolling pin, roll it out until it is about ¼ inch thick and about 20 inches in diameter (any shape is O.K.).

Spread the drained fruit all over the rolled-out dough. Roll it up like a jelly roll. Then fold both ends in toward the center. Press down firmly, and knead all together for a few moments to distribute the fruit evenly. Form the dough into a ball. With a long, heavy knife, cut it carefully into quarters.

Then form each quarter into a ball by holding it in your hands and pulling the sides around to the bottom and pushing them into the center. Let the balls stand for a few moments.

Butter 4 loaf pans that measure 8 × 4 × 2½ inches.

On the floured board with the floured rolling pin, roll one ball of dough into an oblong or oval 7 × about 12 inches. Roll up from a narrow end like a jelly roll. (It should be a nice, even shape, but if not, shape it a bit with your hands. Or, if necessary, reroll it.)

Place the rolled-up dough, seam down, in a buttered pan. Do not press down or flatten the loaf; there will be a little empty space in the pan on both long sides. Prepare all 4 loaves.

Cover the loaves loosely with a lightweight towel and let rise (see Rising, page 221) for 1¼ to 1½ hours; the loaves should rise a generous 1 inch above the tops of 8 × 4 × 2½-inch pans.

About 20 minutes before the loaves have finished rising adjust a rack one-third up from the bottom of the oven and preheat the oven to 350 degrees.

Place the loaves in the oven. They will start to brown rather quickly; when the tops are dark enough, cover them loosely with foil. If the loaves in the back of the oven brown faster than those in the front, reverse the pans from front to back after about 25 minutes. Bake for a total of 50 minutes until done.

As soon as the loaves are removed from the oven they should be turned out onto racks to cool. (A few raisins will probably have popped out on top and become burnt; pick them off.)

Place the loaves, on racks, over foil or wax paper.

After about 10 minutes, while the loaves are still warm, prepare the glaze.

GLAZE

¼ cup heavy cream
1 teaspoon vanilla extract
2 cups strained confectioners sugar

In a small pan over moderate heat, heat the cream until it is hot but not boiling. Remove from the heat. Stir in the vanilla.

In a bowl, mix the hot cream with the sugar until smooth. It should be a thick but pourable mixture.

Brush the glaze heavily over the tops of the warm loaves, letting it drip down the sides.

Let stand until completely dry.

This makes absolutely marvelous toast, but watch it carefully; it browns (burns) unusually fast.

These loaves freeze perfectly.

Stollen

1 LARGE STOLLEN
(2½ POUNDS)

A Stollen is a free-form, long, oval, rich and buttery yeast cake generously studded with a variety of rum-soaked candied fruits and nuts. It comes from Germany; the best ones, I have heard, are from Dresden. Although Stollen are generally made at Christmas and are a popular Christmas gift, they're wonderful any time as coffee cake with breakfast, or with tea, coffee, wine, milk, etc. It is a firm and compact (not light and airy) cake that lasts extremely well (for weeks in the refrigerator or a year in the freezer)—it should be refrigerated for at least a few days before it is served. It makes marvelously crisp and crunchy toast.

For a brunch buffet party, I sliced the loaf a bit thinner than bread slices, placed the slices overlapping on a long, narrow board, and placed the board next to a toaster on a side table near the rest of the food. Everyone toasted his or her own (I should have had three or four toasters).

½ cup diced candied orange rind (I use a
    combination of lemon, orange, and citron)
¼ cup currants
¼ cup light raisins
¼ cup candied cherries, halved
⅓ cup dark rum
2 tablespoons warm water (105 to 115 degrees;
    see Dissolving, page 221)
1 envelope active dry yeast
¼ cup plus 2 tablespoons granulated sugar
½ cup milk
1 teaspoon salt
3 ounces (¾ stick) unsalted butter, at
    room temperature
½ teaspoon almond extract
3 cups unsifted all-purpose flour
1 egg (graded large), at room temperature
Finely grated rind of 1 or 2 fresh lemons
½ cup whole blanched almonds
Additional flour
2 tablespoons additional butter, at room
    temperature (to be used after baking)
Confectioners sugar

The candied citrus fruits, currants, raisins, and cherries should be marinated in the rum for an hour or two, or overnight. It is best to do it in a jar with a tight cover so that you can turn it upside down and from side to side occasionally to soak all the fruits thoroughly (do it on a tray or dish in case it leaks).

Before preparing the dough, pour the fruits and rum into a large strainer set over a bowl to drain. Reserve the drained rum. Let stand.

Rinse a small bowl with hot water to warm it. Do not dry. Pour the 2 tablespoons of warm water into the bowl, sprinkle the yeast over the water, and add a pinch of the sugar. Stir with a fork or a table knife to mix and set aside at room temperature. (After about 10 to 15 minutes it will begin to rise.)

Pour the milk into a small, preferably narrow saucepan. Add the ¼ cup plus 2 tablespoons of sugar, the salt, and the 3 ounces of butter. Stir frequently over low heat until the mixture reaches 105 to 115 degrees on a candy thermometer. Remove from the heat and add the almond extract.

Meanwhile, place 1¾ cups (reserve the remaining 1¼ cups) of the flour in the large bowl of an electric mixer. Add the warm milk-butter mixture, the egg, lemon rind, yeast, and the drained-off rum (reserve the fruits). Beat on moderate speed, scraping the bowl occasionally, for 8 to 10 minutes. Remove from the mixer.

Add the reserved 1¼ cups of flour and stir with a heavy wooden spatula to mix. (Or, if your mixer has a dough hook, you can add the full 3 cups of flour at once and beat with the dough hook for 8 to 10 minutes.)

Flour a large board or smooth work surface, turn the dough out, and knead it (see Kneading, page 222) for a few minutes until smooth. It will be necessary to add a bit more flour so you can handle it; add only enough to keep the dough from sticking.

Now, to incorporate the fruits and nuts: Add about ⅓ cup of them at a time and knead them in. Add more flour as necessary while you are kneading in the fruits and nuts, but not so much more that the dough becomes dry.

Form the dough into a ball, flour it lightly, place it in a large bowl, cover airtight with plastic wrap, and let rise (see Rising, page 221) for about 2 hours until almost double in bulk.

Traditionally, a Stollen is shaped like an elongated monster Parker House roll, but this one is like a fat French bread loaf.

Flour a large board or work surface and a rolling pin. Make a fist and punch down the dough, folding the sides in toward the middle. Then turn it out onto the floured surface. With the rolling pin, roll it into an oval shape measuring 15 × 9 inches. From one long side, roll it up like a jelly roll. Pinch the seam securely to hold it in place; be sure it is tightly sealed. (If it does not want to hold, dampen the edge with a bit of water.) Then, with your hands, roll the Stollen to taper the ends a bit, and then push the long sides together to mound it high in the middle. It should measure 16 inches in length and should be 3 inches across the middle.

If you have a nonstick cookie sheet or jelly-roll pan, place the Stollen on it diagonally. Otherwise, place it on a lightly buttered sheet or pan.

No matter which sheet or pan you have used, now place it on another sheet or pan to prevent the bottom from becoming too dark.

Push the long sides of the cake together again to shape it fat and high.

Cover the Stollen loosely with plastic wrap and let it rise again for 1½ hours (see Rising, page 221) until almost double in bulk.

Shortly before it has finished rising, adjust a rack to the center of the oven and preheat the oven to 350 degrees.

Bake the Stollen for 45 minutes. If it starts to become too dark, cover it loosely with foil.

As soon as the Stollen is done, use a flat-sided cookie sheet to transfer it to a large rack placed over aluminum foil. Brush the additional 2 tablespoons of butter generously all over the hot cake and, without waiting, coat the top generously with confectioners sugar, sprinkling it through a fine strainer; it should be a solid coating of sugar, not just a sprinkling.

Let the cake cool. Wrap it in plastic wrap and refrigerate for at least a few days before serving, or freeze it.

Just before serving, you may want to sugar the top again.

This should be cut into rather thin slices (about ⅜ inch thick). It is best to use a serrated French bread knife.

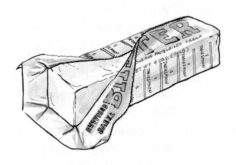

Swedish Leaf Cakes

This recipe will make two sensational-looking, long, narrow, hand-formed coffee cakes that should be planned for a special occasion. They not only look fantastic, but they have a delicious raisin-nut filling and everyone raves about them.

Serve them when they are very fresh, or freeze them.

Do not make these when you are in a hurry; there are two risings, and mixing, kneading, shaping, cutting, twisting, icing, etc. It is all fun to do anyhow, but especially gratifying when you see the beautiful results.

2 LARGE, LONG, NARROW CAKES

DOUGH

1 cup warm water (105 to 115 degrees; see Dissolving, page 221)
½ cup granulated sugar
2 packages active dry yeast
⅓ cup instant nonfat dry milk
1 teaspoon salt
2 eggs (graded large), at room temperature
4 ounces (1 stick) unsalted butter, cut into pieces, at room temperature
5 to 5¼ cups unsifted all-purpose flour

To heat the large bowl of an electric mixer, place it in the sink and let hot water run into it for about a minute. Pour out the water and shake the bowl, then pour in the 1 cup of warm water, 1 teaspoon of the sugar, and the yeast. Twirl the bowl gently to mix the ingredients a bit and then let stand for 5 or 6 minutes.

Add the remaining sugar, the dry milk, salt, eggs, butter, and 2½ cups of the flour (reserve the remaining flour). Beat at high speed for 2 minutes. Then, gradually, on low speed add about another cup of the flour and beat only to mix. Remove from the mixer.

Add another 1¼ cups of the flour (you will still have another ¼ to ½ cup of flour in reserve). With a heavy wooden spatula stir to mix.

Lightly flour a large board or work surface. Turn the dough out onto the floured surface. Knead (see Kneading, page 222) the dough briefly until it is smooth. If it is sticky, add some of the reserved flour—you might not need all of it. Then continue to knead the dough for about 6 or 7 minutes until it is very smooth and elastic.

Lightly butter a deep mixing bowl. Form the dough into a ball, place it in the bowl, turn it around in the bowl to butter all sides, and then cover the bowl with plastic wrap. Let rise (see Rising, page 221) for about 1½ hours or until it doubles in volume.

Meanwhile, prepare the ingredients for the filling.

FILLING

2 ounces (½ stick) unsalted butter
½ cup granulated sugar
4 teaspoons cinnamon
½ teaspoon nutmeg
4 ounces (1 cup) walnuts or pecans, finely
    chopped
5 ounces (1 cup) raisins (they may be dark or
    light, or currants, or a combination of
    any of these)

The above ingredients are to fill two cakes; use half for each cake.

Melt the butter and set it aside.

In a small bowl mix the sugar, cinnamon, and nutmeg and set aside.

Have the nuts and raisins ready; do not stir them into the sugar mixture.

You will need two large cookie sheets or jelly-roll pans (one for each cake). It is best to use nonstick pans, but if you don't have them, butter the pans lightly and set them aside.

When the dough has risen, form a fist and punch it down, turning the edges in toward the center. Form the dough into a ball and cut it in half. Return one half to the buttered bowl, cover, and set aside.

Form the other half into a ball. On the floured surface, with a floured, heavy rolling pin, roll the dough out into a 10 × 15-inch rectangle. If the dough is too elastic and shrinks back each time you roll it, simply cover it lightly with a towel and allow it to stand for 5 or 10 minutes. Then it will be easier to work with. But this is one of those things where you have to remember that you are the boss; be firm, get tough with it if you must.

Brush the rolled-out dough with the melted butter. Sprinkle with the sugar mixture. Then sprinkle on the nuts and raisins, keeping them about an inch away from the farther long side.

Roll up like a jelly roll, starting at the long side where the nuts and raisins go all the way to the end.

Pinch the seam to seal. Then, with your hands, stretch the roll a bit until it is as long as the measurement from one corner of the baking sheet to the diagonally opposite corner.

Place the roll diagonally on the sheet. Now to form the roll into "leaves": Hold a pair of scissors over and at one end of the roll, with the blades pointing toward the roll; the blades should be at about a 45-degree angle. You are going to make slanting cuts about ½ inch apart, without cutting through to the bottom. Here's how:

Open the scissors to straddle the roll and lower the blades until the points are a scant ½ inch from the pan. Make the first cut, bringing the blades together and cutting through all but the lower ¼ to ½ inch of the roll. Continue to cut these slices about ½ inch apart (the narrower the slices are—within reason—the fancier the cake will be).

Next step: Start at one end and, with your fingers, gently move one "leaf" to the right of center and the next one to the left. It is not necessary to move each "leaf" all the way onto its side; just alternate them away from the center. Do not handle too much or the filling might fall out.

Cover lightly with a smooth, lightweight towel or cloth napkin and set aside to rise (see Rising, page 221) for 1 hour.

Meanwhile, prepare the second cake the same way, place it on another sheet, cover, and let rise.

About 20 minutes before baking, adjust a rack one-third up from the bottom of the oven and preheat the oven to 350 degrees.

Bake the cake that was shaped first (let the second cake wait). Bake for 25 to 30 minutes, until golden brown. Do not underbake.

ICING

½ cup strained confectioners sugar
1 tablespoon milk
¼ teaspoon vanilla extract

These amounts are for one cake. Do not mix enough for both cakes at once; the icing should be used shortly after it is prepared.

Simply mix the ingredients until smooth.

When the cake is removed from the oven, bake the second cake.

Let the baked cake stand on the sheet for about 3 minutes. Then, with a firm metal spatula, cut under the cake to be sure it is not stuck to the pan. Carefully (I always appreciate another person's help at this stage), using a flat-sided cookie sheet as a spatula, or two long and strong metal spatulas, or the bottoms of two loose-bottomed quiche pans, transfer the cake to a large rack. Place the rack over a long piece of foil or wax paper.

With a pastry brush, brush the icing all over the hot cake, including the exposed filling.

Let cool completely.

Meanwhile, bake, ice, and cool the second cake.

Place each cake on a long, narrow board (a chocolate-roll board is perfect) or on any long, narrow, flat tray.

Aunt Leah's Raspberry Squares

These are from a wonderful cook and baker, Leah Snider, in Detroit. They are made with a dough that must be refrigerated overnight. But there is no kneading and no rising. They are especially attractive and delicious and equally quick and easy. They are not too sweet and are wonderful as a coffee cake with breakfast or brunch, with a fruit salad at lunch, or at a tea party.

32 SQUARES

¼ cup warm water (105 to 115 degrees; see Dissolving, page 221)
1 envelope active dry yeast
3 cups sifted all-purpose flour
¾ teaspoon salt
3 tablespoons granulated sugar
8 ounces (2 sticks) unsalted butter
1 egg (graded large)
½ cup evaporated milk
Confectioners sugar (to be sprinkled over the baked cakes)

Rinse a small cup in hot water to warm it. Dry it quickly, or just shake it out well. Pour in the warm water and sprinkle the yeast on top. Stir with a fork to mix and set aside.

Mix the flour, salt, and sugar in a large bowl. With a pastry blender cut in the butter until the particles are fine and the mixture resembles coarse meal.

Beat the egg and the milk just to mix, and add, along with the yeast, to the dry ingredients. Stir thoroughly to mix.

(The above steps, mixing the dry ingredients, cutting in the butter, and then mixing in the liquids and yeast, may all be done in a food processor if you wish.)

Transfer the mixture to a bowl, cover airtight, and refrigerate overnight.

FILLING

1 pound (1½ cups) thick raspberry preserves
Finely grated rind of 1 large lemon
2½ ounces (½ cup) blanched almonds,
    chopped into medium-fine pieces

Adjust a rack to the center of the oven and preheat oven to 350 degrees. Lightly butter a 10½ × 15½ × 1-inch jelly-roll pan. It should not be a nonstick pan.

Flour a pastry cloth and a rolling pin. Turn the dough out onto the cloth, form it into a ball, and cut it in half. Set aside and reserve one piece. Shape the other piece into a rectangle, flouring the dough and your hands as necessary. Then, with the rolling pin, roll the dough out to measure 12 × 17 inches, keeping the corners as square as you can, and the sides as straight as you can. Loosely drape it over the rolling pin and transfer it to the buttered pan. With a small, sharp knife, trim the sides of the dough even with the top of the pan.

Mix the filling ingredients and spread over the dough. Go all the way to all edges. Set aside.

Flour the remaining dough, form it into a rectangle, and roll it out to measure about 10½ × 15½ inches. (This time don't worry about the corners or edges.) With a zigzag or a plain pastry wheel or with a pizza cutter, slice the rolled-out dough into lengthwise strips ½ inch wide. Place half of the strips on a diagonal ½ inch apart over the filling, pinching them off level with the rim of the pan. Place the remaining strips crisscrossing in the opposite direction, forming a lattice (or diamond) design. Pinch off those ends also.

With your fingers, fold over the dough around the edges. Fold it in toward the center to form a border about ½ inch wide all around. With a fork, press down on it lightly to seal.

Without waiting for the dough to rise, place the pan in the oven and bake for 25 to 30 minutes until nicely colored.

Cool in the pan.

With a small, sharp knife cut the cake into squares and with a wide metal spatula transfer them to wax paper. Generously sprinkle confectioners sugar over them, sprinkling it through a fine strainer held over the top.

Transfer to a serving plate.

These may be frozen.

Sally Lunn

1 LARGE ROUND BREAD
OR 2 SMALL LOAVES

There was a young lady from England who sold round, flat buns on the streets in the town of Bath toward the end of the eighteenth century. Some say that her name was Sally Lunn and the buns were named after her. Another story is that the round buns looked like the sun and the moon—"soleil et lune" in French. When she cried it out with her cockney accent, it sounded like sally lunn.

Enough history. Now, about this recipe. It is not for buns. It is for a large, light and airy, sweet bread, only slightly sweeter than plain bread—it is rich and delicious.

This is not really a dessert; it is a very plain coffee cake. Or serve it toasted at the table (to toast this, cut it in thick slices and toast in the oven) with room-temperature butter and marmalade or a thick honey spread. Serve it at a brunch, or luncheon, or a tea or coffee party.

This is extremely easy to make.

This can be baked in a 9-inch (10-cup) tube pan with or without (see Note) a fancy design, or in two 9 × 5 × 3-inch loaf pans. But it is especially gorgeous in the black iron kugelhopf pan made by Le Creuset under the name "Cousances." The pan is available at many of the better kitchen shops, or it may be bought at, or ordered by mail from, Cooktique, 9 Railroad Avenue, Tenafly, New Jersey 07670.

4 cups unsifted all-purpose flour
⅓ cup plus 1 tablespoon granulated sugar
2 teaspoons salt
2 packages active dry yeast
1 cup milk
½ cup water

4 ounces (1 stick) unsalted butter, cut into
pieces, at room temperature
3 eggs, at room temperature

In the large bowl of an electric mixer (or any large bowl, if you want to mix this by hand) place 1½ cups of the flour (reserve the remaining 2½ cups to add later). Add the sugar, salt, and dry yeast to the 1½ cups flour. Stir to mix.

In a saucepan, combine the milk, water, and butter. Stir over low heat until the mixture is warm (105 to 115 degrees on a candy thermometer). Don't worry if the butter is not completely melted—it is O.K.

Gradually pour the warm liquids into the dry ingredients, beating on low speed in a mixer, or stirring with a large wooden spatula. When it is incorporated, beat for 2 minutes in a mixer, or stir briskly by hand for 3 minutes.

Add the eggs and 1 more cup of the flour and beat or stir to mix. Then, in a mixer, beat for 2 minutes more, or stir by hand for 3 minutes more. Add the remaining 1½ cups flour and beat or stir to mix until smooth.

Scrape down the sides of the bowl with a rubber spatula. Cover the top of the bowl airtight with plastic wrap and set aside to rise (see Rising, page 221) for about 1 hour or until the dough has doubled in volume.

Meanwhile, prepare a 9-inch (10-cup capacity) tube pan or two 9 × 5 × 3-inch loaf pans as follows: Butter the pan or pans—if the pan is a tube pan with a fancy design, the best way to butter it is with soft, not melted, butter, brushing it on with a pastry brush—then coat the pan or pans all over with fine, dry bread crumbs. Tap to shake out excess crumbs over a piece of paper. Set aside.

When the dough has doubled, with a heavy wooden spatula stir it to deflate it completely; then stir for about half a minute. Pour the dough into the prepared pan or pans. Smooth the top or tops.

Now, to let this rise again: Butter a piece of plastic wrap and place it buttered side down over the top of the pan or pans. Set the dough to rise again (see Rising, page 221) for about 30 to 40 minutes or until double in volume. Even though the plastic wrap is buttered, when the dough rises it might stick, therefore, remove the plastic just before the dough reaches it and let the dough finish rising uncovered. (If you are now asking, "Then why butter it?" the answer is that if it does stick, it will stick less if the plastic is buttered. If the dough rises to touch the plastic, and if it is not buttered, peeling the plastic away might disturb the dough too much and cause it to deflate.) It should rise a scant 1 inch above the top of the pan, but watch it—this is a very lively mixture and it should not rise higher or it might run over the sides during baking.

About 20 minutes before the Sally Lunn is ready to be baked, adjust an oven rack one-third up from the bottom of the oven and preheat oven to 375 degrees. Bake for 35 to 40 minutes; after about 20 minutes of baking, cover the top loosely with foil. When the bread is done, a cake tester inserted in the middle will come out clean and dry, the top of the bread will be richly browned, and if you tap it with your fingertips or knuckles it will make a hollow sound.

(If the bread is baked in a tube pan, during baking it will rise to about 3 inches above the top of the pan; however, when it is done, it will settle down to about 1 inch above the top.)

Cool in the pan or pans for about 3 minutes. Then cover with a rack, turn over pan and rack, remove the pan, and leave the bread upside down to finish cooling.

This freezes perfectly.

NOTE: *If you use a plain tube pan with no design it will probably have three small extensions (legs) on top (presumably to rest the inverted pan on). If so, butter those also, or the dough will cling to them and might not rise evenly.*

VARIATION: *Sally Lunn with walnuts is unusual and delicious and I like it even better than the plain version. Cut or break 1 cup of walnuts into large pieces. Follow the above recipe, and add the nuts when you stir down the dough after the first rising.*

Sweet Breads, Gingerbreads, and Muffins

Sweet Breads

Gingerbreads

Muffins

Sweet Breads

All of the following sweet breads have a special attraction and charm.
They are easy to make, they look good and are wonderful to wrap as gifts,
they are nice to have on hand as a plain tea or coffee cake, or when you
want just a bit of something sweet but not too sweet as dessert. Or serve
them as bread (especially with a fruit or vegetable salad at lunch), or use
them for sandwiches—my favorite combination is Monterey Jack cheese,
crisp bacon, and sliced apple on lightly buttered sweet bread, grilled in a
pan with butter. My husband's favorite is peanut butter and sliced banana
with hot mustard and honey. Or try sliced ham and apricot preserves.
They keep well and can all be frozen; they slice well (they slice best and
taste best if they are made ahead of time and are wrapped and refrigerated
overnight). I think you will love them.

Zucchini Loaf from Seattle

14 TO 16 SLICES

When we stopped at a restaurant named E.A.T.
in Seattle, I spotted several large, dark loaves that
looked homemade. After two thick slices that
turned out to be my lunch, I started asking questions. They told me it was zucchini (I never would
have guessed), they gave me the recipe (which I
have since divided by six), and they said that they
are not connected with any other business by the
same name (they never heard of the one in New
York).

This is sweet enough to be a plain cake or a
coffee cake; it can also be served as a sweet bread. It is deliciously moist,
is wonderful for a gift, and has gotten top ratings from the friends I have
served it to.

3 cups sifted all-purpose flour
Scant 1 teaspoon salt
1 teaspoon baking soda
½ teaspoon double-acting baking powder
3 teaspoons cinnamon
Scant 1 pound zucchini (to make 2 packed
    cups, shredded; see Note)
2 eggs
2 cups granulated sugar
1 cup salad oil
1 teaspoon vanilla extract
4 ounces (generous 1 cup) walnuts, cut or
    broken into medium-size pieces

Adjust an oven rack one-third up from the bottom of the oven and preheat oven to 350 degrees. Butter a 10 × 5 × 3-inch loaf pan, or any other bread-loaf pan that has a 10-cup capacity (measured to the very top of the pan). Or, if you wish, use two smaller pans. Dust the pan or pans with fine, dry bread crumbs and tap to shake out excess crumbs over paper.

Sift together the flour, salt, baking soda, baking powder, and cinnamon and set aside.

Wash the zucchini well under running water, scrubbing with a vegetable brush, and cut off both ends. Now, to grate it, either use the coarse grater attachment of a food processor, or use the large round openings of a metal grater. Either way, the zucchini should be grated into julienne-shaped slivers; it should not be puréed. Do not drain. Press it firmly into a 2-cup measuring cup; you should have 2 firmly packed cups. Set aside.

It is not necessary to use an electric mixer for this but if you would like to you can. In a large bowl, beat the eggs just to mix. Mix in the sugar, oil, and vanilla. Add the sifted dry ingredients and beat/stir to mix. It will be thick. Then add the zucchini along with any juice that has collected and mix thoroughly with a wooden spatula—the zucchini will thin the batter. Stir in the nuts.

Turn into the prepared pan or pans, smooth the top or tops, and bake. In the one large pan it will take 1 hour and 45 to 50 minutes or a few minutes longer; in two smaller pans it will take slightly less time. Either way, bake until a cake tester gently inserted into the middle comes out clean and dry. (It will rise high and form a crack on the top.)

Cool in the pan for 15 minutes. Then cover with a rack, turn over the rack and cake pan, remove the pan and turn over again, leaving the cake right side up.

Let stand until cool.

It will probably be best to cut this with a serrated French bread knife.

NOTE: *You can use any zucchini for this, either young and small or old and large. It is a delicious way to use up zucchini from your garden that has grown to a monster size.*

Date-Nut Loaf

This is an all-American classic—very popular, very delicious, and a wonderful loaf to make as a gift. Although this is sweet enough to be a cake, it is often served as a sweet bread.

1 9-INCH LOAF

8 ounces (1 packed cup) pitted dates
5 ounces (1 cup) raisins (may be half dark and half light, or all dark)
1 teaspoon baking soda
1 cup boiling water
4 ounces (1 stick) unsalted butter
1 teaspoon vanilla extract
1 cup granulated sugar
¼ teaspoon salt
Optional: ½ teaspoon powdered instant espresso or other powdered instant coffee (see Note)
1 egg (graded large or extra-large)
1⅓ cups sifted all-purpose flour
7 ounces (1¾ cups) walnut or pecan halves or large pieces

Adjust a rack one-third up from the bottom of the oven and preheat oven to 350 degrees. Butter an 8 or 9 × 4½ or 5 × 3-inch loaf pan or any loaf pan with at least a 6-cup capacity. Dust all over with fine, dry bread crumbs, then, over a piece of paper, tap to shake out excess crumbs.

Cut the dates into medium-size pieces (each date should be cut into 4 or 5 pieces); if you wish, cut with scissors frequently dipped into cold water to keep them from sticking. Place the dates and raisins in a mixing bowl.

Dissolve the soda in the boiling water and pour it over the dates. Stir to mix, then let stand until tepid.

In the large bowl of an electric mixer, cream the butter. Add the vanilla, sugar, salt, and optional coffee, and beat well. Add the egg and beat well. On low speed add the flour, scraping the bowl with a rubber spatula and beating only until incorporated. Remove from the mixer.

Add some of the liquid from the dates and raisins and stir it in well; add most of the remaining liquid and stir it in. Then add all of the dates and raisins and stir well. Stir in the nuts.

Pour into the prepared pan and smooth the top. The batter might fill the pan to about ½ inch from the top.

Bake for about 1½ hours. About 30 minutes before the baking time is over check to see if the top is becoming too dark; if so, cover loosely with foil. To test for doneness, insert a small, sharp paring knife into the center of the loaf almost all the way to the bottom; when the knife comes out clean the loaf is done.

Cool in the pan for 20 to 30 minutes. Cover with a rack, turn over pan and rack, remove the pan, and carefully turn the loaf right side up to cool. When it is completely cool, wrap in plastic wrap or foil and refrigerate at least overnight, or freeze it for about an hour. (This can be sliced, and even served, while it is frozen.)

NOTE: *If you use granular instead of powdered coffee, dissolve it in the boiling water with the baking soda to pour over dates, instead of adding it to the butter mixture.*

Joan's Pumpkin Loaf

14 TO 16 SLICES

The first time I ate this there was also a huge tray piled high with California crabs and a marvelous string bean salad, and although the whole meal was memorable, I especially remember getting up for more and more slices of this pumpkin loaf that made me an addict with the first bite. It is so good, there ought to be a law . . .

2½ cups sifted all-purpose flour
2 teaspoons baking soda

½ teaspoon salt

1½ teaspoons cinnamon

½ teaspoon cloves

2 eggs (graded large)

2 cups granulated sugar, or light brown sugar,
firmly packed

½ cup salad oil (Mazola, peanut oil, corn oil,
or any one of the health-food oils that
are tasteless)

1 pound (2 cups) canned pumpkin (solid pack,
not pumpkin-pie filling; to use fresh
pumpkin, see Notes, page 159)

8 ounces (1 cup) pitted dates, each date cut
into 2 or 3 pieces—no smaller (see Note)

4 ounces (generous 1 cup) walnuts, cut or
broken into medium-size pieces

Adjust an oven rack one-third up from the bottom of the oven and preheat oven to 350 degrees. Butter a 10 × 5 × 3-inch loaf pan, or any other loaf pan that has a 10-cup capacity, measured to the very top of the pan. Or use two or more smaller pans if you wish. Dust the pan (or pans) with fine, dry bread crumbs, and tap over a piece of paper to shake out excess crumbs.

Sift together the flour, soda, salt, cinnamon, and cloves and set aside.

It is not necessary to use an electric mixer for this although you can if you wish (I do). In any large bowl beat the eggs just to mix. Add the sugar and oil and beat lightly just to mix. Mix in the pumpkin and then the dates. Now add the sifted dry ingredients and stir, mix, or beat only until they are smoothly incorporated. Stir in the nuts.

Turn into the prepared pan (or pans) and smooth the top (tops).

Bake for 1½ hours in the large pan, less time in smaller pans (in two 8½ × 4½ × 2¾-inch [6-cup capacity] pans, bake for 65 to 70 minutes), until a cake tester gently inserted into the middle comes out just barely clean.

Cool in the pan (pans) for 15 minutes. Cover with a rack, turn over the rack and the pan, remove the pan, and then turn the loaf right side up again on a rack. Let stand until cool.

Now, if you can wait, wrap the loaf (loaves) in plastic wrap and refrigerate for a day or two, or freeze.

To serve, cut into slices a generous ½ inch thick. If you do not wait for the loaf to age a day or two, it is best to cut it with a serrated French bread knife.

NOTE: *It will be a more delicious loaf if you use whole dates and cut them yourself rather than using the diced dates that are too sweet and the pieces too small.*

Applesauce Loaf

1 9- OR 10-INCH LOAF

This is one of the first recipes I taught about 20 years ago when I started my cooking school. A friend just told me that she has been making it all these years—I had forgotten it. It is one of the best-looking loaves and one of the most delicious. Dark, firm, solid, compact, loaded with nuts and raisins, it is a delicious plain tea or coffee cake, and may also be served at the table with butter, or used for sandwiches. It is a lovely loaf to make for a gift. (It is made with both white and whole-wheat flour.)

You will need a pan with an 8-cup capacity; I especially like one that measures 10¼ × 3¾ (width at top) × 3⅜ inches (in depth) (see Note), but you can use any other loaf pan with the same capacity.

5 ounces (1 cup) raisins
1 cup unsifted all-purpose white flour (stir to aerate before measuring)
6 ounces (1½ cups) walnuts, halves or large pieces
½ teaspoon salt
1½ teaspoons cinnamon
1 teaspoon double-acting baking powder

1 teaspoon baking soda
1 teaspoon powdered instant espresso or other
    powdered (not granular) instant coffee
4 ounces (1 stick) unsalted butter
¾ cup light or dark brown sugar, firmly packed
2 eggs (graded large or extra-large)
1¼ cups sweetened or unsweetened applesauce
1 cup unsifted all-purpose whole-wheat flour

Adjust an oven rack to the center of the oven and preheat oven to 350 degrees. Butter a 9 × 5 × 3-inch or 10¼ × 3¾ × 3⅜-inch loaf pan with an 8-cup capacity, dust it with fine, dry bread crumbs, and tap to shake out excess over a piece of paper. Set aside.

Place the raisins in a large mixing bowl. Add 2 or 3 tablespoons of the white flour to the raisins (reserving the remaining flour) and, with your hands, toss to coat the raisins with flour. Add the nuts and toss again. Set aside.

Sift the reserved white flour with the salt, cinnamon, baking powder, baking soda, and powdered instant coffee. Set aside.

In the large bowl of an electric mixer, beat the butter until it is soft. Add the sugar and beat to mix. Mix in the eggs and then add the applesauce and beat to mix. On low speed, add the whole-wheat flour and the sifted ingredients and, scraping the bowl with a rubber spatula, beat only until smoothly incorporated. Remove from the mixer and stir in the floured raisins and nuts, and any flour remaining in the bowl.

Turn into the prepared pan, smooth the top, and then, with the back of a spoon, form a shallow trench down the length (it keeps the loaf from rising too high in the middle).

Bake for about 1 hour and 5 minutes until a cake tester gently inserted into the middle comes out clean and dry. (The loaf will form a shallow crack on top—O.K.)

Cool in the pan for 10 minutes, cover with a rack, turn over the pan and the rack, remove the pan, and then very carefully turn the loaf right side up to cool on the rack.

Wrap the cooled loaf and refrigerate it for a few hours or overnight (it slices better if it has been chilled).

NOTE: *The 10¼ × 3¾ × 3⅜-inch pan is available from Bobbi & Carole's Cookshop, 7251 S.W. 57th Court, Miami, Florida 33143.*

Whole-Wheat Banana Bread

Of the many sweet breads, banana bread seems to be the most popular. There is one secret to any banana bread: The bananas must be fully ripened or the bread will not have enough, if any, banana flavor.

This one is quick and easy and deliciously moist.

1 9-INCH LOAF

1 cup sifted all-purpose whole-wheat flour (see Note)
½ cup sifted all-purpose white flour
1 teaspoon baking soda
¾ teaspoon salt
½ teaspoon mace
About 3 ripe bananas (to make 1⅓ cups, mashed)
¼ cup buttermilk
4 ounces (1 stick) unsalted butter
½ teaspoon vanilla extract
¾ cup dark or light brown sugar, firmly packed
1 egg
Finely grated rind of 1 large lemon
4 ounces (1 cup) pecans or walnuts, cut or broken into medium-size pieces

Adjust a rack to the center of the oven and preheat oven to 350 degrees. Butter a 9 × 5 × 3-inch loaf pan and dust it all with wheat germ or with fine, dry bread crumbs. Tap to shake out excess crumbs over a piece of paper. Set aside.

Sift together both flours, baking soda, salt, and mace and set aside.

Mash the bananas either on a plate with a fork, in a food processor, in a blender (in a processor or blender be careful not to really liquify the bananas), or in the small bowl of an electric mixer. You need 1⅓ cups. Stir the bananas and buttermilk to mix and set aside.

In the large bowl of an electric mixer (if you used the mixer for mashing the bananas it is not necessary to wash the beaters), cream the butter. Beat in the vanilla and the sugar. Add the egg and beat well. On low speed, alternately add the sifted dry ingredients in three additions with the banana mixture in two additions, scraping the bowl as necessary and beating only until incorporated after each addition.

Remove the bowl from the mixer and stir in the grated rind and the nuts.

Turn into the prepared pan and smooth the top.

Bake for 50 to 55 minutes until a cake tester inserted into the middle comes out clean and dry.

Let cool in the pan for about 20 minutes.

Cover with a rack, turn the pan and the rack over, remove the pan and very gently (the loaf is delicate—do not squash it) turn the loaf over again, leaving it right side up to cool.

If there is time, wrap the loaf in plastic wrap and refrigerate overnight before serving.

This is especially good sliced rather thick and well toasted—it becomes very crisp and crunchy; it is best to toast it on a cookie sheet under the broiler.

NOTE: *When you sift whole-wheat flour, some of the flour may be too coarse to go through the sifter. That part should be stirred into the part that did go through.*

Cuban Banana Bread

1 10-INCH LOAF

Hundreds of loaves of this were sold at a street festival in Little Havana in Miami (they could have sold many more if they had them), and thick slices of it were served along with small cups of strong black coffee, and everyone loved it. It is moist, dark, chewy, coarse (it has bran in it), crunchy, dense, and not too sweet. Serve it as a coffee cake or a sweet bread, or make cream cheese sandwiches with it, or peanut butter, or peanut butter and bacon. Or make it to give as a gift; it is beautifully shaped, richly colored, and mucho delicious.

1½ cups sifted all-purpose flour
1 teaspoon salt
2 teaspoons double-acting baking powder
½ teaspoon baking soda
2 ounces (½ stick) unsalted butter
1 teaspoon vanilla extract
½ cup dark brown sugar
1 egg
1 cup bran cereal (not flakes—I use
    Kellogg's All-Bran)
3 to 4 medium-size, thoroughly ripe bananas
    (to make 1½ cups mashed—see directions
    in the recipe for mashing)
2 tablespoons water
½ cup raisins
4 ounces (generous 1 cup) walnuts, cut or
    broken into medium-size pieces

Adjust a rack one-third up from the bottom of the oven and preheat the oven to 350 degrees. Butter a 10¼ × 3¾ × 3⅜-inch loaf pan (see page 12 for a source) or any other with at least a 7½-cup capacity. Dust it all with fine, dry bread crumbs, tap to shake out excess crumbs over a piece of paper. Set the pan aside.

Sift together the flour, salt, baking powder, and baking soda, and set aside.

In the large bowl of an electric mixer, beat the butter until soft. Add the vanilla and then the sugar and beat until well mixed. Add the egg and beat until pale in color. Add the bran cereal and beat just to mix. Set aside.

The bananas should be mashed on a large, flat plate with a fork (a processor or blender liquifies them too much); they may be slightly uneven with a few coarse pieces.

Add the water to the bananas and stir to mix. Then add the bananas to the bran mixture, beating only to mix. (The mixture might appear curdled—O.K.)

Add the raisins and nuts and beat only to mix. Then, on low speed, add the sifted dry ingredients, scraping the bowl with a rubber spatula, and beating only until incorporated—do not overbeat.

Turn into the prepared pan and smooth the top.

Bake for 1 hour until a cake tester gently inserted in the middle comes out clean and dry.

Cool in the pan for 10 to 15 minutes.

Turn over onto a rack, remove the pan, and then turn the loaf right side up to finish cooling.

Let stand for several hours or overnight, or refrigerate for at least 1 or 2 hours, before slicing.

French Spice Bread

2 8-INCH LOAVES

In France this is Pain d'Epice, in Belgium it is Ghentsche Peperkoek. It is a sensational small loaf of richly colored, not-too-sweet, eggless and butterless chewy honey cake with an intriguing texture and flavor. The flavor depends very much on which honey you use; generally, darker honey has a stronger flavor. (When I can get it, I especially like a light honey labeled "Golden Nectar [Real Leatherwood] extra-light amber—R. Stephens, Mole Creek, Tasmania, Australia.")

The batter should stand overnight or longer (up to a week) before it is baked (the texture of the cake is better and less rubbery if you let it stand before baking). Then the baked loaves should stand at least a day or longer before serving—they are worth waiting for. The loaves will keep indefinitely wrapped in foil and refrigerated, and probably almost as long at room temperature. Therefore, this is an extremely practical gift; you can wrap it and let it stand way ahead of time.

It is served with tea or coffee, plain or toasted, with or without butter and marmalade. It can be sliced paper thin.

I have made this for many, many years. It is adapted from Mimi Sheraton's original Visions of Sugarplums, which has recently been revised and reprinted (Harper & Row, 1981).

You will need two 8 × 4 × 2½-inch loaf pans (5-cup capacity).

1 tablespoon whole anise seeds

¼ cup candied orange peel

¼ cup candied or preserved ginger

2¾ cups unsifted all-purpose flour (stir to aerate before measuring)

¾ cup unsifted rye flour (I use Old Mill from Deaf Smith, Texas—available at health-food stores)

½ teaspoon cinnamon

½ teaspoon powdered mustard

⅛ teaspoon salt

1 cup honey

1 cup granulated sugar

3 teaspoons baking soda

1 cup hot tap water or coffee

½ teaspoon finely ground black pepper

⅓ cup light raisins

Crush the anise seeds in a mortar with a pestle just to bruise them. Set aside. The candied orange peel and ginger should be cut into pieces about ¼ inch in diameter, no smaller. Set aside. Sift together both flours, the cinnamon, mustard, and salt and set aside.

Place the honey, sugar, baking soda, and hot water or coffee in the large bowl of an electric mixer, and beat to mix. On low speed add the sifted dry ingredients and the pepper and beat only until smooth. Remove from the mixer and stir in the anise seeds, orange peel, ginger, and raisins.

Transfer to a smaller bowl if you wish, cover, and refrigerate at least overnight or up to a week.

Before baking, adjust a rack one-third up from the bottom of the oven and preheat oven to 350 degrees. Butter two loaf pans measuring 8 × 4 × 2½ inches (5-cup capacity). Dust the pans with fine, dry bread crumbs, and tap to shake out excess crumbs over a piece of paper.

The batter will be quite sticky. Spoon it into the pans, smooth the tops, and bake for 60 to 65 minutes until a cake tester gently inserted into the middle and to the bottom comes out clean and dry.

Cool in the pans for 15 minutes. Then cover with a rack, turn over pan and rack, remove pan, and carefully turn the loaf right side up to cool. Then wrap airtight and let stand for a few days or longer. It gets better.

Dutch Honey Bread

This is a beautiful, mildly spiced, interesting sweet loaf, like the ones that come from Holland. It keeps very well, travels well, and makes a nice gift. Soft, tender, fine-grained—it slices beautifully.

1 LARGE LOAF

2 cups sifted all-purpose flour
½ teaspoon ginger
½ teaspoon cinnamon
½ teaspoon cloves
¼ teaspoon salt
½ cup light raisins
8 ounces (1 cup) diced candied orange peel
¼ pound (1 stick) unsalted butter
1 teaspoon powdered instant espresso or other powdered (not granular) instant coffee
1 cup dark or light brown sugar, firmly packed
2 eggs (graded large, extra-large, or jumbo)
½ cup honey
1 teaspoon baking soda
½ cup buttermilk

Adjust a rack to the center of the oven and preheat oven to 350 degrees. Butter a 10 × 5 × 3-inch loaf pan, or any other loaf pan with a 10-cup capacity. Dust it all over with fine, dry bread crumbs, and tap to shake out excess crumbs over a piece of paper. Set aside.

Sift together the flour, ginger, cinnamon, cloves, and salt. In a small bowl, stir and toss the raisins and orange peel with about 2 tablespoons of the sifted dry ingredients. Set aside the fruit and the remaining sifted dry ingredients.

In the large bowl of an electric mixer, beat the butter until it softens slightly. Mix in the powdered espresso and then the sugar and beat to mix. Add the eggs one at a time, beating until incorporated after each addition.

Place the honey in a bowl. Add the baking soda through a fine strainer, stir to mix, then add the buttermilk and stir to mix. (The mixture will foam slightly.)

To the butter mixture, add the sifted dry ingredients in three additions alternating with the liquid in two additions, scraping the bowl with a rubber spatula, and beating on low speed only until incorporated after each addition.

Remove from the mixer and stir in the floured raisins and orange peel.

Turn into the prepared pan and smooth the top.

Bake for about 1 hour and 10 minutes until the top feels semifirm to the touch. If the top begins to brown too much during baking, cover it loosely with foil. (The top will be flat, not rounded.)

Let the loaf stand in the pan for 15 to 20 minutes. Then cover it with a rack, turn the pan and the rack over, and remove the pan, leaving the loaf upside down.

Let the loaf stand until completely cool. Then wrap it in plastic wrap and refrigerate for a few hours or overnight, or freeze it for about an hour.

Cut into thin slices.

Portuguese Sweet Walnut Bread

This beautiful, old-fashioned, moist loaf—packed with walnuts—is like a not-too-sweet pound cake. It is a coffee cake to serve between meals with tea or coffee. It is best to let this stand overnight before serving.

1 LARGE LOAF

2 cups sifted all-purpose flour
1 teaspoon double-acting baking powder
½ teaspoon mace
¾ teaspoon salt
8 ounces (2 sticks) unsalted butter
1½ teaspoons vanilla extract
¾ cup granulated sugar
6 eggs (graded large)

Finely grated rind of 1 large lemon
8 ounces (2 cups) walnut halves or
large pieces

Adjust a rack one-third up from the bottom of the oven and preheat oven to 350 degrees. Butter a loaf pan that has an 8-cup capacity (see Note). Dust it all over with fine, dry bread crumbs, and tap to shake out excess crumbs over a piece of paper. Set aside.

Sift together the flour, baking powder, mace, and salt and set aside.

Beat the butter in the large bowl of an electric mixer just to soften it slightly. Add the vanilla and sugar and beat to mix. Add the eggs, one or two at a time, scraping the bowl with a rubber spatula and beating until incorporated after each addition. On low speed gradually add the sifted dry ingredients, scraping the bowl and beating only until incorporated.

Remove from the mixer and stir in the lemon rind and walnuts.

Turn the mixture into the prepared pan and smooth the top. Then, with a spatula or a spoon, form a trench about ½ inch deep down the length of the loaf. (This keeps the loaf from mounding too high, but it will mound somewhat anyhow and will form a crack on the top. It will be gorgeous.)

Bake for 1 hour and 25 to 30 minutes. You will be able to tell when this is done by pressing gently with a fingertip on the top of the cake; when it is done it will resist the pressure.

Cool in the pan for about 15 minutes. Then cover with a rack, turn over the pan and the rack, remove the pan, and carefully turn the loaf right side up. Let the loaf stand for 8 hours, or wrap the cooled loaf and let it stand overnight. Or freeze it for an hour or two.

Use a very sharp knife for slicing—this slices beautifully—the large pieces of walnuts look wonderful.

NOTE: *I especially like a new pan I recently bought that measures 10¼ × 3¾ inches across the top, and 3⅜ inches in depth. It makes a higher and more narrow loaf than the usual. (See page 12 for a source.) A 9 × 5 × 3-inch pan is all right, but 9 × 5 × 2¾ is too small.*

Georgia Pecan Bread

1 8-INCH LOAF

A luscious little loaf loaded with pecans, gorgeous and delicious.

2 cups sifted all-purpose flour
2 teaspoons double-acting baking powder
½ teaspoon baking soda
½ teaspoon salt
1 teaspoon cinnamon
¼ teaspoon nutmeg
1 egg
1 cup buttermilk
3½ tablespoons unsalted butter, melted
¾ cup light brown sugar, firmly packed
6 ounces (1½ cups) pecans, cut or broken into
    large pieces

Adjust a rack one-third up from the bottom of the oven and preheat oven to 350 degrees. Butter an 8-inch loaf pan, or any pan with at least a 4-cup capacity (the pan should not be much larger or the loaf will be too shallow). Dust the pan all over with fine, dry bread crumbs, and tap to shake out excess crumbs over a piece of paper. Set aside.

Sift together the flour, baking powder, baking soda, salt, cinnamon, and nutmeg, and set aside.

This can be mixed with an electric mixer or by hand. In a large bowl, beat the egg to mix. Mix in the buttermilk, butter, and the sugar. Add the dry ingredients and stir or beat only to mix. Stir in the nuts.

Turn into the prepared pan and smooth the top. (In an 8-inch pan, the pan might seem too full, but if it has a 4-cup capacity it will be all right.)

Bake for 1 hour and 5 to 10 minutes until the top feels semifirm to the touch and a cake tester comes out clean. Do not overbake.

Cool in the pan for 10 or 15 minutes. Cover with a rack and turn the pan and the rack over, remove the pan, and then very carefully turn the loaf right side up to cool.

Wrap the cooled loaf and refrigerate it overnight. (Sometimes I cannot follow that last direction. If you slice it immediately, as soon as it has cooled, use a serrated French bread knife.)

Fresh Apple Bread

This is a plain loaf, not quite as sweet as cake. It has a rather light texture, a mildly spiced flavor, and a beautiful golden-brown crust.

1 9-INCH LOAF

2 cups sifted all-purpose flour
2 teaspoons double-acting baking powder
1 teaspoon baking soda
½ teaspoon salt
1 teaspoon cinnamon
½ teaspoon nutmeg
¼ teaspoon ginger
¼ teaspoon allspice
1 large, firm, and tart apple, or 2 smaller ones
4 ounces (1 stick) unsalted butter
¾ cup plus 2 tablespoons light brown sugar, firmly packed
2 eggs (graded large or extra-large)
2 tablespoons buttermilk or sour cream
Finely grated rind of 1 large lemon
4 ounces (1 cup) walnuts, cut or broken into medium-size pieces

Adjust a rack one-third up in the oven and preheat oven to 350 degrees. Butter a 9 × 5 × 3-inch loaf pan (8-cup capacity), dust it all with fine, dry bread crumbs, and tap to shake out excess over a piece of paper. Set the pan aside.

Sift together the flour, baking powder, baking soda, salt, cinnamon, nutmeg, ginger, and allspice, and set aside.

You will need 1¼ to 1⅓ cups of finely diced apple. Peel, quarter, and core the apple or apples. Dice each piece into ¼- to ⅓-inch squares. Set aside.

In the large bowl of an electric mixer, beat the butter until it is soft. Add the sugar and beat to mix. Add the eggs one at a time, beating until incorporated after each addition. Beat in the buttermilk or sour cream, then the diced apple. Then, on low speed, gradually add the sifted dry ingredients, scraping the bowl with a rubber spatula and beating only until thoroughly incorporated.

Remove from the mixer. Stir in the lemon rind and then the nuts.

The mixture will be very thick. Turn it into the prepared pan, smooth the top, and let stand for 10 minutes before baking.

Bake for about 1 hour until a cake tester gently inserted into the middle comes out clean and dry.

Let the loaf cool in the pan for 10 or 15 minutes. Cover with a rack, turn the pan and the rack over, remove the pan, cover with another rack and turn over again, leaving the loaf right side up to finish cooling.

When completely cool, wrap in plastic wrap and refrigerate overnight or at least for a few hours.

Cut with a very sharp knife into slices about ½ inch thick.

Fig Bread

1 9- OR 10-INCH LOAF

This is a wonderfully chewy and coarse, old-fashioned and kind of healthy-tasting, not-too-sweet loaf. Serve it plain or toasted (super), just by itself or with butter, cheese, thick honey, or marmalade. This is wonderful as a coffee cake— or make a grilled cheese sandwich with it.

12 ounces (1½ packed cups) dried brown figs
   (soft and moist)
1 cup sifted all-purpose white flour
1 teaspoon salt
1 teaspoon double-acting baking powder
1 teaspoon baking soda
1 cup unsifted all-purpose whole-wheat flour
   (stir to aerate before measuring)
½ cup honey
1½ cups buttermilk
2 ounces (½ stick) unsalted butter, melted
4 ounces (1 cup) walnut halves or pieces

Adjust a rack one-third up in the oven and preheat oven to 375 degrees. Butter a 10¼ × 3¾ × 3⅜-inch or a 9 × 5 × 3-inch loaf pan or any loaf pan with at least an 8-cup capacity, and dust it all with toasted wheat germ (toasted wheat germ makes a beautiful brown crust), oatmeal (that makes a nice chewy crust), or with fine, dry bread crumbs, and tap over a piece of paper to shake out any excess. Set aside.

With a knife or with scissors, cut off and discard the stems of the figs and cut the figs into slices about ¼ inch thick or into pieces—the slices or pieces should not be too thin or small; noticeable chunks are delicious. Set aside.

Sift together into a large mixing bowl the white flour, salt, baking powder, and baking soda. Add the whole-wheat flour and stir to mix thoroughly. Add the figs and toss with your fingers to thoroughly separate and coat the pieces.

In another bowl mix the honey, buttermilk, and melted butter (a small wire whisk will blend them easily). Stir in the nuts.

Add the liquids to the dry ingredients and stir lightly only until the dry ingredients are moistened—it will be a thick mixture.

Turn into the prepared pan and smooth the top. The batter will almost fill the pan. Bake for about 50 to 60 minutes until the top is a rich golden brown, semifirm to the touch, and until a cake tester inserted into the middle comes out clean (test it carefully). (The top will be quite flat.)

Cool in the pan for 15 minutes, then cover with a rack, turn over the pan and the rack, remove the pan, cover with another rack and turn over again, leaving the cake right side up to cool. It is best to chill the loaf before you slice it.

Delicious Bran Loaf

1 MEDIUM-SIZE LOAF

This is ridiculously easy and so good I can't stop. It is full of raisins, dates, and nuts and the wonderful taste and chewy quality of bran and whole wheat. It is not too sweet—serve it as bread with a meal—or serve it between meals with tea or coffee. Wrap it as a gift—it keeps well and travels well.

1 cup 100% bran cereal (*I use Kellogg's All-Bran*)

⅔ cup raisins

½ cup dark or light molasses

2 tablespoons unsalted butter, cut into small pieces

¾ cup boiling water

1 egg

4 ounces (generous 1 cup) walnut or pecan halves or large pieces

½ cup dates, cut into pieces

Optional: ¼ cup unsalted sunflower or pumpkin seeds

½ cup unsifted all-purpose whole-wheat flour

½ cup unsifted all-purpose white flour

½ teaspoon baking soda

½ teaspoon salt

½ teaspoon ginger

½ teaspoon cinnamon

Adjust a rack to the center of the oven and preheat the oven to 350 degrees. Butter an 8½ × 4½ × 2¾-inch loaf pan with a 6-cup capacity (see Note). Dust the pan all over with wheat germ, quick-cooking oatmeal, or fine, dry bread crumbs. Tap to shake out excess over a piece of paper. Set aside.

Place the bran, raisins, molasses, and butter in a large mixing bowl. Add the boiling water and stir to mix and to melt the butter. Beat the egg lightly just to mix and stir it in. Stir in the nuts, dates, and optional seeds.

Sift over the bran mixture both flours, baking soda, salt, ginger, and cinnamon. Stir to mix but do not handle any more than necessary.

Turn into the prepared pan and smooth the top.

Bake for about 40 minutes until the top is barely firm to the touch.

Cool in the pan for 10 or 15 minutes. Then cover with a rack and turn over the pan and rack. Remove the pan and very carefully turn the loaf right side up. (The top of the loaf will be quite flat; this can be served either side up.) Let stand until cool.

NOTE: *If you use a larger pan (9 × 5 × 3 inches) the loaf will not fill the pan but it will bake well and will look fine.*

Health-Food Raisin Bread

This is firm, solid, chewy, beautiful, and deliciously satisfying. Serve it plain, or with butter, cream cheese, cottage cheese, jelly, or marmalade. It is too easy to make.

1 8- OR 9-INCH LOAF

2 cups unsifted all-purpose whole-wheat flour
¼ cup unsifted all-purpose white flour
¾ teaspoon salt
1 teaspoon baking soda
6 ounces (1¼ cups) raisins (they may be a
    combination of dark and light,
    or all dark)
¼ cup wheat germ, untoasted or toasted
½ cup milk
1 cup buttermilk
¼ cup honey
¼ cup dark or light molasses

Adjust a rack one-third up from the bottom of the oven and preheat oven to 350 degrees. You will need a loaf pan with a 6-cup capacity. It can be either an 8- or 9-inch pan, about 4½ inches across, and 3 inches deep. Or it can be longer and narrower. Butter the pan and dust it all over with wheat germ (additional to what is called for in the ingredients list—toasted wheat germ makes a very nice crust).

Place both flours and the salt in a large mixing bowl. Add the baking soda through a fine strainer. Stir well to mix. Stir in the raisins, making sure that they are all separated and floured. Stir in the wheat germ. Mix the milk, buttermilk, honey, and molasses. Add the milk mixture to the batter and, with a wooden spatula, stir only until mixed.

Turn into the prepared pan. Smooth the top, and then, with the back of a spoon, form a slight trench down the length of the loaf.

Bake for about 50 minutes until the top feels semifirm to the touch and a cake tester inserted into the middle comes out clean.

Cool in the pan for about 15 minutes.

Cover with a rack, turn the pan and the rack over, and remove the pan. Let the loaf cool either side up.

Gingerbreads

Gynger-brede

16 SQUARES OR
32 SLICES

This is a recipe that was used by Mary Ball Washington, George's mother. It is very spicy. And equally delicious. Serve it as a coffee cake or a tea cake, or serve it with ice-cold buttermilk (a great combination). Or with vanilla ice cream as a dessert.

3 cups sifted all-purpose flour
2 tablespoons ginger
1½ teaspoons cinnamon
1½ teaspoons nutmeg
1½ teaspoons mace
1 teaspoon cream of tartar
½ teaspoon salt
5 ounces (1 cup) raisins
Boiling water
4 ounces (1 stick) unsalted butter
¼ cup dark or light brown sugar, firmly packed
½ cup light molasses ⎱ or 1 cup of either
½ cup dark molasses ⎰   dark or light
½ cup honey
¼ cup bourbon, dark rum, brandy, or sherry
½ cup milk
3 eggs (graded large), beaten to mix
¼ cup orange juice (grate the rind before
    squeezing to use below)
1 teaspoon baking soda
2 tablespoons warm water
Finely grated rind of 1 orange

Adjust a rack one-third up from the bottom of the oven and preheat oven to 350 degrees. Line a 13 × 9 × 2-inch pan as follows: Turn the pan over, and cover it with a piece of foil 17 or 18 inches long. Fold down the sides and the corners of the foil to shape it, remove the foil, turn the pan right side up and put the foil in the pan and carefully press it into place. To butter the foil, place a piece of butter in the pan, place the pan in the oven until the butter melts, then, with a pastry brush or wax paper, spread the butter all over the foil. Set the pan aside.

Sift together the flour, ginger, cinnamon, nutmeg, mace, cream of tartar, and salt. Set aside.

Cover the raisins with boiling water, let stand for about 5 minutes, drain in a strainer, and then spread them on paper towels to dry.

In the large bowl of an electric mixer, cream the butter until soft, add the sugar, and beat to mix. Add the molasses and honey and beat well. Then add the sifted dry ingredients in three additions, alternating with the bourbon and milk in one addition, and the eggs and orange juice in another addition.

Dissolve the baking soda in the warm water and mix into the batter. (This is a very old-fashioned method that still works well.)

Remove the bowl from the mixer and stir in the grated orange rind and the raisins.

Turn into the prepared pan and smooth the top.

Bake for 45 to 50 minutes until the top springs back when lightly pressed with a fingertip.

Let the cake cool in the pan for about 10 minutes. Then cover it with a cookie sheet or a large rack, turn over the pan and the sheet or rack, remove the pan, peel off the foil, cover with a large rack, and turn to finish cooling right side up.

When the cake is cool, carefully slide it onto a board. Use a long, thin, sharp knife to cut it into squares or slices.

West Indies Ginger Cake

1 9-INCH LOAF CAKE

Gingerbread is said to be the oldest sweet cake in the world; The Dictionary of Gastronomy (McGraw-Hill) puts its creation at about 2800 B.C. in Greece. Although it has remained rather popular ever since, it seems to be a craze now.

This Jamaican cake is not the usual ginger cake; this is made with chunks of preserved ginger (delicious), walnuts, honey, and sour cream. Serve it as a tea or coffee cake or as a dessert cake. It keeps well, it freezes well, it is a wonderful gift, it is a wonderful whatever.

2 cups sifted all-purpose flour
1 teaspoon baking soda
1 teaspoon powdered ginger
½ teaspoon salt
8.5 ounces (about ⅔ cup) preserved ginger
with its syrup (see Note)
4 ounces (1 stick) unsalted butter
½ cup light brown sugar, firmly packed
2 eggs (graded large), separated
½ cup sour cream
½ cup honey
3½ ounces (1 cup) walnuts, cut into
medium-small pieces

Adjust a rack one-third up from the bottom of the oven and preheat oven to 350 degrees. Butter a 9 × 5 × 3-inch pan, or any pan of a similar shape with an 8-cup capacity. Dust it all with fine, dry bread crumbs, and tap to shake out excess over a piece of paper. Set aside.

Sift together the flour, baking soda, ginger, and salt and set aside. Place pieces of the ginger on a plate or board and, with a small, sharp knife, cut them one at a time into pieces ¼ to ⅓ inch in diameter (no smaller). Mix together the cut ginger and its syrup and set aside.

In the large bowl of an electric mixer, beat the butter until it is soft. Add the sugar and beat well for a few minutes. Add the egg yolks and beat well. On low speed mix in about a third of the dry ingredients, then all the sour cream, another third of the dry ingredients, all the honey, and then the remaining dry ingredients, mixing only until incorporated after each addition. Remove from the mixer and stir in the ginger with the syrup and nuts.

In a small bowl, beat the egg whites only until they hold a shape but not until they are stiff or dry. Fold them into the batter.

Turn the batter into the prepared pan, smooth the top, and bake for 1 hour and 15 minutes until the top springs back when it is lightly pressed with a fingertip.

Cakes made with honey have a tendency to become too dark on the top; about 20 minutes before this cake is done (or whenever it has formed a top crust, and it begins to look too dark) cover it loosely with foil.

Let the cake cool in the pan for 15 minutes. Then cover it with a rack. Hold the pan and rack carefully together and turn them over, remove the pan, and very carefully (the cake is fragile now) turn the cake right side up to cool on the rack.

When the cake has cooled, wrap it in plastic wrap and place it in the freezer or refrigerator until it is well chilled before slicing it.

NOTE: *The preserved ginger that I buy is put out by Roland in an 8.5-ounce jar. You can use any preserved ginger of approximately that amount.*

Whole-Wheat Yogurt Date-Nut Ginger-bread

1 9- OR 10-INCH LOAF

The name tells it all, except that it has no eggs, no butter, no oil, no sugar. It is a hefty, dense, moist loaf from central Europe. Serve it as a coffee cake, a plain dessert, a sweet bread, or use it to make unusual and wonderful cheese sandwiches (butter the slices lightly, sandwich with sharp cheddar cheese and a bit of mustard).

This is best the day after it is baked.

½ cup unsifted all-purpose white flour
½ teaspoon double-acting baking powder
2 teaspoons baking soda
2 teaspoons ginger
½ teaspoon cloves
¾ teaspoon salt
16 ounces (2 cups) plain yogurt
½ cup dark or light molasses
8 ounces (1 cup) pitted dates, each date cut in half the long way
4 ounces (1 cup) walnut halves or large pieces
2½ ounces (⅓ cup) candied or preserved ginger, cut into small pieces (about ¼-inch size)
2 cups unsifted all-purpose whole-wheat flour (stir to aerate before measuring)

Adjust a rack one-third up from the bottom of the oven and preheat the oven to 350 degrees. Butter a loaf pan with an 8-cup capacity (10¼ × 3¾ × 3⅜ or 9 × 5 × 3 inches). Dust it with fine, dry bread crumbs or wheat germ; tap to shake out excess over a piece of paper. Set the pan aside.

Sift together the white flour, baking powder, baking soda, ginger, cloves, and salt, and set aside.

In a large mixing bowl, stir the yogurt and molasses with a wire whisk until smooth (the yogurt will become thin). With a rubber or wooden spatula stir in the dates and then the nuts and ginger. Then add the sifted dry ingredients and stir just to mix. The mixture will foam up; do not wait for the foam to subside but as soon as the ingredients are mixed add the whole-wheat flour and stir only until thoroughly mixed. It will be a stiff mixture.

Spoon it into the prepared pan and smooth the top.

Bake for 1½ hours; do not underbake. (Testing this the usual ways can be deceiving; it is best to be sure of your oven temperature and bake the specified time.)

Cool in the pan for about 15 minutes.

Then cover with a rack and turn over the pan and the rack. Remove the pan, and then gently turn the loaf right side up to cool.

Wrap and let stand overnight before slicing.

Whole-Wheat Ginger-bread from New Orleans

12 TO 16 SLICES

This is too delicious for words—that is, if you like sharp, spicy, chunky, wonderful gingerbread. Serve it between meals with strong, hot coffee or ice-cold milk or buttermilk. Or serve it as dessert with vanilla ice cream or applesauce. This is baked in a shallow square pan.

¼ pound (1 stick) unsalted butter
1½ teaspoons dry powdered (not granular) instant coffee
2 tablespoons granulated sugar
¾ cup light molasses
2 eggs (graded large, extra-large, or jumbo)
½ cup milk
1 cup sifted all-purpose white flour
1 cup strained or sifted all-purpose whole-wheat flour (see Note)
½ teaspoon salt

¾ teaspoon baking soda

2 teaspoons powdered ginger

½ teaspoon mace

4 ounces (generous 1 cup) walnuts, cut or
broken into medium-size pieces

4 ounces (scant 1 cup) raisins

⅓ cup candied or preserved ginger, cut into
¼-inch pieces

Adjust a rack to the center of the oven and preheat oven to 350 degrees. Prepare an 8 × 8 × 2-inch metal cake pan as follows: Turn the pan upside down, center a 12-inch square of foil over the pan, fold down the sides and corners of the foil, then remove the foil, turn the pan right side up, and place the shaped foil in the pan, pressing it carefully into place. To butter the foil, brush it with melted butter. (Easy, if you place a piece of butter in the pan in the oven to melt; then brush with a pastry brush.) Set aside.

In a 4- to 6-cup saucepan, melt the ¼ pound butter. Remove from the heat, add the coffee and sugar and stir to dissolve. Then stir in the molasses and set aside to cool slightly.

Place the eggs in a bowl and beat just to mix. Mix in the milk and set aside.

Sift both flours, salt, baking soda, powdered ginger, and mace into a large bowl. Add the nuts, raisins, and candied ginger and stir well. Add the melted butter and the egg-milk mixtures and, with a wooden or rubber spatula, stir only until thoroughly mixed.

Transfer to the prepared pan and smooth the top.

Bake for 40 to 45 minutes until the top springs back when it is lightly pressed with a fingertip.

Cool the cake in the pan for about 10 minutes. Then cover with a rack, turn over the pan and rack, remove the pan and the foil lining, cover with another rack and turn the cake right side up to cool.

To keep the cake from drying out, slice only as much as you might need. Cut the cake in half, and then cut each half into 6 or 8 slices.

NOTE: *When you sift whole-wheat flour, some of the flour may be too coarse to go through the sifter. That part should be stirred into the part that did go through.*

Marma-
lade
Ginger-
bread

1 9-INCH LOAF

This is a beautiful, fine-grained, honey-colored loaf—plain, not too sweet, moist, mildly spiced, and delicious. Serve it as a sweet bread with a meal, as a tea or coffee cake, or make thin bread and butter or cream-cheese sandwiches with it.

2 cups sifted all-purpose flour
½ teaspoon salt
1 teaspoon baking soda
1 teaspoon ginger
½ teaspoon nutmeg
Finely grated rind of 2 large lemons
1 tablespoon dark or light rum or Cognac
4 ounces (1 stick) unsalted butter
½ cup honey
1 cup sweet orange marmalade
2 eggs (graded large, extra-large, or jumbo)

Adjust a rack to the center of the oven and preheat oven to 350 degrees. Butter a 9 × 5 × 3-inch loaf pan, dust it all with fine, dry bread crumbs, and tap lightly over a piece of paper to shake out excess crumbs. Set the pan aside.

Sift together the flour, salt, baking soda, ginger, and nutmeg and set aside.

Mix the rind and rum or Cognac and let stand.

In the large bowl of an electric mixer, cream the butter. Add the honey and beat to mix. Mix in the marmalade. On low speed add half the dry ingredients, scraping the bowl and beating only to mix. Then mix in the eggs, one at a time, and then the balance of the sifted dry ingredients. Remove from the mixer and stir in the rind and rum or Cognac.

Turn into the prepared pan and smooth the top.

Bake for 1 hour until the top feels semifirm to the touch and a cake tester inserted into the middle comes out clean. If the loaf begins to brown too much during baking, cover it loosely with foil.

Cool in the pan for about 10 to 15 minutes. Cover with a rack, turn over the pan and the rack, remove the pan, and leave the loaf upside down to cool.

Pumpkin Ginger- bread

This bakes into a beautiful, richly browned, perfectly shaped loaf with a combination of spices giving a mild and deliciously gingery flavor that is just right, and a wonderfully moist texture from the pumpkin. You will be proud of this. It makes a marvelous gift. Serve it with tea or coffee, or milk or buttermilk.

1 LOAF

2 cups sifted all-purpose flour
¾ teaspoon salt
1 teaspoon baking soda
¼ teaspoon double-acting baking powder
2 teaspoons powdered ginger
½ teaspoon nutmeg
½ teaspoon cinnamon
¼ teaspoon cloves
¼ teaspoon dry powdered mustard
4 ounces (1 stick) unsalted butter
1½ cups granulated sugar
2 eggs (graded large, extra-large, or jumbo)
⅓ cup strong prepared black coffee (you can use 1 rounded teaspoon instant coffee in ⅓ cup water)
1 cup mashed cooked pumpkin (see Note)
7 ounces (2 cups) pecans, cut or broken into large pieces

Adjust a rack to the center of the oven and preheat oven to 350 degrees. You will need a loaf pan that has a 7-cup capacity; that may be 9 × 5 × 3 inches (which has an 8-cup capacity), 9 × 5 × 2¾ inches, or it may be longer and narrower. Butter the pan, dust it all over with fine, dry bread crumbs, and tap over a piece of paper to shake out excess crumbs. Set aside.

Sift together the flour, salt, baking soda, baking powder, ginger, nutmeg, cinnamon, cloves, and mustard and set aside.

In the large bowl of an electric mixer, cream the butter. Add the sugar and beat to mix. Add the eggs and beat to mix. On low speed, add half of the dry ingredients, scraping the bowl with a rubber spatula. Beat only until barely incorporated. Mix in the coffee. Add the remaining dry ingredients and beat only until incorporated. Add the pumpkin and, scraping the bowl as necessary, beat only until incorporated. Remove the bowl from the mixer.

Stir in the pecans.

Turn into the prepared pan and smooth the top. Then, with the back of a spoon, form a trench down the middle, about ½ to 1 inch deep. The trench will prevent the middle from rising too high, although it will rise some anyhow, and will form a crack down the length of the cake (it is supposed to), and will be as pretty as a picture.

Bake for 1 hour and 10 to 15 minutes until the top feels slightly firm to the touch and a cake tester inserted into the middle comes out clean.

Cool the cake in the pan for 10 to 15 minutes.

Cover the pan with a rack, turn over the pan and the rack, remove the pan, cover the cake with another rack, and very carefully (do not squash the cake) turn over again (or gently turn it over with your hands), leaving the cake right side up to cool.

NOTE: *If you use canned pumpkin, it should be labeled "solid-pack pump-kin," not "pumpkin-pie filling." A 1-pound can has a scant 2 cups of pumpkin. If you want to double the recipe, the 1-pound can is enough for the 2 loaves.*

To use fresh pumpkin, see Notes, page 159.

Muffins

Blueberry Muffins

12 MUFFINS

Especially light, tender, and delicate, these pale golden muffins are generously spotted with deep purple berries. Quick, easy, delicious, and they freeze well. Serve these either hot or cooled, either as a sweet bread with a meal, or between meals with tea or coffee.

1 cup fresh blueberries
1½ cups sifted all-purpose flour
2 teaspoons double-acting baking powder
½ teaspoon salt
½ cup granulated sugar
1 egg
2 tablespoons unsalted butter, melted
½ cup milk
Finely grated rind of 1 medium-size lemon

Adjust a rack to the center of the oven and preheat the oven to 400 degrees. These can be baked in any muffin forms lined with paper liners. However, without the liners, buttered pans give the muffins a nicer crust. I use a buttered, nonstick muffin pan.

The berries must be washed and thoroughly dried; rinse them in cold water, drain, and spread them out in a single layer on paper towels. Pat the tops with paper, and let stand until the berries are thoroughly dry.

Into a very large mixing bowl, sift together the flour, baking powder, salt, and sugar. Add the dried berries and stir to mix without breaking the berries.

In a mixing bowl, beat the egg lightly with a whisk or a beater just to mix. Mix in the melted butter and then the milk. Stir in the grated rind.

The secret of muffins is not to overmix. Add the liquid ingredients all at once to the dry ingredients and, with a large rubber spatula, stir/fold very little—only until the dry ingredients are barely moistened. It should take only a few seconds. If you do not handle it too much the batter will be lumpy, which is the way it should be.

Spoon into the muffin forms, filling them two-thirds full.

Bake for 20 to 25 minutes until golden.

Cool in the pan for 2 or 3 minutes. Then cover with a rack, turn over the pan and the rack, and remove the pan. Turn the muffins right side up.

Bran Muffins

18 MUFFINS

These are moist, dark, chewy-crunchy, sweet, and very good for you. They can become a delicious habit. My mother made them almost every day, dozens at a time; we ate them for breakfast and lunch and between meals, we took them on picnics and fishing trips and in lunch boxes and to Ebbets Field and Yankee Stadium and to the movies. I can't remember ever being without them for long.

Recently, in beautiful Rancho Santa Fe, California, my husband and I spotted a little sign saying SONRISA BAKERY OPENING SOON. *We quickly made friends with Linn Hadden and Bruce Munter, the wonderful young couple who built Sonrisa (which is Spanish for "smile"). Although they both bake and have many of their own recipes, I gave them this bran muffin recipe. The day their convection oven was installed this was the first thing they baked. They were ecstatic. They said these were the best bran muffins they ever ate and they plan to make them a daily specialty.*

They are quick and easy to make. But if you want them fresh for breakfast, you can prepare everything the night before; mix the liquids in a bowl and refrigerate, sift the dry ingredients and set aside, then put them together in a jiffy in the morning. (See Note.)

2 ounces (½ stick) unsalted butter
½ cup dark brown sugar, firmly packed
¼ cup dark or light molasses or honey
2 eggs
1 cup milk
1½ cups bran cereal (not bran flakes—
    I use Kellogg's All-Bran)
5 ounces (1 cup) raisins
4 ounces (generous 1 cup) walnuts, cut or
    broken into large pieces
½ cup unsifted all-purpose whole-wheat flour
    (stir lightly to aerate before measuring)
½ cup unsifted all-purpose white flour (stir
    lightly to aerate before measuring)
¾ teaspoon salt
1½ teaspoons baking soda

Adjust a rack to the center of the oven. (If your oven is not wide enough for the two muffin pans described below to fit on the same rack, adjust two racks to divide the oven into thirds.) Preheat the oven to 400 degrees. Butter 18 2¾-inch muffin forms (I use one pan with 12 forms and another with 6 forms). Butter them even if you are using a nonstick pan. Or line the forms with paper liners for muffin pans. It is a toss-up as to whether lining the pans or buttering them is best. Buttered pans make a nice crust; lined pans make no crust but the muffins probably keep fresh longer.

Place the butter in a small pan over low heat to melt, and then pour it into a large mixing bowl. Add the sugar and then the molasses or honey, stirring to mix well.

In a small bowl, beat the eggs only to mix. Gradually add the milk and beat to mix.

Slowly add the egg mixture to the butter mixture, stirring with a wire whisk to blend. Mix in the bran and the raisins and let stand for a few minutes (or cover and refrigerate overnight).

Then stir in the walnuts.

Sift together the whole-wheat flour, white flour, salt, and baking soda. Add to the bran mixture. Stir with a rubber spatula very little and very quickly, only until the dry ingredients are moistened.

With a large spoon, spoon the mixture into the prepared cups, filling them about two-thirds of the way.

Bake for 15 minutes just until the tops spring back when they are lightly pressed with a fingertip. (If you are baking on two racks, reverse the pans top to bottom and front to back once during baking to ensure even baking.) If the wet ingredients were mixed ahead of time and refrigerated overnight, the muffins will take about 4 minutes longer to bake. Time these muffins carefully; do not overbake them or they will dry out.

Immediately cover each pan with a rack and turn over the pan and the rack, then remove the pan. If you have used paper liners, turn the muffins right side up, if not, leave them upside down.

NOTE: *It takes only a few minutes to prepare bran muffins from scratch—doing part ahead of time does not actually save very many minutes—but it is a nice feeling and a pleasant experience early in the morning to have both the wet and the dry mixtures, as well as the muffin pans, prepared and ready.*

VARIATIONS: *You can vary these by adding about 12 coarsely cut dates or 6 coarsely cut dried prunes along with the raisins. Or, if you wish, add a few spoonfuls of pumpkin or sunflower seeds (unsalted) along with the nuts. Or sprinkle the tops with sesame seeds before baking.*

Cookies
and Crackers

Cookies

Crackers

Cookies

Christmas Brownies

16 THIN BROWNIES

Of course it's silly to limit these or any Brownies to Christmas. These have this name because they contain diced candied fruits, which are generally more available during the holiday season. These are extra special, very CHOCOLATE, and chewy, even though they are only ½ inch thick. They are crusty on top and wet inside.

2 ounces unsweetened chocolate
2 ounces (½ stick) unsalted butter
2 eggs (graded large or extra-large)
1 teaspoon vanilla extract
1 cup granulated sugar
¼ cup unsifted all-purpose flour (stir to aerate before measuring)
⅓ cup finely diced, mixed candied fruits (see Notes)

Adjust a rack one-third up from the bottom of the oven and preheat oven to 300 degrees. Prepare a shallow 9-inch square metal cake pan as follows: Turn the pan upside down, cover with a 12-inch square of aluminum foil, fold down the sides and the corners to shape the foil, remove the foil, turn the pan right side up, place the foil in the pan and carefully press it into place. To butter the foil, place a piece of butter (in addition to that called for in the recipe) in the pan in the oven to melt. Then, with a pastry brush, brush the butter all over the bottom and halfway up on the sides.

Place the chocolate and the butter in the top of a small double boiler over warm water on moderate heat. Cover until melted. Stir until smooth. Remove the top of the double boiler and set aside to cool slightly.

In the large bowl of an electric mixer, beat the eggs only to mix; they should not be foamy. Add the vanilla and sugar and beat to mix. Beat in the melted chocolate mixture. Then, on low speed, add the flour and beat only until mixed, scraping the bowl as necessary with a rubber spatula.

Remove from the mixer and stir in the diced candied fruit.

Turn into the lined and buttered pan and if necessary tilt the pan to level the batter.

Bake for 35 minutes. A toothpick inserted into the middle of the cake should come out just barely clean, or there may still be a tiny bit of the batter clinging to the toothpick—if necessary, bake for 2 or 3 minutes more.

Remove from the oven and cool in the pan for 5 minutes. Then cover the pan with a rack, turn the pan and the rack over, remove the pan, and carefully peel off the foil. Cover with another rack and carefully turn over again, leaving the cake right side up. This cake has a tendency to stick to the rack now. To prevent that, let it stand right side up for only 5 minutes. Then cover it with another rack and turn the rack and the cake over, cover what was originally the bottom of the cake with a piece of foil or wax paper, cover with a rack again and invert again, leaving the cake right side up on foil. The cake will be about ½ inch thick.

Let stand until completely cool.

Then place in the freezer or the refrigerator long enough to chill. This cuts best when it is cold or even almost frozen.

Transfer to a cutting board. With a long, heavy, sharp knife cut into 16 squares (cutting down with the full length of the blade, not just the point). If necessary, dry the blade after making each cut.

Wrap individually in clear cellophane or wax paper (not plastic wrap) or pack in an airtight box with wax paper between the layers.

NOTES: 1. *These are especially and wonderfully moist; they must be handled more carefully than most brownies or they will squash.*

2. For the candied fruits, I use citron, lemon, orange, and sometimes a bit of candied ginger. See Note on page 85 for the kind I buy and the source. I cut them on a board with a small, sharp knife.

Denver Brownies

64 TINY SQUARES

When my husband and I were on a tour for my chocolate book, I made hot fudge sauce on a Denver TV program. As we left the station, the receptionist handed me a recipe and said, "Since you like chocolate so much, you should have this recipe. When Julia Child was here, one of the men in the station made these for her and she loved them."

They are fancy little bite-size chocolate squares with a layer of white icing which is covered with chocolate icing. They look like elegant candy— make them for a party. They freeze well, but they are not for packing or mailing.

¾ cup sifted all-purpose flour
¼ teaspoon double-acting baking powder
¼ teaspoon salt
⅓ cup honey
2 tablespoons water or black coffee
4 ounces (1 stick) unsalted butter, cut into pieces, at room temperature
6 ounces semisweet chocolate, coarsely chopped
1 teaspoon vanilla extract
2 eggs
6 ounces (generous 1½ cups) walnuts, cut into medium-size pieces
2 tablespoons bourbon, brandy, or rum

Adjust a rack to the center of the oven and preheat oven to 325 degrees. Prepare a 9-inch square cake pan as follows: Turn the pan over, cover it with a 12-inch square of aluminum foil, fold down the sides and the corners of the foil to shape it, remove the foil, turn the pan right side up, place the foil in the pan and carefully press it into place. To butter the foil, place a piece of butter in the pan and place it in the oven to melt. Then brush it over the foil. Set the pan aside.

Sift together the flour, baking powder, and salt and set aside.

Place the honey, water or coffee, butter, and chocolate in a 2- to 3-quart saucepan over moderate heat. Stir until the chocolate and butter are melted. Remove from the heat. With a wooden spatula, stir in the vanilla and then the eggs, one at a time. Mix well. Add the dry ingredients and whisk vigorously with a wire whisk until smooth. Stir in the nuts.

Turn into the prepared pan and smooth the top.

Bake for about 25 minutes until a toothpick inserted into the middle just barely comes out clean—do not overbake.

Remove from the oven and brush the bourbon, brandy, or rum over the hot cake.

Cool to tepid in the pan.

Cover the pan with a rack, turn over the pan and the rack, remove the pan and the foil, cover with another rack and turn over again, leaving the cake right side up. Let stand to cool completely and then transfer to a small board. (The cake will be ¾ inch high.)

WHITE ICING

4 ounces (1 stick) unsalted butter
1 teaspoon vanilla extract
2 cups sifted confectioners sugar

In the small bowl of an electric mixer, beat the butter until soft. Add the vanilla and then gradually add the sugar, beating well until soft and fluffy.

Spread the white icing over the top of the cake. With a long, narrow metal spatula, smooth the top.

Refrigerate.

CHOCOLATE ICING

6 ounces semisweet chocolate, coarsely chopped
1 tablespoon vegetable shortening
(Crisco or other)
1 tablespoon unsalted butter

Place the chocolate, shortening, and butter in the top of a small double boiler over hot water on moderate heat. Cover until partly melted. Then uncover and stir until completely melted and smooth. Remove from the heat.

Pour in a thick ribbon all over the white icing, working quickly before the chilled white icing sets the chocolate. With a long, narrow metal spatula smooth the top.

Refrigerate.

To cut: The chocolate might be so firm that it cracks while you cut it.

Either let it stand at room temperature briefly or score the cutting lines gently and carefully with a long serrated knife, and then cut through with a long, thin knife, cutting straight down (not back and forth). First trim the edges slightly. Then cut the cake into eight 1-inch strips. With a small, sharp paring knife, cut each strip into 1-inch squares.

Place the Brownies in a single layer in a shallow covered box, or place them on a tray; be sure the chocolate is firm and then cover with plastic wrap.

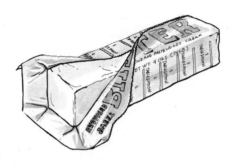

Marjorie Kinnan Rawlings's Chocolate Cookies

25 LARGE COOKIES

Shortly after I finished work on my chocolate book, we were driving through central Florida and stopped for gas in the town of Cross Creek. I was delighted to see a little sign in the garage office that announced "Homemade Brownies 4 Sale." The garage man told me his wife baked them fresh every day and the delivery for that day was expected in an hour. We paid for a dozen Brownies and told him we would be back. After an hour of driving around in circles, we returned just as the Brownies were being delivered. They were drop cookies, not bar cookies. They were unusually good, and certainly worth waiting for. When I asked for the recipe I was told that his wife would not part with it, but his mother-in-law had worked for Marjorie Kinnan Rawlings and this had been Mrs. Rawlings's recipe. I couldn't wait to get home to see if it was in Cross Creek Cookery (Mrs. Rawlings's cookbook). It was. The garage man's wife had made a change (she added the chocolate morsels) and I added the coffee and omitted the baking powder.

They taste like Brownies should: chewy/chocolate/wonderful, and they are quick and easy, and they keep well.

1 cup sifted all-purpose flour
¼ teaspoon salt
Scant 2 teaspoons instant coffee
¼ cup boiling water
2 ounces unsweetened chocolate, coarsely
    chopped
3 ounces (¾ stick) unsalted butter
½ teaspoon vanilla extract
1 cup granulated sugar
2 eggs (graded large or extra-large)
2½ ounces (½ cup) raisins
8 ounces (2 cups) walnuts, cut or broken
    into large pieces
6 ounces (1 cup) semisweet chocolate morsels

Adjust two racks to divide the oven into thirds and preheat oven to 350 degrees. Cut aluminum foil to fit cookie sheets.

Sift together the flour and salt and set aside.

In a small saucepan, dissolve the coffee in the water and add the chocolate, place over low heat and stir with a rubber spatula until smooth; it will be a thick mixture. Set aside.

In the large bowl of an electric mixer, beat the butter until it is soft. Add the vanilla and then the sugar and beat until mixed. Add the chocolate mixture (which may still be warm) and beat until smooth and thoroughly mixed. Then add the eggs one at a time, beating well after each addition. On low speed add the sifted dry ingredients, scraping the bowl with a rubber spatula and beating only until mixed. Remove from the mixer.

Stir in the raisins, nuts, and morsels.

Use a heaping teaspoonful of the mixture for each cookie. Place them on the cut aluminum foil, 2 inches apart; 8 cookies will fit on a 12 × 15½-inch sheet. Slide a cookie sheet under the foil.

Bake for 13 to 15 minutes, reversing the sheets top to bottom and front to back once during baking to ensure even baking. The cookies are done if they just barely spring back (but just barely—do not overbake) when lightly pressed with a fingertip.

If you bake only one sheet at a time, bake on the higher rack.

With a wide metal spatula, carefully transfer the cookies to racks to cool.

Chocolate Hermits

24 LARGE COOKIES

Hermits are very old-fashioned cookies that usually have raisins, nuts, and spices. Some were made in a shallow, oblong pan and cut into squares; some were drop cookies. This yummy chocolate version is a drop cookie. They are large, thick, semisoft, dark, not too sweet, slightly spicy, full of raisins and nuts, and topped with a white sugar glaze.

They keep well; they are great for a lunch box or a picnic, or for wrapping as a gift. Or for just having around.

3 ounces unsweetened chocolate
1¼ cups sifted all-purpose flour
2 teaspoons double-acting baking powder
¼ teaspoon salt
1 tablespoon unsweetened powdered cocoa
1 teaspoon cinnamon
1 teaspoon powdered (not granular) instant coffee
4 ounces (1 stick) unsalted butter
1 teaspoon vanilla extract
1 cup granulated sugar
1 egg
⅓ cup milk
5 ounces (1 cup) raisins
4 ounces (generous 1 cup) walnut or pecan halves or pieces

Adjust two racks to divide the oven into thirds and preheat the oven to 350 degrees. Line two cookie sheets with aluminum foil.

Place the chocolate in the top of a small double boiler over hot water on moderate heat. Cover until partly melted. Uncover and stir until completely melted. Remove the top of the double boiler and set aside to cool slightly.

Sift together the flour, baking powder, salt, cocoa, cinnamon, and coffee, and set aside.

In the large bowl of an electric mixer, cream the butter. Add the vanilla and then the sugar and beat to mix well. Then add the egg and the melted chocolate (which may still be slightly warm) and beat well. Beat in the milk. Then, on low speed, add the sifted dry ingredients, scraping the bowl as necessary with a rubber spatula, and beating only until mixed. Remove from the mixer and stir in the raisins and nuts.

Use a well-rounded tablespoonful of the dough for each cookie (make these large). Place the mounds at least 1 inch apart (place 12 mounds on a 12 × 15½-inch cookie sheet); they spread only slightly.

Bake for 18 to 20 minutes, reversing the sheets top to bottom and front to back once during baking to ensure even baking. The cookies are done when they feel slightly firm to the touch, and just barely spring back when they are lightly pressed with a fingertip. Do not overbake.

While the cookies are baking, prepare the following glaze.

GLAZE

¾ cup sifted or strained confectioners sugar
1 tablespoon unsalted butter, melted
½ teaspoon vanilla extract
1 tablespoon milk or light cream
Pinch of salt

In a small bowl, stir all the ingredients to mix well. The mixture must be smooth. It should be about the consistency of thin and runny mayonnaise; adjust it with more sugar or milk. Cover the glaze airtight until you are ready to use it.

Just as soon as you take the cookie sheet out of the oven, spoon or brush some of the glaze over the tops of the hot cookies. Do not attempt to cover all over the tops—just spread it on the middle and let it run down the sides a bit. Then, with a wide metal spatula, transfer the cookies to racks to cool.

When the glaze has dried and is no longer sticky, the cookies should be stored airtight. If you package them in a box, put wax paper between the layers. I wrap them, two to a package, bottoms together, in clear cellophane.

Big Sur Chocolate-Chip Cookies

These California cookies are 6 inches in diameter —they are the largest homemade chocolate-chip cookies I know (nothing succeeds like excess). They are crisp, crunchy, buttery, delicious. Too good. Irresistible. But because of their size, don't make them for a fancy tea party. Do make them for a barbecue or a picnic, or for any casual affair.

12 TO 15 VERY LARGE COOKIES

1½ cups sifted all-purpose flour
½ teaspoon salt
1 teaspoon baking soda
½ teaspoon cinnamon
6 ounces (1½ sticks) unsalted butter
1½ teaspoons vanilla extract
1 teaspoon lemon juice
⅔ cup light brown sugar, firmly packed
⅓ cup granulated sugar
2 eggs (graded large or extra-large)
¼ cup quick-cooking (not instant) rolled oats
6 ounces (1½ cups) walnuts, cut or broken into medium-size pieces
6 ounces (1 cup) semisweet chocolate morsels

Adjust two racks to divide the oven into thirds and preheat oven to 350 degrees. Cut aluminum foil to fit cookie sheets.

Sift together the flour, salt, baking soda, and cinnamon, and set aside.

In the large bowl of an electric mixer, cream the butter. Add the vanilla and lemon juice and then both of the sugars and beat to mix. Beat in the eggs one at a time. On low speed, add the sifted dry ingredients and then the rolled oats, scraping the bowl as necessary with a rubber spatula and beating only until mixed.

Remove from the mixer and stir in the nuts and morsels.

Now work next to the sink or have a large bowl of water handy so you can wet your hands while shaping the cookies. Spread out a piece of wax paper or foil. Use a ¼-cup measuring cup to measure the amount of dough for each cookie. Form 12 to 15 mounds of the dough, and place them any which way on the wax paper or foil. Wet your hands with cold water, shake the water off but do not dry your hands, pick up a mound of dough, roll it into a ball, flatten it to about ½-inch thickness, and place it on the prepared foil. Do not place more than 4 cookies on a 12 × 15½-inch piece of foil or cookie sheet. These spread to gigantic proportions.

Slide a cookie sheet under the foil.

Bake two sheets at a time for 16 to 18 minutes, reversing the sheets top to bottom and front to back as necessary to ensure even browning. If you bake only one sheet at a time, bake it on the higher rack. Bake until the cookies are well colored; they must not be too pale. Watch these carefully; they might become too dark before you know it.

When you remove these from the oven, let them stand for about a minute until they are firm enough to be moved. With a wide metal spatula, transfer them to racks to cool. If the racks are not raised at least ½ inch from the work surface, place them on a bowl or cake pan to allow more air to circulate underneath.

When cool, wrap them, bottoms together, two to a package, in cellophane or wax paper or in plastic sandwich bags. Then place all of the packages in a freezer box or in one large freezer bag. If you do not plan to serve these soon, freeze them.

Chocolate Pepper Pretzels

24 PRETZEL COOKIES

Pretzel superstitions go back to the time of the Romans. People wore pretzels made of flour and water around their necks to ward off evil spirits. They hung them on fruit trees in the belief that the pretzels would cause the trees to have a prolific yield. And they believed that if you break a pretzel with someone else (like breaking a wishbone) and if you make a wish at the same time, your wish would come true. (Imagine all that and chocolate too.)

All of these reasons have made it a popular custom to hang pretzels on Christmas trees. And, also, it is so easy to thread a ribbon through a pretzel.

These particular pretzel cookies are best when they are not too fresh—another reason to make them for the Christmas tree.

But Christmas aside, these are delicious and adorable. But they aren't as sweet as cookies usually are. They are peppery, but not sharp or harsh. The wonderful dough handles like ceramicist's clay and is just as much fun, if not more, because you get to eat these. A lovely and unusual way to serve these is with wine.

¼ cup unsweetened cocoa powder (preferably
    Dutch process)
1 teaspoon instant coffee
3 tablespoons boiling water
4 ounces (1 stick) unsalted butter
1 teaspoon vanilla extract
½ teaspoon salt
⅛ teaspoon allspice
¼ teaspoon ginger
1 teaspoon finely ground black pepper
¼ cup granulated sugar
1 egg (graded large)
2 cups unsifted all-purpose flour

Place the cocoa and coffee in a small bowl; add the water and stir to dissolve. Set aside to cool slightly.

In the large bowl of an electric mixer, cream the butter. Add the vanilla, salt, allspice, ginger, pepper, and sugar and beat to mix well. Beat in the egg, then the chocolate mixture, and then, on low speed, gradually add the flour and beat until smooth.

Turn the mixture out onto a large board or work surface and shape it into a thick cylinder 6 inches long. Wrap it in plastic wrap and refrigerate for at least half an hour or for as long as a few days.

Before baking, adjust two racks to divide the oven into thirds and preheat oven to 350 degrees. You will use unbuttered, unlined cookie sheets.

With a sharp and heavy knife, cut the dough into six 1-inch slices. Then cut each slice into equal quarters, making 24 pieces. (You can cut the 6 slices but do not separate them; then quarter the whole cylinder.)

To shape pretzels: Roll a piece of the dough on a board or work surface (do not flour the work surface) under the fingers of both hands. Spread your fingers slightly, move them back and forth and gradually out toward the ends of the roll. Each time you do this the roll will increase in length and become thinner. Continue until you have shaped a thin snake 10 inches long.

Form it into a pretzel shape (see illustration) and place each pretzel as it is shaped on an unbuttered cookie sheet.

GLAZE AND TOPPING

1 egg yolk
1 teaspoon water
Crystal sugar (see page 4) or granulated sugar

Beat the yolk and water lightly just to mix, strain the mixture, and with a small, soft brush (I use an artist's water-color brush), brush the glaze over about 4 pretzels at a time. Be careful not to allow the glaze to run down on the sheet or the cookies will stick. (If just a very little runs down it is O.K.)

Using your thumb and forefinger, carefully and slowly sprinkle the crystal or granulated sugar generously over the pretzels.

Bake for about 25 minutes, reversing the sheets top to bottom and front to back once during baking to ensure even baking. Bake until the cookies are thoroughly dry. Do not underbake. If you are not sure, break one to see.

With a wide metal spatula transfer the cookies to racks to cool.

Store airtight. Let stand for at least a day or two before serving.

Giant Oatmeal Spice Cookies

Very large, crisp/crunchy, with a marvelous blend of spices.

You will love them. These cookies should stand for 2 hours after they are shaped, before baking; it will make them bake with a better shape.

20 VERY LARGE COOKIES

1½ cups sifted all-purpose flour
2 teaspoons cinnamon

2 teaspoons allspice

1½ teaspoons cloves

1½ teaspoons ginger

½ teaspoon salt

½ teaspoon finely ground black pepper

½ teaspoon baking soda

8 ounces (2 sticks) unsalted butter

1 teaspoon vanilla extract

1 cup granulated sugar

1 cup light brown sugar, firmly packed

2 eggs (graded large or extra-large)

3 cups quick-cooking (not instant) rolled oats

Cut aluminum foil to fit cookie sheets.

Sift together the flour, cinnamon, allspice, cloves, ginger, salt, black pepper, and baking soda, and set aside.

In the large bowl of an electric mixer, cream the butter. Add the vanilla and then both sugars and beat to mix well. Add the eggs and beat to mix. On low speed beat in the sifted dry ingredients. Remove from the mixer. With a wooden spoon stir in the oats.

Work next to the sink or have a bowl of water nearby so you can wet your hands while you shape the cookies. Spread out a large piece of wax paper or foil.

Use a ¼-cup measuring cup to measure the dough for each cookie. Form 20 mounds of the dough, and place them any which way on the wax paper or foil.

Wet your hands with cold water, shake off the water but do not dry your hands. Pick up a mound of the dough, roll it between your hands into a ball, flatten it between your hands until it is about ½ inch thick, and then place the cookies on the prepared foil, placing only 4 of them on a 12 × 15½-inch piece of foil. (They need a lot of room to spread.)

Let stand for 2 hours before baking.

When you are ready to bake, adjust two racks to divide the oven into thirds and preheat the oven to 375 degrees.

Slide the cookie sheets under the foil and bake for 12 to 13 minutes (no longer), reversing the sheets top to bottom and front to back as necessary to ensure even baking. Bake only until the cookies are nicely browned, but be careful that they do not become too dark on the edges. If it looks as though they might, reduce the temperature by 10 or 15 degrees for the last few minutes of baking. If you bake only one sheet at a time, bake it on the upper rack.

Let the baked cookies stand for a minute or so until they are firm enough to be moved. Then, with a wide metal spatula, transfer them to racks to cool.

Wrap the cookies two to a package (bottoms together) in clear cellophane or wax paper, or in plastic sandwich bags. Then place them all in a box or a large plastic bag.

Crisp Oatmeal Wafers

48 COOKIES

These are the most amazingly and deliciously crisp and crunchy of any cookies I know. Even in my kitchen, in humid Florida, they remain that way for weeks in an airtight cookie jar (the glass jars that have a ground-glass rim on the cover are airtight; those that do not have the ground-glass rim are not airtight).

These cookies are wonderful because they are so plain. They are easy-to-mix drop cookies made without flour. Somehow the flavor reminds me of popcorn and peanut brittle. These are especially appropriate when you want something crisp and crunchy to serve with ice cream, custard, or fruit.

3 eggs (graded large)
1 teaspoon cinnamon
1 teaspoon vanilla extract
½ teaspoon salt
1½ cups granulated sugar
2 tablespoons unsalted butter,
    melted and cooled
4 teaspoons double-acting baking powder
3½ cups quick-cooking (not instant)
    oatmeal (see Note)

Adjust two racks to divide the oven into thirds and preheat oven to 350 degrees. Cut aluminum foil to fit cookie sheets. These must be baked on foil, even if you use a nonstick pan.

In the small bowl of an electric mixer, beat the eggs until foamy. Beat in the cinnamon, vanilla, salt, and sugar, and beat for 2 or 3 minutes until pale and thick. Add the melted butter and beat only to mix. Then add the baking powder (if it is lumpy it should be strained) and beat only for a moment or so to mix. Remove from the mixer, transfer to a larger bowl, and stir in the oats.

Use a rounded teaspoonful of the batter for each cookie, placing them about 2 inches apart, or only 6 on a 12 × 15½-inch piece of foil. Stir occasionally; the liquid settles.

Slide a cookie sheet under the foil. Bake two sheets at a time, reversing them top to bottom and front to back once during baking to ensure even browning. Bake for about 10 minutes. The cookies will rise and then settle down during baking. When they are thin (they will be almost lace cookies) and lightly colored—darker on the rim and lighter in the centers—they are done. You will have to be careful not to bake these either too little or too much; after the first sheet you will know when they are done.

Slide the foil off the sheet. Let stand until the cookies are cool. Slide the cookie sheet under another piece of foil with unbaked cookies on it (it is O.K. if the cookie sheet is warm).

When the cookies have cooled completely it will be easy to peel the foil away from the backs of the cookies. (If it is not easy it means that the cookies were not baked enough.)

These must be stored airtight or they will not remain crisp.

NOTE: *"Old Fashioned Quaker Oats," which cook in 5 minutes, work very well for this recipe. Coarser oats that take longer cooking might not hold together in baking.*

Coconut Oatmeal Cookies

48 COOKIES

This is an old-fashioned, homey, plain and crisp, buttery cookie-jar cookie. They are quick and easy drop cookies that are especially good. The recipe was sent to me as a gift from a bakery in Jacksonville, Florida, where they are baked in huge quantities (700 cookies at a time) and are so popular that the bakery runs out of them every day. If you want to go into the cookie business, this is a good one to start with.

2½ cups sifted all-purpose flour
1 teaspoon double-acting baking powder
1 teaspoon baking soda
¼ teaspoon salt
½ teaspoon cinnamon
8 ounces (2 sticks) unsalted butter
½ teaspoon vanilla extract
1 cup light or dark brown sugar,
    firmly packed
½ cup granulated sugar
2 eggs (graded large, extra-large, or jumbo)
1 cup quick-cooking (not instant) rolled oats
1 cup shredded coconut, firmly packed (it may
    be sweetened or unsweetened)

Adjust two racks to divide the oven into thirds and preheat oven to 350 degrees. Line cookie sheets with aluminum foil cut to fit.

Sift together the flour, baking powder, baking soda, salt, and cinnamon, and set aside.

In the large bowl of an electric mixer, cream the butter. Beat in the vanilla and both sugars and beat to mix well. Beat in the eggs, then on low speed beat in the sifted dry ingredients. Remove from the mixer.

With a wooden spatula, stir in the rolled oats and then the coconut.

Use a rounded teaspoonful of the dough for each cookie. Place them 2 to 3 inches apart (I place only 8 on a 12 × 15½-inch sheet; these spread) on the foil-lined cookie sheets. Do not flatten the tops—they flatten themselves.

Bake for about 14 to 15 minutes, reversing the sheets top to bottom and front to back once during baking to ensure even browning. These will rise and then fall during baking. Bake only until the cookies are a rich golden brown all over; they will still feel soft to the touch, but do not bake any longer. These become crisp as they cool. When they are cool they should be crisp on the edges but slightly chewy in the middle.

Let the baked cookies stand on the sheet for a few seconds to firm up slightly before you remove them. Then, with a wide metal spatula, transfer the cookies to racks to cool.

Coconut Cookies

ABOUT 36 COOKIES

These are plain, old-fashioned, thin, extra-crisp, perfectly wonderful refrigerator cookies. The dough must be refrigerated overnight or longer before baking.

This is a homemade version of a famous coconut cookie that used to be sold in Havana. My Cuban friends tell me this is better.

3½ ounces (1 to 1⅓ cups) shredded coconut
2 cups sifted all-purpose flour
½ teaspoon double-acting baking powder
¼ teaspoon salt
6 ounces (1½ sticks) unsalted butter
1 teaspoon vanilla extract
¼ teaspoon almond extract
1 cup light or dark brown sugar, firmly packed
1 egg

Place the coconut in a shallow baking pan in the center of a preheated 350-degree oven. Stir it occasionally until it is toasted to a golden color. Set aside.

Sift together the flour, baking powder, and salt, and set aside.

In the large bowl of an electric mixer cream the butter. Add the vanilla and almond extracts, then the sugar and beat to mix. Add the egg and beat to mix. On low speed, gradually add the sifted dry ingredients, beating only to mix. Remove from the mixer and stir in the coconut.

Place the mixture in the refrigerator for 20 to 30 minutes to chill a bit. Then flour your hands and a work surface. Turn the dough out onto the floured surface, press it together, and shape it into a cylinder about 6 inches long and 2 to 2½ inches in diameter. Wrap in plastic wrap. Refrigerate overnight. (If this is frozen it becomes difficult to slice thin enough without cracking, but it can be refrigerated for a few days if you wish.)

When you are ready to bake, adjust two racks high in the oven, or adjust them to divide the oven into thirds. If your oven has enough adjustments, higher is better. Preheat the oven to 325 degrees.

With a very sharp knife, cut extra-thin cookies; they should be less than ¼ inch thick. Place the cookies 1 inch apart on unbuttered cookie sheets.

Bake for about 16 minutes, reversing the sheets top to bottom and front to back once during baking to ensure even baking. Watch carefully; if the cookies appear to be browning too much on the bottoms, be prepared to slide an additional cookie sheet under them. Do not underbake. Bake until the cookies are lightly browned. You won't believe how wonderfully crisp these are, but only if they are baked enough. (And then they will only stay that way if they are stored airtight.)

With a wide metal spatula gently transfer the cookies to a rack to cool. As soon as they are cool, package them airtight.

Joe Froggers

16 TO 18 5-INCH
COOKIES

Once upon a time, actually, it was over 100 years ago, in Marblehead, Massachusetts, there was an old man who was called Uncle Joe. He lived alongside a frog pond that was known as Uncle Joe's Frog Pond.

Uncle Joe made the biggest and the bestest molasses cookies for miles around. The local fishermen would swap a jug of rum for a batch of the cookies, which came to be known as Joe Froggers, because they were as big and as dark as the frogs in the pond. The fishermen liked them because they never got hard when they took them to sea.

Uncle Joe said the secret of keeping them soft was that he used rum and sea water. But that was all he said. He would not part with the recipe. When he died people said, "That's the end of Joe Froggers."

However, there was a woman named Mammy Cressy who said she was Joe's daughter. She gave the recipe to a fisherman's wife. And soon most of the women in Marblehead were making Joe Froggers. And they were sold at a local bakery. And the recipe traveled. The last I heard about them, a few years ago, they were still being served with a pitcher of cold milk on Sunday nights in the Publick House in the Colonial Village in Sturbridge, Massachusetts.

With their background, it is obvious that these would be a good choice for mailing or traveling.

Originally they were 6 inches in diameter. I use a plain, round cookie cutter that is 5 inches in diameter (that's my largest one). They can be smaller but they are wonderful large.

The dough should be refrigerated overnight before the cookies are rolled, cut, and baked. Allow plenty of time for baking since they are baked only 4 at a time.

4⅓ cups sifted all-purpose flour
1 teaspoon baking soda
¾ teaspoon salt
2 teaspoons ginger
¾ teaspoon cloves
¾ teaspoon nutmeg
¼ teaspoon mace
¼ teaspoon allspice
Optional: 1 teaspoon finely ground black
     pepper (Uncle Joe did not use the pepper,
     but I do)
6 ounces (1½ sticks) unsalted butter
¾ cup granulated sugar
1 cup dark or light molasses
⅓ cup mixed water (it needn't be sea
     water), coffee, and dark rum (amounts
     can vary to your taste, or use
     all of any one; or try 1 tablespoon instant
     coffee dissolved in 3 tablespoons water,
     and the rest rum)

Sift together the flour, baking soda, salt, ginger, cloves, nutmeg, mace, all-spice, and optional black pepper. Set aside.

In the large bowl of an electric mixer, beat the butter until it softens. Add the sugar and beat to mix. Beat in the molasses. Then, on low speed, add about half of the dry ingredients, scraping the bowl as necessary with a rubber spatula and beating until mixed. Beat in the water or coffee and rum, and then the remaining dry ingredients.

Cover the bowl with plastic wrap or foil and refrigerate until it is firm enough to be handled. Then divide it in thirds and wrap each piece in plastic wrap. Refrigerate overnight.

When you are ready to bake, adjust a rack to the center of the oven and preheat the oven to 375 degrees. Cut aluminum foil to fit cookie sheets (you will need 5 pieces if you have 12 × 15½-inch sheets). Place a piece of the foil on a cookie sheet.

Flour a pastry cloth and a rolling pin, using more rather than less flour. Unwrap one of the packages of dough and place it on the cloth. Pound it a bit with the rolling pin to soften it slightly. Turn it over to flour both sides. Work very quickly because the dough will become sticky and unmanageable if it softens too much. Roll out in all directions until the dough is ¼ inch thick. Quickly cut with a floured 5-inch round cutter (or what-have-you).

Use a wide metal spatula to transfer the cookies to the foil. Quickly and carefully place them about 1 inch apart on the foil. (I place 4 on a 12 × 15½-inch sheet.)

Press the scraps together and rechill (the freezer is O.K.), then reroll and cut.

Bake one sheet at a time for 13 to 15 minutes, reversing the sheet front to back once during baking to ensure even baking. Watch these very carefully. They must not burn even a bit on the bottoms or it will spoil the taste. If they seem to be browning too much on the bottoms be prepared to slide an extra cookie sheet under the one that is baking. Or raise the rack slightly higher in the oven. (But I have found that if I bake these high in the oven, they crack. It is only minor, but it does not happen when they are baked on the middle rack. That is why I bake these only one sheet at a time.)

Be very careful not to overbake these cookies. They will become firmer as they cool, and they should remain a bit soft and chewy in the middle. If you use a smaller cutter the cookies will probably bake in slightly less time.

Slide the foil off the sheet and let stand for a few minutes. (Meanwhile, slide the cookie sheet under another piece of foil with cookies on it and place in the oven.) Use a wide metal spatula or the bottom of a loose-bottomed quiche pan to transfer the cookies to racks to cool. Since these are so large, if the rack is not raised enough (at least ½ inch or more), place the rack on any right-side-up bowl or pan to make more room for air to circulate underneath.

When completely cool, store these airtight. I wrap them, two to a package, bottoms together, in clear cellophane.

Lebkuchen

28 LARGE COOKIES

Lebkuchen are traditional German cookies baked at Christmastime. They are usually the first cookies baked for the holiday season because they not only keep well for weeks, but they get better as they age. There are many varieties, although most contain honey, spices, and candied fruits. And most, like these, stand overnight after they are shaped, before they are baked. These are rolled out with a rolling pin and cut with a knife into oblongs. As soon as they are baked they are brushed with a white sugar glaze. They are very firm and chewy, mildly spiced, and just as delicious in the summer as in the winter.

These take longer to prepare than most cookies do, and they are worth it.

> 6 ounces (scant 1¼ cups) blanched almonds
> 2 eggs (graded large)
> ½ teaspoon double-acting baking powder
> ¼ teaspoon salt
> ½ teaspoon cinnamon
> ½ teaspoon powdered cloves
> 1 cup granulated sugar
> 1 tablespoon plus 1½ teaspoons brandy
> ⅓ cup honey
> ¾ cup (generous ¼ pound) mixed candied citron, lemon rind, and orange rind, finely diced
> About 3½ cups sifted cake flour (use a triple sifter, or sift the flour three times before measuring)

The almonds must be ground to a fine powder; this can be done in a processor, a blender (in which case you might like to add a bit of the sugar to keep the almonds from lumping), or a nut grinder. Set the ground almonds aside.

In the small bowl of an electric mixer, beat the eggs for several minutes until they are slightly thickened. Then, while beating, add the baking powder, salt, cinnamon, cloves, and gradually add the sugar. Continue to beat for a few minutes until the mixture is pale and forms a ribbon when the beaters are raised. Transfer to the large bowl of the mixer. On low speed add the almonds, brandy, honey, and then the diced fruit. Gradually add about 3 cups of the flour, scraping the bowl with a rubber spatula and beating only until incorporated. Remove from the mixer. With a large wooden spatula stir in the remaining flour—it will be a very stiff mixture. (However, if the mixture is too wet or too sticky to be rolled out, add a bit more flour, but not unless you are sure you need it. It is best to first flour a pastry cloth and rolling pin and try to roll about one-third of the dough. If it needs more flour return it to the bowl and work in as much as you need.) Let stand while you prepare the cookie sheets.

These cookies will stick to plain aluminum foil. Therefore it is necessary either to butter and flour the foil, or use baking-pan liner paper. Nonstick cookie sheets will not stick either, but since these stand overnight on the paper or cookie sheets, you might not have enough nonstick sheets. Prepare the foil or paper (cut the foil or paper to fit the sheets; butter and flour the foil), or have the nonstick sheets ready.

Turn the dough out onto a well-floured pastry cloth, flour your hands, form the dough into a heavy cylinder, cut it into thirds, and work with one piece at a time. Form it into an oblong, flour it on all sides, and roll it on the floured pastry cloth with a floured rolling pin. Turn it over as necessary to keep both the top and bottom floured. Roll into an oblong shape ¼ inch thick.

It is easiest to cut the cookies with a large and heavy knife. The blade will become sticky after almost every cut, unless you keep the blade wet. Either wipe it with a damp cloth, or hold it under running water, or dip it in a deep pitcher of water. Cut the cookies into 2 × 4-inch oblongs.

To transfer the cookies, use a wide metal spatula. (If the cookies lose their shape slightly while being transferred, just straighten them with the edge of the spatula.) Place the cookies, as you cut them, on the foil, paper, or nonstick sheets, placing them about ½ inch apart.

Press the scraps together and reroll them.

Cover the cookies loosely with plastic wrap and let stand overnight.

To bake, adjust two racks to divide the oven into thirds and preheat the oven to 325 degrees.

Place one sheet of cookies in the oven, and wait 5 minutes before starting the second sheet, so they do not all finish baking at once.

Bake the cookies for 20 minutes, reversing the sheets top to bottom and front to back once during baking to ensure even baking. Bake until the cookies are lightly colored all over.

While the cookies are baking, prepare the following glaze.

GLAZE

1½ cups strained or sifted confectioners sugar
Scant 1 tablespoon fresh lemon juice
Scant 1 tablespoon boiling water

Stir the ingredients together in a small bowl. The glaze should be thick but fluid; as thick as molasses. If necessary, adjust with more sugar or liquid.

When the cookies are baked, with a wide metal spatula transfer them to racks set over foil, wax paper, or a brown paper bag.

Immediately, with a pastry brush, brush the glaze on the hot cookies. The heat will melt the glaze and make it almost transparent. Let stand to dry.

Store airtight. I wrap these individually in clear cellophane. They will be very crisp, but they will soften, as they should, after a few days.

NOTE: *When I bake these, I double the recipe. But it takes hours, and it spreads out of the kitchen into the living room and dining room.*

Fig Bars

24 COOKIES

A pastry chef on a cruise ship that sails from the port of Miami and cruises through the Caribbean gave me this recipe. He makes it frequently for the passengers to have with tea in the afternoon. These cookies are almost solid figs, a few nuts, and just barely enough batter to hold them together—delicious on land or sea. They are homey, old-fashioned cookies—moist, chewy, yummy, not too sweet. Great for a picnic or lunch box, wonderful to mail.

1 pound (2 generous packed cups) dried brown
    figs (although they are called "dried," they
    should be soft and moist)
½ cup sifted all-purpose flour
½ teaspoon double-acting baking powder
½ teaspoon salt
2 eggs (graded large or extra-large)
½ cup light brown sugar, firmly packed
1 teaspoon vanilla extract
6 ounces (1½ cups) walnuts, cut or broken
    into medium-size pieces
Confectioners sugar (to be used after the
    cookies are baked)

Adjust a rack to the center of the oven and preheat oven to 350 degrees. Prepare a shallow 9-inch square cake pan as follows: Turn the pan upside down, cover it with a 12-inch square of foil, fold down the sides and the corners of the foil, then remove the foil, turn the pan right side up, and place the foil in the pan. To butter the foil, place a piece of butter in the pan and place the pan in the oven to melt the butter. Then, with a pastry brush, brush the butter over the bottom and sides of the pan, and set the pan aside.

With a small, sharp knife, cut off and discard the tough stems on the figs. The figs should now be cut into ¼- to ½-inch pieces; they should not be finely chopped or ground. It can be done with a small, sharp knife or with scissors (I use scissors). Set the prepared figs aside.

Sift together the flour, baking powder, and salt, and set aside.

In a mixing bowl, beat or whisk the eggs just to mix well. Beat in the sugar and vanilla. Add the sifted dry ingredients and beat or whisk until smooth (if necessary, use a mixer). Then stir in the figs and nuts.

Turn into the prepared pan and smooth the top.

Bake for 35 minutes. Cool in the pan until tepid.

Cover with a rack, turn the pan and rack over, remove the pan, peel off the foil, cover with a fresh square of foil or wax paper (these might stick to the rack) and another rack, and turn over again, leaving the cake right side up (on the foil or wax paper) on a rack.

When cool, place in the freezer for about an hour (it is much easier to cut these when they are almost frozen). Transfer to a cutting board and, with a long, sharp, heavy knife, cut into 4 strips. Then cut each strip into 6 bars.

To sugar the cookies, place them on wax paper. Place confectioners sugar in a strainer and sugar them generously. Then turn them over and sugar the other side.

Wrap these individually in clear cellophane or wax paper, or package them in an airtight container.

Anise Seed Cookies

50 TO 60 COOKIES

This is an old Shaker recipe from Ohio; it makes beautiful and delicious cookies that are traditional at Christmastime. They are hard and crunchy with just a hint of anise. They keep well, and should ripen for a few days before they are served. They are perfect cookies for a cookie jar, and they make a wonderful gift.

They are rolled out with a rolling pin, and are cut with a small, round cookie cutter.

The dough should be chilled for half an hour or longer before it is rolled out, cut, and baked.

50 to 60 (scant ½ cup) whole
blanched almonds
1 teaspoon anise seeds (not ground; see Note)
4 ounces (1 stick) unsalted butter
1 teaspoon vanilla extract
1½ cups granulated sugar
¼ teaspoon salt
3 eggs (graded large)
3 cups sifted all-purpose flour
1 egg white
A bit of pearl or crystal sugar (see page 4),
or additional granulated sugar (to be
sprinkled over the tops)

Place the skinned almonds in a small shallow pan in a moderate oven. Shake or stir occasionally until the nuts are just lightly colored.

Crush the anise seeds in a mortar and pestle. Or place them on a board, cover with a towel to keep them from flying around, and whack them with the back of a wide cleaver. They do not have to be fine or powdered or strained. Set them aside.

In the large bowl of an electric mixer, beat the butter until it is soft and smooth. Add the vanilla and then the sugar and beat until well mixed. Add the salt and then the eggs, one at a time, beating after each addition until incorporated. Add the anise seeds and, on low speed, gradually add the flour, scraping the bowl with a rubber spatula and beating only until mixed.

The dough will be soft and sticky. Chill it, in the mixing bowl if you wish, or transfer to foil or wax paper, in the freezer for about half an hour, or longer in the refrigerator, until it is firm enough to be rolled.

Before baking, adjust two racks to divide the oven into thirds and preheat the oven to 350 degrees. Line two cookie sheets with foil. (Or you can bake only one sheet at a time, in which case the rack should be in the center.)

Flour a pastry cloth and a rolling pin. Work with only half of the dough at a time; keep the rest cold. Work quickly before the dough becomes sticky. First flour your hands and knead the dough briefly until it is smooth. Then form it into a ball, flour it lightly, flatten it slightly between your hands, and then roll it on a floured pastry cloth with a floured rolling pin until it is ½ inch thick.

Have flour handy to dip the cutter into. Flour a 1½-inch round cutter and cut rounds of the dough, starting at the outside edge of the dough, and cutting the rounds as close to each other as possible. Place them 1 inch apart (no closer) on the foil-lined cookie sheets.

Press the scraps of dough together, rechill, and reroll them.

Beat the egg white until it is foamy. With a pastry brush, brush it over the tops of the cookies. Then press an almond on its flat side gently into the top of each cookie. Brush over the almond and the top of the cookie again with the beaten egg white. (It will have separated and should be beaten again.)

Sprinkle the tops generously with the pearl or crystal sugar, or with granulated sugar.

Bake for about 20 to 22 minutes, reversing the sheets top to bottom and front to back as necessary to ensure even browning. The cookies will be slightly colored and will feel semifirm to the touch. Do not overbake or they will become too hard.

With a wide metal spatula transfer the cookies to racks to cool. Then store them airtight at room temperature for a few days before serving. They can be frozen but they keep very well at room temperature if they are stored airtight.

NOTE: *Anise seed is a spice, found in the spice department of grocery stores. It has a licorice flavor. The amount called for in this recipe is mild; if you know you like it, it may be increased to 1½ teaspoons.*

Raisin-Nut Cookies

These are especially wonderful, large, semisoft drop cookies full of raisins and nuts, and mildly flavored with a few spices. It is an old recipe from Boston, Massachusetts.

40 LARGE COOKIES

10 ounces (2 cups) raisins
1 cup boiling water
3½ cups sifted all-purpose flour
1 teaspoon double-acting baking powder
1 teaspoon baking soda
1 teaspoon salt
1 teaspoon cinnamon

½ teaspoon nutmeg
8 ounces (2 sticks) unsalted butter
1 teaspoon vanilla extract
1¾ cups granulated sugar
2 eggs (graded large)

4 ounces
   (generous 1 cup)
   walnuts
4 ounces
   (generous 1 cup)
   pecans
} or 8 ounces (2 cups) of either one, cut or broken into medium-size pieces

Adjust two racks to divide the oven into thirds and preheat the oven to 375 degrees. Cut aluminum foil to fit cookie sheets.

Place the raisins in a small saucepan, pour the boiling water over them, place over moderate heat, bring to a boil, and boil for 3 minutes. Remove from the heat and set aside to cool. (Do not drain.)

Sift together the flour, baking powder, baking soda, salt, cinnamon, and nutmeg, and set aside.

In the large bowl of an electric mixer, cream the butter. Beat in the vanilla and then the sugar. Beat to mix. Add the eggs and beat well. Then, on low speed, mix in the raisins and their liquid. On low speed, gradually add the sifted dry ingredients and beat, scraping the bowl with a rubber spatula, until thoroughly incorporated. Remove from mixer and stir in the nuts.

Use a rounded tablespoonful (make these large) of the dough for each cookie. Shape the mounds neatly, and place them 2 inches apart on the aluminum foil. Slide a cookie sheet under the foil.

Bake two sheets at a time, reversing the sheets top to bottom and front to back to ensure even browning. Bake for about 18 minutes until the cookies are golden brown and spring back when they are lightly pressed with a fingertip.

With a wide metal spatula transfer the cookies to racks to cool.

It is best to wrap these individually in clear cellophane or in wax paper (not plastic wrap, because that is too much trouble). Or, if you package them in layers in a box or other container, they must have wax paper between the layers (if these are exposed to humidity they might stick together).

Carrot and Honey Oatmeal Cookies

These are large, thick, chewy, satisfying, not-very-sweet health-food cookies. They taste as though they are related to bran muffins, although they have no bran. They keep wonderfully. They may be mailed. A few of these and a glass of milk make a delicious quick meal; they are marvelous for a lunch box or a picnic.

36 VERY LARGE COOKIES

6 medium-size carrots (about 1½ pounds)
5 ounces (1 cup) raisins
Boiling water
1 cup sifted all-purpose white flour
1 cup sifted all-purpose whole-wheat flour
2 teaspoons double-acting baking powder
½ teaspoon baking soda
½ teaspoon salt
1 tablespoon cinnamon
4 ounces (1 stick) unsalted butter
1 cup honey
½ cup light brown sugar
2 eggs (graded large or extra-large)
2 cups quick-cooking (not instant) rolled oats
    (see Note)
8 ounces (generous 2 cups) walnuts, cut or
    broken into medium-size or large pieces

Adjust two racks to divide the oven into thirds and preheat oven to 325 degrees. Line cookie sheets with aluminum foil.

Wash the carrots (it is not necessary to peel them) and grate them on the coarse side of a four-sided grater (they should not be finer than that) or they may be shredded with the coarse shredder blade of a food processor. You should have 2 generous cups, firmly packed. Set aside.

Pour enough boiling water over the raisins to cover them. Let stand for 2 or 3 minutes, then pour through a strainer to drain, and let stand.

Sift together both of the flours, the baking powder, baking soda, salt, and cinnamon, and set aside.

In the large bowl of a mixer, beat the butter until soft and smooth. Add the honey and sugar and beat until smooth. Add the eggs and beat well until smooth.

Remove from the mixer. With a large wooden spatula stir in, in the following order, the dry ingredients, carrots, oatmeal, nuts, and raisins.

To shape the cookies, work near the sink or have a bowl of water near you so you will be able to wet your hands easily as necessary. Spread out a long piece of aluminum foil. Use a heaping tablespoonful of the dough for each cookie (make these large). Place them in mounds any which way on the foil. Wet your hands with cold water, shake the water off but do not dry your hands. Lift up one of the mounds (if necessary use a metal spatula to lift with) and, between your wet hands, roll the dough into a ball, flatten it to a generous ½ inch thickness, and place it on a foil-lined sheet. Continue to shape the cookies and place them about 1 inch apart (these barely spread, if at all).

Bake two sheets at a time, reversing the sheets top to bottom and front to back once during baking to ensure even baking. Bake for 25 to 30 minutes until the cookies are lightly colored.

With a wide metal spatula transfer the cookies to racks to cool.

Store airtight in a freezer box with wax paper between the layers. Or, better yet, wrap the cookies individually in clear cellophane or in wax paper or aluminum foil.

NOTE: *For these cookies I use Shiloh Farms rolled oats (from Sulphur Springs, Arkansas). I buy them in health-food stores.*

Whole-Wheat Cinnamon-Nutmeg Cookies

These delicious, plain, old-fashioned cookies are easy and fun to make, they keep well, they travel well; make them to keep in a cookie jar, or make them for a tea or coffee party. A gentleman friend always has a jar of these on his huge, shiny desk in his sleek, modern, impressive, mirror-and-chrome office—his young daughter makes them for him and he could not be more proud.

36 COOKIES

2 cups unsifted all-purpose whole-wheat flour
1 teaspoon double-acting baking powder
Scant ½ teaspoon salt
½ teaspoon baking soda
1 teaspoon cinnamon
½ teaspoon nutmeg
4 ounces (1 stick) unsalted butter
1 teaspoon vanilla extract
1 cup dark or light brown sugar, firmly packed
1 egg (graded large)
2 tablespoons milk
Finely grated rind of 1 large lemon

Adjust two racks to divide the oven into thirds and preheat oven to 375 degrees. Line two cookie sheets with aluminum foil.

Through a large strainer set over a bowl, strain the flour (see Note), baking powder, salt, baking soda, cinnamon, and nutmeg and set aside.

In the large bowl of an electric mixer, cream the butter. Add the vanilla and then the sugar and beat to mix. Then beat in the egg, milk, and lemon rind. On low speed gradually add the strained dry ingredients and beat only until mixed.

Lightly flour a large board or work surface. Turn the dough out, knead it slightly, form it into a ball, and cut it in half. Work with one half at a time. On the lightly floured surface roll it into a long and thin roll, 18 inches long and 1 inch in diameter. Cut it into eighteen 1-inch lengths. Repeat with the other half.

Pick up a piece of dough, roll it between your hands into a ball, flatten it slightly between your hands, and place it on a foil-lined sheet. Repeat with the remaining pieces of dough, placing them about 1½ inches apart.

Press the cookies with the back of the tines of a fork, forming ridges in one direction only and flattening the cookies slightly.

TOPPING

1 tablespoon granulated sugar
½ teaspoon cinnamon

In a small cup, mix together the sugar and cinnamon. With a spoon, sprinkle the mixture generously over the tops of the cookies.

Bake for 10 to 12 minutes, reversing the sheets top to bottom and front to back once during baking to ensure even browning. Bake only until the cookies are lightly colored and feel semifirm when gently pressed with a fingertip. Do not overbake.

With a wide metal spatula transfer the cookies to a rack to cool.

If you bake only one sheet at a time, bake it on the higher rack, and it will take a bit less time than when there are two sheets in the oven at once.

NOTE: *Some of the whole-wheat flour will be too coarse to go through the strainer; it should be stirred into the part that did go through.*

Sour
Lemon
Squares

16 COOKIES

This recipe comes from a friend in Scottsdale, Arizona. The cookies have a crisp, buttery base and a soft, custardy, sour-lemon topping. They are more delicate than many other cookies and they are fabulous! Make them to serve with tea (especially) or coffee, or serve them as dessert, or along with a fruit or custard dessert. They may be frozen.

PASTRY BASE

3 ounces (¾ stick) unsalted butter
¼ teaspoon salt
¼ cup light brown sugar, firmly packed
1 cup sifted all-purpose flour

Adjust a rack to the center of the oven and pre-heat oven to 350 degrees. To line an 8 × 8 × 2-inch square pan with foil, turn the pan upside down. Center a 12-inch square of foil over the pan, fold down the sides and corners to shape it, remove the foil, turn the pan right side up, place the foil in the pan and press it into shape. To butter the foil, put a piece of butter (in addition to what is called for in the recipe) in the pan, place the pan in the oven to melt the butter, and then brush the butter over the bottom and halfway up the sides. Let the pan cool and then place it in the freezer (it is easier to press the bot-tom crust into place if the pan is cold).

In a small bowl, cream the 3 ounces of butter. Beat in the salt, sugar, and then the flour. (Or you can do this in a food processor: Place the dry ingredients in the bowl, with the steel blade; cut the butter into pieces and add, then process until thoroughly mixed.) If the mixture does not hold together, turn it out onto a work surface and knead it until it does.

Place the mixture in mounds (each one about a rounded teaspoonful) over the bottom of the cold pan. Then, with your fingers, press it to make a smooth and firm layer on the bottom only.

Bake for about 18 minutes until the crust is lightly colored.

Meanwhile, prepare the Lemon Layer.

LEMON LAYER

Finely grated rind of 2 medium-size lemons
3 tablespoons fresh lemon juice
2 eggs (graded large, extra-large, or jumbo)
¾ cup granulated sugar
2 tablespoons sifted all-purpose flour
¼ teaspoon double-acting baking powder
Confectioners sugar (to be used after the
    cookies are baked)

In a small cup mix the rind and juice and set aside.

In the small bowl of an electric mixer, beat the eggs well. Add the sugar, flour, and baking powder and beat for 1 minute at high speed (see Note). Stir in rind and juice.

Pour the lemon mixture over the hot bottom crust.

Bake for 25 to 30 minutes until the top is lightly colored and dry to the touch; when it is done it will feel spongy and custardy, not dry or stiff.

Cool completely in the pan and then chill in the freezer for about half an hour. Cover the pan with a rack or a small cookie sheet, turn over the pan and rack or sheet, remove the pan, and slowly and carefully peel off the foil. Cover with a small cutting board and turn over the board and the rack or sheet, leaving the cake right side up. The cake will be only about ½ inch deep.

Use a long, heavy, sharp knife and cut the cake into 16 squares. Wipe the blade after making each cut. Place them on wax paper and strain confectioners sugar generously over the tops.

Package these in a shallow box or arrange them on a tray and cover with plastic wrap.

These may be refrigerated and served cold or they may be served at room temperature. When they are cold, the lemon layer is more firm and wonderful; when they are at room temperature the lemon layer is softer and wonderful.

NOTE: *I once made these in a kitchen that did not have an electric mixer or an egg beater. I used a wire whisk, and they were just as good.*

Old-Fashioned Jumbo Lemon Wafers

This is a very old recipe from Connecticut for old-fashioned drop cookies. They are wide, flat, semisoft, crisp and brown on the edges, and they have a gorgeous lemon/mace flavor. Because these are so large and fragile, do not choose them to make for mailing or packing as a gift.

14 4½-INCH COOKIES

1¼ cups sifted all-purpose flour
¼ teaspoon salt
½ teaspoon double-acting baking powder
½ teaspoon mace
6 ounces (1½ sticks) unsalted butter
½ teaspoon lemon extract
¾ cup granulated sugar
1 egg plus 1 egg yolk
Finely grated rind of 2 or 3 lemons
Crystal sugar (see page 4) or additional
    granulated sugar (to sprinkle on the tops)

Adjust two racks to divide the oven into thirds and preheat oven to 350 degrees. Cut aluminum foil to fit cookie sheets.

Sift together the flour, salt, baking powder, and mace, and set aside. In the large bowl of an electric mixer, beat the butter until it is soft. Add the lemon extract and then the sugar and beat well for 2 or 3 minutes. Add the egg and the yolk and beat for 2 or 3 minutes more. Then, on low speed, add the sifted dry ingredients, scraping the bowl with a rubber spatula, and beating only until incorporated. Remove from the mixer and stir in the rind.

Transfer the mixture to a small bowl for easy handling.

Make these very large; use a heaping teaspoonful or a rounded table-spoonful of the dough for each cookie. They will spread considerably in baking; do not place more than 5 cookies on a 12 × 15½-inch piece of foil—1 near each corner and 1 in the center. However, I suggest that you try a sample sheet first with only 3 or 4 cookies so you know just what to expect. (If you bake only one sheet at a time, adjust a rack to the center of the oven.)

Wet a teaspoon in cold water. Press down gently on each cookie with the back of the wet spoon to flatten the cookie to about ¾-inch thickness. Then, with the wet spoon, smooth the edges of each cookie to round it.

Sprinkle the tops generously with crystal sugar or with granulated sugar.

Slide a cookie sheet under each piece of foil.

Bake for about 10 minutes, reversing the sheets top to bottom and front to back once during baking to ensure even browning. When the cookies are done they will have brown rims and the tops will feel semi-firm to the touch. Do not underbake.

With a wide metal spatula transfer the cookies to racks to cool.

Store the cookies airtight, preferably in a plastic freezer box, placing two cookies at a time, bottoms together, with wax paper between the layers.

Toasted Pine-Nut Cookies

This is an easy recipe that makes a small number of dainty butter cookies. They are crisp and crunchy, flavored with rum and toasted pine nuts —delicious. Make them to serve with tea or coffee; or with ice cream, custard, or fruit; or to package as a gift.

24 SMALL COOKIES

3 ounces (½ cup) pine nuts (pignolias)
4 ounces (1 stick) unsalted butter
2 tablespoons honey
2 tablespoons granulated sugar
Pinch of salt
2 tablespoons dark rum, brandy, or whiskey
1 cup sifted all-purpose flour

Adjust two racks to divide the oven into thirds and preheat oven to 375 degrees. Cut aluminum foil to line two cookie sheets, or use nonstick pans.

Toast the nuts by placing them in a wide frying pan over moderate heat (the pan should be dry—the nuts release oil as they become warm). Shake the pan frequently to move the nuts around. Watch carefully; after they become hot and start to color it doesn't take long before they burn. When they are golden brown, remove the pan from the heat and set aside for the nuts to cool. Then chill them in the freezer or refrigerator.

In the large bowl of an electric mixer, beat all the remaining ingredients, adding them in the order listed. Remove from the mixer and stir in the chilled nuts.

Place a large piece of wax paper or foil on a tray or shallow pan. Using two teaspoons (one for picking up and one for pushing off), divide the mixture into 24 equal mounds, placing them any which way on the wax paper or foil. Place in the freezer for about 5 minutes or in the refrigerator a little longer, only until they are not too sticky to be handled.

Then, between your hands, roll the mounds into balls, flatten them very slightly, and place them about 1 inch apart on the cookie sheets. Now, to flatten the cookies still more and to decorate them, dip a fork into cold water and, with the backs of the wet tines, flatten the cookies (pressing in one direction only) until the cookies are about ½ inch thick. Wet the fork before pressing it on each cookie.

Bake for 12 to 15 minutes, reversing the sheets top to bottom and front to back once during baking to ensure even baking. Bake until the cookies are lightly colored; do not underbake—they must be crisp.

With a wide metal spatula transfer the cookies to racks to cool.
Store airtight.

Belgian Almond Cookies

52 COOKIES

These are the famous Pain d'Amandes, *crisp, crunchy, chewy, very delicious and very popular refrigerator cookies (although they must be frozen, not refrigerated, when sliced), made with both ground almonds and whole almonds. They keep very well and are wonderful to package as a gift, to mail, or to keep in a cookie jar. Or keep them unbaked in the freezer and slice and bake them as you need them.*

2¼ cups sifted all-purpose flour
½ teaspoon double-acting baking powder
½ teaspoon cinnamon
⅛ teaspoon salt
10 ounces (2 cups) whole blanched almonds
½ cup plus 2 tablespoons light brown sugar,
    firmly packed

⅓ cup milk
Brandy or whiskey
4 ounces (1 stick) unsalted butter, melted

Sift together into a large bowl the flour, baking powder, cinnamon, and salt, and set aside. Reserve 1 cup of the almonds.

The other cup of almonds must be ground fine. It can be done in a food processor, a blender, or a nut grinder—but they must be fine.

Add the ground almonds to the sifted dry ingredients. Add the sugar.

Pour the milk into a glass measuring cup and add brandy or whiskey to the ½-cup line. Add the milk mixture and the melted butter to the dry ingredients. Stir with a wooden spoon to mix.

Then turn the mixture out onto a work surface and knead it to mix the ingredients thoroughly. It might be a little soft at first but it will become slightly firmer as you work it.

Add the reserved 1 cup of whole blanched almonds and knead the mixture to distribute the almonds.

On a long piece of wax paper, shape the dough into an oblong about 13 inches long, 1½ inches high, and 2½ inches wide.

Wrap it in the wax paper. Slide a flat cookie sheet under it and transfer to the freezer. Freeze for at least several hours or overnight or longer; it must be frozen.

When you are ready to bake, adjust two racks to divide the oven into thirds (or if you bake only one sheet at a time, bake it on the higher rack). Preheat the oven to 350 degrees. These may be baked on unbuttered, unlined cookie sheets, or on cookie sheets lined with foil.

Unwrap the bar of frozen dough and place it on a cutting board. Slicing the cookies is a bit tricky. Try different knives. I have good luck with a very finely serrated knife (much finer serrations than on a bread knife), or with a sharp, strong chef's knife that has a 5½-inch blade.

Slice the cookies ¼ inch thick.

Place them a scant 1 inch apart. Bake for 18 to 20 minutes, reversing the sheets top to bottom and front to back as necessary to ensure even browning. Bake until the cookies are golden on the tops; they will be darker on the edges. Watch them carefully. Do not underbake; they must be crisp. But if they become too dark they will taste burnt.

With a wide metal spatula transfer the cookies to racks to cool.

Some of the large pieces of almonds will fall out of the baked cookies when they are handled—it is to be expected.

Almond Sugar Cookies

These are Swedish; quick and easy, fancy and elegant. Crisp, rich, crumbly, not too sweet. A plain sugar-and-butter dough made with egg yolks and ground almonds is rolled with a rolling pin, cut with a scalloped cookie cutter, decorated with lines made with a fork, and topped with more almonds and sugar. Although they are a snap to make, they are for a fancy tea party or a swank dinner. They keep well, they may be frozen, and the recipe may be multiplied to make more if you wish.

10 VERY LARGE COOKIES

2½ ounces (½ cup) blanched almonds
1 cup sifted all-purpose flour
¼ teaspoon salt
2 ounces (½ stick) unsalted butter
¼ cup granulated sugar
2 egg yolks
½ teaspoon vanilla extract
¼ teaspoon almond extract

Adjust two racks to divide the oven into thirds and preheat the oven to 375 degrees. Cut aluminum foil to fit cookie sheets.

The almonds must be ground very fine. It can be done in a food processor, a blender, or a nut grinder. If you use a processor or a blender add a bit of the sugar to keep the nuts from lumping.

Then all of the ingredients may be combined in one of many ways. If you have ground the almonds in a processor, the remaining ingredients may all be added and processed until thoroughly mixed. Or they can all be mixed together in an electric mixer. Or they can be stirred together by hand in a mixing bowl.

Then turn the mixture out onto a work surface and "break" the dough as follows. First form it into a ball. Then, starting at the side of the ball farthest from you and using the heel of your hand, push off small pieces (about 2 tablespoons), pushing against the work surface and away from you. Continue until all the dough has been pushed off. Repeat "breaking" the dough once or twice until it is smooth.

Do not chill the dough before rolling it out.

Form the dough into a ball, flour it lightly, and flatten it slightly. Place it between two pieces of wax paper. With a rolling pin, roll over the top piece of paper until the dough is a scant ¼ inch thick.

Peel off the top piece of paper just to release it and then replace it. Turn the dough over with both pieces of paper. Then peel off the other piece of paper but do not replace it.

Use a scalloped, round cookie cutter 3¼ inches in diameter (or any other size, shape, or design that you prefer). Cut the cookies, starting at the outside edge of the dough, and cutting them as close to each other as possible. This dough wants to stick; I find that the best way to transfer the cookies is to lift one carefully with a wide metal spatula, turn it over into the palm of my hand, and then place it, either side up, on the aluminum foil.

Press the scraps of dough together and reroll and cut cookies until it is all used.

TOPPING

1 egg yolk
1 teaspoon water
About 2 tablespoons coarsely chopped, or
    sliced or slivered, blanched or
    unblanched almonds
Additional granulated sugar

In a small cup stir the yolk and water just to mix. With a pastry brush, brush the mixture generously over the tops of the cookies.

Then, to form a plaid design completely covering the tops, hold a four-pronged fork as though you were eating with it. Rest the back of the tines lightly on a cookie and pull it across the cookie from one side to the other side to score the top lightly. Repeat, making additional lines, to cover the top of the cookie completely with lines all going in one direction. Then score again, this time at right angles to the first lines.

Now brush a little more of the egg-yolk mixture on the middle of each cookie. Sprinkle a few of the almonds on the middle of each cookie. Then, with your fingertips, sprinkle sugar over each cookie, sprinkling it heavily in the middle and lightly at the edges.

Slide cookie sheets under the aluminum foil.

Bake for about 15 minutes, reversing the sheets top to bottom and front to back as necessary to ensure even browning. The cookies will have a nice golden color and a shine like varnish.

With a wide metal spatula transfer to racks to cool.

Store airtight.

Les Petites

These are dainty, delicate, delicious, fancy little French cookies. There are two cookies sandwiched together with chocolate between them; the top cookie has a hole cut out in the middle for the chocolate to show through. They are nicknamed Black-eyed Susans.

46 SMALL SANDWICH COOKIES

Make these for a wedding reception (there is an old saying that a ring-shaped cookie symbolizes eternal happiness because it has no end), a bridal shower, a tea party, or anything fancy and special.

3¾ ounces (¾ cup) blanched hazelnuts or
    almonds, or a combination of both
6 ounces (1½ sticks) unsalted butter
½ teaspoon vanilla extract
½ cup granulated sugar
Pinch of salt
1½ cups sifted all-purpose flour
5 ounces semisweet chocolate (to be used for
    sandwiching the cookies; see Note)
Optional: confectioners sugar (to be sprinkled
    over the cookies before serving)

Adjust two racks to divide the oven into thirds and preheat oven to 350 degrees. Line two cookie sheets with aluminum foil.

The nuts must be ground fine. This can be done in a food processor, a blender, or a nut grinder. If you use a processor or a blender add a spoonful of the sugar to prevent the nuts from lumping.

The dough can be put together in a mixer or a processor.

In a mixer: Cream the butter, mix in the vanilla, sugar, salt, then the flour and finally the ground nuts, beating until mixed.

In a food processor: After grinding the nuts, do not remove them from the bowl; add the butter, which should be cut into small pieces, and all the other ingredients except the chocolate, and process until the dough holds together.

Do not chill the dough before rolling it; chilling makes it crack when it is rolled.

Flour a pastry cloth and a rolling pin. Use only half of the dough at a time. Form it into a ball and flour it lightly. Flatten it slightly between your hands. Then roll it carefully, flouring the top, the bottom, and the rolling pin as necessary, until it is a scant ¼ inch, or a generous ⅛ inch thick.

You will need a round (preferably scalloped) cookie cutter that measures 1½ inches in diameter. Starting at the outside edge of the rolled-out dough, cut rounds and place them about ½ inch apart on the foil-lined sheets. Then, with a plain round cutter that measures ¾ inch in diameter, cut holes out of the middle of half of the cookies. (Save the cut-out holes and the leftovers and roll them out again to make more cookies.)

Bake for about 10 to 15 minutes or a bit longer (depending on the thickness of the cookies), reversing the sheets top to bottom and front to back as necessary to ensure even browning. Bake until the cookies are sandy colored. Do not underbake.

With a wide metal spatula transfer the cookies to racks to cool.

Coarsely chop the chocolate and place it in the top of a small double boiler over hot water on low heat. Cover until partly melted, then uncover and stir until completely melted. Transfer to a small shallow cup for easy handling.

Turn the cookies that do not have holes in them upside down. With the tip of a small spoon, place a bit (about ¼ teaspoon) of the melted chocolate in a mound in the center of each cookie. Do not spread it out. Then place one of the cookies that has a hole in it over the chocolate with the two undersides together. Press together lightly. The chocolate should not extend out to the edges. Repeat, sandwiching all the cookies.

Refrigerate the cookie sandwiches until the chocolate is firm. Then these may be stored in the refrigerator or the freezer. Or, if the room is not too warm, they may stand at room temperature. If the cookies are going to stand overnight or longer they should be wrapped airtight. Pack them in a box with wax paper between the layers.

The cookies may be sprinkled with confectioners sugar before serving. Place the cookies on a large piece of wax paper. Sprinkle the sugar through a fine strainer held over the tops of the cookies.

NOTE: *I have used both Maillard's Eagle Sweet chocolate and Tobler Tradition—they are both semisweet and both delicious; use any semisweet.*

Pecan Squares Americana

(an updated recipe from my first dessert book)

32 TO 48 (OR MORE COOKIES)

Many years ago a Miami newspaper published a letter to the food editor from the wife of Governor Collins of Florida. She raved about the pecan cookies she had eaten at the Americana Hotel in Miami Beach. She went on to say that she had requested the recipe from the hotel, that they had given it to her, but it did not work for her. The letter included the recipe as she had received it. I ran to the kitchen to try it. The recipe did not work for me either. I called the hotel and asked to speak to the pastry chef. His name was Jacques Kranzlin; he could not have been more gracious or charming, and he invited me to his kitchen to watch him work. It was a treat.

When I got home I was able to make the Pecan Squares. I made them again and again and again. I wrote the recipe. I taught it in my classes. It was unanimously THE BEST! I included the recipe in my dessert book. And when I taught classes around the country, it was one of my favorite recipes to teach because I knew how people would rave about them.

During a class in Ohio, as I started to make this recipe, I explained that there was one hitch: The filling sometimes ran through the bottom crust and stuck to the pan, making it difficult to remove the cookies. A nice lady in the class said, "Since you use so much foil to line so many pans, why not line this one?"

It sounded like a good idea. I tried it right then and it was a good idea. It was terrific! The cookies simply cannot stick to the pan this way. I have always worried about the people who are making this without the foil. Here's the way I do it now.

PASTRY SHELL

8 ounces (2 sticks) unsalted butter
½ cup granulated sugar
1 egg (graded large)
¼ teaspoon salt
Finely grated rind of 1 large lemon
3 cups sifted all-purpose flour

Butter a 15½ × 10½ × 1-inch jelly-roll pan and then line it with aluminum foil as follows: Turn the pan upside down. Center a piece of foil 18 to 19 inches long (12 inches wide) over the pan; check the long sides to be sure there is the same amount of overhang on each side. Fold down the sides and the corners to shape the foil. Remove the foil, turn the pan right side up, place the shaped foil in the pan, and press it carefully into place. Butter the foil with soft (not melted) butter (in addition to that called for in the recipe). Butter the bottom well but butter the sides only lightly (if the sides are heavily buttered the dough will slide down as it bakes). Place the prepared pan in the freezer (it is easier to spread this dough on a cold pan—the coldness will make the dough cling to the pan).

In the large bowl of an electric mixer, beat the 8 ounces of butter until it is softened, add the sugar, and beat to mix well. Beat in the egg, salt, and lemon rind. Gradually add the flour and beat, scraping the bowl with a rubber spatula, until the mixture holds together.

Now you are going to line the pan with the dough; it is important that you have enough dough on the sides of the pan to reach generously to the top of the pan. It will work best and be easiest if you place the dough, one rounded teaspoonful at a time, around the edges of the bottom—that is, just touching the raised sides. (I don't actually use teaspoons for this. It is easiest to lift a generous mound of the dough, hold it in your left hand, and use the fingers of your right hand to break off teaspoon-size pieces.) Place the pieces about ½ to 1 inch apart. Then place the remaining dough the same way all over the rest of the bottom of the pan. Flour your fingertips (if necessary) and start to press the mounds of dough, working up on the sides first and then the bottom, until you have formed a smooth layer all over the sides and bottom. There must not be any thin spots on the bottom or any low spots on the sides (it is best if it comes slightly above the top). Take your time; it is important for this shell to be right.

With a fork, carefully prick the bottom at about ½-inch intervals. Chill in the freezer or refrigerator for about 15 minutes.

Adjust a rack one-third up from the bottom of the oven and preheat oven to 375 degrees.

Bake for 20 minutes. Watch it constantly. If the dough on the sides starts to slip down a bit, reach into the oven and press it with your finger-tips or the back of a spoon to put it back into place. If the dough starts to puff up, prick it gently with a cake tester to release trapped air and flatten the dough. (There have been times when it insisted on puffing up, and it was a question of which one of us would win. I did. Here's how: Place one or more pot holders on the puffed-up part for a few minutes. The puffed-up dough will get the message and will know you mean busi-ness, and it will lie down flat.) After 20 minutes, the edges of the dough will be lightly colored; the bottom will be pale but dry. Remove from the oven but do not turn off the heat. Prepare the topping.

PECAN TOPPING

8 ounces (2 sticks) unsalted butter
½ cup honey
¼ cup granulated sugar
1 cup plus 2 tablespoons dark brown sugar,
    firmly packed
¼ cup heavy cream
20 ounces (5 cups) pecan halves or large pieces

In a heavy 3-quart saucepan over moderately high heat, cook the butter and honey, stirring occasionally, until the butter is melted. Add both sugars, stir to dissolve, bring to a boil, and let boil without stirring for exactly 2 minutes.

Without waiting, remove from the heat, stir in the heavy cream and then the pecans. (Although the original recipe says to do the next step immediately, I have recently decided it is better to wait a bit.) Wait 5 minutes. Then, with a large slotted spoon, place most of the pecans evenly over the crust. Then drizzle the remaining mixture over the pecans so it is distributed evenly—watch the corners. Use your fingers or the back of a spoon to move around any nuts that are piled too high and place them in any empty or thin spots. (It will look like there is not enough of the thin syrupy mixture, but there is.)

Bake at 375 degrees with the rack one-third up from the bottom for 25 minutes. (Now you will see that the syrupy mixture has spread out and boiled up and filled in any hollows.)

Cool in the pan on a rack.

Cover with a large rack or a cookie sheet, hold them firmly together, and turn the pan and rack or sheet over and remove the pan and the foil. If the bottom of the dough looks very buttery you may pat it with a paper towel if you wish, but it is not really necessary, the dough absorbs it as it stands. Cover with a rack or sheet and turn over again, leaving the cake right side up. It is easiest to cut the cake into neat pieces if it is well chilled first; chill it in the refrigerator or the freezer. Then transfer it to a large cutting board. Use a ruler and toothpicks to mark the cake into quarters. Use a long and heavy, sharp knife, and cut straight down (not back and forth). These are very rich, and although most people like them cut into 48 bars, I know several cateresses who make them almost as small as lump sugar. And I have made them larger because I wrap them individually in clear cellophane and it is more fun to wrap cookies that are not too small.

Crackers

The next four recipes are not cookies but I cannot resist including them. They are crackers, to serve with a meal, or with cheese, or just to nibble on, plain, with tea or coffee or wine. They are unusual (some of the directions are strange) and delicious (I don't know of anything that I make that people rave about more than they rave about Corn Melba) and fun to make and I love them.

Corn Melba

96 CRACKERS

About 40 years ago the dining room of the Hampshire House in New York City always had a basket of these on each table. They were unbelievable! They were surely the thinnest (as though they had been made by some special machine—not by a person), the crispest, flakiest, most buttery, most exciting . . . the flavor was bland and mild and simply buttery and simply delicious and I simply had to have the recipe. The hotel would not give it to me. That was the beginning of a hunt that lasted for many years and involved almost everyone I knew from coast to coast. I was getting nowhere.

Sometime before I started my Corn Melba hunt, I had sent 25¢ for a small pamphlet called Menus and Recipes of Famous Hostesses, published by one of the leading fashion magazines. I made a few things from it and put it away in a desk drawer and forgot about it. Years later I came across it, and as soon as I opened it I saw Corn Melba; it even had the same name. I don't remember the name of the famous hostess (I wish I did) who contributed it, but I think she lived on Long Island, and I think her menu included broiled fish, and I think it was for a luncheon.

Serve Corn Melba any time, any place, with or without anything.

Making these is a most unusual experience, different from any other baking I have done. And fun all the way.

Corn Melba keeps well for a week or more. What I mean is, it does not spoil. But it is hard to keep it.

This is baked in jelly-roll pans. The recipe makes six panfuls. If you have only one pan, and therefore bake only one pan at a time, be prepared to spend several hours near the oven. But if you bake three or four pans of it at one time, it can all be completed in about 1½ hours.

2 cups double- or triple-sifted all-purpose flour
    (if your sifter has only one screen, resift the
    flour before measuring; if it is sifted only
    once, you will be using a little more flour,
    and the mixture will be a little too thick)
2 teaspoons double-acting baking powder
½ teaspoon salt
4 ounces (1 stick) unsalted butter, at room
    temperature
2 tablespoons granulated sugar
2 eggs (graded large or extra-large)
1 cup milk, at room temperature
1 cup water, at room temperature
½ cup cornmeal (the cornmeal may be white
    or yellow—I have used both many times—
    but I think that the Melba is slightly
    thinner and crisper with white water-
    ground cornmeal)

This is made in jelly-roll pans that measure 10½ × 15½ × 1 inch. The crackers will be cut into squares in the pans, therefore you should not use pans that have a nonstick finish or you will cut through the finish. You can bake six pans at a time if you have that many pans and oven racks, or you can bake only one or more at a time (the remaining batter should stand at room temperature). Adjust oven racks for as many pans as you have, or adjust a rack to the center for only one pan. Preheat the oven to 375 degrees. Butter the pans (see Note).

Sift together the flour, baking powder, and salt, and set aside.

In the small bowl of an electric mixer, beat the butter until it is soft. Beat in the sugar and then the eggs, one at a time. On low speed add the sifted dry ingredients in three additions alternating with the milk and water in two additions, scraping the bowl with a rubber spatula and beating until well mixed after each addition. Add the cornmeal last and beat only until mixed. The mixture will look curdled during the mixing and might still be lumpy after the mixing. Strain it through a strainer set over a bowl to remove any lumps. It will be a thin mixture.

You will have 4 cups of batter with which to make 6 panfuls of Melba. As closely as I can figure it, that means that for each panful you should use ⅔ cup of batter. Measure it in a glass measuring cup.

Pour the measured amount along one long side of the buttered pan, scraping out the cup with a rubber spatula. Tilt the pan as necessary for the batter to run into a thin, thin layer completely covering the bottom of the pan. Hold the pan almost vertically, turn it one way and then another, and have patience—the batter might run slowly. If, after a reasonable length of time, you see that you simply cannot get the batter to cover the pan, use an extra spoonful or so as necessary.

Bake one or more pans at a time—you can put a second pan in after the first one has started baking. After about 5 to 7 minutes the batter should be firm enough to be cut; remove it from the oven and, with a small, sharp knife, cut the long way to make 4 strips, and then cut crossways to make 16 rectangles.

Return the pan to the oven and continue to bake for about 25 minutes more or until the Melba is crisp all over—part of it might be golden brown or even darker, and part of it may be lighter (although it is best when it is all an even golden color). During baking reverse the pan top to bottom and front to back as necessary to ensure even browning. The crackers will shrink as they bake, and some of the crackers may still look wet and buttery in places but they will dry and crisp as they cool if they have been baked enough.

The crackers will not all be done at the same time; some may be done in 20 to 25 minutes, others might take as long as 45 minutes. Remove them from the oven as they are done.

With a wide metal spatula, transfer the baked crackers to a paper towel to cool. When you run out of room it is all right to place some of them on top of others.

Wash, dry, and butter the pans each time you use them.

Corn Melba is fragile—handle with care. (Before I knew how to make this, we ordered it by mail from New York; when it arrived in Florida it was pretty well broken up—but we were happy to have it anyway.) Store it airtight but don't worry about this getting limp—it stays crisp. It may be frozen if you want to keep it for many weeks or months.

NOTE: *When a friend of mine had trouble with this recipe we talked long distance for hours. We finally found the trouble. She was buttering the pans with melted butter and a pastry brush, and was using much more butter than you use when you spread the butter (not melted) with crumpled wax paper. The excess butter prevented the crackers from baking as they should. The pans should be buttered normally, not extra heavy and not extra thin.*

Ralph's Corn Melba

For many years my husband asked me to add some cayenne pepper to this recipe. I don't know why it took me years to do it. I finally did, and Ralph loves it. If you want to try it, add ¼ teaspoon of cayenne to ⅔ cup of the batter and make one panful.

Swedish Hardtack

This is the name that came with this recipe when I got it from a lady in Michigan. But they are not what I think of when I hear that name; they are rich and buttery and flaky and so delicious you will eat them plain with soup, salad, cocktails, tea or coffee, or nothing. Once, at a large cocktail party, I served a huge bowl of these along with a variety of hors d'oeuvres. These went first, and I had to promise the recipe to all the guests.

You will need a regular rolling pin and also a special type of corrugated rolling pin with deep ridges about ¼ inch apart in the wood that go around the pin like bracelets and make the dough look like matzohs. I was told that it is made for cutting spaghetti—or use it to decorate shortbread-type cookies. It can be bought at, or ordered by mail from, the Perfect Pan, 4040 Goldfinch Street, San Diego, California 92103.

These crackers keep perfectly in an airtight container for weeks.

Do not make these if you are in a hurry; they take a great deal of time and patience. (This is the original Swedish recipe divided by 8—it took me 2 days to make the full amount.) This amount will be enough to serve to 6 people with lunch or cocktails.

The prepared dough must be chilled in the freezer for an hour or two before you use it. While you are making these you can stop in the middle and let the dough wait in the freezer or the refrigerator for days or weeks.

1 ounce (¼ stick) unsalted butter
1 cup plus 1 tablespoon unsifted
    all-purpose flour
¼ teaspoon baking soda
¼ teaspoon salt
2 tablespoons granulated sugar
½ cup buttermilk

338

Sesame seeds (I use the white, or bleached,
seeds, although either those or the natural
ones can be used)

Place the butter in a small pan (or in a custard cup placed in a little water in a small pan) over low heat to melt slowly. Remove from the heat and set aside to cool slightly.

Meanwhile, sift together into a mixing bowl the flour, soda, and salt. Stir in the sugar. Add the buttermilk and the melted butter all at once and stir until smooth.

Wrap the dough in plastic wrap and place it in the freezer for about 1 or 2 hours. (It will become too hard to roll if it is frozen too long. If this happens, let it stand in the refrigerator or at room temperature briefly until you can roll it.)

When you are ready to bake, adjust two racks to divide the oven into thirds and preheat the oven to 350 degrees.

Generously flour a pastry cloth and a plain rolling pin. (Both the cloth and the pin will have to be refloured often to keep the dough from sticking.)

Work with 1 rounded tablespoonful of the dough at a time, keeping the rest in the freezer or the refrigerator. (The dough becomes too sticky to handle at room temperature.) Place the dough on the floured cloth and turn it over to flour all sides. With the floured rolling pin, roll the dough gently until it is about ¼ inch thick—the shape does not matter. The rolled-out dough can be turned over as often as necessary to keep both sides floured, but work quickly.

Sprinkle the top generously with sesame seeds, use more than you think are enough, and then add a few more. Roll over the seeds lightly with the rolling pin to press the seeds into the dough and to roll the dough very thin; it should be as thin as you can make it.

Next, flour the corrugated rolling pin (it is best to do this with a pastry brush) and, very gently, roll over the dough, rolling in one direction only until the dough has ridges all over like matzohs. If you press too hard while you are doing this, the dough will stick to the pin (and be a pain). It is best to press only gently; you can repeat this several times, rerolling as you wish. The outside shape of the dough does not make any difference. And it does not matter if the ridges actually cut through the dough in places.

Now, with a pizza cutter, a pastry wheel, or a long knife, cut the rolled-out dough into halves or quarters. With a wide metal spatula transfer the pieces to unbuttered and unlined cookie sheets, placing them any which way and very close together.

Repeat rolling and cutting the crackers to fill the cookie sheets. (It gets easier and they get thinner and better as you make more.)

Bake for 10 to 25 minutes until the crackers are golden brown, reversing the sheets top to bottom and front to back as necessary during baking to ensure even browning. The crackers will be darker on the edges or wherever the dough is thinner, and they will be barely sandy, or not actually colored at all in other areas. (Some of the flour that was used for rolling will remain white and floury on the crackers; it is O.K., but if there is really a lot it can be brushed off with a pastry brush after the crackers are baked.) The baking time will vary depending on the thickness/thinness of the crackers. Do not underbake.

With a wide metal spatula transfer the crackers to a piece of paper toweling as they are done.

WARNING! *This dough is sticky and difficult to work with. I think it is worth the hassle. Watchpoints: The dough must be as cold as possible without being frozen when you roll it. It is easier to roll a small piece than a large one. Do not be afraid to keep it well-enough floured (within reason) on both sides to keep it from sticking. Mainly, work quickly!*

NOTE: *To make a generous number of these crackers, the following amounts (four times the recipe) will keep you in the kitchen for most of a day. (It is the amount I like to make.)*

4 ounces (1 stick) unsalted butter
4¼ cups unsifted all-purpose flour
1 teaspoon baking soda
1 teaspoon salt
½ cup granulated sugar
2 cups buttermilk
Sesame seeds

Knäckbröd

6 LARGE KNÄCKBRÖD

This is a rather bland, plain, crisp, paper-thin, whole-wheat Scandinavian cracker 12 inches in diameter. Aside from its unusual dramatic looks, it is extra delicious and fun to make and fun to serve. Serve it with cheese (preferably a semisoft cheese like Brie) or as a table bread. Or just have it around for a nibble. Or make it for a sensational house gift if you are going for dinner. A basket of this is gorgeous on a buffet table.

2 cups unsifted all-purpose whole-wheat flour
1 teaspoon salt
1 teaspoon baking soda
1 cup buttermilk
2 ounces (½ stick) unsalted butter, melted
¼ cup unsifted all-purpose white flour
Additional white or whole-wheat flour
Sesame seeds and/or caraway seeds

Measure out the whole-wheat flour and set aside ½ cup. Place the remaining 1½ cups of whole-wheat flour in a large mixing bowl. Add the salt, baking soda, buttermilk, and the melted butter and stir with a rubber or wooden spatula to make a smooth dough. Add the reserved ½ cup whole-wheat flour and the ¼ cup white flour. Stir to mix.

Flour a large board or work surface and turn the dough out onto it. Knead for a few seconds, adding additional white or whole-wheat flour if necessary. You should add just enough flour to keep the dough from sticking but no more.

Form the dough into a thick cylinder 6 inches long. Cut it into 6 even slices. Each slice will be a Knäckbröd.

Adjust one rack to the center of the oven for baking one Knäckbröd at a time, or adjust two racks to divide the oven into thirds for baking two Knäckbröd at a time. Generously butter one or two cookie sheets (or more if you wish; you will bake 6 separate breads, or crackers, each on a buttered sheet—you can bake just one at a time, and roll out the second one while the first one is baking).

Now, you can roll out each piece of dough either on a large board or pastry cloth. Flour the board or cloth and a rolling pin. Roll one piece of the dough into a 12-inch circle; it should be paper thin. While rolling, turn the dough over occasionally to keep both sides floured.

Drape the rolled-out dough over the rolling pin and unroll it onto the buttered sheet.

Prick it all over, at ½- to 1-inch intervals, with a fork. Then, with the dull side of the blade of a long knife, press down on the dough to score it without cutting through the dough into 12 pie-shaped wedges.

Sprinkle the top generously with sesame seeds or caraway seeds. Roll over the seeds with a rolling pin, pressing firmly enough so the seeds will not fall off. Or sprinkle three Knäckbröd with sesame seeds and three with caraway seeds.

Bake for 10 to 12 minutes. If you bake two sheets at a time, reverse them top to bottom and front to back once during baking to ensure even baking. If you bake only one sheet at a time, reverse it front to back. They should be golden brown all over, but don't let them burn anywhere.

They can cool on the sheet or on a rack or on paper.

To store, place the Knäckbröd in a large plastic bag and fasten the top airtight. Store at room temperature or in the freezer.

To serve, they can be broken into pie-shaped wedges in the kitchen, but it is a shame—they look so great before they are broken. Just place them in a shallow basket or on a large, round board or tray and let people break off their own.

Black Pepper Crackers

Delicate, tender, delicious, thin and crisp, all-purpose crackers to serve with soup, salad, or with cheese. I use a conservative amount of pepper—just enough to taste—but it may be increased or omitted. Or you can substitute chili powder, or caraway or sesame seeds. Or garlic or onion powder. Or whatever.

ABOUT 24 CRACKERS

2 cups sifted all-purpose flour
1 tablespoon granulated sugar
¾ teaspoon salt
¼ teaspoon double-acting baking powder
2 ounces (½ stick) unsalted butter, cold and firm, cut into ¼-inch pieces (it is best to cut it ahead of time and refrigerate)
½ cup milk or light cream

Additional milk or light cream
Black pepper (preferably use whole pepper-
corns and a mill, or use ground pepper)

Adjust two racks to divide the oven into thirds and preheat oven to 425 degrees. You will use unbuttered and unlined cookie sheets which may be plain or nonstick.

This may be put together in a food processor or in a bowl with a pastry blender. To do it in a processor (fitted with the steel blade), sift together the flour, sugar, salt, and baking powder, and place them in the bowl of the processor. Add the butter and process very briefly with quick on-and-off "pulses" for about 10 seconds or less only until the mixture resembles coarse meal. Then, through the feed tube, quickly add the milk or cream and process only until the mixture barely holds together.

To do it without a processor, sift together into a large bowl the flour, sugar, salt, and baking powder. Add the butter and with a pastry blender cut in the butter until the mixture resembles coarse meal. Add the milk or cream and stir with a fork to make a stiff dough.

Work with half of the dough at a time. Press it into a square shape, place it on a floured pastry cloth, and roll it with a floured rolling pin. Keep the shape squarish and roll the dough until it is very, very thin, or as thin as you can make it. (The crackers will be good if the dough is not that thin, but they will be better if it is.)

With a pizza cutter, a pastry cutter, or a long, sharp knife, trim the edges square. With a fork, prick the dough all over at ½-inch intervals. Then brush it all lightly with milk or cream. Now grind the black pepper over the dough. Or sprinkle with whatever topping or combination you wish. I use black pepper, and I use enough so you can really taste it (it is delicious) but not enough to make it really harsh. But it is up to you. (It is a good idea to bake one as a sample; it is too bad to bake them all and then say, "They should have had more pepper.")

Now, with the cutter or knife, cut the entire piece of dough into even squares or oblongs. (I make them about the rectangular size of bought graham crackers. And with the edge of a wide metal spatula, I lightly score each cracker through the middle into halves like graham crackers.)

Place the crackers on unbuttered, unlined cookie sheets. Bake for about 18 to 20 minutes, reversing the sheets top to bottom and front to back as necessary to ensure even browning, until the crackers are golden colored. Be sure to bake them long enough for them to be crisp.

Cool on a rack and then store airtight.

Custards, Mousses, Soufflés, etc.

Some of the following custard recipes call for lining the dishes with caramelized sugar. When you melt sugar to caramelize it, do not do it in a tin-lined copper pot because the tin will melt before the sugar does. Also, it is not a good idea to do it in a pan with a black lining because against the black you can't tell how dark the caramel is.

French Baked Custard

This is a classic. It is simple and wonderful. It is baked and served in individual cups, which should be pottery (it bakes better).

6 PORTIONS

2½ cups milk
3 eggs plus 3 yolks (graded large or extra-large)
⅓ cup granulated sugar
1 teaspoon vanilla extract
Scant ¼ teaspoon almond extract (a small amount of almond flavoring is delicious in custard, but the least bit too much can ruin it)
Pinch of salt

Adjust a rack one-third up from the bottom of the oven and preheat the oven to 325 degrees. You will need six 6-ounce (measured to the very tops) custard cups or individual soufflé dishes. Place the cups or dishes in a shallow baking pan that must not be deeper than the cups or dishes. Set aside.

Place the milk in a saucepan, uncovered, over moderate heat. Let stand until you see a slightly wrinkled skin on top or tiny bubbles around the edge.

Meanwhile, place the eggs and yolks in a large mixing bowl. Beat or whisk briefly only to mix, not until they are foamy or light. Gradually mix in the sugar, vanilla and almond extracts, and the salt, beating only to mix.

Very gradually at first, add the hot milk to the egg mixture, stirring or whisking gently only to mix.

Strain the mixture into a wide-mouthed pitcher.

Check the flavoring; sometimes it is necessary to add a bit more salt, which brings out the vanilla and almond flavors.

Pour into the cups or soufflé dishes. Do not fill all the way to the tops, there should be a bit of headroom left. There should not be any foam on the tops; if there is, remove it with a teaspoon.

Carefully pour hot water into the pan up to one-half the depth of the cups. Carefully transfer to the oven and then cover the tops of the cups or soufflé dishes with a cookie sheet.

Bake for 40 to 50 minutes until a small, sharp knife gently inserted about 1 inch into the middle of a custard comes out clean. Testing the custards leaves scars, which become larger as they cool. So test as little as possible with a knife. It is also possible to test without the knife; just tap the side of a cup gently with a knife or spoon—if the custard is not done you will be able to see that it is still liquid, but when it is done you will see that it is no longer runny, and is set. Do not overbake.

Remove the pan from the oven and remove the cups from the water. (Some people use a bulb baster to remove most of the water first. And/or use a wide metal spatula to transfer the cups.)

Let stand until the cups reach room temperature. Then refrigerate for several hours. The custards may be placed in the freezer for about 15 minutes before serving.

These may be served perfectly plain, or they may be topped with a rosette or a spoonful of whipped cream and, if you wish, a candied violet or rose petal, or a very thinly sliced fresh strawberry.

VARIATION: *A cook I know from Kingston, Jamaica, makes this same custard with the following changes: Omit the almond extract and add 1 teaspoon powdered ginger—it is delicious.*

Grape-Nut Custard

The Inn at Saranac Lake in upper New York State was a luxurious resort (and probably it still is), famous for the view, the lake, the climate, fishing and boating, and buffets a mile long. This simple dessert was a specialty, and was always one of the first desserts they ran out of. I have never seen it any other place.

Follow the above recipe for French Baked Custard (see page 347), but before pouring the mixture into the custard cups, place 2½ to 3 teaspoons of Grape-Nuts in each cup; pour the custard over the Grape-Nuts. Bake as directed. Some of the cereal will rise to the top and some will remain in the bottom, where it will form a thicker texture somewhat like bread pudding. It is delicious. Serve it very cold. If you have time and space, place it in the freezer for about 15 minutes before serving.

Orange Custard

Extremely light, delicate, tender, creamy—with a refreshing orange flavor; baked in individual cups and served in the cups. This is a wonderful dessert to serve after a sharp and spicy main course.

8 PORTIONS

5 eggs and 3 yolks (graded large or extra-large)
¾ cup granulated sugar
Finely grated rind of 2 deep-colored oranges
Pinch of salt
1⅓ cups orange juice
1 cup heavy cream

Adjust a rack one-third up from the bottom of the oven and preheat oven to 325 degrees.

Place the eggs and yolks in a large mixing bowl and beat or whisk until they are mixed but not foamy or light. Add the remaining ingredients one at a time, beating or whisking lightly only until everything is well mixed.

Pour through a strainer set over a pitcher with a wide mouth.

Pour into eight 4-ounce custard cups (preferably pottery cups). Place the cups in a large, shallow pan that must not be deeper than the cups. Pour hot water into the pan up to half the depth of the cups.

Place in the oven and cover with a cookie sheet.

Bake for 50 to 60 minutes until the custards just test done. To test, uncover and insert about an inch of a small, sharp knife into the middle of one of the cups. If the knife comes out clean, the custard is done. Or tap on the side of a cup with a knife; you will be able to see when the custard is no longer runny. Do not overbake.

These should be refrigerated for at least a few hours, but if they are refrigerated for more than 24 hours they begin to shrink and will not be attractive. These should be very cold when they are served. (The cups may be placed in the freezer for about 15 minutes before serving.)

These do not need any topping. But, if you wish, top with a spoonful of whipped cream and/or a fresh strawberry.

NOTE: *During baking these might separate into two barely visible layers— a heavier, creamier layer on top and a lighter, juicier layer on the bottom. Yummy.*

Rum and Brandy Custard

This is a famous old recipe from a private club in Lexington, Kentucky. It is too smooth, delicate, and creamy to describe, with a positive rum and brandy flavor. Need I say more? It is baked in individual, caramelized custard cups that are unmolded before serving.

You will need six 4-ounce cups, preferably the heavy pottery ones.

6 PORTIONS

½ cup plus ⅓ cup granulated sugar
¾ cup milk
1 cup heavy cream
3 eggs and 2 egg yolks (graded large or extra-large)
⅛ teaspoon salt
½ teaspoon vanilla extract
2 tablespoons dark rum
2 tablespoons Cognac or brandy

To caramelize the custard cups: Place ½ cup of the sugar (reserve the remaining ⅓ cup) in a heavy frying pan over moderate heat. Just as soon as the sugar barely begins to melt, stir it constantly with a wooden spatula until it is all melted and turns a nice rich caramel color. Do not let it become too dark, or it will taste burnt.

Pour the caramelized sugar into six 4-ounce custard cups and immediately, before it hardens, use pot holders and twirl and tilt the cups to run the caramel about halfway up on the sides; continue to move the cups until the caramel stops running. Set the cups aside.

Adjust a rack one-third up from the bottom of the oven and preheat oven to 350 degrees.

Place the milk and cream in an uncovered saucepan over moderate heat until it is scalded, or until a slight skin forms on the top, or tiny bubbles form around the edge.

Meanwhile, in a bowl, beat or whisk the eggs, yolks, salt, and the reserved ⅓ cup of sugar only until they are well mixed but not until they are foamy or light.

Very gradually at first, stir in the hot milk and cream, and then add the vanilla, rum, and Cognac or brandy.

Pour the mixture through a fine strainer into a wide-mouthed pitcher.

Then pour the custard into the prepared cups (there should be ¼ to ½ inch of space above the tops of the custards).

Place the cups in a shallow baking pan that must not be deeper than the cups. Pour hot water into the pan, up to half the depth of the cups.

Carefully transfer the pan to the oven and cover with a cookie sheet.

Bake for about 35 minutes or until a small, sharp knife inserted into the middle comes out clean. Or test by tapping a cup gently with a knife or spoon; when it is done you will be able to see that the custard is no longer runny, and is set. Do not overbake.

Remove the pan from the oven. Let stand for 2 or 3 minutes and then carefully remove the cups from the water. Let cool to room temperature.

Refrigerate the custards for at least a few hours or all day. If you really must, you can let this stand overnight. This should be very cold when it is served. (The custards may be placed in the freezer for about 15 minutes before serving.)

Just before serving, carefully cut around each custard with a small, sharp knife to release. Cover with a chilled dessert plate, and turn the plate and the custard over. The custard will slip out and it will have a caramel sauce that will run onto the plate.

Coconut Custard

8 PORTIONS

This is an especially fine custard, smooth, creamy, lighter than others in this collection, baked in one large caramelized dish. It is elegant; make it for a dinner party. And make it at least 10 hours before serving, or a day ahead. Do not double the recipe for one large dish (the custard is too delicate to hold up); bake two separate custards instead.

You will need a 7½ × 3-inch soufflé dish, or any other straight-sided ovenproof dish with a 6-cup capacity.

3½ ounces (1 to 1⅓ cups) shredded coconut
1½ cups granulated sugar
4 cups milk
3 eggs plus 3 egg yolks (graded large or
    extra-large)
½ teaspoon vanilla extract
Scant ½ teaspoon almond extract
⅛ teaspoon salt

To toast the coconut (this can be done anytime ahead of time) spread it out on a large, shallow baking pan (a cookie sheet or jelly-roll pan) and place it in the middle of a preheated 350-degree oven. Stir it every 2 or 3 minutes; do not let it become too brown. Bake only until it is golden; it will take about 10 minutes. Set aside.

Adjust a rack one-third up from the bottom of the oven and preheat the oven to 350 degrees.

To caramelize the dish: Place 1 cup of the sugar (reserve the remaining ½ cup) in a large, heavy frying pan over moderate heat. As soon as the sugar barely begins to melt, stir it constantly with a wooden spatula until it is completely melted and smooth. (The sugar will start to caramelize before it is all melted—that's O.K.—just continue to stir constantly.) Cook and stir until the sugar is golden brown; if it is too dark, it does not taste good.

Pour the caramelized sugar into the 6-cup soufflé dish and, using two pot holders, immediately tilt the dish in all directions to coat the bottom and the sides of the dish thoroughly. Run the caramel as close to the top of the dish as you can (¼ to ½ inch from the top is good). Continue to tilt and turn the dish until the caramel stops running and then set the dish aside.

Place the milk in an uncovered saucepan over moderate heat to scald. Meanwhile, in a large mixing bowl with a wire whisk, or in the large bowl of an electric mixer, beat the eggs, yolks, remaining ½ cup sugar, vanilla and almond extracts, and the salt just to mix well, but not until it is light or foamy.

When the milk barely forms a slightly wrinkled skin on top or tiny bubbles around the edge, gradually (very slowly at first) pour the hot milk onto the egg mixture, stirring constantly. Strain into a large pitcher. Stir in the toasted coconut.

Place the soufflé dish in a large, shallow pan or baking dish. Pour the custard into the dish. Pour hot water about 1½ inches deep into the pan. Carefully transfer to the oven.

Bake uncovered for 1½ hours. To test, gently insert a small, sharp paring knife 1 to 1½ inches deep (no deeper) into the middle of the custard. When the blade comes out clean, the custard is done.

Remove from the oven, let stand for about 5 minutes. It is helpful now to remove most of the water with a bulb baster and then carefully remove the dish from the hot water, place it on a rack, and let stand until the bottom of the dish reaches room temperature.

Then refrigerate for about 10 hours or overnight.

Do not unmold this until just before serving (it only takes a minute to unmold it and the caramelized sugar is shiniest as soon as it is unmolded).

You will need a flat serving platter with a bit of a rim (the caramelized sugar will have become a liquid sauce). With a small, sharp knife carefully cut around the sides of the custard to release. Place the serving dish over the custard, centering it carefully. Hold the serving dish and the custard dish firmly together, and turn both over.

Wait a few seconds and then carefully lift off the custard dish.

To serve, cut into portions with a sharp knife and transfer them with a pie server to flat dessert plates. Serve with a fork and spoon for each guest.

NOTE: *This needs longer chilling than some of the other custards because it is a lighter custard and must be chilled this long to hold its shape.*

Crème Renversée

8 PORTIONS

This is the elegant, classic French caramelized baked custard. It is made in a ring mold and is served either with or without fresh or stewed fruit, and either with or without whipped cream. The custard is silky smooth and is indescribably delicious. You will need a 5- to 6-cup metal ring mold, and since the mold must be placed in water during baking, you will need something large enough to hold it (it can be deeper than the mold if necessary, although it only needs to be deep enough for 1½ to 2 inches of water). This has to be refrigerated for at least 3 or 4 hours before serving, or it may stand overnight.

TO CARAMELIZE THE MOLD

¾ cup granulated sugar
3 tablespoons water
⅛ teaspoon cream of tartar

Place the sugar, water, and cream of tartar in a heavy 1-quart saucepan over moderate heat. Stir with a small wooden spatula until the sugar is dissolved and the mixture comes to a boil. Wash down the sides with a pastry brush dipped in water to remove any undissolved crystals. Let boil without stirring until the mixture barely begins to caramelize. (It takes about 8 minutes.) If it starts to darken in one spot, twirl the pan gently. Then stir with the wooden spatula briefly until the mixture becomes a lovely caramel color. (If it is too pale, it will not have any flavor; if it is too dark, it will taste bitter.)

Immediately pour the boiling syrup into the mold. Hold the mold carefully with pot holders and tilt it gently in all directions to make the caramel run all over the bottom and up the sides to about ½ inch from the top of the mold. Continue to tilt and turn the dish until the caramel stops running. You will not be able to make the caramel run up on the center tube—that's O.K.

When the caramel stops running and is cool, butter the center tube to make it easier to unmold the custard.

FRENCH CUSTARD

2½ cups milk
1 cup light cream

4 eggs plus 4 egg yolks (graded large or
    extra-large)
½ cup granulated sugar
¾ teaspoon vanilla extract
Scant ½ teaspoon almond extract
Pinch of salt

Adjust a rack one-third up from the bottom of the oven and preheat the oven to 325 degrees.

Scald the milk and cream in an uncovered saucepan over moderate heat just until a slight skin forms on top or tiny bubbles form around the edge.

Meanwhile, in a large mixing bowl, stir the eggs, yolks, sugar, vanilla and almond extracts, and the salt with a wire whisk to mix thoroughly; do not beat until light or foamy.

When the milk and cream are ready, pour them very gradually at first into the egg mixture, stirring steadily to mix.

Pour through a rather fine strainer into a large, wide-mouthed pitcher.

Check the flavoring; sometimes it is necessary to add a bit more salt, which brings out the vanilla and almond flavors.

Place the caramelized mold in a larger pan (see introduction). Carefully pour the custard into the mold. Then carefully pour hot water into the larger pan until it comes halfway up the sides of the mold.

Transfer the pan to the oven.

Bake uncovered for 35 to 40 minutes until a small, sharp knife gently inserted into the custard comes out clean.

Remove from the oven and let stand for 5 or 10 minutes. Then, carefully remove the mold from the water and let stand uncovered at room temperature to cool.

Refrigerate for 3 or 4 hours or overnight, but no longer.

Do not unmold the custard any earlier than necessary. (The beautiful, shiny caramel will become dull if it stands too long—about 1 hour is not too long.) To unmold: With a small, sharp knife carefully cut around the outside edge of the custard to loosen. Then cut around the tube to be sure it is not stuck. Cover the mold with a large, flat dessert platter that has a small rim; be sure the platter is centered. Hold the platter and the mold together and carefully turn them over. Don't rush—be patient—the custard will slip out of the mold. The caramel will have melted into a sauce and will coat the top of the custard and run onto the plate.

Return to the refrigerator.

If you serve whipped cream, the amount to use depends on the number of people you are serving. For four, 1 cup is enough; for six or eight use 2 cups. Use 2 tablespoons of granulated or confectioners sugar for each cup of cream, and about 2 tablespoons of kirsch, rum, or Cognac or ½ teaspoon vanilla extract for each cup of cream. Whip the cream, sugar, and flavoring in a chilled bowl with chilled beaters only until the cream holds a soft, not stiff, shape. If you whip the cream ahead of time, refrigerate it and then stir it a bit with a wire whisk just before serving (to blend it if it has separated slightly).

It is best to serve the cream separately and spoon or pour it alongside each portion.

It is not necessarily traditional to serve fruit with this, but it is good; it goes wonderfully with the custard and with the caramel, and you will like it. It may be served separately and spooned alongside each portion, or it may be placed around the rim of the mold or piled up in the center. This has been one of my favorite desserts for many years and I have always served it with fruit. Many guests prefer a generous amount of the fruit, and just a small serving of the custard. It is wonderful with fresh strawberries or raspberries, or with stewed pears, or with any brandied fruits.

Use a wide cake server or spatula for serving the custard.

Lemon Mousse

8 PORTIONS

This is food for angels; it is like eating a sweet, lemon-flavored cloud, like a glass of delicious nothingness. Plan it for any luncheon or dinner; you will love it! Make it at least 4 hours ahead or the day before. It is prepared in individual glasses that should have at least a 10-ounce capacity, although they can be larger if you wish.

1 envelope unflavored gelatin
2 tablespoons cold water
Finely grated rind of 2 large lemons
½ cup plus 1 tablespoon fresh lemon juice
1 cup granulated sugar

1 cup egg whites (about 8 whites; they may be
    whites that were left over from other
    recipes, frozen and then thawed)
⅛ teaspoon salt
⅛ teaspoon cream of tartar
1 cup heavy cream

Sprinkle the gelatin over the water in a small cup and let stand for a few minutes.

Meanwhile, place the rind, juice, and ¾ cup (reserve the remaining ¼ cup) of the sugar in a small saucepan and stir with a wooden spatula until the sugar is dissolved and the mixture just comes to a boil. Add the softened gelatin, stir to melt, remove from the heat, and pour the mixture into a rather large mixing bowl (preferably metal—it will chill faster).

Partially fill a larger bowl with ice and water and place the bowl of lemon mixture into it; stir constantly until the mixture is cool (test it on the inside of your wrist) but not until it starts to thicken. Remove the bowl from the ice water temporarily (but reserve the ice water) and set aside.

Place the whites in the large bowl of an electric mixer. Add the salt and the cream of tartar and beat until the whites hold a soft shape. Reduce the speed to moderate and gradually add the reserved ¼ cup of sugar. Then, on high speed again, beat only until the whites barely hold a definite shape; they should not be stiff or dry. Set aside.

In a small, chilled bowl with chilled beaters, whip the cream until it just barely holds a definite shape; it should not be stiff or dry. (If the cream or whites are beaten too much the finished dessert will not be as good.) Set aside.

Replace the bowl with the lemon mixture over the bowl of ice water and scrape the bowl constantly with a rubber spatula until the mixture thickens to a syrupy consistency. Remove from the ice immediately before it really stiffens and quickly fold about one-quarter of it into the whipped cream. Then fold in a second quarter. And then a third. If you have a large-size rubber spatula, use it now. Then, in either bowl, briefly fold the cream and the remaining lemon mixture together. Next, fold about a cupful of the beaten whites into the cream—do not be too thorough. Then another cupful. Finally, in either bowl, fold the cream and the remaining whites only until barely blended. Do not handle any more than necessary.

With a large spoon, spoon the mixture into eight wine glasses or straight-sided old-fashioned glasses (that is, the drink "old-fashioned").

If you can cover the glasses with plastic wrap without having it touch the mousse, do so.

Refrigerate for 4 hours or overnight. These do not need any decoration. I like them plain. Or with a tiny sprinkling of crumbled candied violet or rose petals sprinkled on top, or a few very thin slices of fresh strawberries.

It is nice if you can get some large, flat green leaves to place under the glasses on the dessert plates. (Here in Florida, I pick sea grape leaves outside of either door. In other areas it might be necessary to get them from a florist—I have used a few lemon leaves from a florist on each plate.)

Tangerine Mousse

8 PORTIONS

This Florida mousse is as light as air, as delicate as a soft breeze, and as fresh and delicious as if you just picked the tangerines yourself. Tangerines are in season during the winter; remember this recipe when you see them. It is prepared in individual glasses, and should be made at least 4 hours before serving or it may stand overnight.

1½ teaspoons unflavored gelatin
2 tablespoons water, Grand Marnier, kirsch, or
    additional tangerine juice
6 eggs (graded large or extra-large), separated
⅔ cup granulated sugar
⅓ cup tangerine juice (grate the rind to use
    later before squeezing the juice)
2½ tablespoons lemon juice
Finely grated rind of 2 or 3 large, deep-colored
    tangerines
1 cup heavy cream
Pinch of salt

Sprinkle the gelatin over the 2 tablespoons water (or other substitute liquid) in a small cup and let stand.

Place the egg yolks in the top of a large double boiler off the heat.

With a wire whisk, stir to mix well. Measure out the sugar. Remove and reserve 3 tablespoons; add the remaining sugar to the yolks and beat briskly with the whisk until foamy. Mix in the tangerine juice and the lemon juice.

Place over the bottom of the double boiler partly filled with hot water on moderate heat. Stir and scrape the bottom and sides almost constantly with a rubber spatula until the mixture thickens enough to coat a metal or wooden spoon. When it is just right it will register 170 degrees on a candy thermometer, and will look like soft, fluffy mayonnaise. Do not overcook.

Remove the top of the double boiler, add the gelatin and stir to dissolve, stir in the grated rind, and transfer the mixture to a large mixing bowl. Stir occasionally until cool.

Then, in a chilled bowl with chilled beaters, whip the cream only until it holds a soft, not stiff, shape and set aside.

In the large bowl of an electric mixer (or in a large copper bowl with a wire whisk) add the salt to the egg whites and beat only until the whites hold a soft shape. Reduce the speed to moderate, gradually add the reserved 3 tablespoons of sugar, then increase the speed to high again and continue to beat until the whites barely hold a definite shape, not until they are stiff and dry.

Fold about one-third of the whites into the yolks. Then add the remaining whites and the whipped cream and fold gently and carefully only until the mixtures are barely blended; do not fold until they are completely blended or you will lose some of the air. It is all right if you still see a few slight streaks of whipped cream or egg whites and a few streaks of the tangerine mixture.

With a large spoon gently transfer the mousse to dessert bowls or wine glasses or straight-sided old-fashioned glasses. Cover airtight with plastic wrap and refrigerate for at least 4 hours.

These do not need any topping; they may be served quite plain, or each one may be topped with a thin slice or wedge of kiwi fruit and/or a thinly sliced strawberry, or a few blueberries, or a bit of candied violet or rose petal, or a fresh mint leaf. Whatever, it should be delicate.

Orange Mousse with Blueberries

This is a very pretty molded mousse—light, creamy, tender, delicate, and delicious.

You will need a metal mold with an 8-cup capacity; it can be a round-bottomed bowl, a charlotte mold, or a loaf pan. (If the pan has a design, it must not be a small, detailed design.) The prepared mousse should be refrigerated 4 to 10 hours before serving.

6 TO 8 PORTIONS

1 cup fresh blueberries (approximately)
1 envelope plus 1½ teaspoons
    unflavored gelatin
⅓ cup cold water
⅓ cup boiling water
1 cup granulated sugar
3 tablespoons lemon juice
1 cup orange juice
3 egg whites
Pinch of salt
1 cup heavy cream

Wash, drain, and dry the berries. Place them in a plastic bag in the freezer for about 30 minutes; it is best if they are very cold or almost but not quite frozen when you use them.

Sprinkle the gelatin over the cold water in a small bowl. Let stand for 5 minutes. Then add the boiling water and stir with a metal spoon to dissolve. (Examine it carefully; if it is not completely dissolved, place it in a little hot water over low heat and stir to dissolve.)

Transfer the gelatin to a large mixing bowl. Add ¾ cup of the sugar (reserve the remaining ¼ cup), the lemon juice, and the orange juice. Stir until the sugar is dissolved.

Place the bowl in a larger bowl of ice and water. Stir occasionally until the gelatin mixture thickens slightly.

While the gelatin mixture is chilling, prepare the egg whites and the heavy cream. In a small bowl, beat the whites with the salt until they hold a soft shape. On low speed gradually add the reserved ¼ cup of sugar, then beat on high speed again until the whites hold a firm shape, but not until they are stiff and dry. Set aside. In a small, chilled bowl with chilled beaters, whip the cream until it holds a shape; it should be rather firm but not stiff. Set aside.

When the gelatin mixture thickens enough so that it does not completely flatten out if some of it is dropped back onto itself, whip it briskly with a large wire whisk or with a beater.

Gradually fold in the beaten whites and then the whipped cream. If the mixture appears to separate slightly (the gelatin part is heavier and it might sink) pour the entire mixture gently back and forth from one large bowl to another. If it still separates, place it in the freezer briefly, and then fold again.

Fold in the very cold blueberries. (The very cold berries will help to set the mousse.)

Quickly rinse an 8-cup, plain (not fancy) metal mold with ice water. Shake it out; do not dry it. Pour the mousse into the wet mold.

Refrigerate for at least 4 hours or all day.

When you are ready to unmold the dessert, which should be as close to serving time as possible (1 to 1½ hours is all right), lightly oil (with tasteless salad oil) an area the size of the mold on a flat serving platter— the oil will make it possible for you to move the mousse if necessary.

Cut around the top of the mousse with a small, sharp knife to release the edges. Quickly dip the mold for only a moment or so (actually, count slowly to three if the mold is thin metal; count to six if it is heavy metal) in hot (not boiling) water at least as deep as the mold. Then quickly place the mold on a towel to dry it, place the dessert platter over it, and holding the mold and the platter firmly together, turn them both over. If the mousse does not slip out easily, bang both the platter and the mold against the counter top. If it still does not slip out easily, it may be necessary to dip it in hot water again. (If so, be careful while turning the mold upright again. It has happened that a dessert was ready to come out, had actually started to come out, when the mold was raised to be turned upright for another hot-water dip. And it did indeed come out, but not on the platter. Therefore, to turn the mold upright again, keep the platter over it and invert both together.)

If the mousse is not in the center of the plate, use your hands to move it very slowly and gently.

VARIATIONS: 1. *This does not want whipped cream; it is perfect just as it is. However, fresh strawberries are terrific with it. Either place a ring of washed and drained, but unhulled, berries around the mousse; or hull the berries, slice them thick, sprinkle with a bit of sugar and some Grand Marnier, let stand for about an hour or more and then serve the berries separately, spooning them alongside each portion.*

2. Here's another way I have made this—a sort of fruit-cup mousse; it was wonderful. I mixed the blueberries into the mousse and poured about two-thirds of it into the mold. Then I added a layer of strawberries (not too many). And I folded some orange sections into the remaining mousse before pouring it on top of the strawberries.

3. If you wish, either of the versions of this mousse can be prepared individually in large wine glasses; it is easier and equally nice.

Grapefruit Mousse

6 PORTIONS

This recipe comes from a lady fishing guide in the Florida Keys who used to take my father tarpon fishing. My father supplied roast chickens and vegetable salad; the lady guide brought dessert and the fishing bait.

This is light, creamy, sweet-and-sour, deliciously refreshing. Prepared in individual glasses.

2 large, sweet grapefruits
¼ cup cold water
1 envelope unflavored gelatin
3 eggs (graded large), separated
¾ cup granulated sugar (see Note)
Finely grated rind of 2 deep-colored oranges
1 cup heavy cream
Generous pinch of salt

Peel and section the grapefruits (see page 19). They should be puréed in a food processor or a blender (or, as was told to me, cut up and then mashed with a potato masher in a large bowl). You should have 1¾ cups of purée.

Place the cold water in a small cup and sprinkle the gelatin over the top. Let stand.

Place the egg yolks in the top of a large double boiler off the heat. Measure out the sugar and remove and reserve 2 tablespoons; add the remaining sugar to the yolks. Stir briskly with a small wire whisk. Then, with a wooden or rubber spatula, gradually stir in the grapefruit purée.

Place over boiling water on moderate heat and cook, stirring frequently, until the mixture thickens slightly. It will not thicken as much as most custard sauces do. It will take about 5 to 7 minutes. A candy thermometer inserted into the mixture should register 180 degrees.

Add the softened gelatin and stir to dissolve.

Remove from the hot water. Stir in the orange rind. Transfer to a wide mixing bowl. Place the bowl in a larger bowl partly filled with ice and water. Stir occasionally until the mixture barely starts to thicken. Remove it from the ice water and set aside.

In a chilled bowl with chilled beaters, whip the cream until it holds a shape, but not until it is really stiff. Set aside.

In the small bowl of the electric mixer, beat the egg whites with the salt until the whites hold a soft shape when the beaters are raised. Add the reserved 2 tablespoons of sugar and continue to beat the mixture until the whites barely hold a definite shape, but do not beat them until they are stiff or dry.

The grapefruit mixture should be thick enough to mound slightly when some of it is dropped back into the bowl; if necessary, stir it a bit more over the ice. (The ideal condition for incorporating these three mixtures is to have them all the same consistency.) With a whisk or a beater, beat the grapefruit mixture briefly.

Fold one-quarter of the grapefruit mixture into the whipped cream. Fold in another quarter without being too thorough. Then fold the cream into the remaining grapefruit mixture. If some of this seems heavier than the rest and sinks to the bottom of the bowl, pour it all gently back and forth from one large bowl to another to blend the mixtures.

Then fold one-quarter of the grapefruit-cream mixture into the whites. Now fold the whites into the remaining grapefruit-cream. Again, if some of the mixture sinks to the bottom, pour it all gently from one large bowl to another to blend. Whatever you do, try not to lose the air that was beaten into the whites and the cream.

Gently transfer the mousse to a wide pitcher and pour it into six 8-ounce wine glasses. Cover them with plastic wrap. Refrigerate for at least 4 hours or overnight.

Serve these plain. Or, if you want to top them with something, it should be fruit: a few thinly sliced strawberries, a few raspberries, a slice of kiwi fruit, or a few canned black Bing cherries. Or a sliced preserved kumquat.

NOTE: *If the grapefruits are extra sour, add an additional 1 to 2 tablespoons of sugar.*

Sour Lime Mousse with Straw- berries

6 PORTIONS

This is light and airy, tender and delicate, and it is sour. Which makes it a perfect hot-weather dessert, or serve it after a big meal in any weather. Make it at least a few hours before serving or as long as a day ahead. It is prepared in individual glasses.

6 eggs (graded large or extra-large), separated
¾ cup granulated sugar
Finely grated rind of 1 large lime
¾ cup fresh lime juice
1½ tablespoons unsalted butter
1½ teaspoons unflavored gelatin
½ teaspoon vanilla extract
Pinch of salt

Combine the egg yolks, ½ cup of the sugar (reserve the remaining ¼ cup of sugar), lime rind, ½ cup of the lime juice (reserve the remaining ¼ cup of juice), and the butter in the top of a large double boiler. Place over hot water on moderate heat. While the mixture cooks, continuously scrape the bottom and sides with a rubber spatula.

Meanwhile, sprinkle the gelatin over the reserved ¼ cup of lime juice in a small cup, and let it stand.

Cook the egg-yolk mixture until it thickens slightly, or until it registers about 180 degrees on a candy thermometer.

Remove the top of the double boiler, add the softened gelatin, stir to melt the gelatin, and set aside to cool to room temperature.

Stir in the vanilla.

In the large bowl of an electric mixer (or in a large bowl with a balloon-type wire whisk) beat the egg whites and the salt until the whites hold a soft shape. Gradually add the reserved ¼ cup of sugar and continue to beat until the whites hold a definite shape but not until they are stiff or dry.

Fold about one-quarter of the yolk mixture into the whites. Then fold in another quarter. And then fold the remaining yolk mixture and the whites together only until they are barely blended.

Gently pour the mixture into a wide-mouthed pitcher and pour it into six wine glasses that have a 10-ounce capacity. Do not fill the glasses all the way; leave room for the berries.

Cover the glasses with foil or plastic wrap and refrigerate for at least a few hours or overnight.

This may be served with a topping of just barely thawed and partially drained frozen strawberries. Or with the following fresh strawberries.

STRAWBERRIES

About 4 cups fresh strawberries
3 tablespoons granulated sugar
3 tablespoons Curaçao, kirsch, Grand Marnier,
or dark rum

Wash the berries quickly, hull, drain thoroughly, and then cut each berry into 3 or 4 slices.

In a bowl, toss the berries gently with the sugar and liquor. Let stand at room temperature, stirring occasionally, for about half an hour. Then cover and refrigerate until serving time.

Just before serving, spoon the berries over the mousses.

Zabaglione Freddo

8 PORTIONS

Mama mia! That's amore! It is a sweetened egg-yolk and wine mixture with Cognac and lemon, and a small amount of gelatin (just barely enough —the way it should be) and a generous amount of whipped cream folded in, and it is a bit of Italian heaven served in individual wine glasses.

If you are serving an Italian dinner, serve this for dessert. Or if it is any other dinner—French, Chinese, seafood, what-have-you—serve this for dessert. It is the fluffiest, lightest, airiest mixture of sweetness ever.

To be serious for a moment, if I can come back to earth after the zabaglione cloud I have been flying on, zabaglione is traditionally served hot (without gelatin), the moment it has cooked and risen to beautiful proportions (timed like a hot soufflé). It is a headwaiter's show-stopper in the finest Italian restaurants. This version is different. "Freddo" or "cold" is the difference—this should chill for at least 4 hours.

As fabulous as this is—and it is—it is easy. The one most important thing is a double boiler in which the top has more than a 9-cup capacity (9 cups is exactly the capacity of my largest one and it is not quite large enough). Unless yours is larger, find a bowl or saucepan, preferably with a round bottom, that you can set over a saucepan of shallow hot water to make your own double boiler. A capacity of 10 or 11 cups should be large enough, but even larger is O.K.

Finely grated rind of 1 small lemon
1 tablespoon lemon juice
1 tablespoon cold tap water
1 teaspoon unflavored gelatin
8 egg yolks
½ cup granulated sugar
1 cup dry Marsala
2 tablespoons boiling water
¼ cup Cognac or other brandy
2 cups heavy cream

Mix the rind and juice in a small cup and set aside.

Place the cold water in a small custard cup and sprinkle the gelatin over the top; set aside to soften.

In the small bowl of an electric mixer, beat the yolks and sugar at high speed for 5 minutes until very pale and thick. On lowest speed slowly add the Marsala, scraping the bowl with a rubber spatula and beating only until incorporated.

Transfer the mixture to the top of a large double boiler or any bowl with at least a 10-cup capacity. Place over a little hot water on *low* heat. Beat with a portable electric mixer for about 10 minutes or until the mixture has risen and holds a soft shape when the beaters are raised.

Immediately (to stop the cooking) transfer to the large bowl of an electric mixer.

Add the boiling water to the softened gelatin and stir until dissolved. Then, while beating on low speed, gradually add the gelatin to the yolk mixture; beat only to mix. Remove from the mixer. Add the lemon-juice and rind mixture and gradually add the Cognac, while folding gently and lightly with a large rubber spatula. Set aside until cool.

Meanwhile, in a chilled bowl with chilled beaters, whip the cream until it holds a shape but not until it is stiff or dry.

Fold about half of the egg-yolk mixture into the whipped cream and then fold the cream into the remaining egg-yolk mixture.

Transfer to a wide-mouthed pitcher and pour into eight 8- or 10-ounce wine glasses or straight-sided old-fashioned glasses. If the zabaglione is below the tops of the glasses, cover them with foil or plastic wrap; if not, just leave them uncovered.

Refrigerate for 4 to 8 hours.

Do not add anything to decorate this; it is too classic and simple and wonderful just as it is.

Raspberry Bavarian

6 PORTIONS

There are some parties that must be pink for one reason or another; this is the dessert to make—it is a gorgeous color. (But unless you have one planned soon, don't wait for a pink party to make this.) It is wondrously smooth, creamy, and refreshing, with an intense and irresistible raspberry flavor. And it is so easy you will be tickled pink.

It can be made in a mold or in wine glasses. You will need a blender. Make it at least 4 or 5 hours before serving or the day before. To double the recipe, see Notes at the end of the recipe.

1 10-ounce box frozen raspberries, in syrup
3 tablespoons fresh lemon juice
1 envelope unflavored gelatin
¼ cup milk
2 egg yolks
Pinch of salt
1 cup heavy cream
1 cup crushed ice (see Notes)

Place the frozen berries and the lemon juice in a bowl and let stand until the berries have thawed. (Or, if you are in a hurry, place the plastic bag or waterproof package of berries in warm water for about 10 or 15 minutes to thaw, then turn it into a bowl and add the lemon juice.) As the berries start to thaw, you can help them along by breaking the frozen block into small pieces with a fork. When it is completely thawed, pour it into a strainer set over a bowl. Let the juice drain. You should have ⅔ cup or a little more.

Sprinkle the gelatin over the milk in a small custard cup, stir with a fork, and let stand for 5 minutes.

Meanwhile, place the drained juice in a small, uncovered saucepan over moderate heat and bring it to a boil. Then add the softened gelatin, stir to dissolve (the mixture might not look smooth but it is O.K.), transfer to the container of a blender, and blend at high speed for 1 minute.

Remove the cover of the blender, add the raspberries, egg yolks, and salt, and blend at high speed for 5 seconds. Then add the cream and crushed ice and continue to blend for 10 or 15 seconds until perfectly smooth. (Easy?)

Now, to remove the seeds, strain the mixture through a wide strainer set over a bowl or a wide pitcher (a small strainer will take forever, and it might seem slow even in a wide strainer—work the mixture through with a rubber spatula).

If you have strained the mixture into a bowl, and if you are going to prepare it in individual glasses, transfer it to a pitcher and pour it into six 6- or 8-ounce wine glasses. Cover airtight and refrigerate for at least 4 hours.

If you are preparing this in a mold, use a thin metal mold (it is easier to unmold than a heavy pottery one) with a 4-cup capacity and not too much detail in the mold; you might like a plain round bowl or ring mold best. Rinse the mold with ice water, shake it out but do not dry it, and pour the mixture into the mold. Refrigerate until set, then cover with plastic wrap and refrigerate for at least 5 hours or overnight.

To unmold, lightly oil a large, flat dessert platter with tasteless salad oil. This will make it easy to move the unmolded dessert if necessary to center it on the platter. (It also makes it easier to serve; the dessert doesn't cling to the plate. No one will see or taste the oil.) Cut around the top of the mold with a small, sharp knife. Then dip the mold into a large bowl or dishpan of hot tap water up to ½ inch from the top, hold the mold in the water for 8 or 9 seconds, remove from the water, dry the mold quickly, place the oiled platter over the mold, center it carefully, and, holding the mold and the platter firmly together, turn them both over. Bang the mold and the platter a few times on a heavy folded towel on the counter top. The dessert should slide out after a few seconds. If not, raise the mold slightly and bang it against the plate a few more times. Or, as a last resort, tilt the mold on a slight angle—sometimes it will slip out more easily on an angle than it will drop straight down. If it is still in the mold, carefully turn it upright and dip it again in hot water but only for a few seconds.

Dry the platter around the mold and immediately place the Bavarian in the refrigerator.

WHIPPED CREAM

1 cup heavy cream
2 tablespoons confectioners or granulated sugar
2 tablespoons kirsch or framboise
  (raspberry brandy)

In a chilled bowl with chilled beaters, whip the above ingredients until they just hold a shape. If the Bavarian is in glasses, place a large spoonful of the cream on each portion. If it has been molded, the cream may be served separately or, better yet, place it in a pastry bag fitted with a medium-size star-shaped tube and form a border of whipped-cream rosettes around the base of the mold. And maybe a few on top also. Or use it on the top only.

If, by some good luck, fresh raspberries are available, of course it is lovely to serve some with the Bavarian; but if not, don't worry—this is great as it is.

NOTES: 1. *To double this recipe: If you are making it in a mold, prepare it once, set it aside, prepare it again, mix the two batches and pour it into a wet 8-cup bowl or simple mold. If possible, refrigerate this larger amount overnight. If you are making it in glasses, prepare it once, pour into 6* glasses, prepare it again, and pour into 6 more glasses. In other words, blenders are not large enough to handle double the amount in one load.

2. If you do not have an ice crusher, crush the ice in a processor, or put ice cubes in a canvas or heavy plastic bag. Work on a board or outdoors. Pound the ice with a hammer to crush it. Place the bag in the freezer until you are ready for it.

Cognac-Coffee Mousseline

6 TO 8 PORTIONS

A mousseline is an airy mixture made with beaten egg whites, like a mousse; the difference is that a mousseline also always contains whipped cream.

Although the ingredients call for Cognac, coffee, eggs, cream, and gelatin, the main ingredient is air. This is utterly delicious. I made this many years ago for my husband's restaurant; now, years later, I meet people who still rave about it.

It is prepared in individual glasses and should be made about 6 to 12 hours before serving, although there were times at the restaurant when it was served only a few hours after it was made (in that case it was placed in the freezer for about half an hour just before serving).

You will need six to eight wine glasses, each with a 6- to 8-ounce capacity.

2 tablespoons instant coffee (powdered or granular)
½ cup boiling water
1 envelope unflavored gelatin
¼ cup cold water
4 eggs (graded large), separated
1 cup granulated sugar
Scant ¼ teaspoon salt
1 teaspoon vanilla extract
¼ cup Cognac, brandy, or Irish whiskey
1 cup heavy cream

Dissolve the coffee in the boiling water and set aside.

Sprinkle the gelatin over the cold water and let stand.

Place the egg yolks in the top of a large double boiler off the heat, stir just to mix, and very gradually stir in the prepared coffee (which may still be warm). Then add ½ cup of the sugar (reserve the remaining ½ cup of sugar) and the salt, and stir to mix well.

Place over hot water on moderate heat. Cook, scraping the pan continuously with a rubber spatula, until the mixture thickens slightly. It is thick enough when a candy thermometer inserted in the mixture registers 180 degrees; do not overcook or it will curdle.

Remove from the hot water, stir in the softened gelatin to dissolve, then stir in the vanilla and Cognac and set aside.

In a chilled bowl with chilled beaters, whip the cream only until it barely holds a shape but not until it is stiff or dry. Set aside.

In the small bowl of the electric mixer, or in a copper bowl with a large whisk, beat the egg whites until they hold a shape. Reduce the speed slightly and gradually add the reserved ½ cup of sugar. Then increase the speed again and beat until the mixture resembles a thick, stiff marshmallow fluff. Set aside.

Place some ice and a bit of water in a large mixing bowl. Place the bowl of the gelatin-coffee-Cognac mixture in the ice water. Stir constantly with a rubber spatula until the mixture thickens slightly (do not wait for it to mound, that would be too thick).

The gelatin mixture will thicken more as it stands, so work quickly now. Fold about half of the gelatin mixture into the beaten whites and fold the other half into the whipped cream. Then, in a large bowl, fold the two mixtures together.

Transfer the mixture to a wide-mouthed pitcher and pour it into six to eight wine glasses.

Refrigerate from 6 to 12 hours.

If you wish, top each glass with a bit of whipped cream and a few candied violet or rose petals. Or, as I did for the restaurant, top with a few chocolate shavings made with semisweet chocolate. Or a bit of whipped cream and a few chocolate coffee-bean candies.

Cold
Praline
Soufflé

Make this for an important occasion—it is elegant, swanky, gorgeous, and delicious. Make it early in the day for that night, or the day before. You will need a 5-cup soufflé dish.

PRALINE

The praline may be prepared months ahead of time if you wish, or just before making the soufflé.

¾ cup whole blanched almonds or
    blanched hazelnuts
1⅓ cups granulated sugar
6 tablespoons water
¼ plus ⅛ teaspoon cream of tartar

Place the almonds in a single layer in a shallow cake pan in the middle of a 350-degree oven. Bake for about half an hour, shaking the pan occasionally to stir the nuts, until they are toasted to a rich golden brown. Remove from the oven and set aside.

If you use hazelnuts, you will have toasted them during the blanching process. If you buy them already skinned but not toasted, they should be toasted in the oven the same as the almonds.

Prepare a jelly-roll pan or any rectangular metal pan by lining it with one long piece of foil, and set it aside.

Place the sugar, water, and cream of tartar in a saucepan with about a 1-quart capacity over high heat. Stir constantly with a wooden spatula until the sugar is dissolved. Wash down the sides of the saucepan with a pastry brush dipped in cold water to remove any undissolved granules. Then let the syrup boil without stirring until it turns the color of dark molasses (while it is boiling, lift the pan a bit and swirl it a few times to move the ingredients). Add the nuts, stir to mix, and pour out into a thin layer on the foil-lined pan.

Let the mixture cool. Then peel the foil away from the back. With your hands break the praline into pieces. Then, in a blender or a processor, blend or process until the praline is finely powdered (in a blender it may be necessary to do it in two or three batches).

If you prepare the praline ahead of time, it must be stored airtight or it will absorb moisture and become wet and sticky. I store it airtight in a double plastic bag in the freezer. You will use the full amount of this for the soufflé.

SOUFFLÉ

⅓ cup water
1 envelope plus 1½ teaspoons
    unflavored gelatin
3 eggs (graded large or extra-large), separated
¾ cup milk
¼ cup dark rum
½ teaspoon vanilla extract
¼ teaspoon almond extract
1½ cups heavy cream
Pinch of salt

Prepare a 5-cup (6¾ × 3-inch) soufflé dish by folding a 24-inch length of wax paper in half the long way. Wrap it around the dish, folded edge to the bottom. Tie the paper tightly with string, wrapping the string about ½ inch below the top of the dish. Secure the top of the overlap with a pin or paper clip. (Do not butter or oil the dish or the wax paper.) Set the dish aside.

Place the water in a small, heatproof glass custard cup and sprinkle the gelatin over it. Let stand for a few minutes. Then place the cup in shallow hot water in a small pan on low heat. Stir with a metal spoon to see when the gelatin is dissolved, or pick up the cup and twirl it a bit; you will be able to see against the glass when the gelatin is dissolved. If your cup is not glass, dip a metal spoon in. The gelatin will show on the metal.

Place the egg yolks, milk, rum, vanilla and almond extracts, and the warm dissolved gelatin in the container of a blender or a processor (fitted with the metal blade). Blend or process for about 10 or 15 seconds. Add the powdered praline and blend or process for a few seconds.

Transfer the mixture to a rather large mixing bowl and set aside.

Whip the cream until it just barely holds a shape and set aside.

In a clean bowl add the salt to the whites and, with clean beaters, beat only until the whites barely hold a firm shape—not until they are stiff or dry—and set aside.

Place the bowl of praline mixture into a larger bowl partially filled with ice and cold water. Stir constantly with a rubber spatula, scraping the bottom, until the praline mixture thickens slightly (it will take only a few minutes). Immediately remove the bowl from the ice and water before the mixture actually starts to set. (It is best if the praline mixture, the whipped cream, and the egg whites are all the same consistency.)

Immediately add the whipped cream to the praline mixture, fold them together, then add the whites and fold together. Do not handle any more than necessary.

Turn the soufflé into the prepared dish and smooth the top (it should stand about an inch or so above the top of the dish).

Refrigerate 6 to 8 hours or overnight.

DECORATION

2 to 3 tablespoons melted and strained
   apricot preserves
⅓ cup blanched almonds, lightly toasted in the
   oven, or blanched hazelnuts, chopped into
   fine pieces (these should be chopped by
   hand, not ground to a powder)
½ to 1 cup heavy cream
Granulated or confectioners sugar
Vanilla extract

When you are ready to finish the dessert (which may be just shortly before serving or several hours before), cut the string, and gently and carefully remove the wax-paper collar. Wipe the sides of the dish and place it on a large piece of wax paper.

With a pastry brush, brush the sides of the soufflé with the strained apricot preserves. Then, with your fingers, place the almonds or hazelnuts into the preserves to cover the sides. Many of the nuts will fall onto the wax paper. Use a long, narrow metal spatula to pick them up and transfer them to the sides of the soufflé.

The amount of cream will depend on how you want to use it. To use it as a decoration with a pastry bag and a star tube you will probably need only ½ cup (with 1 tablespoon sugar and ¼ teaspoon vanilla). Whip the ingredients until they hold a shape and decorate as you wish. The easiest—and it is pretty—is a border of small rosettes around the rim.

If you do not use the cream as decoration but want to serve it as a sauce, whip the ingredients (1 cup cream, 2 tablespoons sugar, and ½ teaspoon vanilla) only until the cream is lightly thickened—no stiffer. Place it in a bowl and serve it separately.

Cold Orange Soufflé

Cool and refreshing, extremely light, creamy, and delicate.

Gelatin desserts should be just barely stiff enough to hold their shapes. They are best as soon as they become firm, they toughen slightly if they stand overnight, and they become rubbery if they stand longer. It is best to make this during the day for that night; it should be refrigerated for at least 4 hours before serving.

This is a festive dessert, make it for a party.

Finely grated rind of 2 large, deep-
    colored oranges
Finely grated rind of 1 large lemon
⅓ cup lemon juice
1 envelope plus 1 teaspoon unflavored gelatin
1 cup plus 2 tablespoons granulated sugar
4 eggs (graded large, extra-large, or
    jumbo), separated
1½ cups orange juice
1½ cups heavy cream
⅛ teaspoon salt

You will need a straight-sided soufflé dish with a 5-cup capacity; the classic white china French one with that capacity measures 6¾ inches in diameter and 3 inches in depth.

To prepare a wax-paper collar: Tear off a piece of wax paper long enough to wrap around the dish and overlap itself by a few inches (for a 6¾-inch dish you need 24 inches of paper). Fold the paper in half the long way and wrap it around the dish, placing the folded edge even with the bottom of the dish. Wrap string around the collar about ½ inch below the top of the dish and tie it securely. Fasten the top overlapping ends with a straight pin or a paper clip. Set aside.

Place both grated rinds and the lemon juice in a small cup and set aside.

Place the gelatin and ¾ cup plus 2 tablespoons of the sugar (reserve the remaining ¼ cup) in the top of a large double boiler off the heat. Stir to mix and set aside.

In a bowl beat the yolks just to mix them well. Gradually mix in the orange juice, beating to mix well, and then pour this mixture over the gelatin and sugar, and stir to mix. Let stand for about 3 minutes to soften the gelatin.

Place the top of the double boiler over hot water on moderate heat and stir almost constantly with a rubber spatula until the gelatin and sugar are dissolved (it takes about 5 minutes—test by dipping a metal spoon in and out; undissolved granules show up against the metal).

Remove the top of the double boiler and stir in the grated rinds and lemon juice.

Place the top of the double boiler in a large bowl of ice and water. With a rubber spatula, scrape the bottom and stir frequently until the mixture cools and begins to thicken.

Meanwhile, in a chilled bowl with chilled beaters, whip the cream until it holds a soft shape (it should not be stiff or it will make the soufflé heavy). Set aside.

Also meanwhile, in the small bowl of an electric mixer (or in a large copper bowl with a large wire whisk), beat the egg whites with the salt until they barely hold a soft shape. Reduce the speed to moderate and gradually add the reserved ¼ cup of sugar. Then increase the speed to high again and continue to beat briefly only until the whites resemble a thick marshmallowlike fluff, not stiff or dry.

When the orange mixture thickens to the consistency of a soft mayonnaise, transfer it immediately to a mixing bowl (if you leave it in the cold top of the double boiler it will continue to set and will quickly become too firm).

With a rubber spatula, gradually (not all at once) fold about half of the orange mixture into the whites and then gradually fold the other half into the whipped cream. Then, in a large bowl with a large rubber spatula, fold the two mixtures together. Handle as little as possible. If necessary, pour gently from one bowl to another to ensure thorough blending.

Pour the mixture into the prepared soufflé dish (it will come about 1½ inches above the top), smooth the top, and refrigerate for at least 4 hours.

OPTIONAL ACCOMPANIMENTS

⅓ cup apricot preserves
1½ tablespoons Grand Marnier, Cognac,
    rum, or water
2 or 3 dry almond macaroons (I use
    Amaretti)

In a small saucepan over moderate heat, stir the preserves occasionally until melted. Mix in the Grand Marnier, press through a strainer set over a bowl, and set aside.

Coarsely break up the macaroons and then process them in a food processor, or grind them in a blender, to make fine crumbs. Set aside.

Before serving (as close to serving time as is comfortable) remove the string and pin or paper clip, and slowly and carefully peel away the wax-paper collar; have a small, sharp knife handy in case the paper needs a little encouragement.

Place the crumbled macaroons on a large piece of wax paper. Support the soufflé dish on the palm of your left hand, hold it over the crumbs, pick up a generous amount of the crumbs in the palm of your right hand, turn your hand toward the soufflé and place the crumbs on the side of the soufflé, allowing excess crumbs to fall back onto the others. Repeat, coating the sides all around with the macaroon crumbs. Wipe the sides of the dish clean.

With a pastry brush, gently and lightly brush the thinned and strained preserves over the top of the soufflé to make a beautifully shiny layer.

This may be served just as it is, or with almost any delicious fresh, stewed, or frozen fruit on the side. Following are two suggestions.

FROZEN RASPBERRIES (sauce)

2 10-ounce boxes frozen raspberries in
    syrup, thawed
1 tablespoon honey
2 tablespoons kirsch or framboise
    (raspberry brandy)

Strain 1 box of the berries; set the berries aside—you will not use the drained syrup for this recipe.

Purée the other box of berries with their syrup in a food processor, a blender, or a food mill. Pour it through a wide but fine strainer set over a bowl to remove the seeds.

Mix the puréed and strained berries with the whole berries and the honey and kirsch or framboise. Refrigerate.

FRESH STRAWBERRIES

About 4 cups (1 pound) strawberries
(generally called a 1-pint box)
2 to 3 tablespoons granulated sugar
2 to 3 tablespoons kirsch or brandy

Wash, hull, and drain the berries. Slice them thin, mix with the sugar and kirsch or brandy, and refrigerate for at least an hour.

NOTE: *If you wish, whip ½ cup heavy cream and use it to decorate the top of the soufflé. Fit a pastry bag with a medium-small star-shaped tube, place the whipped cream in the bag, and press out either a border of rosettes or a lattice design.*

Hot Lemon Soufflé

4 TO 6 PORTIONS

This is one of the recipes that I often taught in cooking courses because it is quick and quite easy, very delicious, and because it rises into a dramatically high, photogenic, picturesque, show-off dessert. Many of the people in the classes told me that they had been afraid of soufflés, but that they had made this right after seeing it in class, and it was wonderful and they were thrilled.

Part of this can be made a few hours ahead of time; the mixture can stand at room temperature until about 40 minutes before serving, when you beat the whites and fold them in. But I have a theory about soufflés. I do not think you should be concerned about rushing breathlessly into the kitchen at some point to finish the soufflé, timing it carefully so you will be able to serve it without keeping your guests waiting. I think it is better to announce, "We are having a soufflé for dessert; I am going in to finish it now, then we will have a little wait, during which I wish you would all pray for the soufflé to rise." It adds to the fun and the excitement and makes it all more dramatic.

This does not have the usual flour and butter base; the ingredients are few and simple.

6 eggs plus 1 additional egg white (graded
large), separated (the additional white may
be one that was left over, frozen and then
thawed)
½ cup granulated sugar
⅓ cup lemon juice (grate the rind before you
squeeze the juice to use below)
Finely grated rind of 2 large or 3 small lemons
Generous pinch of salt
Optional: confectioners sugar (to sprinkle on
before serving)

Adjust a rack to the lowest position in the oven and preheat the oven to
375 degrees. Butter a 2-quart soufflé dish (7½ × 3¼ inches). Tear off a
piece of aluminum foil long enough to wrap around the dish and overlap
itself a few inches. Fold the foil in half the long way. Butter one-half of
the length (along the open end, not along the fold). Wrap the foil tightly
around the dish, open end up, with the fold lined up with the bottom
of the dish. Fasten it securely by wrapping string about ½ inch below
the top of the dish and tying it tightly. Shake granulated sugar (additional
to that called for in the ingredients) around in the dish to sugar both the
dish and the foil. Shake out excess sugar, and set the dish aside.

Place the yolks in the small bowl of an electric mixer. Add ¼ cup
of sugar (reserve the remaining ¼ cup) and beat at high speed for about
5 minutes until the mixture is pale and thick and forms a wide ribbon
when the beaters are raised. On low speed gradually mix in the juice.
Remove from the mixer, stir in the grated rind, and set aside. (The recipe
may be prepared up to this point a few hours ahead of time. If you want
to do this ahead, cover tightly and let this mixture and the egg whites
stand at room temperature.)

To finish the soufflé: In the large bowl of the mixer, with clean beaters, or in a large copper bowl with a large wire whisk, beat the 7 egg
whites and the salt until the whites hold a soft shape. Reduce the speed
to moderate and gradually add the reserved ¼ cup of sugar. Increase the
speed to high again and continue to beat only until the whites hold a
shape but not until they are stiff or dry.

In three additions carefully fold the egg-yolk mixture into the whites,
folding only until the mixtures are barely incorporated—do not handle
any more than necessary.

Turn the mixture into the prepared dish. (It will reach to the top of the dish.) Smooth the top. Place the dish in a large pan that must be wider than the dish but must not be deeper. Pour about 1 inch of hot water into the large pan. Place in the oven immediately.

Bake for 30 minutes until the soufflé is well risen and browned on the top. Quickly sprinkle the top with the optional confectioners sugar through a strainer.

Now, I have another theory about soufflés. You can quickly and carefully remove the string and the collar in the kitchen and then quickly and carefully carry the soufflé to the table. But my theory is that it is more fun and more exciting to take the dish right to the table and remove the string and the foil at the table.

Have a plate or tray ready to put the soufflé on, have scissors ready for cutting the string, have flat dessert plates ready to serve on (they should be warm), and don't waste any time.

Serve with one of the following sauces, which you should either pass and let the guests help themselves to (so you can quickly get on with serving), or have someone else spoon out while you serve the soufflé. It is best to serve the sauce alongside, rather than on top of the soufflé.

MARMALADE SAUCE

This is the easiest. Simply stir some marmalade to soften, and add a few spoonfuls of Grand Marnier, Cointreau, or orange juice. Serve at room temperature.

STRAWBERRY AND RASPBERRY SAUCE

Slice about a cup of fresh strawberries rather thin. Sprinkle with 2 tablespoons of granulated sugar and 2 tablespoons of kirsch or framboise (raspberry brandy). Let stand at room temperature, stirring occasionally. Meanwhile, thaw and drain a 10-ounce box of frozen raspberries (they should be whole raspberries packed in syrup, although you will not use the drained syrup for this recipe). Purée them in a processor or a blender, or force them through a food mill. Strain to remove the seeds. Stir the strained raspberries with the sliced strawberries. Serve at room temperature.

Soufflé Grand Marnier

Serving a hot soufflé is generally considered a great compliment to your guests; it is always festive, and this one is the most luxurious, elegant, and swanky.

(Please read the introduction to the previous Hot Lemon Soufflé [page 378] about making part of this ahead. And the paragraph near the end about removing the foil collar.)

4 TO 6 PORTIONS

6 eggs plus 1 additional egg white (graded large), separated (the additional white may be one that was left over, frozen and then thawed, or it may be left over if you make the Sauce Grand Marnier, see page 382)
½ cup granulated sugar
⅓ cup Grand Marnier
1 tablespoon lemon juice (grate the rind to use below before you squeeze the juice)
Finely grated rind of 1 lemon
Finely grated rind of 1 deep-colored orange
Generous pinch of salt
Optional: confectioners sugar (to sprinkle on before serving)

Adjust a rack to the lowest position in the oven and preheat the oven to 375 degrees. Butter a 2-quart soufflé dish. Tear off a piece of foil long enough to wrap around the dish and overlap itself by a few inches (a dish 6½ inches in diameter needs a 24-inch length of foil). Fold the foil in half the long way. Butter one-half of the length (along the open end, not along the fold). Wrap the foil tightly around the dish, open end up, with the fold lined up with the bottom of the dish. Fasten it securely by wrapping a string about ½ inch below the top of the dish and tying it tightly. Shake granulated sugar (additional to that called for in the ingredients) around in the dish to sugar both the dish and the foil. Shake out excess sugar, and set the dish aside.

Place the yolks in the small bowl of an electric mixer. Add ¼ cup of sugar (reserve the remaining ¼ cup) and beat at high speed for about 5 minutes until the mixture is pale and thick and forms a wide ribbon when the beaters are raised. On low speed gradually beat in the Grand Marnier and lemon juice. Remove from the mixer and stir in the lemon and orange rinds and set aside. (The recipe may be prepared up to this point a few hours ahead of time. If that is what you are going to do, cover tightly and let both this mixture and the egg whites stand at room temperature.)

To finish the soufflé: In the large bowl of the mixer, with clean beaters, or in a large copper bowl with a large wire whisk, beat the 7 egg whites and the salt until the whites hold a soft shape. Reduce the speed to moderate and gradually add the reserved ¼ cup of sugar. Increase the speed to high again and continue to beat only until the whites hold a shape but not until they are stiff or dry.

In three additions carefully fold the egg yolks into the whites, folding only until the mixtures are barely incorporated—do not handle any more than necessary.

Turn the mixture into the prepared dish. (It will reach the top of the dish.) Smooth the top. Place the dish in a large pan that must be wider than the dish but must not be deeper. Pour about 1 inch of hot water into the large pan. Place in the oven immediately.

Bake for 30 minutes until the soufflé is well risen and browned on the top.

Quickly sprinkle the optional sugar through a strainer over the top and quickly remove the foil collar either in the kitchen or at the table and serve at once.

Serve with the following Strawberries Grand Marnier and/or Sauce Grand Marnier.

If you go all out and serve both the strawberries and the sauce (in which case this will make 6 or 8 portions), one person should serve the soufflé while someone else serves the berries and sauce in order to save time. The berries should be placed on one side of the soufflé and the sauce on the other side.

STRAWBERRIES GRAND MARNIER

For each cup of washed, hulled, drained, and thinly sliced berries, add 1 tablespoon of granulated sugar, and 1 tablespoon each of Grand Marnier and Cognac or brandy. Let stand at room temperature, stirring occasionally, for about an hour or a little longer. Serve at room temperature.

SAUCE GRAND MARNIER

Except for folding in the whipped-cream just before serving, this can be made hours ahead, or a day ahead.

1 egg plus 3 egg yolks
¼ cup honey
Pinch of salt
1 cup heavy cream
3 tablespoons Grand Marnier (or 1½ tablespoons Grand Marnier and 1½ tablespoons
  Cognac or brandy)

Place the egg and yolks, honey, salt, and ½ cup of the cream (reserve remaining ½ cup) in the top of a small double boiler off the heat. Whisk or beat until well mixed but not light. Place over hot water on moderate heat. Stir and scrape the bottom constantly with a rubber spatula until the mixture thickens enough to coat a spoon—it should register 170 degrees on a candy thermometer.

Remove the top of the double boiler, strain the mixture into a bowl, stir occasionally until cool, then stir in the Grand Marnier. Cover and refrigerate until serving time.

Meanwhile, whip the reserved ½ cup of cream until it holds a shape. Cover and refrigerate. It will probably separate slightly while standing; whisk it a bit with a wire whisk just before using.

Shortly before serving, fold the sauce gradually into the whipped cream.

Serve the sauce cold. Spoon or pour it alongside, not over, the portions of soufflé.

Floating Iceberg

4 OR 5 PORTIONS

Sensational! This is a frozen Floating Island, not too rich, very popular, and easy. It is a meringue "iceberg" served in a sea of custard sauce. The sauce can be made a day or two ahead; the meringue should be made about 3 to 8 hours before serving.

CUSTARD SAUCE

1¾ cups light cream, half-and-half, or milk
4 egg yolks
Pinch of salt
⅓ cup granulated sugar
½ teaspoon vanilla extract
2 tablespoons Grand Marnier

Place the cream or milk in a heavy saucepan, uncovered, over moderate heat to scald.

Place the yolks in the top of a large double boiler off the heat. (It is not necessary to beat the yolks now.) When you see a slightly wrinkled skin on top of the cream, gradually add the hot cream to the yolks, stirring constantly. Stir in the salt and sugar. Place over a little hot water in the bottom of the double boiler on moderate heat.

Cook, stirring constantly and scraping the bottom and sides of the pan with a rubber spatula, until the mixture thickens enough to coat a wooden spoon; that will be 180 degrees on a candy thermometer.

Remove the top of the double boiler, stir in the vanilla, cool slightly, stir in the Grand Marnier, and then cool completely.

Place the cooled sauce in a covered container and refrigerate. The sauce should be as cold as possible when it is served. (I place the jar of sauce in a bowl of ice in the refrigerator for several hours before serving.)

MERINGUE

4 egg whites
Pinch of salt
½ cup granulated sugar
½ teaspoon vanilla extract
⅓ cup thinly sliced almonds, toasted, and
  coarsely chopped (see Notes)

Adjust a rack one-third up from the bottom of the oven and preheat the oven to 300 degrees. Butter a 6½ × 2¾-inch soufflé dish or any other similar ovenproof container (it can be a round-bottomed mixing bowl) with a 1-quart capacity. Dust the buttered dish with granulated sugar and shake out excess sugar over a piece of paper. Set the prepared dish aside. When you are ready to bake, you will also need a large baking dish or roasting pan or any large pan big enough to hold the soufflé dish. It must not be deeper than the soufflé dish.

Place the whites and the salt in the small bowl of an electric mixer and beat at high speed until the whites hold a soft shape. Reduce the speed to moderate and start adding the sugar, 1 tablespoonful at a time— beating for about 10 to 15 seconds between additions. After the sugar is added, add the vanilla, increase the speed to high again, and continue to beat until the meringue is thick and marshmallowlike and holds a stiff shape when the beaters are raised or when some of the meringue is lifted on a rubber spatula.

Remove from the mixer, fold in the almonds, and turn into the prepared dish. Since the meringue is stiff, push it into the pan to avoid air holes. The baked meringue will be served upside down, therefore you must be sure that the top (which will become the bottom) is a smooth surface or the meringue will not stand straight.

Place in a shallow baking dish or pan, pour hot water about 2 inches deep into the larger pan. Bake for 30 to 35 minutes until the top is puffed up, golden brown, and almost firm to the touch.

Remove from the hot water and let stand until completely cool.

The meringue will shrink as it cools, and there may be a little bit of liquid in the bottom of the soufflé dish—it is probably from the sugar coating on the pan and it is O.K.

Cover the cooled meringue with a serving plate (the plate does not need to have a much larger diameter than the meringue has). Center the plate carefully; the turned-out meringue cannot be moved. Invert the serving plate and the dish or pan of meringue. Lift off the dish or pan and place the meringue in the freezer for 3 to 8 hours.

To serve, cut the meringue (it slices beautifully) at the table in pie-shaped wedges with a sharp knife and, with a pie or cake server, transfer the wedges to flat dessert plates. Then either pour the icy cold sauce from a pitcher or ladle it from a gravy boat and serve it generously over the tops of individual portions.

NOTES: 1. *To toast the almonds, place them in a shallow baking dish or cake pan in a 300-degree oven. Shake or stir occasionally until the nuts are golden-colored. Let cool. Then place the almonds on a chopping board* and, with a long, heavy knife or with a Chinese cleaver, chop them coarsely.

2. To prepare this recipe for 8 to 10, double all the ingredients. Mix the meringue in the large bowl of the mixer. Bake in an 8- to 10-cup container at 300 degrees for 50 to 60 minutes.

Straw-berry Iceberg

Strawberries are wonderful with Floating Iceberg; so are raspberries, blackberries, etc. Serve them separately and spoon them onto the individual dishes. Or place them in a ring around the meringue on the serving plate. Or, if you have a large ring mold with a large space in the middle, bake the meringue in that and fill the middle space on the serving plate with the berries.

Crème Fraîche

This is a homemade version of a natural heavy cream that exists in France, different from any we have here. It is slightly tart and very thick. It is wonderful to serve with any fresh fruit, heaven with raspberries, strawberries, sliced bananas, or seedless grapes, etc. It is easy to make—there is nothing to it. But it must be made ahead of time. It takes from 1 to 3 days, then it can be kept for about 4 weeks. Multiply the ingredients as you wish; allow 1 cup of cream for 2 or 3 portions.

1 cup heavy cream
1 teaspoon buttermilk

Place the cream in a jar with a cover. Add the buttermilk and stir to mix. Cover the jar and let stand at room temperature from 1 to 3 days until it is as thick as our commercial sour cream.

Refrigerate at least 24 hours or up to 4 weeks, or for as long as it still tastes good. In the refrigerator, after a day or so, it will thicken quite a bit more and will become very firm; stir it to soften or use it as it is.

Gingered Crème Fraîche

1 cup Crème Fraîche (see page 386)
2 tablespoons honey
2 to 4 tablespoons finely chopped candied or
    preserved ginger

Mix the above ingredients. This is delicious with apple or pumpkin pie. Or with almost any fresh or stewed fruit or with baked apples. Or just with a spoon.

California Cream

Here's a substitute for Crème Fraîche that can be made in a moment—it is thicker than the real thing.

2¼ CUPS

1 egg yolk
4 ounces cream cheese, at room temperature
1 cup sour cream
1 cup heavy cream
Optional: 1 teaspoon honey or
    granulated sugar

Place all the ingredients in the bowl of a food processor fitted with the steel blade, or in the jar of a blender. Process or blend until perfectly smooth.

    Ladle over berries or pass separately with fruit pies or tarts or with baked apples.

Ginger-Marmalade Yogurt

This has a tantalizing and fascinating flavor. The texture—a smooth, jellied yogurt studded with tiny chunks of chewy ginger—is sensational! Serve this any time, anywhere, any way; it is probably most appropriate as a summer dessert, but I could eat it for breakfast, lunch, and dinner; as appetizer, entrée, and/or dessert. The recipe can be multiplied by any number. It is prepared in individual glasses or individual soufflé dishes.

4 PORTIONS

⅓ cup orange juice
2 teaspoons lemon juice
1 envelope unflavored gelatin
⅓ cup sweet orange marmalade
3 to 4 tablespoons finely chopped crystallized ginger, firmly packed (see Note)
3 tablespoons light or dark brown sugar, firmly packed
1 pint (2 cups) unflavored yogurt

Place the orange juice and lemon juice in a custard cup. Sprinkle the gelatin over the top. Let stand for 5 minutes to soften.

Meanwhile, place the marmalade, ginger, and brown sugar in a bowl and stir to mix. Set aside.

Place the yogurt in another bowl and stir until it is softened and smooth. Set aside.

Now place the cup of gelatin mixture in a little hot water in a pan over low heat. Stir occasionally with a metal spoon until the gelatin is dissolved.

Then add the gelatin to the marmalade mixture and stir until thoroughly mixed. Gradually add the gelatin mixture to the yogurt, stirring well after each addition until well mixed.

Place the mixture (preferably in a metal bowl because it chills faster) into a larger bowl of ice and water. Stir constantly and gently with a rubber spatula until the mixture thickens enough to keep the ginger and the marmalade from sinking.

Transfer to a wide-mouthed pitcher and pour into four 6-ounce glasses or dessert cups.

Refrigerate for 2 to 3 hours or all day.

This does not need any topping; it can be served as is. But if you want to make it more colorful and festive, top each portion with a very thinly sliced strawberry, or with a thin slice of peeled kiwi fruit cut into four or six pie-shaped wedges.

These may also be unmolded. Prepare them in custard cups. When they are firm, cut around the sides to release. Then dip the cup in hot water and hold it for 2 or 3 seconds, cover with a flat plate, turn the plate and cup over; the molded yogurt should slip right out. It is pretty surrounded by a border of very thinly sliced strawberries.

NOTE: *This will have a good gingery flavor with 3 tablespoons of chopped ginger—but if you love ginger as I do, you will want to use 4 tablespoons.*

Yogurt Cheese

This might be as old as recorded history. The Bulgarians and Turks and Armenians, et al., have probably made it for as long as they have been making yogurt. But it is new to me. And so good! If you like yogurt, you will be wild about this. It is simply unflavored regular or low-fat yogurt that has drained and is like cream cheese with a yogurt flavor. Serve it with crackers as an hors d'oeuvre or serve it as a dessert cheese with fresh fruit; it is delicious and unusual; spread it on sliced apples or pears—or use it to make the following Milk-and-Honey Yogurt Cheese.

This must drain for 6 to 24 hours, but then it can be refrigerated for 2 weeks.

You will need a large strainer, a large bowl, cheesecloth, and yogurt— as much or as little as you want. I use Dannon low-fat yogurt.

Here goes: Place a large, wide strainer over a large bowl. Line the strainer with a double thickness of wet cheesecloth (if the cheesecloth is tubular, it should be split down one side to make it wide enough).

Empty the yogurt into the lined strainer. You might like to try this first with only ½ pint (1 cup) of yogurt. If so, you can use a smaller strainer, although it doesn't hurt if the strainer is too large. I use 6 half-pints (6 cups) in a 9-inch strainer. Cover with an inverted bowl or a flat plate and let stand at room temperature or in the refrigerator if there is room for 6 to 24 hours. After 3 or 4 hours stir the yogurt very lightly to encourage all of the whey to drain off. Occasionally, as the whey collects in the large bowl, it may be emptied out (it should be emptied if it is touching the strainer). The longer the yogurt drains, the drier the cheese and the sharper the taste.

When drained, transfer the cheese to any container and refrigerate.

You will have about 2 cups of cheese from 6 half-pints (6 cups) of yogurt if it has drained the full time; more if it has drained less time.

Two cups of yogurt cheese should serve 6 to 8 people, if I am not one of them.

NOTE: *A technicality—the older the yogurt is, the more tart the cheese will be. Good either way, but I use the freshest I can get.*

Milk-and-Honey Yogurt Cheese

This is a slightly thinned and barely sweetened version of the preceding Yogurt Cheese. It has a custard consistency; the silkiest, smoothest texture; an elusive, mild, and delicate flavor; it is heavenly and then some.

For each ½ cup of Yogurt Cheese, stir in 2 tablespoons of milk or cream (light or heavy) and 2 tablespoons of honey. Taste it; you might like a bit more honey. And, depending on how you will serve it, you might like it a bit thinner. Make it as sweet, and as thin, as you wish. (I like it best not too sweet and not too thin.)

Transfer to a covered container and refrigerate for several hours.

Whisk/stir it just before serving to soften it to a sauce consistency and spoon it generously over fresh berries, sliced peaches, sliced bananas, or what-have-you.

Or it may be poured into small pots de crème cups (make the portions small), refrigerated for a few hours until it is about as firm as a custard, and served right in the cups.

Fruit Desserts

Some honey or sugar and kirsch or Cognac can improve the flavor of fresh fruit—but only to a degree. The dessert you serve depends on the quality of the fruit you use—no matter what you do to it. The secret is to use fresh fruit when it is in season and delicious.

ABOUT STRAWBERRIES

First of all, there seems to be much confusion about how much to buy and how much you get when you buy a 1-pint box. Actually, if you measure the berries in a glass measuring cup, the little box or basket of berries that is called 1 pint will measure 1 quart. And it will weigh 1 pound. To be sure we understand each other, every time I call for a 1-pint box, I also say "1 pound." And if you measure it, it will be 1 quart. O.K.?

To wash strawberries: Strawberries will lose their flavor if they soak in water. Either dip them, just a few at a time, quickly in and out of cold water, or, if you work quickly enough, gently turn them all into a large bowl of cold water (the sand will settle to the bottom, so do not agitate the water) and pick them out quickly. If they do not seem clean enough, hold them, a few at a time, under running water. Remove the hulls after the berries have been washed. Then drain on paper towels.

It has recently become popular to grind a little black pepper over strawberries, either in recipes where the berries are mixed with other ingredients, or when they are eaten just by themselves. And some people sprinkle a tiny bit of mild vinegar (for instance, raspberry vinegar) over the berries. Me, I like both—pepper and vinegar.

Fresh Straw- berries with Sour Cream

4 TO 6 PORTIONS

This is one of the easiest and also one of the most popular desserts that I know. Years ago, when I told the chef at the Pier House in Key West about this dessert, he made it often and later told me that it was the most requested dessert he served.

2 pint boxes (2 pounds) fresh strawberries
2 cups thick sour cream
⅔ cup dark brown sugar, firmly packed

Wash the berries by placing them briefly in a large bowl of cold water. Pick them out quickly, one at a time, and as you do, remove the stems and hulls. Place the berries on paper towels to drain; let them stand until they are thoroughly dry.

Place the berries in a wide, shallow serving bowl. Cover with the cream and smooth the top. With your fingers sprinkle the sugar over the cream. Refrigerate for 3 to 6 hours. (If it stands overnight the sugar will melt too much and will lose its dark color and generally be less attractive.) The sugar will melt into a very dark, thin layer of deliciousness resting on the white cream (with the red berries showing through the bowl if you have used a glass bowl).

The secret of this dessert is to handle the cream as little as possible so it remains thick.

This can be prepared in individual shallow dessert bowls instead of one large serving bowl, in which case you will probably have to use more sugar to cover all of the cream.

Straw-berries De Luxe

This is quick and easy and terrific! It should be prepared about 3 or 4 hours before serving. It is prepared in individual glasses, and makes a marvelous dinner-party dessert.

6 PORTIONS

2 pint boxes (2 pounds) fresh strawberries
Optional: 2 tablespoons granulated sugar
Optional: 5 tablespoons kirsch or Cointreau
3 ounces cream cheese, at room temperature
3 tablespoons Grand Marnier
3 tablespoons mild honey
1 cup heavy cream
Optional: a few fresh mint leaves

Wash the berries quickly in a large bowl of cold water. Hull them and drain well on paper towels. If the berries are very large, cut them in halves or quarters. (Taste the berries; if they are wonderful, leave them alone. But if they are flat, place them in a bowl, sprinkle with 1½ tablespoons granulated sugar and 5 tablespoons kirsch or Cointreau. Toss gently, and let stand for about an hour.)

In the small bowl of an electric mixer, beat the cream cheese until it is soft and smooth. Beat in the Grand Marnier and honey. Remove from the mixer.

In a small bowl, whip the cream until it holds a shape.

Fold the whipped cream into the cheese mixture.

Divide the berries among six large wine glasses or wide champagne glasses. Pour the cheese mixture on top.

Refrigerate for 3 to 4 hours.

OPTIONAL: *Top each portion with a small sprig of fresh mint. (Or you could use a chocolate leaf, a bit of candied violet or rose petals, a few seedless grapes, or what-have-you.)*

Brandied Straw- berries with Cream

This is elegant and easy; the preparation can be done several hours before serving.

1 cup heavy cream
3 tablespoons kirsch
1 cup sour cream
2 pint boxes (2 pounds) fresh strawberries
¼ cup dark or light brown sugar, firmly packed
3 ounces brandy or Cognac

6 PORTIONS

In a small chilled bowl with chilled beaters, whip the heavy cream until it just holds a shape. In a small bowl stir the kirsch into the sour cream and mix until smooth. Fold both creams together. Cover and refrigerate.

Wash the berries quickly in cold water, hull, and drain thoroughly on paper towels.

Place the berries in a bowl. Add the sugar and brandy. Stir gently with a rubber spatula. Let stand for about an hour, stirring occasionally. Then cover and refrigerate.

To serve: The berries may be at room temperature or cold; the cream should be very cold. Place the berries in wine glasses or individual dessert bowls; pour on any remaining marinade. Stir the cream gently and spoon it generously over the berries.

NOTE: *The brandied berries alone, without the cream, are perfectly wonderful over coffee ice cream.*

South-ampton Straw-berries

This is a Long Island version of Strawberries Romanoff; it is very pretty, elegant, and easy. The preparation may be completed about 3 hours before serving, but it must be put together at the last minute; however, that takes only a minute to do.

6 PORTIONS

2 pint boxes (2 pounds) fresh strawberries
3 tablespoons granulated sugar
4 tablespoons Cognac
3 tablespoons Grand Marnier
1 cup heavy cream
½ teaspoon vanilla extract
1 cup vanilla ice cream
Optional: candied violet leaves or rose petals

This should be served at the table from a shallow bowl (preferably crystal or silver, with about a 2-quart capacity). The bowl should be placed in the freezer ahead of time so it will be frosty at serving time.

To wash the berries, place them (1 box at a time) in a large bowl of cold water for only a few moments. Quickly lift them from the water, remove the hulls, and drain on paper towels.

About 3 hours before serving, slice each berry into two or three slices and place them in a bowl with 2 tablespoons of the sugar (reserve the remaining 1 tablespoon of sugar), 3 tablespoons of the Cognac (reserve remaining 1 tablespoon Cognac), and the Grand Marnier. Mix gently. Cover with plastic wrap or foil and refrigerate.

Whip the cream with the reserved 1 tablespoon sugar, the reserved 1 tablespoon Cognac, and the vanilla, whipping only until it holds a soft shape—not stiff. Refrigerate.

About half an hour before serving, place the ice cream in the refrigerator to soften a bit.

Immediately before serving, mix the ice cream and the berries only slightly—they should each retain their own identity—and place in the chilled serving bowl.

Check to see if the whipped cream has separated a bit; if it has, beat it slightly with a small wire whisk. Pour the whipped cream over the berries and ice cream.

Sprinkle with the optional candied leaves or petals.

Serve in shallow dessert bowls (which also may have been chilled in the freezer).

Fresh Straw-berries with Raspberry Sauce

(made with frozen raspberries)

4 TO 6 PORTIONS

This is easy, unusual, and delicious. The sauce may be prepared a day or two ahead of time, if you wish.

SAUCE

1 10-ounce package frozen raspberries, packed in syrup
2 tablespoons granulated sugar
1 tablespoon lemon juice
1 tablespoon kirsch

Thaw the berries. Drain the juice, but reserve it. In a blender or a food processor, purée the berries with the sugar, lemon juice, and kirsch.

Strain the mixture to remove the seeds.

Stir in a bit of the drained juice (you will not use all of it) to thin the sauce slightly.

Refrigerate.

STRAWBERRIES

4 to 6 cups strawberries
1 tablespoon kirsch
1½ tablespoons granulated sugar

Wash the berries quickly in cold water, remove the hulls, and drain thoroughly on paper towels.

When they are thoroughly dry, place them in a bowl. Add the kirsch and sugar, stir gently, and let stand, stirring occasionally, for about an hour.

Transfer the berries to individual wine glasses or to a serving bowl. Cover and refrigerate.

Shortly before serving prepare the whipped cream.

WHIPPED CREAM

1 cup heavy cream
½ teaspoon vanilla extract
⅓ cup raspberry, strawberry, or
currant preserves

In a chilled bowl with chilled beaters, whip the cream and the vanilla until the cream holds a shape but not until it is really stiff. In a small bowl stir the preserves with a small wire whisk to soften them. Add about one-quarter of the cream and stir to mix. Then add the preserves to the remaining cream and fold together, but do not be too thorough; it does not have to be completely blended.

Refrigerate.

To serve: Just before serving, pour the sauce over the berries and the whipped cream over the sauce. Or the whipped cream may be passed separately in a pitcher, to be poured over each portion.

Fresh Straw- berries in Honeyed Raspberry Sauce

(made with fresh raspberries)

6 PORTIONS

This is quick, easy, and elegant. The sauce can be prepared a day ahead, if you wish.

SAUCE

1½ to 2 cups fresh raspberries
¼ cup honey

Unless the berries really need it, do not wash. But if they do, dip them quickly in and out of a bowl of cold water. Spread on paper towels to drain.

Press the berries through a food mill or process them in a food processor to purée. Strain to remove the seeds. Stir in the honey.

If you plan to use this within a few hours, it is not necessary to refrigerate it. If you want to keep it for a day or two, refrigerate, and then bring it to room temperature before serving. Or, although many people are positive that it must be served at room temperature, you may serve it cold. I think it is delicious either way.

STRAWBERRIES

4 to 6 cups strawberries

Quickly rinse the berries, remove the hulls, and drain well on paper towels.

Place the berries in wine glasses or dessert bowls and spoon or pour the sauce over them.

Serve at room temperature or refrigerated.

NOTE: *In a nouvelle cuisine kitchen, the chef might grind a bit of black pepper over the berries and add a bit of raspberry vinegar to the sauce. Both wonderful. Or you can add a very little bit of kirsch to the sauce.*

Rhubarb Straw- berries

4 PORTIONS

The rhubarb and strawberries should both be fresh—it is not as good with frozen fruit. This is very easy, and it is a delicious dessert to serve after a big meal. And it can be made a day ahead. It consists of fresh strawberries mixed with baked rhubarb; it has a slightly tart flavor and a beautiful color. It is very pretty served in small wine glasses. This recipe may be multiplied by any number.

1 pint box (1 pound) fresh strawberries
1 pound rhubarb
½ cup granulated sugar
2 tablespoons lemon juice

Adjust a rack to the center of the oven and preheat oven to 350 degrees.

Wash the berries quickly in a large bowl of cold water; do not let them soak. Remove the hulls and let the berries drain on paper towels. Refrigerate.

Cut the leaves and the ends off the rhubarb stalks (unless you buy them already trimmed). Brush them with a vegetable brush under cold running water. Do not peel unless they are very tough, and in that case they would probably not be good for this recipe anyhow. Cut the stalks into 1-inch pieces (there should be about 4 cups). Place them in a pot or an ovenproof casserole that has a tight cover. Add the sugar and lemon juice. Cover tightly.

Bake for 25 to 30 minutes, stirring occasionally, until the rhubarb is tender. Test it with a toothpick. As it becomes tender it will fall apart somewhat as you stir it; that is to be expected.

As soon as the rhubarb is done, pour it into a bowl and add the cold berries; stir gently with a rubber spatula. Don't worry about the rhubarb losing its shape and falling apart.

Cover and refrigerate.

Spoon into small wine glasses or dessert bowls.

NOTE: *This can also be served as a sauce over vanilla ice cream. It is a perfect combination, tart and sweet. It is tantalizing.*

Honeyed Grapes

4 PORTIONS

Helen McCully was one of the country's leading cookbook authors and food editors for many years when she was associated with Ladies' Home Journal *and then with* House Beautiful. *I had the greatest respect for her knowledge of food and for her recipes. I was thrilled when she invited me and my husband to her apartment in New York City for dinner. She served poached striped bass at room temperature with homemade mayonnaise, cucumber salad, sourdough rolls, and several wonderful desserts. This was one.*

It is the easiest thing to make. Helen said it should be put together a day ahead, but it is also delicious as soon as it is mixed.

1 pound seedless green grapes
¼ cup honey
2 tablespoons rum or Cognac
1 teaspoon lemon juice

½ cup crème fraîche (see page 386), sour
cream, or unflavored yogurt (see Note)

Remove the grapes from the stems (there should be about 2½ cups of grapes), wash and drain them, then spread them on a towel to dry thoroughly.

In a bowl mix the honey, rum or Cognac, and the lemon juice. Add the grapes. Turn carefully with a rubber spatula. Refrigerate overnight, stirring occasionally. Or serve sooner.

Divide the grapes among four wine glasses or dessert bowls and spoon a bit of the crème fraîche, sour cream, or yogurt over the tops.

NOTE: *Helen used sour cream; I have since tried yogurt and also crème fraîche—they are equally delicious.*

Cassis Raspberries

6 PORTIONS

Raspberries do not have to be washed, and they are best at room temperature.

1 quart raspberries
2 tablespoons granulated sugar
¼ cup crème de cassis
Optional: crème fraîche (see page 386)

Place the berries in a wide, shallow bowl. Sprinkle the sugar over them and then the cassis. Stir gently with a rubber spatula and let stand for about an hour. If you prepare this hours ahead of time, refrigerate it and then remove it to room temperature for about an hour before serving.

Serve in wine glasses or shallow dessert bowls with an optional spoonful of crème fraîche over each portion.

Cassis Grapefruit

This is a simple and delicious way with grapefruit. Do not make it unless the fruit is wonderful. Use 1 large grapefruit for 2 portions. Peel and section the grapefruit (see page 19). For each grapefruit add 1 tablespoon honey and 2 tablespoons cassis (black currant syrup) or crème de cassis (black currant brandy). Stir gently to mix without breaking the fruit. Taste, and add a bit more honey and/or cassis if necessary, but it is best if the flavoring is mild. Cover and refrigerate for at least several hours or overnight, stirring occasionally.

Serve in wine glasses or shallow dessert bowls, dividing all of the liquid over the fruit.

Broiled Grapefruit

This is wonderful either as dessert or as a first course. It may be prepared ahead of time but must be broiled immediately before serving and must be served without delay.

It is best to use large, juicy fruit. The combination of flavors—honey, butter, rum, and grapefruit—is delicious. Although this is usually made without the butter, the first time we had it this way was at Chalet Suzanne, a restaurant in Lake Wales, Florida (they are famous for their wonderful soups, which are distributed all over the world), and we were immediately converted.

Grapefruit (pink or white—preferably large and seedless)
Unsalted butter, melted
Honey (either liquid, or thick and butterlike)
Optional: rum

Use half a grapefruit for each portion, but before halving the fruit, trim the ends very slightly if they are uneven, so that the halves will stand upright without tilting. Then cut them in half crosswise and, with a curved and serrated grapefruit knife, cut around each section to loosen it completely (but do not remove it); remove any seeds.

Brush each half with a generous teaspoon of melted butter, or simply drizzle the melted butter on. Then, if you are using liquid honey, drizzle a generous tablespoonful over each half; if you are using honey as thick as a spread, smooth a generous tablespoonful over each half. (Some thick honeys are sticky and difficult to spread on wet grapefruit; it does not have to be spread evenly or all over—the heat will melt it and it will run.)

These may be broiled immediately, or refrigerated and broiled later on.

Before broiling, adjust a rack to the top position under the broiler and preheat the broiler until red hot.

Place the fruit in a shallow metal pan, pour water about ½ inch deep in the pan, and broil for about 7 or 8 minutes until the top is well colored (it will not brown evenly, it will be spotty) and the fruit is very hot.

Meanwhile, if you have large, round fresh green leaves, place one on each dessert plate.

Then transfer each grapefruit half to a plate, and sprinkle with the optional rum (I use Myers's dark rum—about 1 to 2 tablespoons per portion).

Serve immediately.

California Fresh Figs

Fresh figs are very scarce. If you are among the lucky ones who can get them, here's an easy, delicious, and unusual way of serving them.

6 PORTIONS

12 fresh figs
3 tablespoons granulated sugar
3 tablespoons Cognac or rum
1 cup crème fraîche (see page 386)
⅓ cup Curaçao

Cut the figs in half the long way through the stems. Place them cut side up on a large plate or tray. Sprinkle with the sugar and then with the Cognac or rum. Cover and refrigerate for at least half an hour or longer.

Mix the crème fraîche and the Curaçao and refrigerate.

At serving time, place the figs and their liquid in shallow dessert bowls, and pour the cream over the tops.

Stewed Peaches

This is from my first dessert book. The peaches are stewed and served whole with the pits in.

6 PORTIONS

6 large freestone peaches, ripe but firm
1½ cups water
1 cup granulated sugar
1 vanilla bean, 6 to 8 inches long

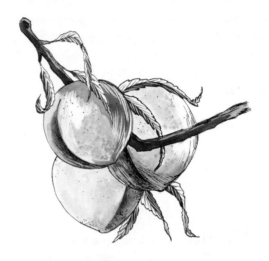

To peel the peaches: Have ready a large bowl of cold water, a slotted spoon, and a saucepan of boiling water deep enough to cover the peaches.

With the slotted spoon, place the peaches in the boiling water, two or three at a time. If the peaches are fully ripe they will need only about 15 seconds in the boiling water; if they are not quite ripe they will need more. With the slotted spoon, raise a peach from the water and move your thumb firmly over a small section of the skin. If the skin has loosened enough it will wrinkle and feel loose from the fruit. At that point transfer the peach to the ice water for at least a moment.

Then peel the peach with your fingers, starting at the stem end. Return the peeled fruit to the ice water. Partially peeled peaches may be returned to the boiling water for additional time, if necessary. Continue blanching and peeling the remaining peaches.

In a saucepan wide enough to hold the peaches in a single layer, place the water and sugar. Slit the vanilla bean the long way and scrape the seeds into the water; add the pod also. Bring to a boil, stirring, and let boil about 5 minutes to make a syrup.

With the slotted spoon add the peaches and adjust the heat so the syrup simmers gently. Cook, covered, turning the peaches a few times with two rubber spatulas in order not to mar them. Baste occasionally with the syrup.

Test for doneness with a cake tester. Do not overcook. When just barely tender, transfer the peaches gently with the slotted spoon to a large, wide bowl or casserole.

Raise the heat and boil the syrup rapidly for a few minutes to reduce slightly. Taste the syrup and continue to boil until it tastes right—sweet enough and not watery.

Pour the hot syrup over the peaches. Do not remove the vanilla bean. Let stand to cool, basting occasionally with the syrup.

Cover with plastic wrap or transfer to a covered container. Refrigerate and serve very cold.

Serve in dessert bowls with a generous amount of the syrup.

Stewed Peaches with Brandy

Prepare the preceding plain Stewed Peaches (page 404). After the peaches have been removed from the syrup, boil the syrup down about 10 minutes longer to reduce it more. Then add ½ cup brandy, or ¼ cup brandy and ¼ cup kirsch, and simmer gently for only 1 or 2 minutes. Pour the hot syrup over the peaches, and spoon the syrup over the peaches occasionally as they cool.

Stewed Apricots with Brandy

Follow the above recipe, substituting about 1½ to 2 dozen fresh apricots for the peaches. Do not peel the apricots—poach them briefly, and follow the above directions.

Brandied Fresh Peaches

These are not the stewed peaches usually found under this name; these are raw. Brandy and honey with almost any delicious fresh fruit is heavenly; especially so with peaches. They may be prepared a few hours before serving.

Blanch and peel the peaches (see page 404) and slice each peach into about 8 wedges.

For 3 large peaches mix about ¼ cup honey and ¼ cup brandy or Cognac. Stir the peaches gently in the mixture, cover with plastic wrap directly on the peaches, and refrigerate for an hour or two. Stir them gently a few times.

Serve as is, or with vanilla ice cream. If the peaches are being served alone as dessert, allow 1 large peach for each portion. If they are being served with ice cream, 1 peach will serve two.

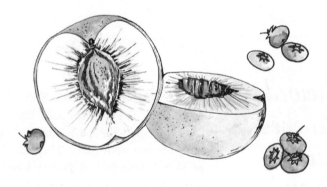

Peach and Blueberry Casserole

6 PORTIONS

This combination of peaches and berries is baked with cinnamon sugar and the crispest, crunchiest topping ever. It can be served immediately while it is piping hot and is so good you can't wait for it to cool even if it burns your tongue, or it can be served at room temperature or refrigerated and it will be just as wonderful. But do try it hot (see Note).

1 pint (1 pound) fresh blueberries
2 pounds (6 or 7 medium peaches) ripe
    freestone peaches

¾ cup plus 3 tablespoons granulated sugar
1 cup sifted all-purpose flour
1 teaspoon double-acting baking powder
½ teaspoon salt
1 egg
2⅔ ounces (5⅓ tablespoons) unsalted
    butter, melted
1 teaspoon cinnamon

This must be baked high in the oven. Adjust a rack one-third down from the top, and preheat the oven to 375 degrees. You will need a wide and shallow 2-quart ovenproof casserole (mine is 12 × 9 × 2 inches). Generously butter the casserole and set it aside.

Wash and drain the berries and set them aside.

Blanch and peel the peaches (see page 404) and slice each peach into 6 to 8 wedges (the wedges should be large rather than small).

Place the peaches in the casserole. Cover with the berries. Sprinkle with 2 tablespoons of the sugar (reserve the remaining ¾ cup plus 1 tablespoon of sugar) and set aside.

Into a mixing bowl, sift together the flour, ¾ cup of the sugar (reserve the remaining 1 tablespoon of sugar), baking powder, and salt. Add the unbeaten egg. With a fork, stir/cut/fluff the mixture (almost as though the egg were butter and you were making pie crust). You do not want the mixture to go together in one mass. When it appears to be partially mixed, you can change the fork for a pastry blender and chop until most of the dry ingredients are coarsely blended. When it is ready there will be very little or none of the dry ingredients unincorporated. Do not handle any more.

With a large spoon, sprinkle the topping evenly over the berries; it should be a very thin, uneven layer. There may be a few spots that are not covered at all—O.K.—but the topping must not be too thick anywhere or it may not cook through.

Drizzle the melted butter all over the topping.

Mix the cinnamon with the remaining 1 tablespoon of sugar and sprinkle over the top.

Bake uncovered for 15 minutes. Then increase the temperature to 400 degrees and bake for 12 to 15 minutes more until the topping is lightly browned.

NOTE: *This can all be prepared hours ahead. Refrigerate it, and then let it stand at room temperature for about half an hour, and bake it while you are having dinner. Serve it straight from the oven.*

Island Pineapple

4 PORTIONS

Try to get Hawaiian pineapple for this scrumptious combination. It is delicious. I could eat it all day. The green peppercorns do not taste too peppery or spicy; they just give it a tang.

Both the pineapple and the sauce can be prepared a day before serving. Or they can be served as soon as an hour after they are prepared.

2 to 3 cups diced fresh pineapple
1 teaspoon (about 20 peppercorns) green
    peppercorns, packed in wine vinegar
    (available in specialty food stores)
¼ cup honey
¼ cup kirsch

Place the pineapple in a bowl. In a small cup, mash the peppercorns with the back of a spoon to purée (they are soft); they do not have to be mashed until smooth. Stir in the honey and kirsch. Pour over the pineapple. Stir occasionally until thoroughly marinated.

Refrigerate for an hour or more.

ISLAND SAUCE

When you taste this, you might want to double the recipe.

1 cup plain yogurt
¼ cup honey
2 tablespoons light or dark rum
¼ cup Grand Marnier

In a small bowl, stir the yogurt to soften. Mix in the remaining ingredients. Cover and refrigerate.

To serve: Divide the pineapple and any juice among six wine glasses or small dessert bowls.

Immediately before serving, spoon the sauce over each serving of the pineapple.

This may be served just as it is, although in Hawaii it was originally decorated with a slice of fresh mango and one strawberry on each portion. Aloha.

Portuguese Pineapple

Everybody should have a recipe like this up their sleeve for the times they want something very fancy and elegant, but easy. You can prepare the ingredients from 1 to 10 hours before serving; then put it together in just a few minutes right before serving.

I am not giving amounts, since they are flexible. But 1 pineapple, 4 cups of berries, and 1 pint of ice make 6 generous portions.

Fresh pineapple
Granulated sugar
Kirsch
Fresh strawberries
Grand Marnier or Curaçao
Strawberry, Lemon, or Orange Ice (bought
    or homemade, see pages 440 and 441)
Optional: candied violets or rose petals

Peel the pineapple, removing all the eyes. With a long, thin, very sharp knife cut the pineapple into very thin rings (⅛ to ¼ inch). Place the rings on a large, shallow platter, sprinkle lightly with a bit of sugar and kirsch. Let stand at room temperature for about half an hour, turning the rings over occasionally to flavor them all. If necessary, add a little more sugar and kirsch after the rings have been turned.

Wash the berries quickly in a large bowl of cold water, remove the hulls, and drain thoroughly on paper towels. Place the berries in a wide, shallow bowl and sprinkle them lightly with sugar and Grand Marnier or Curaçao. Let the berries stand at room temperature, turning occasionally, for about half an hour.

With an ice-cream scoop, form the ice into balls, place them on a shallow tray, cover, and place in the freezer.

Cover the pineapple and the berries and refrigerate.

Choose large, flat plates for serving this. If you have room, place the plates in the freezer to chill well.

Immediately before serving arrange 2 or 3 rings of the pineapple overlapping on each plate. Place a mound of the berries on one side and a scoop of the ices on the other side. Place a few of the optional violets or rose petals into the top of the ices.

Serve with a knife and fork.

Oranges à la Grecque

One of the most popular desserts to serve after a big meal. Or any time. You must have large, juicy, seedless oranges. You can make this a day or two ahead.

6 TO 8 PORTIONS

10 large, deep-colored, thick-skinned seedless oranges
1½ cups granulated sugar
¼ cup red currant jelly
¾ cup water

With a vegetable parer, peel the thin colored rind from 4 or 5 of the oranges, removing it in long strips rather than short ones. Pile two or three of the strips one on top of the other on a cutting board and with a very sharp knife cut the rind into thin slivers; make them as long as you can and about ⅛ inch wide.

Place the slivered rind in a saucepan over high heat, cover with boiling water, boil for 10 minutes, and then drain. Return the rind to the saucepan, cover with boiling water again, and boil again for 10 minutes. Repeat for three boilings in all. Drain in a strainer.

While the rind is boiling, prepare the oranges. Peel and cut them into sections (see page 19). Pour over the oranges any juice that remains.

Place the sugar, jelly, and water in a 6-cup saucepan. Stir over moderate heat until the sugar is melted and the syrup comes to a boil. Raise the heat and let boil without stirring for 5 minutes.

Pour the hot syrup over the oranges and let stand for 10 or 15 minutes. Then pour through a large strainer set over the saucepan. Transfer the orange sections to a bowl. Boil the syrup again for 10 minutes more. Add the drained rind to the hot syrup, and pour rind and syrup over the orange sections. Stir gently with a rubber spatula. Cool and then refrigerate.

This must be as cold as possible when it is served. (If possible, place it in the freezer for 20 to 30 minutes just before serving.)

Serve in shallow glasses or dessert bowls, spooning the rind and sauce generously over each portion.

VARIATION: *Before pouring the hot syrup over the oranges, drain the juice off the oranges (do not use it for this variation). Sprinkle ¼ to ⅓ cup Grand Marnier, Curaçao, rum, Cognac, or whatever over the oranges. Then proceed with the directions. Or follow the above recipe and just before serving pour a little Grand Marnier (or whatever) over each portion.*

Saidie Heatter's Apple Fritters

This was one of my mother's specialties. She made them for breakfast, brunch, lunch, or supper, either as an entrée or as dessert. Whatever and whenever, they were always a special treat.

These fritters are fried in deep fat and then they are glazed under the broiler. They should be served as soon as they are done, but they don't take long to prepare.

I have made these fritters, all ready to fry, an hour or so ahead of time. When you add the apple slices be sure they are all coated with the batter (it is best to add them one at a time), that way they will not discolor. Cover and refrigerate. Or, if you want to start it hours ahead, or the night before, prepare the egg-yolk mixture, cover, and refrigerate it; cover the whites and let them stand at room temperature for a few hours, or refrigerate them for longer. Then complete the mixing and add the apples shortly before frying.

Deep fat for frying (Crisco in a can, or Crisco, Mazola, or Wesson oil)
1 cup sifted all-purpose flour
2 teaspoons double-acting baking powder
½ teaspoon salt
2 eggs (graded large), separated
⅔ cup milk
1 tablespoon brandy
2 tablespoons unsalted butter, melted
4 large, tart, crisp apples
Granulated sugar (to be used after the fritters are fried)

Pour the fat about 1 inch deep in a wide, deep frying pan (or you can use two pans if you wish). Heat the fat to 375 degrees on a frying thermometer. Adjust the heat to maintain the correct temperature. (Do not fry at a lower temperature or the fritters will be greasy.)

Adjust a rack about 10 inches below the broiler and preheat the broiler.

Butter a large jelly-roll pan and set aside.

Resift the flour with the baking powder and salt, and set aside.

In a small bowl, beat the egg yolks until thick and pale. Gradually mix in the milk, brandy, and butter. Add the sifted dry ingredients and beat only until the mixture is smooth. Set aside.

Peel and core the apples (with an apple corer) and slice them crossways into rings about ⅓ inch thick.

Beat the egg whites until they hold a shape but not until they are stiff or dry, and fold them into the yolk mixture.

Add several slices of the apples to the batter, thoroughly coating the slices with the batter.

Use a fork with two or three long prongs or a wooden or metal skewer, place it through the hole in an apple ring, raise the ring and hold it briefly so that a bit of (but not too much) excess batter runs off, and then slip it gently into the 375-degree fat. Add as many slices as there is room for.

Fry on one side until golden brown, then turn the rings without piercing them and brown the other sides. As the rings finish frying, drain them briefly on brown paper and then transfer them to the buttered jelly-roll pan. Do not let them cool off any more than necessary—work quickly. With your fingers, sprinkle the slices generously with granulated sugar (there is no sugar in the batter) and place the pan under the broiler.

WATCH THEM VERY CAREFULLY!!! Broil until the sugar melts; it may begin to caramelize (delicious), but do not let the sugar turn black anywhere.

As soon as the rings are done, place them on warm plates and serve immediately.

VARIATION: *If the broiled sugar topping seems to be more than you want to bother with, you can eliminate it and simply sprinkle the fried and drained rings generously with confectioners sugar, sprinkling it through a strainer held over the slices.*

Banana Fritters

Follow the preceding recipe, using bananas instead of apples. Use bananas that are not overripe; they must not be too soft. Peel and cut them crosswise into 1½-inch pieces. Use a wide fork, a flat wire whisk, or a slotted metal spoon for turning and transferring the banana fritters.

Saidie often served a combination of apple and banana fritters; since the bananas fry more quickly, they were fried after the apples.

Ginger-Honey Baked Apples

6 PORTIONS

These are especially gorgeous. Try to get large and beautiful apples: Rome Beauties are generally recommended for baking because they hold their shape better than some others. Spy, Jonathan, Cortland are among others that are good for baking. These baked apples will have a richly colored, shiny glaze. And, although there are several flavors in the recipe, you will only taste delicious baked apples. These are a perfect dessert for almost any meal.

6 large baking apples
3 tablespoons finely chopped candied ginger
½ cup honey
1 cup water
1 teaspoon cinnamon
3 tablespoons granulated sugar
¼ cup preserves (see Note; to be used when the apples are almost finished baking)

Adjust a rack to the center of the oven and preheat the oven to 350 degrees.

Have a shallow ovenproof baking dish ready; there should be a little room around the apples—it is best if they are not touching.

Wash the apples and remove the cores with an apple corer, but do not cut all the way down; leave the bottoms of the apples intact. With a vegetable parer, remove the peel from the top halves of the apples. Now score the peeled part of the apples to make a design on them. Here's how: Place an apple on the counter top. Use a four-pronged fork. Gently insert the tips of the prongs slightly into the apple and rotate the apple slowly, so the fork makes a spiral pattern on all of the peeled section.

My mother always decorated baked apples this way, but I remember times when she crosshatched the lines, making them go around and then up and down. And I remember times when each apple had a different design. Fun!

Place the apples in the baking dish. Place the ginger in the cavities of the apples and then fill the cavities with honey. There will be some remaining honey.

Pour the water and the remaining honey into the bottom of the dish. Mix the cinnamon and sugar and sprinkle over the tops of the apples.

Place in the oven and bake uncovered. Use a bulb baster to baste the apples about every 10 minutes. Total baking time may be about 45 minutes to 1 hour. However, after about 30 minutes start testing the apples with a cake tester and bake until they are almost but not completely tender.

Now use the bulb baster to transfer all of the liquid, including what is in the cavities of the apples, to a 1-quart saucepan. Allow the apples to continue to bake without the liquid. Place the saucepan of liquid over high heat and boil uncovered until the liquid reduces to about half its amount; it will take about 7 to 10 minutes. Then add the preserves, stir well, and boil for 2 minutes.

Pour the hot glaze over the tops of the apples. The apples should be completely tender now; be careful not to overbake or they will squash and lose their shape. The liquid should be slightly thickened and very shiny.

Place the apples under the broiler for a few minutes to caramelize the glaze on top slightly.

Set aside to cool. When cool, the liquid will thicken to a soft jelly.

Serve at room temperature or refrigerated. It is best to serve these on flat dessert plates with a knife and fork for each person. Serve some of the jellied liquid over or alongside each portion.

NOTE: *The preserves can be almost any kind; the apples will look quite different depending on the preserves. Apricot preserves or sweet orange marmalade (do not strain) will give a nice shine. But if you use red currant or some other red berry jam or jelly, it will also color the apples beautifully. I have made these often, and have varied the preserves depending on what was on hand. Today I used a mixture of half marmalade and half strawberry, and I wish you could see them.*

Apple Bread Pudding

This is a great dessert for a buffet party. Bread pudding can be served, as it often is, tepid, cooled, or chilled. But for it to be really super-duper, serve it very hot, right out of the oven. Here's how: Prepare the entire recipe but do not bake it. Cover and refrigerate for several hours or overnight. Remove it from the refrigerator about 2¼ hours before baking. Place it in the oven to bake about 1¼ hours before you plan to serve it.

8 TO 12 PORTIONS

You will need a 13 × 9 × 2-inch ovenproof casserole, or any shallow casserole with a 12-cup capacity. Butter it well.

1 pound Italian or French bread (the commercial loaves are generally ½ pound each)
4 to 5 medium-large tart and crisp apples (1½ to 2 pounds; Granny Smith are good)
4 ounces (1 stick) unsalted butter
¾ cup plus 2 tablespoons granulated sugar
1 teaspoon cinnamon
½ cup raisins
4 eggs plus 2 yolks (graded large or extra-large)
4½ cups milk
2 teaspoons vanilla extract
⅛ teaspoon nutmeg
⅛ teaspoon salt

To make it easier to handle the bread, cut each loaf so it is only half as long. With a sharp knife remove the crusts. Slice the bread a generous ½ inch thick (do not slice too thin). If the bread is very fresh, place it right on an oven rack in a very low oven (about 200 degrees) for a little while to dry out a bit, but it should not become hard. Meanwhile, prepare the apples and the custard.

Peel, quarter, and core the apples. Cut each quarter into 3 wedges.

Place 2 ounces (½ stick) of the butter, reserving the remaining 2 ounces, in a very large frying pan to melt. Add the apples and 2 tablespoons of the sugar, reserving the remaining ¾ cup. Cover and cook over moderate heat for about 2 minutes. Then remove the cover, stir gently and carefully, and continue to cook for about 6 minutes more (8 minutes altogether) until the apples are just barely tender; test them with a tooth-pick. They should not be cooked until they fall apart or get mushy.

Sprinkle the cinnamon all over the apples, stir gently (turning the apples with a wide metal spatula helps) until the cinnamon is absorbed. Set aside uncovered.

Place one layer of the bread slices in the buttered baking dish, pack-ing them close together. Sprinkle with half of the raisins. Spread the apples and all of their juice over the top. Sprinkle with the remaining raisins. Make another layer of bread. (Use only enough bread to make the two layers—you will probably have a few slices left over, depending on how thick/thin you sliced it.) Set aside.

In a mixing bowl, beat or whisk the eggs and yolks lightly just to mix. Add the milk, vanilla, nutmeg, salt, and ½ cup of the remaining sugar, reserving the remaining ¼ cup. Mix thoroughly. Pour into a pitcher.

Pour the custard slowly and evenly all over the top layer of bread, being careful to wet it all thoroughly. While pouring the custard over the bread, stir the custard occasionally from the bottom—the sugar settles.

Cover the top with a large piece of wax paper and, with the palms of both hands, press down on the paper gently to push the bread down into the custard. You can use a weight (or a few small ones) if you wish, but be careful that it is not so heavy that it makes the custard run over the sides of the dish. Or you can just do it with your hands—about 10 minutes is long enough.

Set aside, or refrigerate, or bake (see introduction).

When you are ready to bake, adjust a rack to the center of the oven and preheat the oven to 350 degrees.

Melt the reserved 2 ounces of butter and drizzle it all over the bread. Then, carefully sprinkle the reserved ¼ cup of sugar over the top.

Place the dish of pudding in a larger, shallow baking pan. Pour about 1 inch of hot water into the larger pan. Carefully transfer to the oven and bake uncovered for 60 to 70 minutes. To test for doneness, insert the tip of a small, sharp knife into the middle of the pudding; it is done just as soon as the knife comes out clean. Do not overbake.

The bread will have puffed up and started to brown slightly on top. Place it under the broiler briefly (watch it every second because the butter and sugar on top will brown very quickly) until the top becomes gorgeous—crisp and golden honey-colored.

Remove from the hot water.

Serve immediately or let stand.

To serve: Use a small, sharp knife to cut the pudding into portions, and use a wide metal spatula to transfer each portion to an individual flat dessert plate.

NOTE: *Bread Pudding is often served with a sauce. If this one is served piping hot, it is so good as it is that it does not need a sauce. However, after it has cooled or been refrigerated, it becomes more firm and compact and then you will probably like a sauce with it. Cold Custard Sauce (see Floating Iceberg, page 384) is always good, regardless of the temperature of the pudding. Or serve the following, which is very quick and easy.*

APRICOT SAUCE (GENEROUS 1 CUP)

12 ounces (1 cup) apricot preserves
1 tablespoon water
3 tablespoons rum, kirsch, brandy, bourbon,
    or orange juice

In a small saucepan, stir the preserves and water over moderate heat until the mixture comes to a low boil.

Strain the mixture and then stir in the liquor or orange juice.

Serve warm or at room temperature.

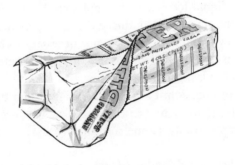

Almond-Apple Pudding

8 PORTIONS

This is a wonderful old Swedish dessert. It consists of sliced apples that are barely cooked on top of the stove, placed in a shallow casserole, and topped with a buttery, macaroonlike mixture made with ground almonds. It is baked and served slightly warm or at room temperature, but it is best while it is very fresh. If you wish, the apples can be prepared, including their preliminary cooking, the day before. Then the rest is quick and easy.

6 medium-large, tart apples (2½ pounds;
    Granny Smith apples are delicious for this
    recipe)
3 tablespoons granulated sugar
⅓ cup water
2 tablespoons fresh lemon juice
Freshly grated nutmeg, or about ¼ teaspoon
    powdered nutmeg

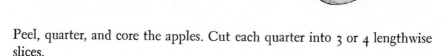

Peel, quarter, and core the apples. Cut each quarter into 3 or 4 lengthwise slices.

Place the sugar and water in a wide frying pan that has a cover, and stir over moderate heat until the sugar is melted. Add the apples and the lemon juice. Cover for 1 minute. Then uncover, raise the heat to high, and cook, agitating constantly—use something like a wide metal or wooden spatula to move and turn the apples without breaking them—and cook until the apples are barely tender and the juice is just evaporated. If there is still much liquid left when the apples are tender, remove the apples and boil down the juice until it thickens slightly, then pour it back over the apples; if they are almost dry it is not necessary to boil down the juice.

This can now be cooled, covered, and refrigerated if you plan to bake it the next day. Or it can be baked now.

Before baking, adjust a rack one-third up from the bottom of the oven and preheat the oven to 350 degrees. You will need a shallow casserole with an 8-cup capacity (mine measures 8 × 11 × 2 inches). Butter the casserole.

Place the cooked apples (which may be warm or chilled) any which way in the casserole; press on the top slightly to level it a bit.

Grate a bit of whole nutmeg over the apples, or sprinkle with the powdered nutmeg.

ALMOND TOPPING

2 ounces (½ cup) blanched almonds
3½ ounces (1 stick minus 1 tablespoon)
    unsalted butter
Scant ¼ teaspoon almond extract

½ cup plus 3 tablespoons granulated sugar
2 eggs, separated, plus 1 additional white (it
     may be a white that was left over from
     another recipe, frozen and then thawed)
Pinch of salt

The almonds must be finely ground. This can be done in a processor, a blender, or a nut grinder—they should be powdery. If you use a processor or blender, add a bit of the sugar to prevent lumping. Set aside.

In the small bowl of an electric mixer, cream the butter. Add the almond extract and then ½ cup of the sugar, reserving the remaining 3 tablespoons of sugar, and beat for a minute or two until well mixed. Add the 2 egg yolks and beat well. Add the ground almonds and beat only to mix.

In a clean small bowl with clean beaters, beat the 3 egg whites and the salt until the whites hold a soft shape. Reduce the speed slightly and gradually add the reserved 3 tablespoons of sugar, increase the speed to high, and continue to beat until the whites hold a definite shape but not until they are stiff or dry.

Stir about one-quarter of the whites into the yolk mixture. Then, in two additions, fold in the remaining whites.

Pour the mixture in a thick ribbon over the apples and then spread it to cover the apples completely.

Bake for 40 minutes until the top is a rich golden color.

Serve while still slightly warm or at room temperature. Serve as is, or with ice cream.

Connecticut Apple Betty

4 TO 6 PORTIONS

This is the way my mother made it on our farm, Valley Ridge, in Brookfield Center, Connecticut. She used apples from our own trees; I don't know what kind they were but I have been using Granny Smith apples and the Betty is too good.

The big difference in this recipe from others is that this calls for small squares of bread, not crumbs. The crumbs turn to mush but the squares don't.

Firm, thin-sliced, white or whole-wheat bread
(Pepperidge Farm, Arnold, or any similar
firm sandwich loaf; you will need enough
to make 4 to 4½ cups of ¼-inch squares)
2⅔ ounces (5⅓ tablespoons) unsalted butter
1 cup light brown sugar, firmly packed
1 teaspoon cinnamon
½ teaspoon mace
Finely grated rind of 1 lemon
½ cup orange juice
2 tablespoons lemon juice
5 medium-size apples (about 2 pounds)
½ cup raisins (see Note)
Optional: ½ cup walnuts, cut into medium-
size pieces

Adjust a rack to the center of the oven and preheat the oven to 375 degrees. You will need a 2 to 2½-quart ovenproof casserole; mine is round, 8 inches in diameter and 3½ inches deep. Butter the casserole well.

Cut the bread (it is not necessary to remove the crusts) into ¼- to ⅓-inch strips. Then cut it crossways making ¼- to ⅓-inch squares. You will need 4 to 4½ cups of squares. Place them in a large, shallow pan in the heated oven. Shake or stir occasionally only until the bread is dry; do not bake until it browns.

Melt the butter. Place the bread in a mixing bowl. Add the butter, drizzling it over as much of the bread as possible instead of pouring it all on one spot, stirring the bread with a spatula or a fork as you add the butter.

Place the sugar, cinnamon, and mace in a bowl and stir to mix. Mix in the lemon rind and set aside.

Mix the orange juice with the lemon juice and set aside.

Peel, quarter, and core the apples. Cut each quarter into 4 or 5 slices. You should have about 6 cups of loosely packed sliced apples.

In a large bowl thoroughly mix the apples with the sugar mixture, raisins, and optional nuts.

Place about one-third of the buttered bread squares over the bottom of the casserole. Cover with one-half of the apple mixture. Then another third of the bread, and then the remaining apple mixture. Now pour the orange juice mixture over the apples, and cover with the remaining bread. If any raisins are exposed place them under some of the apple slices or they will burn.

Cover tightly with aluminum foil, sealing the edges well—it should be airtight.

Bake for 30 minutes.

Remove the foil. If the apples gave off much juice use a bulb baster to baste the top of the Betty. Then bake uncovered for about 30 minutes (total baking time is about 1 hour) until the apples are tender when tested with a cake tester and the top is golden brown. If the top becomes too brown before the apples are done, replace the foil on top.

If it still seems too juicy by the time the apples are tender, don't worry about it. Most of the juice will be absorbed as it stands, and it is best if it is juicy—not dry.

Traditionally, Apple Betty is served warm with a pitcher of cold heavy cream or with whipped cream or ice cream. Or with the following Old-Fashioned Lemon Sauce. I try to serve it warm with very cold sauce. But it is good at any temperature.

NOTE: *If you wish, the raisins may be marinated in rum, brandy, Grand Marnier, or any orange liqueur for several hours or overnight. Any of the marinade not absorbed by the raisins may be used as part of the orange juice.*

OLD-FASHIONED LEMON SAUCE
(1⅓ cups)

This is from my first dessert book.

⅓ cup granulated sugar
1 tablespoon plus 1 teaspoon cornstarch
⅛ teaspoon salt
1 cup hot water
2 tablespoons unsalted butter, at room
    temperature
Finely grated rind of 1 large lemon
2 to 3 tablespoons lemon juice (to taste)

Mix the sugar, cornstarch, and salt in a heavy 1-quart saucepan. Gradually stir in the water. Cook over moderate heat, stirring gently and constantly with a rubber spatula, for about 5 minutes until the mixture comes to a boil and becomes thick and clear. Reduce the heat and boil very slowly, stirring gently, for 2 minutes.

Remove from the heat. Add the butter and stir gently until melted. Stir in the rind and juice.

Serve warm, at room temperature, or refrigerated. This can be refrigerated for about a week. It can be reheated in the top of a small double boiler over hot water.

Ginger Pears

6 PORTIONS

These are whole pears poached in a ginger syrup. Unusual and light, they are a good dessert after chili or curry. They are a snap to make and can be made a day or two before serving. It is important to use pears that are not soft; they get mushy when they are poached. Comice and Bartlett are two good choices; but whichever, they must be firm and not overripe.

1 cup water
1½ cups granulated sugar
Finely grated rind of 2 lemons
3 tablespoons lemon juice
Generous 2 to 3 tablespoons finely diced
    candied or preserved ginger
6 medium-size firm pears
⅓ cup orange marmalade
2 tablespoons Cognac, rum, or bourbon

Use a saucepan that has a cover and is large enough to hold the pears upright in a single layer. Place the water, sugar, rind, and juice in the saucepan and stir over moderate heat until the sugar dissolves and the mixture comes to a boil. Stir in the ginger and set aside.

With a vegetable parer, peel the pears. If necessary, trim the bottoms a bit so they will stand upright. Place the pears in the syrup, cover, and cook over moderate heat. Baste the pears frequently (a ladle is handy for this since the ginger might get stuck in a bulb baster). Do not overcook. Test with a cake tester or a toothpick. When they pierce easily they are done. Start testing after 20 minutes.

When the pears are just tender, transfer them with a slotted spoon to a shallow bowl.

Add the marmalade to the syrup and let boil for 5 minutes. Then add the Cognac, rum, or bourbon, and pour the hot sauce over the pears.

With a ladle or a large spoon, baste occasionally until cool. Cover and refrigerate.

Serve each pear standing upright in a compote or dessert bowl, with several spoonfuls of the syrup.

Ginger- Pear Crisp

6 TO 8 PORTIONS

This can be made without the ginger and it is very good, but ginger and pears are a special combination—each complements the other. This can be served hot, warm, cooled, or chilled; but if you love it hot, and everyone seems to, try the following procedure. Prepare the topping as much ahead of time as you wish and refrigerate it. Cut up the ginger, mix the lemon juice and water, butter the casserole, and have the spices ready. Then, the last thing before dinner (it can be about 2 hours before), peel and cut the pears, put it all together and bake. After it is baked it will keep warm for about an hour, but if necessary, you can put it back in the oven for 5 or 10 minutes just before serving.

CRUMB TOPPING

¾ cup unsifted all-purpose flour
1 cup granulated sugar
4 ounces (1 stick) unsalted butter, cold and
 firm, cut into small pieces

This can be made in a food processor or by hand with a pastry blender. In a processor (fitted with the steel blade), place all of the ingredients in the bowl and process on-and-off, quickly, 6 or 7 times. Then let the machine run for only a few seconds until the mixture resembles coarse meal; it should not hold together.

If you do it with a pastry blender, place all of the ingredients in a mixing bowl and cut with a pastry blender until the mixture resembles coarse meal.

Then, whichever way you have arrived at this stage, now you must work it slightly with your hands. If you have used a processor, transfer the mixture to a roomy bowl. Use both hands and work (squeeze) the ingredients through your fingers to form it into a lumpy, crumbly mixture—not powdery and not smooth. Set aside.

> ¼ cup candied ginger
> ¼ cup lemon juice
> ¼ cup water
> 3 to 3½ pounds firm, fresh pears (about 8;
>   Anjou, Comice, or Bartlett—they must
>   not be overripe, or the least bit soft)
> 2 teaspoons cinnamon
> ½ teaspoon nutmeg

Adjust an oven rack to the center of the oven and preheat the oven to 375 degrees. Butter a shallow ovenproof casserole with an 8-cup capacity (8 × 11 × 2 inches) and set aside. Cut the ginger into dice about ⅛ inch, and set aside. Mix the lemon juice and water and set aside.

With a vegetable parer, peel the pears, cut them into quarters, cut out the cores, and then cut each piece in half the long way. If the pears are small, leave them in quarters—the pieces should not be too small. Work quickly before the pears discolor. Place them in a large bowl, add the cinnamon and nutmeg, toss well to thoroughly coat the pieces with the spices, turn them into the casserole, and press down or rearrange to flatten the top. Drizzle the lemon juice and water all over them. Sprinkle the ginger over the top.

If the topping was refrigerated, work it with your hands a bit to make it crumbly. Sprinkle the topping all over; it should just cover all the fruit. Do not press it down or flatten it.

Bake for 1 hour or until the fruit is barely tender (not mushy) when tested with a cake tester or a toothpick, and the topping is a rich color—it should not be pale. If the fruit is tender and the topping is still pale, place the casserole about 6 inches below the broiler and broil, watching it constantly, only until nicely browned.

Serve this as is or with vanilla ice cream or with sweetened and vanilla-flavored whipped cream.

Mangoes, Key-West Style

Mangoes taste like peaches/pears/apricots/ pineapple. This way of serving them, which I learned in Key West, is so gorgeous that I would be a mangophile even if it did not taste like all the delicious fruits rolled into one.

As far as I know, the only mangoes that are grown commercially in this country are in an area just south of Miami. They come in all sizes from plum size to large ones that weigh two to three pounds. The larger the mango is, the more dramatic and impressive this presentation will be. There are many varieties of mangoes; the Hayden is the best known and probably the most delicious.

Mangoes must be thoroughly ripe in order to have the most and the best flavor. (Green mangoes are used like green apples, for pie.) To ripen, just let the fruit stand at room temperature. To test ripeness, the fruit should "give" to the touch slightly more than a ripe peach does. As it ripens, it might develop black spots on the skin the way bananas do. Some varieties might be green when ripe, and others might be green, gold, and red.

When you are quite sure that the fruit is ripe, refrigerate it either long enough to chill, or for a few days.

Before serving, rinse the fruit under running water to wash it.

Mangoes are not freestone. On the contrary, the fruit clings tenaciously. To such a degree that Floridians who are quite familiar with mangoes (and adore them) are divided into two groups. Those who say the only way to eat a mango is leaning over the kitchen sink, and those who opt for a bathtub.

The seed is long and flat (it reaches the top and the bottom of the fruit and almost two sides). Hold a mango upright, resting it on a work surface. Use a long, sharp knife and, cutting parallel with a long, flat side of the fruit, cut from the top to the bottom (a straight cut, not curved), cutting off a piece that is a scant half of the fruit (you should be cutting right next to—and barely touching—the seed). Then do the same on the other side of the fruit, starting the cut about ¾ inch (which is the width of the seed) from the first cut.

You now have two halves of the fruit and the seed with a bit of fruit clinging to it, which is not part of this recipe. (Incidentally, for some other time, the two halves may be peeled and sliced or diced, or you can eat the fruit from the halves with a spoon like melon.)

Cut each half as follows: Rest it, cut side up, on the work surface. With the tip of a small, sharp paring knife, cut completely through the fruit but not through the skin. Cut straight down into the flat side of the fruit, making cuts from the top to the bottom ¾ inch apart. Then repeat, making cuts ¾ inch apart at right angles to the lengthwise cuts. It is a checkerboard effect.

Now, for the fun. Hold the fruit cut side (flat side) up. Hold the fingers of both hands (except the thumbs) underneath, touching the skin. Gently, with both hands, push the skin up to make it convex. This will cause the fruit to open up in a bold, dramatic pattern of ¾-inch squares.

Serve the mango on a flat dessert plate (which may first be covered with a large fresh green leaf, or a few lemon leaves) either just as it is or with a wedge or a half of a lime, an optional sprinkling of rum, and a shaker or a bowl of confectioners sugar. And with a fork and a sharp knife for each portion.

If the mangoes are large, one will make two portions. If they are small, serve two halves to a portion.

NOTE: *You can prepare the fruit before dinner, but do not press the bottoms up to open the squares until right before serving. Wrap the prepared halves in plastic wrap; they will not discolor.*

By the way, about that center slice that has the seed in it: Peel it, hold it with both hands, bend over the sink, and eat around the seed, pulling the fruit through your teeth.

Brandied Prunes

ABOUT 8 PORTIONS

Dried prunes soaked in flavored Cognac for at least a week or two, served over vanilla ice cream. The prunes absorb so much of the Cognac they remind me of a line in one of Mildred Knopf's wonderful cookbooks. She had made a dessert with a huge amount of liquor. When she served it, a guest said the dessert stood up and announced, "I can lick any man in the house."

12 ounces pitted dried (but soft) prunes
A 2-inch piece of vanilla bean
1 large slice candied ginger or 1 whole piece
    preserved ginger
½ cup Cognac
¼ cup honey
7 tablespoons strong black coffee, tea, or water

Place the prunes in a jar with a tight-fitting cover. Slit the vanilla bean the long way and then crossways, and add it to the prunes. Chop the ginger rather fine and add to the prunes. Add the Cognac, honey, and coffee, tea, or water. Cover the jar tightly.

Turn the jar from top to bottom and from side to side once or twice a day, and let the prunes marinate for at least a week or two. But this will keep for a month.

After the vanilla bean has softened, the seeds seem to float out into the syrup. However, if you think they need some help, you can scrape the seeds out into the syrup. But leave the bean itself in the jar also.

If this stands for a long time and if the prunes absorb most of the liquids, add a little more of either or all of them; it should have some juice and should not be dry.

This is sensational by itself but it is really best over vanilla ice cream. Or serve the prunes with fresh grapefruit sections—it is an exotic and wonderful combination.

NOTES: 1. *If the prunes are very large, they may be cut in half either before or after marinating to make them easier to eat.*

2. *This same recipe can be made with a combination of prunes and dried apricots.*

3. *A pretty jar of this makes a wonderful gift.*

Ice Cream and Other Frozen Desserts

ABOUT ICE-CREAM CHURNS

If no one ever told you that you would love to have an ice-cream churn, I am telling you now. I wish someone had told me. Now that I know what it is like, I am sorry about all the years I did not have one. I thought it was too much work and difficult. It is not either one. It is great fun and exciting, and I become transported to ice-cream heaven every time I use the churn.

Mine is a 4-quart electric churn; I think this is a good size. Any of the following recipes can be divided for a smaller churn.

NOTE: *When the churning is finished the ice cream should be semifirm or soft-frozen—not really firm. At this stage, manufacturers of ice-cream churns direct you to remove the dasher and complete the freezing in the canister of the churn. But I prefer to transfer it to plastic freezer containers before it becomes thoroughly firm, and finish the freezing in the freezer part of the refrigerator. Work quickly; do not allow the partially frozen ice cream to melt.*

TO SOFTEN ICE CREAM OR ICE

Some of these recipes may become too firm if they are frozen for a few days. Here's how to make them way ahead of time (a week or two) and still serve them at their very best.

Immediately before serving, or as long as an hour or two (or three) before serving, use a large, strong, firm kitchen spoon to cut up the too-firm ice cream or ice so it can be transferred. Then use either an electric mixer or a food processor.

In a mixer: Chill the large bowl of the mixer and the beaters ahead of time. Place the cut-up ice cream or ice in the chilled bowl. Beat until fluffy and creamy but not until melted. Use a rubber spatula or a wooden spoon to continually push the hard mixture into the beaters.

In a food processor: Chill the bowl and metal blade ahead of time. With the motor running, add pieces of the frozen mixture through the feed tube, adding a few pieces at a time, and processing until smoothly softened but not until melted. Do not process too much at once; refreeze each batch immediately.

After softening the too-hard mixture either in a mixer or in a processor, serve it immediately in chilled cups, or replace it in the freezer in a chilled container. It will retain its wonderful texture for an hour or two or three (recipes vary).

This procedure can be repeated again days or weeks later, as often as you wish.

Fantastic Vanilla Ice Cream

Rich, luxurious, extravagant, delicious, de luxe, smo-o-oth; the best! This fabulous ice cream will not freeze too hard to serve easily—it will remain creamy and heavenly and perfect—even after days in the freezer.

3 PINTS (1½ QUARTS)

4 cups heavy cream
8 egg yolks (from eggs graded large, extra-large, or jumbo)
1 cup granulated sugar
2 teaspoons vanilla extract

Place 2 cups of the cream (reserve remaining 2 cups) in the top of a large double boiler (8-cup capacity) over hot water on moderate heat. Let stand, uncovered, until a slightly wrinkled skin forms on the top of the cream.

Meanwhile, in the small bowl of an electric mixer, beat the yolks for a few minutes until they are pale and thick. On low speed gradually add the sugar. Then beat on high speed again for 2 or 3 minutes more.

When the cream is scalded, on low speed, very gradually, add about half of it to the beaten yolks and sugar mixture. Scrape the bowl well with a rubber spatula. Then add the yolk mixture to the remaining cream. Mix well, and place over hot water again, on moderate heat.

Cook, scraping the bottom and sides frequently with a rubber spatula, until the mixture thickens to a soft custard consistency. It will register 178 to 180 degrees on a candy thermometer. (When the mixture starts to thicken, scrape the bottom and sides constantly with the rubber spatula.)

Remove from the hot water, transfer to a larger bowl, stir occasionally until cool, mix in the vanilla and the reserved 2 cups of heavy cream.

It is best to chill this mixture for an hour or more before freezing it.

Freeze in a churn, following the manufacturer's directions (see Note, page 431).

NOTE: *To double this recipe you will need an extra-large double boiler. It will probably be necessary to concoct one yourself, by placing a large, wide, round-bottomed mixing bowl over a saucepan of shallow hot water. The rim of the bowl should rest on the rim of the saucepan.*

Ginger Ice Cream

This is a plain, old-fashioned vanilla ice cream with tiny chunks of candied or preserved ginger all through it; the flavor is only mildly gingery.

3 QUARTS

3 cups milk
6 cups heavy cream
1½ cups granulated sugar
3 tablespoons sifted all-purpose flour
¾ teaspoon salt
5 egg yolks
¾ cup chopped candied or preserved ginger
  (see Note)
2¼ teaspoons vanilla extract

Place the milk and 2 cups of the cream, reserving the remaining 4 cups cream, in the top of a large double boiler over hot water on moderate heat, or in a heavy saucepan over low heat. Cook, uncovered, until scalded, or until you see a slightly wrinkled skin on top or small bubbles around the edge.

Meanwhile, sift or strain the sugar, flour, and salt together and add them to the hot milk mixture, stirring well.

In a bowl, stir the yolks slightly just to mix. Gradually add about 2 cups of the hot milk mixture, stirring constantly. Then gradually stir the yolks into the remaining hot milk mixture. Cook, uncovered, stirring and scraping the bottom and sides almost constantly with a rubber spatula, for about 15 minutes until the mixture barely coats a wooden spoon; it should register 180 to 185 degrees on a candy thermometer.

Remove from the heat. To stop the cooking, transfer the mixture to a bowl, or stir over ice and water. Let stand until completely cool.

Stir the ginger and vanilla into the cooled mixture.

In a large chilled bowl, with chilled beaters, whip the reserved 4 cups heavy cream until it holds a shape but not until it is really stiff.

Then gradually fold the milk and ginger mixture into the whipped cream.

Freeze in a churn following the manufacturer's directions (see Note, page 431).

This does not need a sauce, but a nice and easy one, if you wish, is sweet orange marmalade; just stir it to soften.

NOTE: *Chop the ginger either on a board with a sharp knife or in a small, round chopping bowl with a knife that has a rounded blade. Either way, do not chop it all too fine; leave some chunky pieces to really bite into.*

Palm Beach Orange Ice Cream

2½ QUARTS

This delicate and refreshing ice cream has a beautiful pale orange color and a mild and creamy flavor. A scoop of it is delicious on a fresh fruit salad for luncheon. Or serve it for dessert, either plain or in combination with vanilla ice cream, a small scoop of each. It was served to us after a festive dinner party in large, wide, shallow glasses on tall stems. Each portion had a few thin wedges of peeled kiwi fruit on one side, a few small strawberries on the other side, and a perfect white gardenia on the top. Pretty as a picture.

1½ cups milk
Finely grated rind of 2 or 3 oranges
Finely grated rind of 1 or 2 lemons
6 egg yolks
¾ cup granulated sugar
⅔ cup light corn syrup
¼ teaspoon salt
1½ cups heavy cream
3 cups fresh orange juice
2 tablespoons fresh lemon juice

Place the milk in the top of a large double boiler over hot water on moderate heat. Add the grated rinds and let cook uncovered until small bubbles form around the edge.

Meanwhile, in a small mixing bowl, stir the yolks lightly with a whisk just to mix them. Then, stirring constantly, gradually mix in about half of the scalded milk. Add the yolk mixture to the remaining milk, stirring well. Add the sugar, syrup, and salt.

Stir over hot water until the mixture thickens slightly and barely coats a metal spoon; it will register 180 degrees on a candy thermometer.

Strain the mixture (if you leave the grated rinds in, they will collect in one lump on the edge of the dasher during the churning) and set aside to cool.

Add the cream and both juices. Chill in the refrigerator or freezer.

Freeze the ice cream in a churn, following the manufacturer's directions (see Note, page 431).

Pumpkin Ice Cream

This is a wonderful recipe. It is most unusual, a beautiful color, and everybody is wild about it. It has no season.

2 QUARTS

6 egg yolks
1 cup mashed cooked pumpkin (about half
    a 1-pound can of solid-pack pumpkin, not
    pumpkin-pie filling)
1 cup granulated sugar
¼ teaspoon salt
½ teaspoon cinnamon
½ teaspoon nutmeg
½ teaspoon ginger
4 cups heavy cream

In the small bowl of an electric mixer, beat the yolks until they are pale, thick, and creamy.

Place the pumpkin in the top of a large double boiler. Add the beaten yolks, sugar, salt, cinnamon, nutmeg, and ginger. Place over hot water on moderate heat.

Cook, stirring and scraping the bottom with a rubber spatula, for about 10 minutes or until slightly thickened.

Remove the top of the double boiler and set aside, stirring occasionally until completely cool. (If you wish, set the top of the double boiler in a bowl of ice and water and stir constantly until cool.)

In a large chilled bowl with chilled beaters, whip the cream until it holds a soft shape. (If you beat until the cream is stiff it will make the ice cream heavy and buttery instead of light and creamy.)

In a large bowl, fold the pumpkin mixture and whipped cream together.

Freeze according to the manufacturer's directions for your churn (see Note, page 431).

Blueberry Ice Cream

2 QUARTS

This has one of the most beautiful red-purple colors I have ever seen in food. But even if it were colorless, it would be magnificent. Smooth/ creamy/rich/de luxe/delicious—a memorable ice cream.

2 1-pint boxes fresh blueberries
1 cup granulated sugar
⅛ teaspoon salt
3 cups heavy cream
3 tablespoons lemon juice
3 tablespoons kirsch, crème de cassis,
    or brandy

Wash and drain the berries. Place them in a wide and heavy saucepan or frying pan. Add the sugar and stir to mix. Cover, and place over low heat. Cook for 5 minutes to soften the berries a little and partially melt the sugar. Then raise the heat to moderate, uncover the pan, stir until the mixture comes to a boil, and let boil for 5 minutes, stirring and pressing the berries against the sides of the pan to mash them.

Set aside to cool for a few minutes, then strain through a large, large-mesh strainer set over a large bowl. Do not use a strainer that has fine openings; even with a coarse strainer some of the fruit will not go through. However, press through as much as you can.

Place the puréed berry mixture in the freezer or refrigerator until very cold.

Stir in the salt, cream, lemon juice, and kirsch, crème de cassis, or brandy.

If the mixture is less than very cold, chill it in the freezer or refrigerator.

Freeze in a churn following the manufacturer's instructions (see Note, page 431).

When you serve this, you may wish to pass kirsch, crème de cassis, or brandy to be poured over each portion.

Because of the alcohol, this does not freeze too hard to serve directly from the freezer.

NOTE: *Homemakers hint—the blueberries will stain both rubber and wooden spatulas; don't use anything you will feel sad about if this happens to it.*

Cranberry Ice Cream

4 QUARTS

This has an exquisite bright rosy-pink color, and an equally exquisite taste and texture—creamy and tart, not too sweet; extraordinary! Start this ahead of time; the mixture must chill well before it is churned. To make this amount of ice cream you will need a 4-quart churn.

2 pounds (about 10 cups) cranberries, fresh
    or frozen
2 cups water
2 cups orange juice
2 envelopes unflavored gelatin
⅓ cup cold water
1 cup light corn syrup
½ cup water
2 cups light brown sugar, firmly packed
1 cup honey
2 cups heavy cream

Wash and drain the berries. Place them in a large saucepan with the 2 cups of water and the orange juice. Bring to a boil over moderate heat, then reduce the heat and let simmer, uncovered, for 10 minutes. Cool a bit and then purée in a processor or a blender. Press the mixture through a large strainer set over a large bowl. Set aside.

Sprinkle the gelatin over the ⅓ cup cold water in a small cup. Set aside.

Place the corn syrup and ½ cup water in a 1- to 2-quart saucepan over moderate heat. Bring to a boil; boil gently, uncovered, for 5 minutes. Add the softened gelatin and stir to dissolve. Add the brown sugar and stir to dissolve, then stir in the honey.

In a mixing bowl, combine the cranberry mixture with the honey mixture. Set aside to cool. Cover and refrigerate for several hours or overnight, or chill it quickly in the freezer.

When you are ready to churn the ice cream, in a chilled bowl with chilled beaters whip the cream until it holds a soft shape but not until it is stiff. Gradually fold the cranberry mixture into the cream. If the berry mixture sinks to the bottom, pour it all gently from one bowl to another to incorporate.

Then churn the mixture, following the manufacturer's directions for your churn (see Note, page 431).

This stays semifirm for several hours after it is churned. It is best at that consistency. If it freezes longer and becomes too hard, place it in the refrigerator for about half an hour before serving; check it after 15 or 20 minutes.

Grapefruit Ice

This is white and looks somewhat like vanilla ice cream; the flavor is tantalizing. I am crazy about it.

2 QUARTS

1 envelope unflavored gelatin
¼ cup cold water
2 cups granulated sugar
1 cup boiling water
⅛ teaspoon salt
5 cups fresh grapefruit juice

Sprinkle the gelatin over the water in a small cup and let stand. Meanwhile, mix the sugar and boiling water in a saucepan over high heat. Stir with a wooden spatula until the mixture comes to a boil. Boil without stirring for 2 minutes.

Remove from the heat, add the softened gelatin, and stir to dissolve. Add the salt. Stir the sugar mixture into the grapefruit juice. Cool to room temperature and then chill well before churning.

Freeze according to the manufacturer's directions for your churn (see Note, page 431).

NOTE: *This does not become too hard to serve, even after several days in the freezer. But it does lose its creamy consistency and becomes a little dry (see To Soften Ice Cream and Ice, page 431). It will be sensationally creamy immediately after the extra beating, and it will remain sensational for an hour or two. It is definitely worth the little extra handling; you will be pleased if you did it.*

Straw-
berry
Sorbet

3 QUARTS

*This light sherbet is quite incredible. The straw-
berry flavor seems stronger and more intense than
in strawberries alone. When I served this at a
dinner party it caused a run on ice-cream churns
the following day; everyone wanted to make this.*

*Fresh raspberries can be used in place of the
strawberries to make a raspberry sorbet, or you can
use some of each for a combination that is
wonderful.*

4 1-pint boxes (4 pounds) fresh strawberries
3 cups granulated sugar
¼ teaspoon salt
2 tablespoons fresh lemon juice
2 cups cold water

Place the berries (only 1 box at a time so they do not soak too long) in a
large bowl of cold water; quickly pick them out, remove the hulls, and
drain on paper towels.

Slice the berries in half and place them in a roomy bowl. Add the
sugar and salt and stir to mix. Let stand, stirring occasionally, for about
2 hours until the sugar is dissolved and the berries are soft.

Purée the mixture, about one-quarter at a time, in a food processor or
a blender.

Now, a question: To strain or not to strain? I do, but it is a job. You
must use a rather fine-meshed strainer or the seeds will go through. Do not
attempt to strain this in a narrow-diameter strainer; it must be a wide one
or you will be at it for hours. If you examine the strained mixture, you will
see that a few seeds have gone through anyhow—that can't be helped. And
you will have quite a large number of seeds in the strainer to be discarded.

Add the lemon juice and cold water.

Freeze in a churn according to the manufacturer's directions (see
Note, page 431).

Lemon Ice

Extra sour, extra wonderful, extra special—and so easy I can't believe it.

3 QUARTS

As much as I love to use grated lemon rind, I do not use it for this recipe. It settles in lumps on the dasher, and even if you stir it around to mix it in after the ice is churned, frozen grated lemon rind in this recipe is not so great.

8 cups warm water
4 cups granulated sugar
2¾ cups fresh lemon juice

Combine the water and sugar in a saucepan over high heat. Stir with a wooden spatula until the sugar is dissolved and the mixture comes to a boil. Boil without stirring for 5 minutes.

Remove from the heat and let stand until completely cool. Stir in the lemon juice.

If you chill this well before freezing it, it will save churning time.

Freeze in a churn following the manufacturer's directions (see Note, page 431).

Don't be surprised when you remove the cover of the churn to see that this is white, not yellow.

Some people especially enjoy this with a splash of gin, vodka, crème de menthe, or rum poured on it.

NOTE: *As soon as this is churned, and for several hours after, it has a terrific texture—just firm enough but not too firm. After a day or two in the freezer it becomes too firm (see To Soften Ice Cream or Ice, page 431).*

Orange Ice

This is as cool and refreshing as a dip in a cool mountain lake. The flavor is mild; the color is pale, pale orange—only enough to give barely a hint of the flavor. But wait until you taste it.

2 QUARTS

Delicious! Serve a scoop on a fruit salad. Or, for true luxury, serve a combination of this and Strawberry Sorbet (see preceding page).

1 envelope unflavored gelatin
4¼ cups water
2 cups granulated sugar
2 cups fresh orange juice (grate the rind of
    1 large orange to use below before
    squeezing the juice)
¼ cup fresh lemon juice (grate the rind to use
    below before squeezing the juice)
¼ cup Cointreau
Finely grated rind 1 large orange
Finely grated rind of 1 large lemon
⅛ teaspoon salt

Sprinkle the gelatin over ¼ cup of the water in a small cup and let stand.

Combine the remaining 4 cups of water with the sugar in a saucepan. Stir over moderately high heat, bring to a boil, and let boil without stirring for 5 minutes. Remove from the heat, add the softened gelatin, and stir to dissolve.

Pour into a bowl or pitcher and let stand for about 5 minutes. Then add the orange juice, lemon juice, Cointreau, grated rinds, and salt. Stir to mix.

Let stand until cool, then strain through a fine strainer. Chill briefly in the freezer or refrigerator.

Freeze in a churn, following the manufacturer's directions (see Note, page 431).

Frozen Grand Marnier Mousse

12 PORTIONS

This is a dream recipe. It is easy to make, it does not call for a churn, it is elegant and delicious, it is prepared in individual soufflé dishes, custard cups, or coffee cups, it is served directly from the freezer with no last-minute attention, and it may be frozen for a month. It does not freeze hard; it is a light and creamy mousse, lighter than ice cream, sprinkled with a mixture of Grand Marnier and macaroon crumbs. Although this makes 12 portions you should plan on serving seconds.

MACAROON MIXTURE

6 ounces Amaretti or any dry almond
    macaroons (to make 1¼ cups crumbs)
2 tablespoons orange juice (grate the rind
    before squeezing the juice and reserve
    it for the mousse)
3 tablespoons Grand Marnier

The macaroons must be ground fine. To grind them in a food processor (fitted with the metal blade) or in a blender, crumble them coarse and then process or blend to make fine crumbs. Without a processor or blender, place the macaroons in a strong bag and pound them with a hammer or any heavy tool. You should have about 1¼ cups of crumbs.

In a small bowl, mix the orange juice and Grand Marnier. Add the crumbs and mix thoroughly; it will be a crumbly mixture. Set aside.

MOUSSE

5 eggs (graded large), separated
½ cup plus 3 tablespoons granulated sugar
Finely grated rind of 1 large, deep-colored
    orange (see ingredients for macaroon
    mixture above)
3 tablespoons Grand Marnier
2 cups heavy cream
Pinch of salt

In the small bowl of an electric mixer, beat the egg yolks with ½ cup (reserve the remaining 3 tablespoons) of sugar for several minutes until very pale and thick.

Mix the grated rind and the Grand Marnier. Remove the yolk mixture from the beater and stir in the grated rind mixture. Set aside.

In a chilled bowl with chilled beaters, whip the cream until it holds a shape, but not until it is really stiff. Set aside.

Add the salt to the whites and beat until the whites hold a soft shape. On low speed, gradually add the reserved 3 tablespoons of sugar; then increase the speed and beat only until the whites hold a shape but not until they are stiff or dry.

In a very large mixing bowl, with a large rubber spatula, fold together the egg-yolk mixture, the whipped cream, and the beaten egg whites, folding all three mixtures together at once and handling lightly only until the mixtures are barely blended.

Line up twelve individual soufflé dishes, custard cups, or coffee cups, each with about a 6-ounce capacity.

Spoon half of the mixture into the cups, filling them only about halfway; do not smooth the tops. With your fingertips sprinkle about half of the prepared macaroon mixture over the mousses. Top with the remaining mousse mixture, do not smooth the tops, and sprinkle with the remaining macaroon mixture.

Place the mousses in the freezer for about an hour until they are firm enough to be covered. Then cover each one with a piece of plastic wrap large enough to fold under the bottom; do not pull it so tightly that it squashes the top.

Freeze for at least 3 or 4 hours or as long as 3 or 4 weeks. Serve directly from the freezer.

Plum Sorbet

1½ PINTS

For many years, when plums were in season (or using plums from Brazil when they were not in season here), I made honeyed plum sauce, especially to serve over sliced fresh or stewed peaches (a luscious combination) or over vanilla ice cream (exotic) or simply to eat with a spoon or drink from a glass. Once, when I had made a large amount of the sauce, we suddenly decided to close the house and go for a long trip. I put the sauce in the freezer, thinking that I would let it thaw when we returned. But I did not let it thaw; I ate it with a spoon and found that it was a wondrous sorbet. It is slightly tart; very, very good; unusual, and too easy (no churning).

> 2 pounds red plums (about 12; I use President, or Santa Rosa plums)
> ⅓ cup honey
> ¼ cup water
> 2 tablespoons maraschino liqueur (I have only used maraschino, but in place of it, I would think you can use any liqueur or brandy, such as kirsch)

Cut the plums into halves or large pieces and remove the pits. Place the plums, honey, and water in a heavy saucepan. Cover and cook over low-moderate heat, stirring occasionally, until the plums begin to soften. Then uncover and continue to cook, stirring occasionally, until the plums fall apart and are completely softened (it might take about 20 minutes).

Press the mixture through a strainer set over a bowl. At the end, work through as much of the thickened remains as you can (still, some will not go through and will have to be discarded).

Stir in the maraschino liqueur.

Place the mixture, uncovered, in a bowl or container in the freezer until it is firm. Then cover it with plastic wrap, placing the plastic directly on the top of the sorbet.

It might take 5 to 10 hours to freeze solid, depending on the container and whether the mixture is shallow or deep.

Now, this frozen mixture must be beaten once sometime before serving. It may be done immediately before, or hours before. I love it immediately after it is beaten, but, although it becomes firmer as it stands in the freezer, the texture remains nice for many hours. This beating may be done in a food processor fitted with a metal blade or in the large bowl of an electric mixer. Either way, chill the bowl and blade or beaters. In a mixer you can beat it all at once. In a processor, do it in small batches, adding the frozen mixture by spoonfuls through the feed tube.

Process or beat until the mixture is slightly lighter in color, very smooth, and a little fluffy, but not until it melts or becomes runny.

Serve immediately or return to the freezer.

NOTE: *Always cover with plastic wrap directly touching the sorbet, otherwise ice will form in the space between the sorbet and the covering.*

Sorbet Cassis

3 PINTS

This is from my friend Betty Rossbottom, a wonderful cook and cooking teacher (her school is La Belle Pomme at Lazarus Square in Columbus, Ohio). She served this (the main course was Julia Child's delicious Sauté de Veau Marengo) when she invited us to her home for dinner. After the first bite, I asked, "Can I please have the recipe?" It is a sherbet made without a churn. It has a most delicious flavor and a sensational purple color. You need room in the freezer for a large bowl.

> 2 1-pound cans blackberries (Betty and I use Oregon brand) packed in syrup
> 1 cup granulated sugar
> ½ cup plus 2 tablespoons fresh lemon juice
> ½ cup water
> ½ cup cassis liqueur or crème de cassis (cassis is black currant)
> 4 eggs (graded large or extra-large)

Drain the berries in a strainer set over a bowl and reserve the juice (you will need 1 cup of drained blackberry juice).

Purée the berries in a food processor fitted with the metal blade or in a blender. Strain through a large, rather coarse strainer to remove the seeds. Stir in the sugar, lemon juice, 1 cup of drained blackberry juice, water, and cassis. Beat the eggs to mix them well and stir them into the blackberry mixture. Mix thoroughly.

Now strain it all again either through the same strainer or preferably through one with slightly smaller openings.

Place the mixture in a large bowl (stainless steel works best because it gets very cold; the bowl should be large enough to give you plenty of room to stir vigorously), cover with plastic wrap or foil, and place in the freezer.

When it starts to harden (when about 1 inch is frozen around the edge), use a large, strong wooden spatula and stir the mixture vigorously. Refreeze and stir again when it gets to the 1-inch rim stage. Repeat the freezing and stirring at least four times—the more the better (it should be at about 45-minute intervals). Then cover airtight and return to the freezer for at least 6 hours or overnight.

Sometime before serving, which may be right before or up to 3 hours before, beat the sorbet either in an electric mixer or in a processor. The bowl and beaters or metal blade should be chilled first. If you use a processor, process in small batches, adding the frozen sorbet by spoonfuls through the feed tube. Beat or process only until the mixture becomes fluffy and slightly lighter in color, but not long enough for it to melt—it should remain firm enough to hold its shape.

Serve immediately or return to the freezer for up to 2 or 3 hours—the sorbet will remain soft-frozen for 2 or 3 hours.

If this is frozen for several days, it should be beaten or processed again before serving.

It is nice to pass the bottle of cassis at the table to be poured over individual portions.

Betty often serves this piled high in large, scooped-out lemon shells (cut a thin slice off the bottom so it will stand straight) with a sprig of fresh mint in the top of each; it is a riot of colors—purple sorbet, yellow lemon, and green mint.

Joan's Frozen Lemon Mousse

12 TO 16 PORTIONS

This wonderful fix-ahead frozen dessert is a recipe from my friend Joan Borinstein. It resembles ice cream, prepared in a crumb crust. It is easy to slice, and is a deliciously light and refreshing dessert to serve after a dinner party. It must be prepared at least a day ahead; it can be prepared 2 weeks ahead. If you prepare it far ahead, wrap it airtight in plastic wrap to store in the freezer. You will need an 8 × 3-inch spring-form pan.

CRUST

1 12-ounce box vanilla wafers (to make 3¼
   cups crumbs)
4 ounces (1 stick) unsalted butter

Butter the sides only of an 8 × 3-inch spring-form pan. (It is easier to transfer if the bottom is not buttered, or, if you are serving it on the bottom of the pan, it makes it easier to serve.) Make fine crumbs of the wafers, either in a food processor fitted with the metal blade, or in a blender, or by placing them in a strong bag and pounding firmly with a rolling pin.

Melt the butter and add it to the crumbs; mix thoroughly until completely blended.

Now, it is easier if you do not put all of the crumb mixture into the pan at once; work with about one-quarter of the mixture at a time. First press a firm layer on the sides of the pan, up to the top of the pan, and then on the bottom.

FILLING

4 eggs (graded large or extra-large), separated
1 cup granulated sugar
½ cup fresh lemon juice (grate the rind of
   3 or 4 lemons before squeezing the
   juice to use below)
Finely grated rind of 3 or 4 lemons
Pinch of salt
1½ cups heavy cream

In the small bowl of an electric mixer, beat the yolks until they are pale. Add ¼ cup, reserving remaining ¾ cup, of the sugar and beat at high speed for a minute or two. On low speed, gradually add the lemon juice, scraping the bowl with a rubber spatula and beating only until smooth. Remove from the mixer and stir in the grated rind. Set aside.

In a small clean bowl with clean beaters, beat the egg whites with the salt until they hold a soft shape. Reduce the speed to moderate and gradually add the reserved ¾ cup of sugar, adding only 1 or 2 tablespoons at a time. Increase the speed to high again and continue to beat until the whites and sugar become thick and marshmallowlike. Do not beat until stiff. Set aside.

In a chilled bowl with chilled beaters, whip the cream until it holds a shape but not until it is stiff.

In several small additions fold the yolks into the whites. Then, in several additions, fold the yolks and whites into the whipped cream.

Turn into the crumb-lined pan and smooth the top. Freeze for a few hours until firm. Then cover airtight with plastic wrap or aluminum foil. Freeze overnight or up to 2 weeks.

To remove the side of the pan: Use a 5- or 6-inch firm-bladed (not flexible), sharp and heavy knife; cut around the sides between the crust and the pan, pressing the blade firmly against the pan. Release and remove the side.

Then, to remove the dessert from the bottom of the pan, cut between the bottom and the crust to release. With a wide metal spatula transfer the dessert to a large, flat serving plate.

This can be served immediately, or it can be replaced in the freezer. Use the same firm-bladed knife to slice portions.

OPTIONAL SAUCE

1 10-ounce box boysen-
    berries, packed in
    syrup   or any other
1 10-ounce box frozen   fruits or
    blackberries, packed   combination
    in syrup

Thaw the fruit and purée it with its syrup in a blender or a processor. Strain it through a fine strainer to remove the seeds. Pass the sauce separately.

NOTE: *The filling can also be prepared in individual glasses, without any crust.*

Frozen Lemon-Rum Soufflé

6 to 8 portions

This is a powerful concoction—very rummy, very tart, and very sensational! It can be served 3 or 4 hours after it is made or it can wait in the freezer a day or two. You will need room in the freezer for a soufflé dish with a 3-inch collar.

1 envelope plus 1½ teaspoons
    unflavored gelatin
½ cup cold tap water
1 cup fresh lemon juice (grate the rinds of
    2 of the lemons before squeezing to
    use below)
8 egg yolks
2 cups granulated sugar
⅔ cup dark rum (I use Myers's rum)
Finely grated rind of 2 large lemons
2 cups heavy cream

Prepare a 1-quart soufflé dish as follows: Tear off a piece of foil long enough to wrap around the dish and overlap by at least a few inches. Fold it in half the long way; the fold will be the bottom. Very lightly spread a thin layer of tasteless salad oil over the upper (open) half of the length. Wrap the foil around the dish. Tie it securely with a piece of string. Place it on a plate and set aside (see Notes).

Sprinkle the gelatin over the cold water in a heatproof bowl or cup; let stand for about 5 minutes.

Meanwhile, in the large bowl of an electric mixer, beat the lemon juice and egg yolks at high speed for 5 minutes. Add the sugar and rum and continue to beat at high speed for about 5 minutes more until the sugar is dissolved. Reduce the speed slightly if necessary to avoid splashing.

Meanwhile, place the cup of gelatin in a little hot water in a saucepan on low heat. Stir occasionally with a metal spoon until the gelatin is dissolved.

Reduce the mixer speed to low, add the gelatin, and beat until thoroughly mixed. Remove from the mixer and stir in the grated rind.

The mixture must now be chilled until it thickens slightly. It can either be done by placing the bowl in the freezer, or by placing the bowl in a larger bowl partly filled with ice and water. Either way, it should be stirred occasionally to be sure it thickens evenly.

Meanwhile, in a chilled bowl with chilled beaters, whip the cream until it holds a shape but not until it is really stiff. Transfer the whipped cream to a large mixing bowl.

When the gelatin mixture begins to thicken, gradually fold it, in several additions, into the whipped cream. It is best to fold with an extra-large rubber spatula. If the gelatin mixture seems to sink to the bottom, place the whole bowl in the freezer (or in a larger bowl of ice) briefly and fold occasionally until the gelatin no longer sinks. Then pour the mixture into the prepared soufflé dish.

Freeze for at least 3 hours until the soufflé is firm.

If the soufflé is going to stand and you want to cover the top, wait until the soufflé is completely frozen, then cover it with plastic wrap.

Immediately before serving, remove the foil collar. (It will be easy.) The top of the soufflé will be about 2 inches above the top of the dish— beautiful.

This can be decorated any way you wish: rosettes of whipped cream, candied violet or rose petals, chopped unsalted green pistachio nuts, chocolate shavings, etc. But it is such a super dish that I think adding anything is unnecessary. However, it is nice with a side dish of cold Custard Sauce (see Floating Iceberg, page 384) or with softly whipped cream flavored with sugar and vanilla. And, if you wish, pass a bowl of plain or brandied black Bing cherries (see Notes).

NOTES: 1. *Once when I made a cold soufflé for a party, I went to the kitchen just before dinner to remove the foil collar and decorate the soufflé. I had oiled the inside of the foil collar and I guess I had used too much oil. I took the dish out of the freezer, holding one hand on each side of it, and was shocked to see the whole thing, except the foil, slide gracefully out of my hands and land on the floor. Since then, I have always placed the soufflé dish on a plate for putting it into and taking it out of the freezer.*

2. To make your own brandied cherries, drain canned pitted black Bing cherries. Add about ¼ cup each kirsch and Cognac or brandy. Let stand, stirring occasionally, for a day or more in the refrigerator.

San Francisco Ice-Cream Pie

We had this sensational dessert at Fourno's Ovens, a wonderful restaurant in the Stanford Court Hotel on Nob Hill at the corner of California and Powell streets where San Francisco's cable-car lines cross. One entire wall of the dining room is lined with charming French Provincial blue-and-white tiles, and set into the wall are numerous ovens. Our table faced the ovens, like a ringside table at a nightclub. We watched roasts of various sizes and shapes going into and coming out of ovens as we had dinner—a delicious floor show. And we ordered the specialty of the house for dessert.

8 TO 10 PORTIONS

It consists of a baked pie crust that is filled with a praline ice cream (which you make yourself with bought ice cream and a few goodies) and it is covered with a thick layer of meringue. It is baked briefly just to brown the meringue, then it is frozen for a few hours or more, and it is served with a rum custard sauce that is unbelievably good.

It can be made 2 or 3 days before serving. It is well worth every minute it takes to prepare, and is not difficult or temperamental. Make it for a very special occasion.

Although it can all be made in the morning (if you get a very early start) and served that night, it is better to start part of it ahead of time. The pie crust can be shaped in the pan and frozen for days (or longer) before it is baked. It can then be baked and filled with the ice cream a few days (or longer) before serving. The sauce can be made a day ahead. The meringue can be made and baked at least 4 hours before serving, or a day or two before.

You must make room in the freezer for this—with the meringue it is 4½ inches high.

PIE CRUST

Bake a 9-inch Extra-deep Pie Shell (see page 135). This must be extra deep because the ice cream might melt a little while the meringue is baking; if the crust is not deep enough, or if there are any low spots on the sides, the ice cream might run over, running to the bottom of the plate where it will refreeze and make serving difficult.

PRALINE ICE CREAM

5 ounces (1¼ cups) pecans
½ cup light brown sugar, firmly packed

1 ounce (2 tablespoons) unsalted
   butter, melted
½ cup heavy cream
2 teaspoons vanilla extract
3 pints vanilla ice cream (I use Häagen-Dazs®—
   get the best you can)

The pecans must be finely chopped or coarsely ground, but they should not be powdered; it is best if there are a few uneven pieces to crunch. If you chop them in a food processor, be careful not to overdo it. Set aside until you have melted the sugar.

Place the sugar in a 4- to 6-cup heavy saucepan over high heat. Stir with a wooden spatula until the sugar is all melted. Reduce the heat gradually to moderate as the sugar melts. Continue to stir until the melted sugar is smooth (all lumps must be melted) and just turns a slightly darker shade. Immediately stir in the butter and cream. The mixture will become lumpy; continue to stir until it melts again and is smooth. Then stir in the pecans and remove from the heat. Stir in the vanilla. Set aside until completely cool.

When the pecan mixture is cool, it will be stirred into the ice cream. If you allow the ice cream to soften until it is melted, it will lose the air that was beaten into it when it was churned and it will not be as good. It is best to cut the firm ice cream into small pieces and place it in the large bowl of an electric mixer (chilled). Mix only until the ice cream has barely softened, not until it is melted. (This can also be done in any large bowl, stirring it with a heavy wooden spatula.) Quickly stir in the pecan mixture and immediately place it in the freezer until it is firm enough to use, but not until it is hard.

Turn the ice cream into the baked pie crust, spread it quickly, mounding the top slightly, and immediately place it back in the freezer. When it is frozen (which takes at least 4 hours or longer, due to the addition of the brown-sugar mixture) it may be topped with the meringue (recipe follows) and baked, or it may be covered with plastic wrap and wait for several days in the freezer.

Meanwhile, prepare the sauce.

RUM SAUCE

1½ cups heavy cream
6 egg yolks (from eggs graded large; you will
    use the whites for the meringue)
¼ cup granulated sugar
Pinch of salt
1 teaspoon vanilla extract
2 tablespoons dark rum

Place the cream in a saucepan over moderate heat, uncovered, until a slightly wrinkled skin forms over the surface or until you see steam rising from the cream.

Meanwhile, place the yolks in the top of a large double boiler off the heat. Stir lightly with a wire whisk or a spatula just to mix. Gradually stir in the sugar and the salt.

When the cream is ready, pour it very gradually into the yolks, stirring constantly.

Place the yolk and cream mixture over hot water in the bottom of the double boiler on moderate heat. Stir constantly, scraping the bottom and sides of the pan with a rubber spatula, until the mixture thickens to the consistency of a light cream sauce. It will take about 8 minutes, and a candy thermometer inserted into the mixture will register 170 degrees.

Remove the top of the double boiler. Pour the sauce through a fine strainer set over a small bowl.

Stir in the vanilla and the rum. Stir occasionally until cool.

Cover airtight and refrigerate for at least several hours but preferably overnight. (If there isn't time to refrigerate the sauce overnight, either place the bowl into a larger bowl of ice and water and stir frequently, or place the bowl in the freezer for about an hour and stir frequently.) The sauce will thicken more as it chills. It must be very cold when it is served. Stir it slightly just before serving.

MERINGUE

¾ cup egg whites (from 6 eggs, graded large)
⅛ teaspoon salt
1 teaspoon lemon juice
½ cup granulated sugar
1½ teaspoons vanilla extract

Make room in the freezer and set the freezer control to coldest. Adjust an oven rack one-third up from the bottom of the oven. Preheat the oven to 450 degrees.

Place the whites in the small bowl of an electric mixer. Add the salt and beat at high speed until foamy. Add the lemon juice and continue to beat until the whites hold a soft shape.

Reduce the speed to moderate and continue to beat, adding the sugar about 1 tablespoon at a time, beating about 15 seconds between additions. Then increase the speed to high again, add the vanilla, and continue to beat. It might be necessary at about this stage to transfer the mixture to the large bowl of the mixer.

Beat at high speed for several minutes, scraping the bowl as necessary with a rubber spatula, until the mixture is very stiff—it should take about 3 minutes.

Work quickly now. Take the frozen pie from the freezer. Place about half of the meringue on top. Use the back of a teaspoon to spread the meringue around the edges and make sure it touches the crust all around— it must touch the crust or the meringue will shrink during baking.

Then quickly place the remaining meringue on top and spread it with a rubber or metal spatula or with the back of a large spoon, forming it into a dome; it may be smooth or pulled up in peaks. Continue to work quickly; this ice cream melts faster than plain ice cream.

IMMEDIATELY place the pie in the oven and bake for 4 or 5 minutes just until the meringue is golden (if the meringue is peaked it will remain white in the crevices).

Freeze for at least 4 hours before serving. If you do not freeze it long enough the ice cream will be too soft; it should be firm.

Do not store more than 2 or 3 days before serving.

To serve: Since this ice cream melts quickly, it is a good idea to chill the plates (in the freezer if there is room). And be ready to serve as soon as you remove the pie from the freezer. Use a strong, heavy knife.

Place the sauce in a chilled dessert bowl or a pitcher and ladle or pour it alongside, not over, each portion.

NOTE: *If you serve this from 5 to 10 hours after baking the meringue, it will be at its most delicate, delicious, airy best. But my official taster (my husband) says that even after 2 (or 3) days it is still fantastic.*

Lalla
Rookh

This was named for the heroine of a series of oriental tales by Thomas Moore. I seem to have had this recipe forever. It is easy, fun, and everyone loves it. It is hollowed-out ice cream filled with Cognac and covered with whipped cream.

Vanilla ice cream
Heavy cream
Sugar
Vanilla extract
Cognac
Optional: grated semisweet chocolate

The ice cream can be homemade or bought. It should be soft enough so you can work with it, but not softer. The best way is to cut it into chunks and beat it in the large bowl of an electric mixer or in the bowl of a food processor fitted with the metal blade. Beat or process briefly; do not let it melt.

Quickly place a large round scoop of the ice cream in parfait glasses, wine glasses, or tall champagne glasses. Form a hollow with a teaspoon in the middle of each serving. It should be rather deep (this is for the Cognac). The ice cream might not hold its shape now while it is soft—the hollow might disappear—but you can fix it when the ice cream is refrozen.

Immediately place the glasses in the freezer until the ice cream is firm again.

With a teaspoon, correct the hollow. The diameter of the scooped-out space should not be too wide, but the space can be deep if you wish. Return to the freezer.

This part can and should be done way ahead of time. Cover and let stand in the freezer until you are ready for it.

Shortly before serving (an hour or two if you wish) whip the cream with a bit of sugar and vanilla, whipping until it holds a definite shape but not until it is really stiff. Refrigerate. If you do not use it very soon it will probably separate a bit while it stands; just beat it a little with a small wire whisk before you use it until it is right.

Immediately before serving pour the Cognac into the hollowed-out space in the ice cream. (It is easiest if you pour the Cognac into a small pitcher and pour it from the pitcher.) You should use about 1 to 2 tablespoons of Cognac in each portion. Then carefully place a large spoonful of the whipped cream on the top of the Cognac and ice cream. If the scooped-out hollow is not too wide, the whipped cream will rest on the top.

Optional: Sprinkle with grated semisweet chocolate.

This procedure and general recipe opens up a whole world of other combinations. Homemade Palm Beach Orange Ice Cream (see page 434) and Amaretto are delicious. Or marinate some raisins in rum and fill coffee ice cream with the raisins and rum. Et cetera.

Index

A Note About the Author

Maida Heatter, author of Maida Heatter's Book of Great Desserts, Maida Heatter's Book of Great Cookies, and Maida Heatter's Book of Great Chocolate Desserts, is the daughter of Gabriel Heatter, the radio commentator, and has been cooking all her life. She studied fashion illustration at Pratt Institute and has done fashion illustrating and designing, made jewelry, and painted, but her first love has remained cooking. She taught it in classes in her home and gave demonstrations in department stores. And for eight years she prepared all the desserts for a popular Miami Beach restaurant once owned by her husband, Ralph Daniels. More recently she has taught cooking at various stores and schools across the country.

Ms. Heatter has one daughter, Toni Evins, a painter and illustrator, who did the drawings for Maida Heatter's Book of Great Desserts, Maida Heatter's Book of Great Cookies, and Maida Heatter's Book of Great Chocolate Desserts, as well as those in the present volume.

A Note on the Type

The text of this book was set in Electra, a type face designed by William Addison Dwiggins for the Mergenthaler Linotype Company and first made available in 1935. Electra cannot be classified as either "modern" or "old-style." It is not based on any historical model, and hence does not echo any particular period or style of type design. It avoids the extreme contrast between thick and thin elements that marks most modern faces, and is without eccentricities that catch the eye and interfere with reading. In general, Electra is a simple, readable type face that attempts to give a feeling of fluidity, power, and speed.

Composed by Maryland Linotype Co., Inc., Baltimore, Maryland.

Printed and bound by The Maple Press, York, Pennsylvania.

Typography and binding design by Virginia Tan.